Mountain Bike
AMERICA™

ARIZONA

Contact

Dear Readers:

Every effort was made to make this the most accurate, informative, and easy-to-use guidebook on the planet. Any comments, suggestions, and/or corrections regarding this guide are welcome and should be sent to:

Outside America™
c/o Editorial Dept.
300 West Main St., Ste. A
Charlottesville, VA 22903
editorial@outside-america.com
www.outside-america.com

We'd love to hear from you so we can make future editions and future guides even better.

Thanks and happy trails!

Mountain Bike AMERICA™

ARIZONA

An Atlas of Arizona's Greatest
Off-Road Bicycle Rides

by Paul Beakley

The Globe Pequot Press

Guilford, Connecticut

Published by
The Globe Pequot Press
P. O. Box 480
Guilford, CT 06437
www.globe-pequot.com

Produced by
Beachway Press Publishing, Inc.
300 West Main St., Ste A
Charlottesville, VA 22903
www.beachway.com

Mountain Bike America is a trademark of Beachway Press
Publishing, Inc.

Editorial Assistance given by Layne Cameron

Production Assistance given by David Robinson, Gillian
Field

Cover Design Beachway Press

Photographer Paul Beakley

Maps designed and produced by Beachway Press

Cover Photo:
Arizona White-Knuckle Adventures founder Bruce Leadbetter
riding at the north end of Submarine Rock, Sedona, AZ.

Find Outside America™ at **www.outside-america.com**

Library of Congress Cataloging-in-Publication Data
is available

ISBN 0-7627-1224-4

Manufactured in the United States of America
First Edition/First Printing

Acknowledgments

Arizona is a really big state. I'd be a grizzled old bike rat by the time I'd discovered all the state's great rides on my own, and this book wouldn't be in your hands now. I have a lot of people to thank for hooking me up with the best local information I could ever hope for.

In Phoenix, Robert Chilton (my model and compadre for most of the Phoenix rides), Don Knapp, Greg Watley and his "OTB" group, Jeff Harnisch and the ClubMTB.com folks, Heidi Richter for surviving the dreaded Seven Springs ride with me, and Sonia Overholser at MBAA. Special thanks to tour guide extraordinaire Bruce Leadbetter at Arizona White-Knuckle Adventures, who took me way further on a bike than I had any right to think I could ride. Thanks, bro.

One more special mention in Phoenix: Bill, J.R., Nick, Vanessa, Brian, and Jim at Landis Cyclery (Price and Southern, in Tempe) for keeping my machine up and running.

In Tucson, thanks to Tony Krauss, Steve Andresen, Andy Friefeld, and Daniel Meyer and the annual Ruby ride crowd. Most of all, many thanks to C.J. and MaryEllen at Way Out West Treks N' Tours for their hospitality and terrific local knowledge.

In the White Mountains, Chris Tippie, Rene Hokans, Tom Barrett, and Dave Mathews at Pinetop Parks & Rec. Rye Sluiter at Eagar Parks & Rec. deserves special thanks, not only for showing the way in an amazing part of the state, but also for a great job putting on the Valle Redondo Fat Tire Fiesta every year.

In Flagstaff, Steve Garro and the folks at Sinagua Cycles for knowing everything about everything within 75 miles of town; Troy Marino, Don Laury, Sean & Sage, and the rest of the Moqui crowd; Mo and David; and everyone else who unexpectedly hooked up with me at the trailhead for a ride in the thin air.

In the far-flung reaches of the state, Levi Zurcher and John Gallant in Kingman, Bill Hatcher and DuWayne Fritz in Yuma, and Chris Guibert on the North Rim. These guys prove what I've long believed: Throw a dart at the Arizona state map, and you'll find bike trails within a 20-minute drive of that spot.

At Beachway, Scott, Ryan, Brandon, Layne and the rest of the pros who helped pull this mess together. Thanks for the opportunity.

And finally, my greatest debt of gratitude goes to Susan, for supporting me in every way while I worked on this book and others.

Here's hoping we all get to be grizzled old bike rats some day.

Table Of

Contents

Colorado River Country

Sky Islands

Rim Country

White Mountains

The Art of Mountain Biking

RIDES AT A GLANCE

1. South Mountain Trails (Desert Classic Trail)

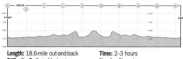

Length: 18.6-mile out-and-back **Time:** 2–3 hours
Difficulty Rating: Moderate **Nearby:** Phoenix

2. Charles M. Christiansen Memorial Trail 100

Length: 21.2-mile out-and-back **Time:** 3-4 hours
Difficulty Rating: Moderate **Nearby:** Phoenix

3. Estrella Loop

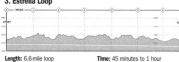

Length: 6.6-mile loop **Time:** 45 minutes to 1 hour
Difficulty Rating: Moderate **Nearby:** Goodyear

4. The Mine Loop – Hawes Pass Area

Length: 7.7-mile loop **Time:** 1.5-2 hours
Difficulty Rating: Moderate to Difficult **Nearby:** Mesa

5. Pima and Dynamite

Multiple Route Options

Length: 5 miles to 50 miles **Time:** Varies
Difficulty Rating: Moderate to Difficult **Nearby:** Scottsdale and Carefree

6. Trail 4 at Seven Springs

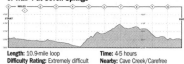

Length: 10.9-mile loop **Time:** 4-5 hours
Difficulty Rating: Extremely difficult **Nearby:** Cave Creek/Carefree

7. White Tank Sonoran Loop

Length: 3.8-mile circuit **Time:** 30-45 minutes
Difficulty Rating: Easy to Moderate **Nearby:** Phoenix

8. Spruce Mountain

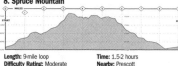

Length: 9-mile loop **Time:** 1.5-2 hours
Difficulty Rating: Moderate **Nearby:** Prescott

9. Granite Basin

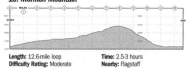

Length: 9-mile loop **Time:** 1 hour
Difficulty Rating: Moderate **Nearby:** Prescott

10. Oak Creek Canyon Trails

Multiple Route Options

Length: Varies by route taken **Time:** 1.5-4 hours
Difficulty Rating: Easy to Difficult **Nearby:** Oak Creek

11. Schnebly Hill to Seven Sacred Pools (East Sedona)

Length: 13-mile loop **Time:** 2-3 hours
Difficulty Rating: Moderate **Nearby:** Sedona

12. Teacup Trail to the Cockscomb (West Sedona)

Multiple Route Options

Length: Varies by route taken **Time:** 1-5 hours
Difficulty Rating: Moderate to Difficult **Nearby:** Sedona

13. Mormon Mountain

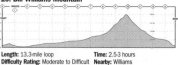

Length: 12.6-mile loop **Time:** 2.5-3 hours
Difficulty Rating: Moderate **Nearby:** Flagstaff

14. Walnut Canyon and Marshall Lake

Multiple Route Options

Length: Varies by route taken **Time:** 3.5-5 hours
Difficulty Rating: Moderate to Difficult **Nearby:** Flagstaff

15. Mount Elden

Length: 5-30 miles (depending on loop) **Time:** 1-7 hours
Difficulty Rating: Moderate to Difficult **Nearby:** Flagstaff

16. Bill Williams Mountain

Length: 13.3-mile loop **Time:** 2.5-3 hours
Difficulty Rating: Moderate to Difficult **Nearby:** Williams

17. Moqui Stage Route

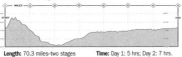

Length: 70.3 miles–two stages
Difficulty Rating: Easy to Moderate
Time: Day 1: 5 hrs; Day 2: 7 hrs.
Nearby: Flagstaff and Tusayan

18. North Rim Loop

Length: 37 miles
Difficulty Rating: Moderate to Difficult
Time: 6-7 hours
Nearby: Jacob Lake

19. Page Rimview Trail

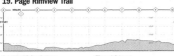

Length: 10.3 mile loop
Difficulty Rating: Easy
Time: 1-2 hours
Nearby: Page

20. Camp Beale Loop

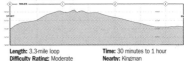

Length: 3.3-mile loop
Difficulty Rating: Moderate
Time: 30 minutes to 1 hour
Nearby: Kingman

21. Moss Wash Mines

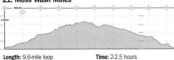

Length: 9.6-mile loop
Difficulty Rating: Moderate
Time: 2-2.5 hours
Nearby: Kingman

22. Gila Mountain

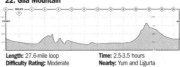

Length: 27.6-mile loop
Difficulty Rating: Moderate
Time: 2.5-3.5 hours
Nearby: Yum and Ligurta

23. Marty's Ridge to Liberty Bell

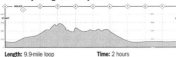

Length: 9.9-mile loop
Difficulty Rating: Moderate
Time: 2 hours
Nearby: Yuma

24. Starr Pass–Yetman Wash

Length: 7.8-mile loop
Difficulty Rating: Moderately difficult
Time: 1 hour
Nearby: Tucson

25. Chiva Falls

Length: 7.8-mile loop
Difficulty Rating: Moderate to Difficult
Time: 1-2 hours
Nearby: Tucson

26. Mount Lemmon Top to Bottom

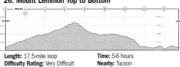

Length: 17.5-mile loop
Difficulty Rating: Very Difficult
Time: 5-6 hours
Nearby: Tucson

27. 50 Year Trail

Multiple Route Options

Length: Varies by route taken
Difficulty Rating: Moderate to Difficult
Time: 2 hours
Nearby: Oro Valley

28. The Tortolitas

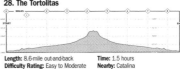

Length: 8.6-mile out-and-back
Difficulty Rating: Easy to Moderate
Time: 1.5 hours
Nearby: Catalina

29. Cobre Ridge

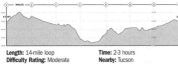

Length: 14-mile loop
Difficulty Rating: Moderate
Time: 2-3 hours
Nearby: Tucson

30. Gold Country

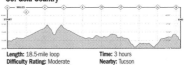

Length: 18.5-mile loop
Difficulty Rating: Moderate
Time: 3 hours
Nearby: Tucson

31. Brown Canyon

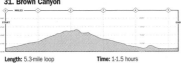

Length: 5.3-mile loop
Difficulty Rating: Moderate
Time: 1-1.5 hours
Nearby: Sierra Vista

32. Mount Graham

Multiple Route Options

Length: 10 miles
Difficulty Rating: Moderate to difficult
Time: 3 hours
Nearby: Safford and Willcox

RIDES AT A GLANCE

33. Cypress Thicket

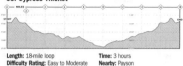

Length: 18-mile loop **Time:** 3 hours
Difficulty Rating: Easy to Moderate **Nearby:** Payson

34. Houston Mesa Horse Camp Trails

Length: 6.8-mile loop **Time:** 1.5 hours
Difficulty Rating: Moderate to Difficult **Nearby:** Payson

35. Strawberry Mountain

Length: 15-mile loop **Time:** 2-2.5 hours
Difficulty Rating: Moderate to Difficult **Nearby:** Pine

36. Highline to Christopher Creek

Multiple Route Options

Length: Varies by route taken **Time:** 2-2.5 hours
Difficulty Rating: Moderate to Difficult **Nearby:** Christopher Creek

37. Willow Springs Lake

Length: 15.8-mile loop **Time:** 2 hours
Difficulty Rating: Moderate **Nearby:** Heber

38. Buena Vista Trail 637

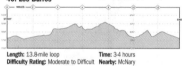

Length: 10.4-mile loop **Time:** 2 hours
Difficulty Rating: Moderate **Nearby:** Show Low

39. Indian Spring/West Fork

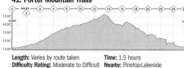

Length: 13.6-mile loop **Time:** 3 hours
Difficulty Rating: Moderate **Nearby:** Eagar

40. Los Burros

Length: 13.8-mile loop **Time:** 3-4 hours
Difficulty Rating: Moderate to Difficult **Nearby:** McNary

41. Porter Mountain Trails

Length: Varies by route taken **Time:** 1.5 hours
Difficulty Rating: Moderate to Difficult **Nearby:** Pinetop-Lakeside

42. South Fork Shuttle

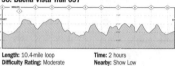

Length: Varies by route taken **Time:** Varies by route taken
Difficulty Rating: Moderate to Difficult **Nearby:** Eagar

43. South Pinetop (Springs, Blue Ridge, Country Club)

Multiple Route Options

Length: Varies by route taken **Time:** 45 minutes to 3 hours
Difficulty Rating: Moderate **Nearby:** Pinetop-Lakeside

Best Singletrack

50 Year Trail *(p. 210)*
Brown Canyon *(p. 234)*
Granite Basin *(p. 70)*
The Mine Loop – Hawes Pass *(p. 32)*
Highline Trail *(p. 274)*
Indian Spring/West Fork *(p. 302)*
Los Burros *(p. 308)*
Mt. Graham *(p. 240)*
Oak Creek Canyon Trails *(p. 76)*
Schultz Creek at Mount Elden *(p. 110)*
South Fork Shuttle *(p. 320)*

Best Climbs

Bill Williams Mountain *(p. 118)*
Mount Elden *(p. 110)*
Mt. Ord – Sunflower *(p. 286)*
Spruce Mountain *(p. 66)*

Best Technical Challenges

Bill Williams Mountain *(p. 118)*
Mormon Mountain *(p. 98)*
Mount Lemmon *(p. 204)*
National Trail at South Mountain *(p. 14)*
Seven Springs *(p. 44)*
South Fork Shuttle *(p. 320)*
Spruce Mountain *(p. 66)*
Strawberry Mountain *(p. 268)*
Sunrise Ski Resort – *(p. 332)*
Sunset Trail at Mt. Elden *(p. 110)*
Walnut Canyon *(p. 104)*

Best Views

Buena Vista Trail *(p. 296)*
North Rim Trail *(p. 142)*
Oak Creek Canyon Trails *(p. 76)*
Page Rimview Trail *(p. 148)*
Schnebly Hill to Seven Pools *(p. 84)*
Teacup to Cockscomb *(p. 90)*

Best Date Rides

Cypress Thicket *(p. 258)*
Papago Park *(p. 54)*
Pyramid Mountain *(p. 56)*
Usery Mountain *(p. 54)*
Willow Springs Lake *(p. 280)*

Best Training/Learning Rides

Camp Beale Loop *(p. 162)*
Chiva Falls *(p. 200)*
Desert Classic at South Mountain *(p. 14)*
Estrella Mountains *(p. 26)*
Marty's Ridge to Liberty Bell *(p. 178)*
McDowell Mountain Park *(p. 55)*
Pima and Dynamite *(p. 38)*
Porter Mountain Trails *(p. 314)*
Slaughterhouse Canyon *(p. 184)*
South Pinetop Trails *(p. 326)*
Starr Pass *(p. 194)*
Tortolitas *(p. 216)*
Trail 100 *(p. 20)*
White Tank Mountains *(p. 50)*

Best History Lessons

Deadhorse Ranch State Park *(p. 135)*
Gold Country/Kentucky Camp *(p. 228)*
Moqui Stage Route *(p. 124)*
Moss Wash Mines *(p. 168)*

Best Loooong Rides

Cobre Ridge *(p. 222)*
Crown King to Lake Pleasant *(p. 133)*
Elephant Head *(p. 246)*
Gila Mountain *(p. 172)*
Moqui Stage Route *(p. 124)*
North Rim *(p. 142)*
Seven Springs *(p. 44)*

HOW TO USE THIS BOOK

Take a close enough look and you'll find that this little guide contains just about everything you'll ever need to choose, plan for, enjoy, and survive a ride in the state of Arizona. We've done everything but inflate your tires and put on your helmet. Stuffed with 368 pages of useful Arizona-specific information, *Mountain Bike America: Arizona* ™ features 43 mapped and cued rides and 39 honorable mentions, as well as everything from advice on getting into shape to tips on getting the most out of mountain biking with your children or your dog. And as you'd expect with any Outside America™ guide, you get the best maps man and technology can render. With so much information, the only question you may have is: How do I sift through it all? Well, we answer that, too.

We've designed our Mountain Bike America™ series to be highly visual, for quick reference and ease-of-use. What this means is that the most pertinent information rises quickly to the top, so you don't have to waste time poring through bulky ride descriptions to get mileage cues or elevation stats. They're set aside for you. And yet, an Outside America™ guide doesn't read like a laundry list. Take the time to dive into a ride description and you'll realize that this guide is not just a good source of information; it's a good read. And so, in the end, you get the best of both worlds: a quick-reference guide and an engaging look at a region. Here's an outline of the guide's major components.

WHAT YOU'LL FIND IN A MOUNTAIN BIKE AMERICA™ GUIDE. Let's start with the individual chapter. To aid in quick decision-making, we start each chapter with a Ride Summary. This short overview gives you a taste of the mountain biking adventure at hand. You'll learn about the trail terrain and what surprises the route has to offer. If your interest is piqued, you can read more. If not, skip to the next Ride Summary. The Ride Specs are fairly self-explanatory. Here you'll find the quick, nitty-gritty details of the ride: where the trailhead is located, the nearest town, ride length, approximate riding time, difficulty rating, type of trail terrain, and what other trail users you may encounter. Our Getting There section gives you dependable directions from a nearby city right down to where you'll want to park. The Ride Description is the meat of the chapter. Detailed and honest, it's the author's carefully researched impression of the trail. While it's impossible to cover everything, you can rest assured that we won't miss what's important. In our Miles/Directions section we provide mileage cues to identify all turns and trail name changes, as well as points of interest. Between this and our Route Map, you simply can't get lost. The Ride Information box is a hodgepodge of information. In it you'll find trail hotlines (for updates on trail conditions), park schedules and fees, local outdoor retailers (for emergency trail supplies), and a list of maps available to the area. We'll also tell you where to stay, what to eat, and what else to see while you're hiking in the area. Lastly, the Honorable Mentions section details all of the rides that didn't make the cut, for whatever reason—in many cases it's not because they aren't great rides, instead it's because they're over-crowded or environmentally sensitive to heavy traffic. Be sure to read through these. A jewel might be lurking among them.

Map Legend

We don't want anyone, by any means, to feel restricted to just the routes and trails that are mapped here. We hope you will have an adventurous spirit and use this guide as a platform to dive into Arizona's backcountry and discover new routes for yourself. One of the simplest ways to begin this is to just turn the map upside down and ride the course in reverse. The change in perspective is fantastic and the ride should feel quite different. With this in mind, it will be like getting two distinctly different rides on each map.

For your own purposes, you may wish to copy the directions for the course onto a small sheet to help you while riding, or photocopy the map and cue sheet to take with you. Otherwise, just slip the whole book in your backpack and take it all with you. Enjoy your time in the outdoors and remember to pack out what you pack in.

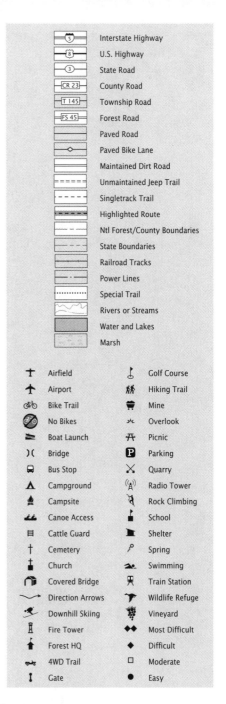

Interstate Highway
U.S. Highway
State Road
County Road
Township Road
Forest Road
Paved Road
Paved Bike Lane
Maintained Dirt Road
Unmaintained Jeep Trail
Singletrack Trail
Highlighted Route
Ntl Forest/County Boundaries
State Boundaries
Railroad Tracks
Power Lines
Special Trail
Rivers or Streams
Water and Lakes
Marsh

✝	Airfield	⚲	Golf Course
✈	Airport	炔	Hiking Trail
🚲	Bike Trail	⛏	Mine
🚫	No Bikes	↓	Overlook
🛥	Boat Launch	🎋	Picnic
)(	Bridge	🅿	Parking
🚌	Bus Stop	✕	Quarry
▲	Campground	((🄰))	Radio Tower
⚱	Campsite	⚐	Rock Climbing
▲▲	Canoe Access	🏫	School
⊟	Cattle Guard	▮	Shelter
✝	Cemetery	⌁	Spring
✚	Church	⊶	Swimming
🏠	Covered Bridge	🌾	Train Station
⤳	Direction Arrows	🦃	Wildlife Refuge
⛷	Downhill Skiing	🍇	Vineyard
Ⅱ	Fire Tower	◆◆	Most Difficult
♠	Forest HQ	◆	Difficult
⚙	4WD Trail	□	Moderate
‡	Gate	●	Easy

HOW TO USE THESE MAPS

1 Area Locator Map

This thumbnail relief map at the beginning of each ride shows you where the ride is within the state. The ride area is indicated with a star.

2 Regional Location Map

This map helps you find your way to the start of each ride from the nearest sizeable town or city. Coupled with the detailed directions at the beginning of the cue, this map should visually lead you to where you need to be for each ride.

3 Profile Map

This helpful profile gives you a cross-sectional look at the ride's ups and downs. Elevation is labeled on the left, mileage is indicated on the top. Road and trail names are shown along the route with towns and points of interest labeled in bold.

Map Descriptions

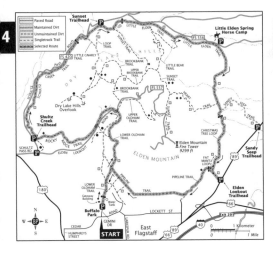

4 Route Map

This is your primary guide to each ride. It shows all of the accessible roads and trails, points of interest, water, towns, landmarks, and geographical features. It also distinguishes trails from roads, and paved roads from unpaved roads. The selected route is highlighted, and directional arrows point the way. Shaded topographic relief in the background gives you an accurate representation of the terrain and landscape in the ride area.

Ride Information (Included in each ride section)

🕿 Trail Contacts:

This is the direct number for the local land managers in charge of all the trails within the selected ride. Use this hotline to call ahead for trail access information, or after your visit if you see problems with trail erosion, damage, or misuse.

🕐 Schedule:

This tells you at what times trails open and close, if on private or park land.

$ Fees/Permits:

What money, if any, you may need to carry with you for park entrance fees or tolls.

🅝 Maps:

This is a list of other maps to supplement the maps in this book. They are listed in order from most detailed to most general.

Any other important or useful information will also be listed here such as local attractions, bike shops, nearby accommodations, etc.

A note from the folks behind this endeavor...

We at Outside America look at guidebook publishing a little differently. There's just no reason that a guidebook has to look like it was published out of your Uncle Ernie's woodshed. We feel that guidebooks need to be both easy to use and nice to look at, and that takes an innovative approach to design. You see, we want you to spend less time fumbling through your guidebook and more time enjoying the adventure at hand. We hope you like what you see here and enjoy the places we lead you. And most of all, we'd like to thank you for taking an adventure with us.

Introdu

Introduction

**W**elcome to the adventurous thrill of mountain biking in Arizona! An amazing state in which to enjoy this awesome sport, Arizona offers up some of the most varied landscapes and weather found in North America. Where else can you ride in locations as diverse as low desert, grasslands, dark forests, and high alpine terrain—all within a few hours' drive of each other?

Arizona Weather

Riding through an Arizona summer in the desert is one of the most brutal things you can inflict on your body. Between the heat, the UV index, and the total lack of humidity, you'll dehydrate, sunburn, and suffer heat stroke in no time at all—that is, unless you go into it prepared *(see page 346 for hints on hot desert riding)*.

Generally, summers in the desert—Phoenix, Tucson, and low-lying towns like Yuma and Casa Grande—don't get below about 80 degrees Fahrenheit at night and early morning, and reach well above 100 at midday. There's also not much shade in the desert, except for the occasional mesquite or palo verde tree, neither of which really qualify as shade trees. Winters, late falls, and early springs are heavenly riding weather in the desert, with lows in the 50s and highs no higher than 80 or so. Night riding is a good option any time of the year.

Meanwhile, the mountainous majority of the state—the Sonoran Desert makes up less than half of Arizona, despite the state's appearance in movies and TV—enjoys extremely mild summers. Flagstaff, Prescott, and Payson, all major riding destinations, hit lows in the 50s and highs in the 80s and (rarely) low 90s. Glorious Sedona is a bit warmer in the summer, sometimes breaking 100 degrees but not until late in the day. The major mountain destinations—Mt. Elden in Flagstaff, Mt. Lemmon in Tucson, and the White Mountains—are typically 15 degrees (or more) cooler than their nearby towns.

As a rule of thumb, the temperature drops about four degrees Fahrenheit for every 1,000 feet of altitude rise. The math is easy once you know where you are and where you're thinking about riding.

The Mogollon Rim, which bisects the state into north and south halves, catches most of the rain that rolls through the state. Monsoons hit hardest halfway up the Rim east of Payson, but the effects can be felt as far west as Prescott and as far east as Springerville. The White Mountains, in particular, are the wettest (and coolest) part of the state all year long.

Winters in the high parts of the state mentioned above often mean either snow or heavy rain, making trails unrideable. But some winters bring freak weather, when major ski destinations stay closed all winter due to total lack of precipitation. So don't write off your favorite Flagstaff ride just because it's

December—but please call ahead to the forest ranger office or local bike shops first to ask about trail conditions. Then there was a year when so much snow fell in June that Flagstaff opened for some late-spring skiing. Weather in Arizona can be quite unpredictable, except for the endless sunny-and-hot days that take up so much of the year.

Because the winters are so mild, and cool rides are so easily accessible during the summer, Arizona mountain bikers enjoy a year-round riding season. Even during the monsoon and winter rain seasons, there's rarely enough rain to close trails for more than a day or so.

One important note on pollution: It's bad, really bad, in metro Phoenix. Thanks to the basin, which is surrounded by mountains on all sides, and the massive "heat island" created by the city's asphalt and concrete, the city sometimes experiences a "thermal inversion," during which a cap of air holds in all the city's pollution for days or weeks at a time. This can happen at any time of the year, but most often in the winter. During these periods, stay off the bike or drive out of town.

Flora and Fauna

Arizona has a remarkable array of distinct life zones. To understand the dramatic climate range of Arizona, look at the transition from the top of the San Francisco Peaks, the highest point in Arizona at 12,670 feet, to the floor of the Verde Valley, about 40 miles as the crow flies. In this 40-mile stretch, you'll find every possible climate life zone of the world except the wet tropical. Above the timberline on the peaks, the climate is Arctic-Alpine, with an extremely short growing season supporting only mosses and similar plants. Just below that is the Hudsonian, home to Englemann spruce and flourishing foxtail pine. Then comes the Canadian zone, with its Douglas fir, aspen and white fir. The Transitional zone in which the ponderosa pine thrives follows this in the descending altitude scale. Below this is the Upper Sonoran zone, supporting piñon and juniper trees. And finally, on the valley floor, the Lower Sonoran climate is the norm, with its cactus and mesquite vegetation.

The Sonoran Desert is the low desert that stretches from the foothills below the Mogollon Rim all the way south to the Mexican border. Here you'll find forests of cactus. Massive saguaros are found further south, but chollas and barrel cactus can be found throughout the desert and sometimes even into the dry foothills climbing out of the desert, such as those found south of Payson. Cactuses, or cacti if you prefer (it's an ongoing linguistic argument), are important vegetation for mountain bikers to be aware of—more specifically, for us to keep our tires away. Because there's such a huge array of sharp, spiky plant life in the desert, tube sealants are strongly recommended (*for other hints about desert-specific riding and equipment, see page 346*).

Other common plants found in the desert are the mesquites, ocotillos, and palo verdes, all spindly, tall trees that are completely unsuitable for shade cover. Along streambeds you'll find clusters of cottonwood trees, as well as denser collections of mesquites, hoarding what little moisture the stream might be hiding in a shaded bend.

Perhaps even more remarkable than these hardy plants is the wildlife of the desert. Coyotes, javelina, and rattlesnakes are among the most dangerous critters you'll run across in the desert, although most would rather stay away from people altogether. Spotting a family of shy javelina in the McDowell Mountains or South Mountain Park is a rare treat. More likely, you'll see plenty of rabbits, kangaroo mice, prairie dogs, and other small fuzzy critters.

Another wildlife danger worth noting is the poisonous desert bug life. Scorpions are the most likely threat along the trail, as they aren't interested in setting traps like the infamous black widow spider and would rather go wandering off in search of munchies and water. There's also plenty of wasps, bees, and some of the biggest ant colonies you'll ever see.

The mountain peaks that suddenly jut from the desert floor, called "sky islands," each have their own eco-systems. Even though two mountains might have similar altitudes, the distance between them has allowed their own distinct versions of everything from mice to owls to trees to evolve. Sometimes the differences are so subtle as to be academic, while in other cases, such as the Mount Graham Squirrel or the Kaibab Squirrel (found only on the North Rim of the Grand Canyon), the differences are obvious even to the untrained eye.

Wilderness Restrictions/Regulations

Arizona has nearly five million acres of designated wilderness, broken into 92 units managed by four different federal agencies: the Fish and Wildlife Service, the National Park Service, the Forest Service, and the Bureau of Land Management. The smallest is the tiny 2,065-acre Baboquivari Peak Wilderness, southwest of Tucson; the largest is the 803,418-acre Cabeza Prieta National Wildlife Refuge Wilderness.

In all cases, bikes are strictly prohibited from entering any wilderness area. Don't mess with this rule—while some riders might flirt with poaching social trails on non-wilderness public lands, it's flagrant abuse of the wilderness rules that have the greatest potential to give mountain bikers a bad name. Unfortunately, wilderness boundaries are sometimes poorly marked (such as the case with some of the trails in Sedona). If you're thinking about exploring a new trail, always check first with the Forest Service or a topo map to determine whether you're about to break the law.

Thanks for purchasing *Mountain Bike America: Arizona!*
Have a great ride!

Paul Beakley
October 2001

3

Getting Around Arizona

☎ AREA CODES

The area code **520** covers Tucson and most of southern Arizona. In Phoenix area code **602** is now split with **480** in the East Valley and **623** in the West Valley. The area code for northern, eastern, and western Arizona is **928**.

⊜ ROADS

For road conditions, contact the **Arizona Department of Transportation**, call 1–888–411–7623 (ROAD) or visit *www.dot.state.az.us* for current road closings and openings, traffic updates, and road construction plans and timetables.

✈ BY AIR

Sky Harbor Airport (PHX) is Arizona's main point of entry, *www.phxskyharbor.com*. A number of smaller airports throughout the state have connections through Sky Harbor. Your travel agent can best advise you on the cheapest and/or most direct way to connect from wherever you're departing. Shared ride vans and taxis serve the metro Phoenix area. Frequent scheduled vans serve Tucson, Prescott, Sedona, and Flagstaff. Most of these services will carry boxed bicycles. **Valley Metro** buses serve downtown Phoenix and Tempe. All Valley Metro buses have bike racks. Valley Metro information can be found at *www.valleymetro.maricopa.gov*.

Tucson International Airport (TIA) serves greater Tucson and southeast Arizona and can be found on the internet at *www.tucsonairport.org* Shared ride vans and taxi's serve Tucson and the surrounding areas. The airport is also served locally by **Sun Tran**. All Sun Tran buses have bike racks. Sun Tran information can be found at *www.suntran.com*.

To book reservations on-line, check out your favorite airline's website or search one of the following travel sites for the best price: *www.cheaptickets.com*, *www.expedia.com*, *www.previewtravel.com*, *www.priceline.com*, *http://travel.yahoo.com*, *www.travelocity.com*, and *www.trip.com*—just to name a few.

⊟ BY BUS

Greyhound serves most major towns and cities in Arizona including Phoenix, Tucson, Flagstaff, Prescott, and Yuma. Schedules and fares are available online at *www.greyhound.com* or by phone at 1–800–231–2222. Bikes cost $15 and must be boxed. **Nava-Hopi Bus** connects Sky Harbor Airport, North Phoenix, and the Flagstaff Amtrak Station with the Grand Canyon. Schedules and fares are available online at *www.navahopitours.com*. Bikes are free but a box is required.

⊞ BY TRAIN

Phoenix takes honors for being the largest city in the country not directly served by **Amtrak**. However two cross-country routes serve Arizona. The Southwest Chief train runs daily to Flagstaff from Chicago, Los Angeles, and Albuquerque, NM. The combined Sunset Limited/Texas Eagle train services Tucson and Yuma every day from Los Angeles and Dallas and three times a week from Orlando and New Orleans.

Amtrak offers connecting bus service to the old Phoenix Amtrak station from Tucson and Flagstaff. Bikes are carried only to and from stations with checked baggage and it costs $12 each way. The stations at Phoenix, Flagstaff, and Tucson handle bicycles. Amtrak information and reservations are available online at *www.amtrak.com* or by phone at 1–800–872–7245. Oh, and you could ride the **Grand Canyon Railway** from Williams to the Grand Canyon, but your bike can't.

❷ VISITOR INFORMATION

For visitor information or a travel brochure, call the **Arizona Office of Tourism** at 1–800–842–8257 or visit their website at *www.arizonaguide.com*.

The Rides

Central
ARIZONA

Charles M. Christiansen Memorial Trail 100 overlooking smoggy Phoenix.

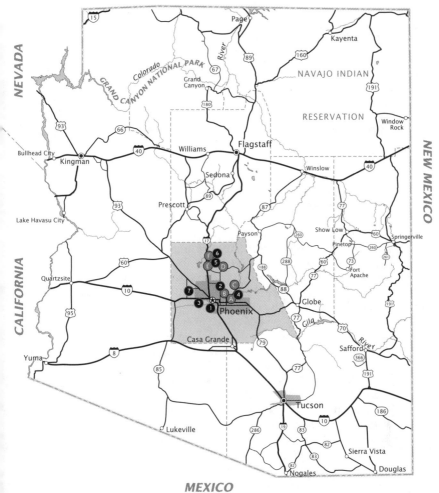

The Rides

South Mountain Trails (Desert Classic Trail) **1.**
Charles M. Christiansen Memorial Trail 100 **2.**
Estrella Loop **3.**
The Mine Loop – Hawes Pass Area **4.**
Pima and Dynamite **5.**
Trail 4 at Seven Springs **6.**
White Tank Sonoran Loop **7.**

Honorable Mentions

A. Usery Mountain Recreation Area
B. Papago Park
C. McDowell Mountain Park
D. Sheep Bridge
E. Pyramid Mountain
F. Cave Creek Recreation Area

Central Arizona

Known as the Valley of the Sun, metro Phoenix, its surrounding cities and suburbs, and the outlying hills and mountains make up what, in this book, is considered Central Arizona. This area is rich with easily accessible mountain bike trails for cyclists of every level, most of which are free and all are within an easy drive, thanks to an extensive freeway system, from anywhere in the Valley.

South Mountain Park, the nation's largest municipal park, is *the* destination for most local cyclists, and visitors from out of town come here to see what all the commotion is about. The bulk of South Mountain's rides start at the eastern end of the mountain, although trails crisscross the park throughout its length, providing additional points of access. The rides here tend to be rocky, sandy, and often dangerous to the uninitiated. As one tour guide told me, "Riding in South Mountain is like skiing on the East Coast—if you can do it here, you can do it anywhere." The same could be said for nearly any ride in Central Arizona. The rocks, the cacti, the sudden drops and sandy washes—it all builds character and makes you a stronger rider.

As a biking-friendly community, metro Phoenix is decidedly mixed. There are abundant bike shops of all degrees, from low-end stores dedicated to ripping off poor college students to high-end bike boutiques that serve and sponsor the strongest racers in the state. Clubs are nonexistent, except for group rides organized by various shops around town. And, as of yet, there is no central, activist, go-to mountain bike organization in metro Phoenix. Yet, there are a whole lot of mountain bikers in town, from fully sponsored pros to weekend warriors.

A trip to South Mountain on any weekend will probably reveal literally hundreds of bikers doing the same thing as you. The scene is repeated at the other central riding areas—North Mountain, Hawes Pass, Pima and Dynamite—and dissipates only when traveling for a ride to the far outskirts of town. If you don't want to be hassled by the crowds, hop in your car and make the trip out to Estrella Mountain Park, Usery Park, or the McDowell Mountains.

Despite the straight roads, numerous bike paths, wide sidewalks, and generous shoulders, bicycling anywhere in metro Phoenix can be terrifying. Take this as a fair warning: You may be safer driving your SUV to the trailhead than riding your bike there. I live just three miles from South Mountain, and have near-miss experiences (and at least a couple real scrapes) at least twice a week. Die-hard roadies agree with this bitter assessment. Who knows, maybe it's the heat.

Speaking of the heat, summers in Central Arizona are not to be trifled with. Daytime temperatures can easily break 110°F all summer long; and 120°F + days are no longer that rare. With all of the concrete and asphalt being poured into the desert to expand metro Phoenix, developers have created what's called a "heat island," trapping heat in the ground even at night. Night rides these days can sometimes mean braving 90°F + temperatures. During the winter, the stark sun, low humidity, and lack of shade on *any* trail also means dehydrating faster in this part of the country than almost anywhere else you'll ever ride a bike. However much water you drink on the trail, it never seems to be enough. And as much as your canine companion may love mountain biking with you, it may be best, in this case, to simply leave him at home.

Section Overview

South Mountain Trails

South Mountain Park features a network of exceptional singletrack just off the freeway and within 30 minutes of the entire valley. The Desert Classic Trail, located along the southern edge of the park, is an excellent introduction to this biking playground, featuring fast singletrack that dives into and out of numerous arroyos. A few technical challenges make the trail fun for experienced riders, but won't overwhelm those who need to walk through them. As a more challenging alternative, cut through the middle of the park to the National Trail, a beast of a whole different stripe. Dangerous, steep, and difficult in

every measurable way, riding (and clearing) the National Trail is postgraduate work for skilled, dedicated riders. This trail features tight switchbacks, big drops, super-steep rock faces, and staircases. (*See page 14.*)

Charles M. Christiansen Memorial Trail 100

Trail 100, another great singletrack ride right in the heart of metro Phoenix, forms the backbone of a larger skeleton of trails that wind through the North Mountains, Shaw Butte, and Squaw Peak. Some riders venture just a few miles from either end of Trail 100, get bored, and turn back. But take my advice and keep going—the good stuff is several miles into this ride (just past Cave Creek) and is worth the time it takes to get there. (*See page 20.*)

Estrella Loop

People have often made a lot of misleading statements about this wonderful, underused county park: "It's just a race loop." "It's all flat." "It's too far away." But what they don't tell you is that hidden behind the ridge, there's a sweet network of fast, buffed singletrack, some lung-burning climbs, and sandy washes that will suck your bike down into their gritty depths. This ride is less than an hour long, and is great for multiple laps if you feel so inclined. (*See page 26.*)

The Mine Loop – Hawes Pass Area

The Hawes Pass area is maybe—just maybe—the best riding available in the Valley of the Sun. It's a big area, the trails are challenging yet fast, and it's boring as heck for hikers. Mountain bikers rule the day at Hawes Pass, at least for now. If cyclists are looking for gut-busting climbs, tight switchbacks, and fast, rolling trails, look no further. (*See page 32.*)

Pima and Dynamite

Way north of central Phoenix, almost to Carefree, is a network of singletrack and doubletrack that, if laid end-to-end, would be more than 300 miles long. Pima and Dynamite (as it's known to mountain bikers and motorcyclists alike) is a vast region of crisscrossing trails of every imaginable difficulty rating. All the trails are gravelly, bermed and, in many cases, extremely fast. Intrepid explorers will find nearly vertical granite rock faces from which to drop, insanely technical climbs and descents, and a host of other off-road horrors further north toward

Bartlett Lake. The trails are on Arizona State Trust land, so you're legally required to have either a $15 recreation pass or a hunting license to ride here. (*See page 38.*)

Trail 4 at Seven Springs

Trail 4 at Seven Springs was featured in a 1998 issue of *Bicycling* magazine as a "Top Ten Swimming Hole" ride. The first portion of Trail 4 is pretty and mostly rideable singletrack along the sycamore-shaded edge of Cave Creek (the actual creek, not the town). And then the ride gets hard. And harder still. And then it's so hard, and cyclists will have gone so few miles in so many hours, that they'll wonder if it was worth the trip. The views atop Skunk Ridge are proof of a worthy payoff. (*See page 44.*)

Central Arizona

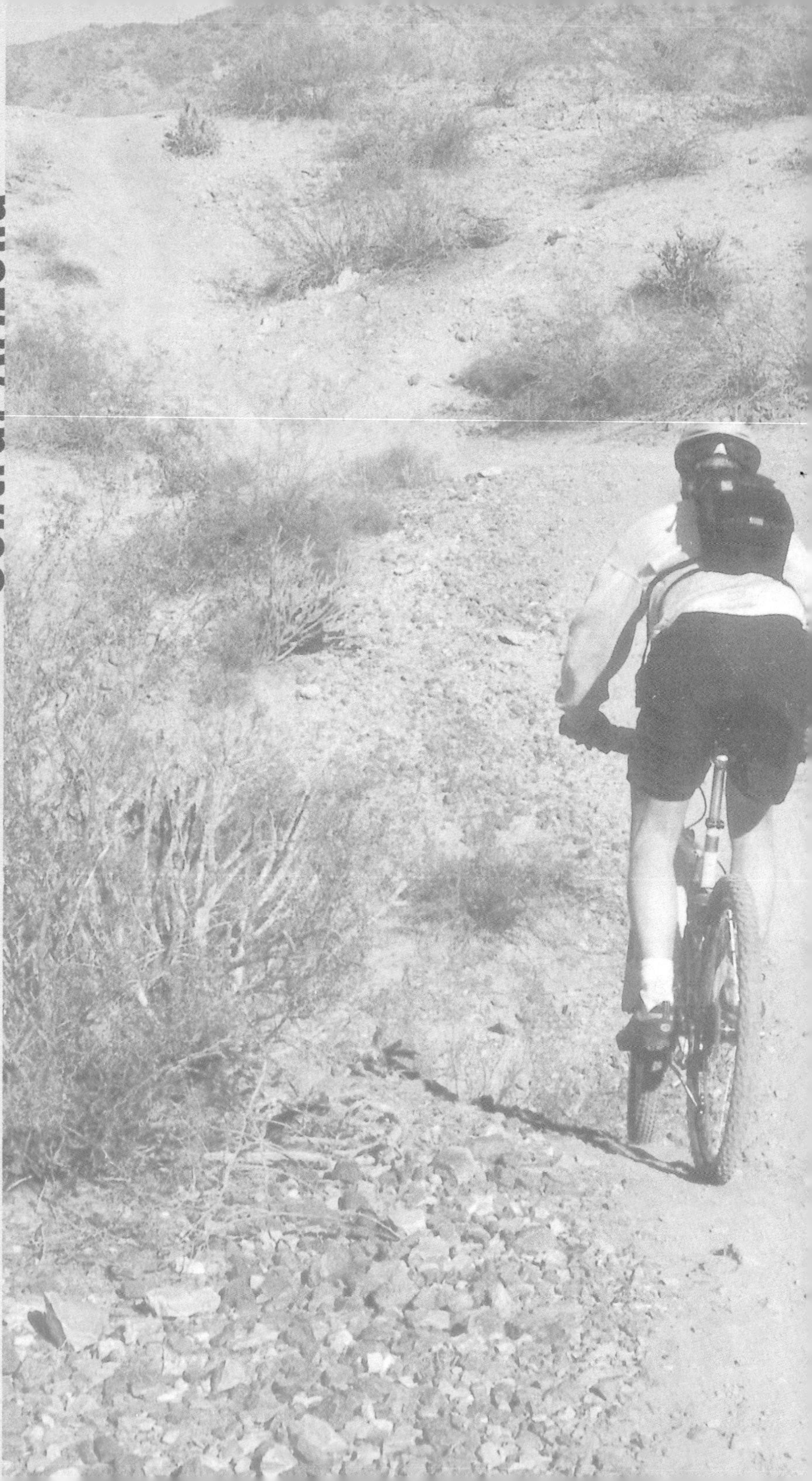

White Tank Sonoran Loop

Home to MBAA's annual White Tank Whirlwind race as well as the beginning of Maricopa County's Dirt Devil race series, the Sonoran Loop at White Tank Mountain Regional Park is one of the few rides in town where cyclists have explicit permission to go as fast as they possibly can. The views of the White Tanks from this short loop are tremendous, and riders tired of speed can work on their technical skills along nearly a mile of challenging terrain called the "Technical Loop." *(See page 50.)*

South Mountain Trails
(Desert Classic Trail)

Ride Specs

Start: From the trailhead at Pima Canyon parking lot

Length: 18.6-mile out-and-back

Approximate Riding Time: 2-3 hours

Difficulty Rating: Moderate. The Desert Classic Trail is technically and aerobically easy, with some moderate-to-difficult transitions into and out of arroyos (washes) along the way. There are some long, but not steep, climbs as well. If you ride Desert Classic Trail all the way to its conclusion, consider it moderate.

Trail Surface: Winding singletrack

Lay of the Land: Lower Sonoran Desert

Elevation Gain: 1,284 feet

Land Status: Municipal park

Nearest Town: Phoenix, AZ

Other Trail Users: Hikers, equestrians

Canine Compatibility: Dogs permitted

Wheels: Hardtails and hybrids are okay on Desert Classic Trail and some of the minor trails to the north of the park.

Getting There

From Phoenix: Head south on I-10 toward Baseline Road. From Exit 155 (Baseline Road and I-10), go west on Baseline Road toward Pointe Parkway, which is the second light about 300 yards west of the overpass. The intersection is across the street from Fry's Electronics store to the north. Turn south on Pointe Parkway, into the Pointe Hyatt Resort, and take the first right (S. 48th Street) that exits the rotunda immediately south of the light. Drive up S. 48th Street and turn right onto East Pima Canyon Road into South Mountain Park (the last right turn before the intersection with Guadalupe Road). Drive up to the Pima Canyon parking lot and park. The parking lot holds about 50 cars. *DeLorme: Arizona Atlas & Gazetteer:* Page 57 B/C 5

A t 16,500 acres, Phoenix's South Mountain Park is the largest municipal park in the world. South Mountain itself stretches several miles along the southernmost reaches of the city, and separates new housing to the south from metro Phoenix to the north.

The South Mountain region's earliest use was as an Indian hunting ground and a site of sacred shrines. The first European to visit Arizona, Franciscan priest Marcos de Niza, passed through the area in 1539 in search of the fabled Seven Cities of Cibola. The entrance to the Desert Classic Trail is marked by the Marcos de Niza inscription rock, where it's believed the priest left his inscription.

Today, South Mountain Park is, among other things, an extremely popular mountain biking playground. A web of singletrack crisscrosses the eastern end of the park, providing nearly endless opportunities to explore and create your own loops. The park's trails run the gamut from smooth to sandy to rugged to nearly impassable by all but the most experienced riders.

True to its name, the Desert Classic Trail provides a cross-section of classic Sonoran desert. South Mountain Park is home to more than 300 species of plant life and a variety of fauna, including rabbits, foxes, coyotes, snakes, lizards, and birds.

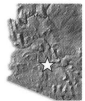

Tarantulas make their appearance in late spring but disappear by the time summer starts. These large spiders are generally shy and harmless, but you still don't want to pick them up.

The Desert Classic Trail, which runs along the southern face of South Mountain, is an excellent introduction to what the park has to offer. It's a favorite local training run, offering a long and moderately challenging ride of nearly 20 out-and-back miles.

You'll start from the east parking lot, at the entrance adjacent to the southernmost of two ramadas (covered picnic table area). After an immediate, short hill, you'll drop back to the desert floor and follow singletrack as it winds along the edge of South Mountain. Numbered posts along the way will help keep you from straying off the trail—and if you do stray, don't worry. Most of the offshoots eventually reconnect to the Desert Classic Trail.

At just under four miles you'll hit a sudden and very steep climb to a water tank. This is a popular rest spot for bikers—expect an audience to watch your attempts to climb the loose, dusty trail up to the tank.

Beyond the tank, the trail becomes a fast roller coaster, and then begins a slight descent. See the mileage breakdown for specifics. By about the sixth mile, you'll come to another nice rest spot. Many local riders choose this spot as their final destination—beyond this the trail becomes much more difficult, with plenty of technical climbing and some tricky switchbacks. Nobody will fault you for stopping here. If you

care to hike-a-bike through this rough patch (not more than 100 yards), the Desert Classic Trail once again becomes a fast and smooth ride across the desert floor.

After heavy monsoon rains, the Desert Classic's character changes from mild-mannered trail to monstrous path. The trails often wash out and become rocky and rutted. Within a week of these rains, though, the swarms of riders will have returned the trails to their normal state as thousands of bike tires wear away the ruts and disperse the loose sand.

The Desert Classic is one of the most heavily traversed trails in all of Phoenix, used by hundreds of mountain bikers every day, not to mention hikers and equestrians. Be careful to keep your speed in check, as you share this trail with so many others.

MilesDirections

Desert Classic Trail

0.0 START from Pima Canyon parking lot. Look for the singletrack heading due south from behind the southern ramada (covered picnic table area). Just beyond the trailhead is an uphill walking trail that takes you to the Marcos de Niza Rock; it's too steep for bikes. The Desert Classic Trail continues around the base of the mountain and goes up a hill.

1.0 Reach the first metal post, marked "11." Continue straight ahead on the singletrack. *[Side-trip. A rugged singletrack splits off to the right, goes up a very steep hill, and eventually descends and hooks up with the wide National Trail dirt road.]*

3.0 Arrive at metal marker 26. *[Side-trip. A singletrack joins from the left, and is a less difficult route to the water tank (see map).]* Continue to the right and into the wash.

3.4 Now at marker 27. A singletrack joins from the left; continue on the right, heading toward the water tank atop a low hill.

3.7 Climb a short, steep hill and arrive at the water tank (marker 31). If needed, take a little rest, and continue along the trail as it winds around the north side of the water tank.

5.0 Come to marker 46. The trail splits left and right. Turn left at the marker. *[Side-trip. Heading right leads to Corona de Loma, a moderately difficult loop option that either goes up and down a hill, reconnecting to the Desert Classic (at mile 5.8), or connects with the National Trail. Add 1.2 miles.]*

5.2 Reach the second split in the trail. Veer right heading due west. *[Bailout. Heading left is an unnamed trail that leads back to Warpaint Drive.]*

5.8 Corona de Loma Loop (see side-trip, mile 5.0) rejoins the Desert Classic Trail from the right. Continue ahead.

6.1 Arrive at marker 52 and a large rest area at the top of a shallow, rocky climb. Continue on the singletrack that heads due west.

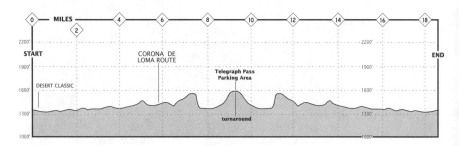

16

6.6 Now at marker 54. Trail forks; veer right. *[Side-trip.* Heading left takes you to the Highline Trail and the Helicopter Pad. In about 1.0 mile, the trail will reach the top of a saddle and fork; one trail will continue ahead and down, the other will split to the right and go up. The right is the Highline Trail; the left heads down a hill and into a neighborhood. The Helicopter Pad is about 1.5 miles up the Highline Trail from here. Once at the Helicopter Pad, you can either ride back down the Highline Trail or down the super-sketchy Goat Trail, and reconnect with the Desert Classic.]*

7.4 Arrive at marker 59. A trail comes down the hill from the left and joins the Desert Classic Trail. Continue ahead and down into the valley. *[Side-trip.* This trail from the left is the other end of the Goat Trail (see side trip, mile 6.6). Ride/hike your bike up two steep climbs. At the top of the second climb, turn right for a minute and visit the Helicopter Pad. Check out the views of endless red tile roofs below. Turn back east and head down the Highline Trail, a twisty, narrow path along the mountain's edge. You'll come out at a saddle, intersecting a trail that goes left and right. The

left will take you back to the Desert Classic Trail at mile 6.6; the right heads down into a neighborhood. This very worthy side trip adds 1.5 miles].*

7.9 At marker 60, the trail forks; veer right. The left dead-ends at somebody's backyard fence.

8.0 The trail goes up a short hill and appears to terminate at a doubletrack that runs behind a neighborhood. Don't stop here! The Desert Classic Trail actually turns at the top of the climb, goes around an old power pole, and continues back down into the wash. There are a couple of singletrack options from here. Look for the leftmost trail (due west, marked with marker 62) and continue.

8.9 Come to an intersection with Telegraph Pass, a hike-a-bike connector with the National Trail. Take the paved, wide trail heading due south (left) to reach the second parking lot, which is this ride's turn-around point.

9.3 Arrive at the second parking lot. Turn around here and head back the way you came.

18.6 Reach the Pima Canyon parking lot.

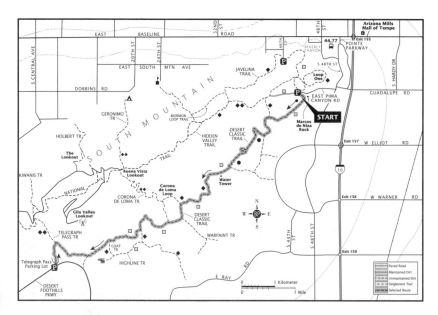

Once you've accomplished riding the Desert Classic Trail, there are many, many other trails to explore in South Mountain Park. One notable ride is the National Trail, widely considered one of the top rides in the nation. However, the National Trail is incredibly difficult and often choked with hikers, especially on the weekend. If you do choose to tackle the National Trail, the climb to the top of the mountain will require practice, patience, and trials-like finesse, as does the descent down Telegraph Pass back to the Desert Classic Trail.

To the north of the Desert Classic trailhead, you can find other technical riding opportunities. Loops One and Two, both accessible by heading due north out of the ramadas at the Pima Canyon parking lot, are excellent, albeit short rides that connect to one another (see map). Beverly Canyon and the Javelina Canyon trails share a parking lot off 46th Street and Baseline; both are moderately technical and difficult

MilesDirections Sidebar

An Epic Alternative:
Mormon Loop-National Trail-Telegraph Pass-Desert Classic

Length: The National Trail is 8.5 miles out to Telegraph Pass (17 miles round trip), although most people prefer the mellower ride up Mormon Loop and immediately down National Trail (14 miles round trip)

Difficulty Rating: National Trail is technically and aerobically difficult to extreme.

Wheels: On the National Trail bring as much suspension as you own—there are many big drops and rugged passages. That said, don't be surprised to see some hardcores out riding the National Trail on their rigid single speeds.

As an epic alternative to the already-challenging Desert Classic ride, this excellent but difficult route is much beloved by Arizona's skilled and super-fit riders. Starting in the Pima Canyon parking lot, ride up to the National Trail (either up the National Trail itself—*ugh*—or up the Mormon Loop, which splits off just past the stone buildings at the end of the gravel road). *[FYI. The Mormon Loop joins the National Trail but is somewhat easier to traverse.]* The National Trail is well marked all the way to Telegraph Pass; ride up into South Mountain until you hit the Buena Vista Lookout. Once at the lookout, the singletrack continues north but becomes nearly unrideable for all but the most skilled riders. *[Option. Take the paved road down to Telegraph Pass.]*

Once at Telegraph Pass, the singletrack bombs down the side of South Mountain. It's very, very hard, featuring two- to three-foot steps all the way down, as well as major foot traffic on the weekends. Again, only the most skilled riders make it all the way down unscathed. If you own body armor, wear it.

Telegraph Pass Trail joins with the Desert Classic Trail (see mile 8.9 in the Desert Classic cues), which you will then ride east all the way back to the Pima Canyon parking lot.

The National Trail is an epic ride on its own, featuring several discrete "problems," interesting technical challenges with names like *The Waterfall* and *The Bermuda Triangle*, to be ridden or walked along the way. Another popular option that allows you to descend the National Trail is to start at the 46th Street parking lot, ride up Javelina Trail to the Mormon Loop, and then down the National Trail and the Beverly Canyon Trail back to the 46th Street parking lot.

trails. One popular loop connects the Pima Canyon parking lot to the Beverly Canyon parking lot, up Javelina Trail; back down the wide dirt road, reconnecting with Loop Two, and then Loop One, creating a figure-eight journey in epic single-track riding.

You can spend your whole biking lifetime exploring various combinations in South Mountain Park and never get bored. And except for the upper reaches of the National Trail, you're never too far from help should things go wrong.

Ride Information

❂ Trail Contacts:
City of Phoenix Parks and Recreation, Phoenix, AZ (602) 262–6861 or www.ci.phoenix.az.us/PARKS/hike soth.html

❂ Schedule:
Open year round. Fair warning: Summers are extremely hot!

❂ Fees/Permits:
No fees or permits required

❂ Local Information:
Greater Phoenix Chamber of Commerce, Phoenix, AZ (602) 254–5521 or www.phoenixchamber.com

❂ Local Events/Attractions:
IMAX at Arizona Mills Mall, Tempe, AZ (480) 897–1453 • Phoenix Rock Gym, Tempe, AZ (480) 921–8322 or www.phoenixrockgym.com - Arizona's largest indoor rock gym

❂ Restaurants:
Four Peaks Brewery, Tempe, AZ (480) 303–9967 or www.fourpeaks.com

❂ Organizations:
Mountain Bike Association of Arizona (MBAA) (603) 351–7430 or www. mbaa.net - MBAA is the state's leading mountain biking advocacy group. They also run the NORBA mountain biking race circuit here.

❂ Local Attractions:
Tovrea Castle, Phoenix, AZ (602) 262–6412 or www.ci.phoenix.az.us/ PARKS/ tovrea.html - Visible for miles in every direction, this wedding-cake-shaped "castle" has been a Phoenix fixture since its construction in 1929. City of Phoenix Parks & Recreation recently restored the castle's gardens to their original design, and is now restoring the castle's interior. Call ahead • Heritage Square, Phoenix, AZ (602) 262–5071 or www.azcentral.com/community/points/ heritage.html - a collection of historic homes

❂ Other Resources:
The Map: Trails of West Phoenix is the excellent full-color map used in the Parks and Recreation Department's official map kiosks. This map features South Mountain Park. Available in bike shops and most bookstores.

❂ Local Bike Shops:
Landis Cyclery, Tempe, AZ (480) 839–9383 or www.landiscyclery.com

❂ Maps:
USGS maps: Laveen, AZ; Lone Butte, AZ; Guadalupe, AZ

2

Charles M. Christiansen Memorial Trail 100

Ride Specs

Start: There are numerous parking lots along Trail 100. The trail described here starts from the parking lot at Central Avenue, south of Thunderbird Road. There are also lots at 7th Avenue and Peoria Avenue, Dreamy Draw Park (off Northern Avenue east of the Squaw Peak Parkway), and at the far eastern end of the trail, on Tatum Boulevard, south of Shea Boulevard.

Length: 21.2-mile out-and-back

Approximate Riding Time: 3-4 hours

Difficulty Rating: Moderate, with a couple technically difficult climbs. It's a long trail, so cyclists should be in good aerobic shape to complete this ride as an out-and-back.

Trail Surface: Singletrack

Lay of the Land: Sonoran Desert

Elevation Gain: 2,094 feet

Land Status: Municipal park

Nearest City: Phoenix

Other Trail Users: Hikers and equestrians

Canine Compatibility: Dogs permitted

Wheels: Hardtail is fine, however full suspension could come in handy on the fast descents.

Getting There

From Phoenix: From I-17, head east from Exit 210 on Thunderbird Road toward Central Avenue (which is a minor neighborhood road north of North Mountain). Turn left on Central Avenue and enter the neighborhood. Continue on Central Avenue until the road ends at the North Mountain Preserve parking lot and trailhead. There is room for about 20 cars here. The surrounding neighborhood has had trouble with people parking on its streets, so now a permit or a neighbor's permission is required. If parking here is ever in question, go instead to Mountain View Park (7th Avenue, south of Peoria) and start your ride there. *DeLorme: Arizona Atlas & Gazetteer:* Page 57 A5

Shuttle Option: One good option in order to avoid the return ride back is to park a second vehicle at the corner of Tatum Boulevard and Shea Boulevard. At the end of the ride, head north on Tatum to your shuttle vehicle and catch a ride back to the start.

Public Transportation: From Central Station take the Blue Line to 36th Street and Shea Boulevard. Now on your bike, proceed south on the 36th Street bike lanes and turn right onto Mountain Road. Continue on Mountain View Road to the Dreamy Draw Bikeway entrance. Proceed on the bikeway for 1.2 miles to the Trail 100 intersection at Dreamy Draw Park. Start the ride at mile 6.5. Valley Metro buses stop near many of the trailheads, therefore one-way trips are possible and parking is not an issue.

North Mountain Preserve is a very popular destination for bikers, hikers, and equestrians from across the Valley. Nestled right in the middle of Phoenix, the park is surrounded by neighborhoods. There are at least five trailheads feeding into North Mountain.

Because of the preserve's heavy use, wildlife sightings are few and far between. However, several coyote families still live here. Ride in the early morning and you might find two or three coordinating their efforts to capture a rabbit.

Starting from the north parking lot off Thunderbird Road and Central Avenue, cyclists will pass through the narrow gate and begin pedaling south. The trails are very easy for this segment, and the urge to kick it into high gear will be hard to fight. However, the neighborhoods surrounding this segment are a good indication that this area of the park is often congested with hikers and even equestrians. So be cautious and courteous.

Like many trail networks in Phoenix's municipal parks, there are ample opportunities to lose the intended trail. The Charles M. Christiansen Memorial Trail 100, named for the man who was instrumental in establishing the Phoenix Mountain Preserve in the 1970s, is fairly well marked with posts.

Upon entering the park, riders pass a dirt dam—on the way back, it's fun to take bets on who can pedal back up the dam without dabbing. Just past the dirt dam, take the first left—this is Trail 100. The trail dips into some shallow arroyos but is otherwise level. The trail is quite wide and smooth, lending credence to the local myth that it's an "easy" trail. Keep riding east to dispel that myth.

Riding along the trail with Phoenix in the distance.

Pass through a tunnel under 7th Street and come out next to Pointe Tapatio Resort's tennis courts and stables for Maricopa County Sheriff's Office horses. Zip up some tight switchbacks, bomb down a short, rocky hill (watch for horses!), and continue straight through the trail intersection. This section is slightly more difficult.

Continue selecting trails to the left while working around the back of "Horse Hill." As cyclists cross the north face of the hill, a protracted, mellow climb leads to a saddle between two peaks. The view of Phoenix is spectacular from the saddle.

The drop out of the saddle starts as a fast and slightly dangerous catwalk. Pick up speed while approaching Cave Creek Road, where riders will pass under a second tunnel and climb a short, super-steep transition. This third segment of the trail is what many cyclists have been waiting for—especially those into technical singletrack.

Cross over the paved road just past the tunnel—look for the singletrack continuing on the other side. At this point, bear left and take Trail 100A, a slightly easier alternate to the heart-attack-inducing path Trail 100 follows up, up, up the side of the mountain. Trail 100A travels around the backside of the mountain, passes behind some very expensive houses, and suddenly becomes more difficult.

This difficult bit of trail continues for several miles until it rejoins with Trail 100 atop another saddle, and another great view of the city. Beware of the hairy descent, and grunt up the steep ascent that leaves cyclists overlooking Dreamy Draw Park and Squaw Peak's north face. Carefully drop into Dreamy Draw Park, consult your computer, and congratulate yourself for completing seven miles of rugged terrain.

From here, Trail 100 continues east to Tatum Boulevard for nearly eight more miles. The portion of the trail from Dreamy Draw Park through the first few valleys provides a lot of shallow climbing on loose trail surfaces: But remember, what goes up *must* come down, and the payoff is worth it (Dreamy Draw Park is also the trailhead to several other trail networks, notably Trail 1A (Perl Charles)). All told, following the entirety of Trail 100 out-and-back clocks in at just under 22 miles.

The alternate start for this trail is from Mountain View Park (also known by local as "Duck Park" for the bronze statue of a duck at its entrance). Head north out of Mountain View Park and take all right turns until you connect with the Trail 100. This route is longer than the original by about two miles, and features more climbing than if starting from the original start point as described in the "Getting There" section of this chapter.

Ride Information

🕐 Trail Contacts:
City of Phoenix Parks & Recreation, Northeast District, Phoenix, AZ (602) 262–7901 or *http://copwww.ci.phoenix.az.us/PARKS/parkidx.html*

🕐 Schedule:
Open year round – but very hot in the summer; bring lots of water

💲 Fees/Permits:
No fees or permits required

❓ Local Information:
Phoenix Mountains Preservation Council: *www.phoenixmountains.org*

📧 Bus Information:
Valley Metro: (602) 253–5000 or *www.valleymetro.maricopa.gov*

🚲 Local Bike Shops:
Slippery Pig Bike Shop, Phoenix, AZ (602) 263–5143 • **Bicycle Showcase,** Phoenix, AZ (602) 971–0730 • **Bike Barn,** Phoenix, AZ (602) 956–3870

Ⓝ Maps:
USGS maps: Sunnyslope, AZ; Paradise Valley, AZ

MilesDirections

0.0 START at the Thunderbird Road and Central Avenue parking lot. Look for the trail heading due south out of the parking lot.

0.2 Just past the dirt dam, there's a metal signpost. The trail splits left and right; take the left, in front of the dam and down into a wash. Pass through three washes and come to another metal signpost. The trail splits left and right; the left goes up the dam, so go to the right and deeper into the park. Just beyond that turn, the trail splits again. Take the left heading southeast.

0.5 The trail turns and heads due east. A trail joins from the right, from the Mountain View

Park trailhead. This trail leads to the alternate start at Mountain View Park (see map).

0.9 Enter a tunnel and pass beneath 7th Street. You'll exit the tunnel next to the Pointe Tapatio Resort's tennis courts. Continue ahead.

1.0 Pass the Pointe's tennis courts and the Maricopa County Sheriff's Office's horse corrals, and arrive at the top of a short hill. At the base of the hill is a crossroads. Pass through the crossroads heading due east and up the hill to the other side.

1.3 Come to a metal signpost to your left. Continue ahead on the trail, due east.

MilesDirections

1.4 Just past the last trail split, you'll come to another signpost. The sign points up a trail that says "Trail 100" to your right; this is a very steep climb. For now, take the easy route straight ahead and up the hill on the doubletrack.

1.9 Join with the difficult portion of Trail 100 that split a half-mile back. Turn left at the top of the hill and head due north for a bit before heading down the hill.

2.7 At the bottom of the long hill pass through a tunnel beneath Cave Creek Road. There's a sudden right turn then a steep incline. Go up this hill, cross Cortez Road (a paved road), and pick up the singletrack on the other side. Immediately past Cortez Road, the singletrack splits several times. Any combination of trails will get you around the mountain.

3.3 Once around the mountain, begin working your way toward a saddle between two hills west of the neighborhood. There are several trail options; it doesn't matter which ones are taken as long as you're working westward toward the saddle.

4.8 Reach the saddle. Trail 100 splits left and right. Go left. [*Side-trip. The right connects with a very difficult portion of Trail 100 that split back around mile 2.5 or so.*] As you round the corner around a house's backyard, you'll come upon numerous trail options. There is a single, best-marked and most-obvious trail dead ahead, which passes down into a wash. Take this trail.

5.3 Steep climb to another saddle.

5.7 At the bottom of a steep descent, the trail splits left and right. Take the left, heading due south toward Squaw Peak Parkway (AZ 51).

6.3 After a short descent, the trail splits left and right. Go right, away from the neighborhood and toward Squaw Peak Parkway. At the bottom of the descent, go through a tunnel and pass under Squaw Peak Parkway. Take the first right turn past the tunnel and enter Dreamy Draw Park. Ride up to the bathrooms on top of the hill. Just past the bathrooms, a paved bike pathway travels east and west. Turn right (west) on the bike path and continue.

6.9 Take a hard left off the bike path at the kiosk and pick up Trail 100 again. Avoid the trail that doubles back and travels east (this is just a minor loop within Dreamy Draw Park). About 20 yards up, there's a signpost for Trail 100.

7.1 Trail 100 splits left and right. Go up the hill, to your right. Turning left takes you to a difficult wash and a hike-a-bike ascent up Trail 220.

7.3 Arrive at the top of a hill. Several trails join from the right; continue ahead.

7.4 A metal signpost indicates that Trail 1A (Perl Charles) splits off to the right from here. Continue on Trail 100, to the left. After arriving at the top of a hill, the open desert valley below is crisscrossed with numerous marked and unmarked trails. Continue heading due east on Trail 100 [*FYI. The trail is (usually) marked with Trail 100 markers.*]

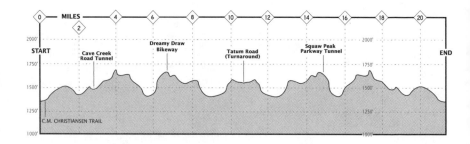

10.6 Reach the end of the trail, at the Tatum Boulevard parking lot. Turn around and head back the way you came or head to your shuttle car on Shea Boulevard. Keep your eyes open for Trail 100 signposts along the way back if you chose to ride.

21.2 Return to the Central Avenue parking lot.

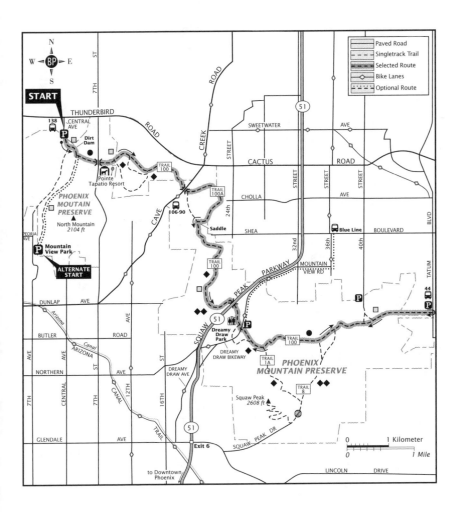

3

Estrella Loop

Ride Specs

Start: Equestrian center in Estrella Mountain Park
Length: 6.6-mile loop
Approximate Riding Time: 45 minutes to 1 hour
Difficulty Rating: Moderate, with a difficult climb and some descents that are very easy to take dangerously fast
Trail Surface: Singletrack
Lay of the Land: Lower Sonoran desert
Elevation Gain: 604 feet
Land Status: Municipal park
Nearest Town: Goodyear
Other Trail Users: Hikers and equestrians
Canine Compatibility: Dogs permitted
Wheels: Hardtail is fine

Getting There

From Phoenix: Going west on I-10, turn south on Litchfield Road (Exit 128). Drive south four miles on Litchfield Road and turn right (about 45 degrees, SW) on Main Street, also called Route 84. There's a convenience market on the opposite corner and an airfield (the Airport Commerce Center) to the right. In

about one mile, look for the brown Estrella Mountain Park signs that point to the left (south). Turn left on Bullard Avenue and head toward the mountains. Once across the bridge, look for another brown sign that points to the right on Vineyard Drive. In about 500 yards, there will be more brown signs. Turn left on Casey Abbott Road just before the turnoff to the Estrella Golf Course. Once through the tollbooth (there's a $3 entrance fee), follow Casey Abbott Road until it reaches a T-intersection. Turn right at the intersection and drive to 143rd Drive, which parallels 143rd Avenue on the inside of the park's fence. Take another right and drive to the equestrian center. Park in the large gravel parking area near the trailhead at the south end of the parking lot. *DeLorme: Arizona Atlas & Gazetteer:* Page 57 B4

The West Valley is a mystery to many mountain bikers. The excellent riding in the East Valley, and the critical mass of riders at Arizona State University and Tempe in general, keep many riders from venturing much further west than Central Avenue. Yet cyclists fight for parking spaces every weekend at South Mountain Park, wait in line at the Cactus Cup race loops, or vie with crowds of equestrians and hikers at North Mountain.

Look west from any part of the Valley, and, smog levels permitting, you'll notice several massive mountain ranges out there. One of these ranges, to the southwest of South Mountain, hides some of the most excellent, and overlooked riding in town.

The Sierra Estrellas are dark, jagged, angry-looking mountains, all granite and dotted with dense Sonoran plant life. The softer, older mountains elsewhere in the Valley, especially South Mountain and the Hawes Pass area, are more inviting than

Beginning the descent from "Boy Scout Hill."

the Estrellas. And at first glance, the Estrella's schist and dark granite appear unmanageably rugged for bikes. Keep looking.

Locals know the Estrella Mountain Regional Park primarily for the annual Hedgehog Hustle mountain bike race (which served as an Olympic qualifying race in 2000). Like most racetracks in Arizona, however, the Hedgehog Hustle loop is pretty boring doubletrack: Fast, wide, repetitive. Such is the racing in Arizona.

The Estrella Loop trail, however, is ideal singletrack for mountain biking, albeit a bit short. The ride starts out heading up a newly graded dirt service road, but quickly turns into a rocky singletrack climb. The top of the climb terminates in a nigh-impossible wash/gulch, which leaves many cyclists walking. The more this wash is ridden, though, the more rideable it becomes—give it the old college try and see for yourself.

There's a long, fast descent on the other side of the wash, with unmarked and unnumbered trails joining and diverging the whole way down. The views in the interior of the park are spectacular, with the bulk of the Sierra Estrellas and Butterfly Mountain visible to the south. And quiet! Except for the occasional airplanes from the nearby regional airport. At just 15 minutes off the freeway, you'll feel as far from civilization as you can get.

MilesDirections

0.0 START from the equestrian center's parking lot. Once out of the parking area, go around the gate and travel south down the gravel road. *[FYI. This gravel road is a recent addition to the park; although it appears to be car-friendly, and despite the generous parking space at the end of the gravel road, it is apparently not open to the public.]*

1.0 Arrive at the second parking area at the end of the gravel road. Look for the singletrack to the left, at the south end of the parking area. Cross over a dirt berm.

1.6 Careful as the trail dives into a steep arroyo; the climb back out the other side is very tough.

2.9 Pass a singletrack trail that merges from the right. Continue on the singletrack as it bends to the left.

4.5 Begin a steep climb. At the top of this climb look for a sign posted from an old Boy Scout project. Head down the descent and take a left, about 15 yards down the hill (the right is a more difficult, unmaintained option). *[FYI. There are several trail options that will get you back to the parking lot; keep heading north and you can't miss it. The remaining cues are for the largest and most obvious trail back to the lot.]*

6.2 Pass through a sandy wash and reconnect with the wide gravel road.

6.6 Arrive back at the parking lot.

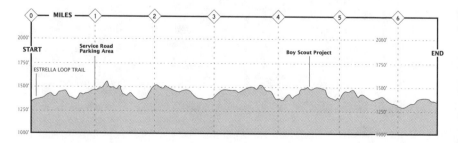

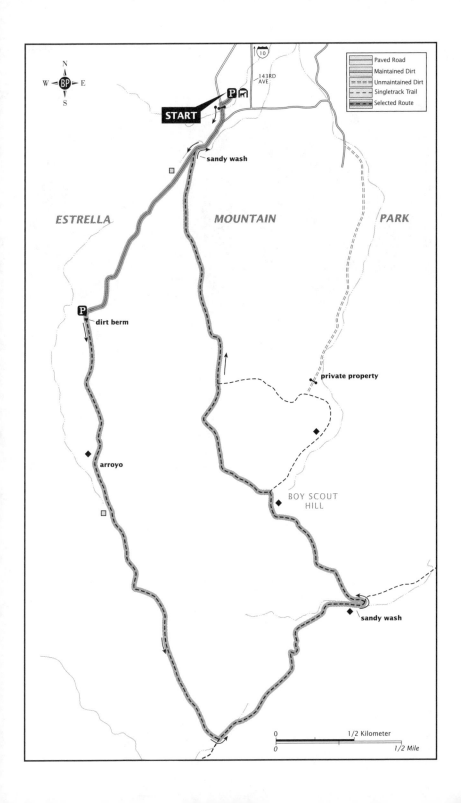

N
W — BP — E
S

10
143RD
AVE

P

START

sandy wash

ESTRELLA   MOUNTAIN   PARK

	Paved Road
	Maintained Dirt
	Unmaintained Dirt
	Singletrack Trail
	Selected Route

P
dirt berm

private property

arroyo

BOY SCOUT
HILL

sandy wash

0   1/2 Kilometer
0   1/2 Mile

Sierra Estrellas in the background.

Most cyclists bang out the seven miles of Estrella Loop in just under an hour. However, there are many offshoots and other trails to explore once done with this loop. Look for official county maps of the park at the trailhead kiosk to find out more about these trails.

Most of the 60,000-acre Sierra Estrellas lie within the Gila River Indian Reservation. There's a 14,000-acre wilderness area—no bikes allowed—deep within the range. The most hospitable part of the range lies within the Estrella Mountain Park, administered by Maricopa County and home to an extensive equestrian center and water-sucking golf course.

The Sierra Estrellas are home to mule deer, javelinas, coyotes, mountain lions, and a small band of desert bighorn sheep. Several species of raptors—Coopers hawks, prairie falcons, and golden eagles—are often visible in the sky.

Some of the Estrella Loop follows a trail called the Gadsden Trail built by the Arizona State Parks department. Portions of the Gila River, once the boundary between the United States and Mexico, are visible from this trail—cyclists will drive over the Gila River to get to the park. The Gadsden Purchase of 1854 relocated the boundary further south, to its present location.

As housing continues to spread ever westward, expect the Estrellas to become increasingly popular. Get in now before it becomes another crowded circus like South Mountain.

Ride Information

🕓 Trail Contacts:
Estrella Mountain Regional Park Ranger Station, Goodyear, AZ (623) 932–3811

🕐 Schedule:
Open year round

💲 Fees/Permits:
$3 per car

❓ Local Information:
Tri-City West Chamber of Commerce (623) 932–2260 or *www.tricitywest-cofc.org* • **Maricopa County Parks & Recreation's information** about Estrella Mountain Regional Park at *www.marico-pa.gov/rec_svc/estrella/est_history.asp*

🔱 Local Events/Attractions:
Hedgehog Hustle, Surprise, AZ (602) 351–7430 or *www.mbaa.net* – *usually early March; part of MBAA's annual NORBA mountain bike race series* •

Estrella War, Phoenix, AZ: *www.estrellawar.org* – *Members of the Society for Creative Anachronism suit up in plate mail every President's Day weekend to bash each other senseless with wooden swords and rubber hammers, re-enacting medieval-style battles in the Arizona desert* • **Phoenix International Raceway,** Phoenix, AZ : *www.phoenixintl-raceway.com* – *One of the two major racecourses in metro Phoenix (the other is Firebird Raceway, south of Chandler on I-10), PIR is home to the NASCAR Winston Cup Series.*

🚲 Local Bike Shops:
Bicycle Warehouse, Phoenix, AZ (602) 265–0660

🅝 Maps:
USGS maps: Avondale SW, AZ; Avondale SE, AZ • County maps available at trailhead kiosk

4

The Mine Loop – Hawes Pass Area

Ride Specs

Start: From the gravel parking area on North Power Road

Length: 7.7-mile loop

Approximate Riding Time: 1.5-2 hours

Difficulty Rating: Physically moderate, with some difficult climbs. Technically moderate, with some difficult passages due to steep climbs and dangerous switchbacks.

Trail Surface: Singletrack

Lay of the Land: Lower Sonoran desert

Elevation Gain: 1,065 feet

Land Status: National forest

Nearest Town: Mesa

Other Trail Users: Hikers and, only occasionally, equestrians

Canine Compatibility: Dogs permitted

Wheels: Full suspension strongly recommended

Getting There

From Mesa: From U.S. 60 (Superstition Freeway) and Power Road (Exit 188), head north on Power Road (a.k.a. Bush Highway). The last light you'll go through is Thomas; continue north past this as the road becomes Bush Highway proper and enters the Tonto National Forest. Follow Bush Highway down to Granite Reef Recreation Area, about four miles past the last light on Power Road. Park anywhere in the recretion area and begin there. *DeLorme: Arizona Atlas & Gazetteer:* Page 58 B1

The Hawes Pass area of Tonto National Forest is sandwiched between the Usery Pass Recreation Area to the south and the Salt River and the Granite Reef Recreation Area to the north.

The hills around which this mountain bike playground wind were heavily prospected a hundred years ago. The Mine Loop got its name from the large, deep, unmarked mine shaft cyclists ride ever so carefully around on the way down the mountain. And this isn't the only mineshaft. There are many prospecting holes all along the trail, especially further up in the mountains. Miners prospected for everything from silver to mica, but never found a profitable enough vein to continue. The hills ultimately remained undeveloped, and were eventually brought under the protection of Tonto National Forest.

The Usery Mountains, which make up the eastern edge of this riding area, are named after King Usery (King refers to his name, not his title). Usery was a cattleman, bandit, and horse thief who homesteaded the area in the 1870s.

Not too many years ago, a small circle of experienced mountain bikers jealously guarded the Hawes Pass Mine Loop. There's certainly nothing to suggest that any rides exist in the region at all: no signs, no trailhead, nothing. Some East Valley bike shops changed the status of these "exclusive" trails and started sending their customers to the trail. The advent of full-suspension bikes also contributed to the influx of riders by lowering the bar for relatively new riders to try more technically chal-

The mine, after which the trail is named.

Ride Information

Trail Contacts:
Tonto National Forest, Mesa, AZ (480) 610-3300 or *www.fs.fed.us/r3/tonto*

Schedule:
Open year round

Local Attractions:
Ghost Town of Goldfield, Goldfield, AZ (480) 983-0333 or *www.arizonaguide. com/goldfieldghosttown* – Located at the base of the Superstitions (a few miles east of the Hawes Pass area),

Goldfield is the only authentic ghost town located in the Valley. You can take underground mine tours, learn about local mining and railroad history, and book helicopter tours of the Superstitions from here.

Local Bike Shops:
Bike Chalet, Mesa, AZ (480) 807-2944 or *www.bikechalet.com*

Maps:
USGS maps: Granite Reef Dam, AZ; Buckhorn, AZ

lenging stuff. The Mine Loop exploded in popularity, much to the detriment of the trail. Today, erosion and over-riding are conspiring to destroy some of the most delicate and dangerous parts of the trail, particularly the switchbacks that go down the backside of the mountain and past the mine hole itself.

Mine Loop's singletrack is fast and a little gravelly, particularly in the corners. The grav-

> ### Red Mountain
>
> The massive red mountain that is visible from all of the Hawes Pass area is known to virtually everyone as "Red Mountain," including housing developers who use it in their advertising. However, the mountain is actually Mt. McDowell (confusing since the McDowell Mountains, north of Scottsdale, are a whole different range) and is located entirely on the Salt River Indian Reservation.

el surface makes some of the climbs very difficult, and some of the descents a bit sketchy. Finding the way around the park can be hard, too: There are no signs, trail markers, or metal posts to guide you. Three aids to help keep your bearings straight are the big red mountain, North Power Road, and the Salt River—all of which are always in view.

Mine Loop is just one of many excellent rides in this area. If riders cross North Power Road and go south about 50 yards to the first power line with a single pole, they can pick up a whole other network of singletrack on the west side of the road. This network of trails is commonly called the "TRW Trail," for the TRW plant at the far western edge of this piece of desert. Sadly, this network will not be around forever: It runs right through the middle of the proposed Red Mountain Freeway route. Enjoy it while it's there because this singletrack will more than likely disappear in a few years.

MilesDirections

NOTE: You'll need to head south on Bush Highway (there's a good shoulder with plenty of room) from Granite Reef Recreation Area where you parked and ride to the north edge of the canal that crosses beneath the road. Across the road, on the west (left) side, look for the trailhead. Ride across the road and begin down the trail.

0.0 START from a wooden pole at the trailhead and make a quick descent onto the trail.

0.1 As you come down the initial hill, the trail splits left and right. Continue to the right and around the bend, following Hawes Trail. *[FYI. The trail to your left is your eventual exit point of the loop.]*

1.0 Pass through a wide wash. Just past the wash, there's a fork in the trail. Go to the right, heading south and up the hill. *[Side-trip/option. The trail to your left is Big Saguaro Trail, which cuts across the Hawes Pass area and eventually reconnects at the base of the Mine Loop climb; see mile marker 3.3 in the cues.]*

2.2 Reach the top of the ridge. Continue on the established trail straight ahead. *[Side-trip. There appears to be a trail off to the left from the top of the ridge; it's just a lookout point, but feel free to check it out.]*

2.6 About 75 yards past a white wooden post to your left, the trail splits. Keep your eyes peeled for this, since it's not marked!

MilesDirections *continued*

Turn left here on the Mine Trail. *[Side-trip/option. Continuing straight here continues following the Hawes Trail, and eventually hooks up with Hawes Road in 1.3 miles. The climb up to Hawes Road is very steep and difficult.]*

3.3 The Mine Trail is joined by the Big Saguaro Trail from the left. This is the shortcut that comes out of the valley below. Continue on the Mine Trail directly ahead.

3.7 Reach the top of a saddle with a large cluster of rocks to your right. *[Note. Be careful here. This is the beginning of some dangerous switchbacks.]*

4.1 The trail you've been on joins with another trail that goes to your left and right. Turn left, heading up the hill *[FYI. Turning right goes down to North Power Road.]*

4.8 Reach another saddle between two peaks. As you leave the saddle, the trail appears to split left and right. Take the right, heading toward the big red mountain.

5.7 At the bottom of the switchbacks, keep your eyes peeled for a split in the trail to the left; this is the Cutacross Trail. It's a little bit hidden, and doubles back tighter than 90 degrees as it goes down a short hill. Turn onto the Cutacross Trail and head down into a wash. If you head straight, you'll end up on North Power Road in about a quarter-mile.

6.2 As you come up a small rise, you'll intersect with a trail going left and right. Turn left, away from North Power Road and back into the desert.

6.6 As you climb another short hill, the trail splits left and right. Turn right onto the Ridge Trail, continuing up the short, steep climb. *[Side-trip. The left option of the Ridge Trail eventually connects with the Big Saguaro Trail, in less than one mile.]*

7.6 The Ridge Trail rejoins with the Hawes Trail near the trail entrance. To get back to your car, turn to the right here and hammer up the hill.

7.7 Arrive back at your car.

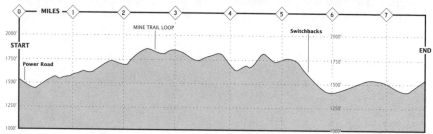

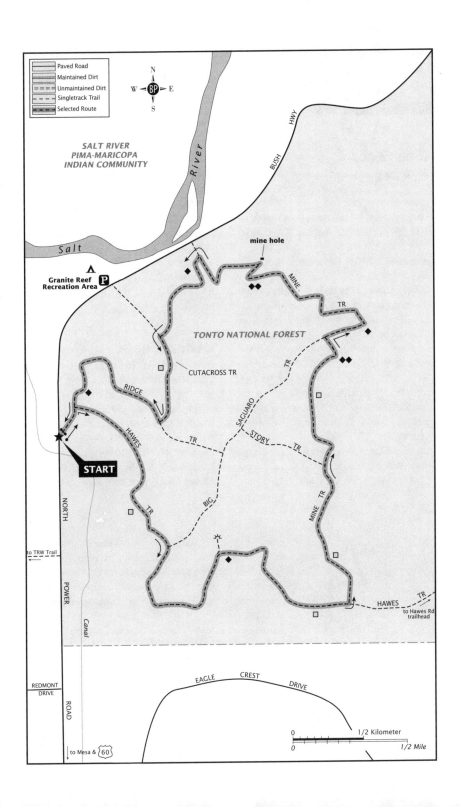

Paved Road
Maintained Dirt
Unmaintained Dirt
Singletrack Trail
Selected Route

N
W — BP — E
S

SALT RIVER
PIMA-MARICOPA
INDIAN COMMUNITY

BUSH HWY

River

Salt

mine hole

Granite Reef
Recreation Area

TONTO NATIONAL FOREST

MINE TR

CUTACROSS TR

RIDGE

SAGUARO

TR

STORY

TR

TR

HAWES

TR

START

NORTH

TR

BIG

MINE TR

to TRW Trail

POWER

Canal

HAWES TR
to Hawes Rd
trailhead

REDMONT
DRIVE

ROAD

EAGLE CREST DRIVE

to Mesa & 60

0   1/2 Kilometer
0   1/2 Mile

Pima and Dynamite

Ride Specs

Start: From the gravel lot at the southeast corner of the intersection of Pima Road and Dynamite Boulevard.

Length: Varies, but can range from 5 miles to 50 miles. There are as many as 300 miles of trails in the entire area.

Approximate Riding Time: Varies. Explore as long as you want!

Difficulty Rating: The trails in this area cover the range from easy to very hard. There are some long, shallow climbs on some trails in the area, as well as long stretches of sandy wash and super-steep arroyos that will prove challenging to climb out of. Also note that some trails feature rocky drops and rutted portions that are more technically difficult.

Trail Surface: Singletrack, with occasional doubletrack (usually as access to other singletrack trails).

Lay of the Land: Sonoran desert, laced with many granite boulders

Land Status: Arizona State Trust land

Nearest Towns: Scottsdale and Carefree

Other Trail Users: Motorcycles, ORVs, equestrians.

Canine Compatibility: Dogs permitted, but keep in mind that there are many motorcycles in the area. Either keep the pooch under control or leave him at home.

Wheels: Hardtail is fine for most of the rides; full suspension is recommended for the far-north trails.

Getting There

From Phoenix: Heading east on the Superstition Freeway (U.S. 60) from Phoenix, head north at Exit 177 on Loop 101. Get off at the Pima Road exit just north of the Scottsdale Municipal Airport and head north on Pima Road to Dynamite Boulevard. Park in the gravel lot at the southeast corner of Pima Road and Dynamite Boulevard. *DeLorme: Arizona Atlas & Gazetteer:* Page 49 D6

As you head north out of the endless sprawl that Scottsdale has become, the desert begins to sprout boulders. By the time cyclists reach Tonto National Forest, the boulders have taken over and it's easy to forget this is still the Sonoran Desert. Luckily for mountain bikers, each little gap between these boulders makes terrific singletrack on which to ride.

The area of boulder-ridden desert north of Dynamite Boulevard at Pima Road has been a hangout for motorcyclists and other motorized ORV riders for decades. Motocross cyclists have cut a network of trails that crisscross the land—all private, but managed as state trust land—for more than 300 miles. It would take many months of dedicated riding to explore every little trail in the area, and new trails sprout up all the time. Because it's state trust land, nobody is responsible for trail management. The motorcyclists run the show, and they know it. Forget IMBA laws and get out of the way

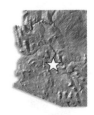

when you hear an engine revving behind you. Common etiquette is to hold up a number of fingers indicating how many riders are in your group as the motorcycles pass.

That said, you could ride more-or-less in peace the further north you go. After traveling about five miles up the Power Line Trail (the service road that passes beneath the power lines up to Bartlett Dam), you leave private land and enter Tonto National Forest. The trails are similar in the national forest, except there are no motorcycles allowed and they seem to become much more difficult. Cyclists can more directly access these northern trails by parking off Bartlett Dam Road, just east of where the road turns off Cave Creek Road.

The slopes of the 4,000-foot high McDowell Mountains, just to the south of Pima and Dynamite, capture more rain than the rest of the desert. Everything you might normally find in the Sonoran Desert grows here, only much bigger: Looming ocotillo and cholla, blooming creosote, palo verdes, and mesquites. Summer or winter rains create explosive color in the desert, contrasting against dramatic boulders and offering up some great photo-ops along the way.

The trails at Pima and Dynamite are a little different than typical hardpack desert singletrack. Its trails are often sandy, though this is decomposing granite and not the

super-silty stuff found in washes. Take care not to wash out on tight turns when going fast; otherwise, it's an excellent surface on which to rip. Many trails also are rutted out, or have little whoop-de-dos that get worse after each rain. With a little speed, these dips act like moguls and can surprise some riders by kicking them into a big jump. Excessive speed combined with washed-out corners and collapsing berms can make these trails dangerous, and in many cases it's very easy to go fast here. So just be careful.

Although motorcyclists should be thanked for creating the network of trails at Pima and Dynamite, they've entered a Faustian bargain: The more the motorcycles ride the trails, the worse they get. Donuts cut into the desert seem to be everywhere. Shredded landscape where mud might have collected becomes a magnet for aggressive throttle-twisters and 4x4 truck drivers. Great trails, all, but there's little evidence that anyone cares to preserve them.

As state trust land, it's just a matter of time before developers replace singletrack with country clubs, and this area's 300 miles of trail with 5,000-square foot homes. There are efforts to preserve as much of this land as possible, by placing it in a private trust called the McDowell Sonoran Land Trust. Unfortunately, however, some of the area has already been cordoned off and marked with colored tape in preparation for development.

Ride Information

📞 Trail Contacts:
Arizona State Land Department, Phoenix, AZ: www.land.state.az.us • **Mountain Bike Association of Arizona (MBAA):** (602) 351-7430 or www.mbaa.net

🕐 Schedule:
Open year round – Summers are extremely hot.

💲 Fees/Permits:
Arizona State Trust land requires you either buy a $15 recreational permit from the State Land department or have a hunting license. Call (602) 542-4631 for more information on how to obtain a permit or license.

❓ Local Information:
Scottsdale Chamber of Commerce, Scottsdale, AZ (480) 945-8481 or www.scottsdalechamber.com

💡 Local Events/Attractions:
Rawhide: (480) 502-1880, 1-800-527-1880 or www.rawhide.com – Gunfights, saloons, a great restaurant, and other touristy Old West activities

ⓓ Other Resources:
McDowell Sonoran: www.highsonoran.com/land.htm • **The Arizona Sonoran Desert Museum:** www.desertmuseum.org – Although it's based in Tucson, the museum's web site will give you a lot of information about the flora of the McDowells.

🚲 Local Bike Shops:
Bicycle Ranch, Scottsdale, AZ (480) 391-3888 or www.bicycleranch.com • **Landis Cyclery,** Scottsdale, AZ (480) 948-9280 or www.landiscyclery.com

Ⓝ Maps:
USGS maps: Cave Creek, AZ; Curry's Corner, AZ; Wildcat Hill, AZ; McDowell Peak, AZ • Arizona Mapping Kompany's *The Map: Trails of East Phoenix* – available at most area bike shops for $13.50

MilesDirections

The Pima and Dynamite area is a vast network of trails, with one local shop estimating there to be more than 300 miles of singletrack and dirt roads in the area open to cyclists. Those who have been riding the area for years, mostly motorcyclists, have named a handful of the trails and know their way around quite well. However, most of the trails remain either unnamed or called as many different names as there are different groups riding them.

The accompanying map shows some of the major trails that comprise just the southern end of Pima and Dynamite. Cutting northeast from the corner of Pima Road and Dynamite Boulevard is the Power Line Trail, a broad, sometimes sandy, dirt road that closely follows the major power lines heading northeast. This is an excellent place to start exploring, and a quick bailout at the end of each ride.

It's hard to get lost in this southernmost region of Pima and Dynamite. The power lines are always visible, and point directly back to the parking lot. The western boundary is Pima Road while Dynamite Boulevard acts as the area's southern perimeter (although you'll run into housing developments well before you reach that road).

The most visible landmarks, other than the power lines, are the two mountains to the east of Power Line Trail. The smaller, more westward one is Cone Mountain. The larger mountain to the northeast is Slant Mountain. Their names make perfect sense once you see them.

Look for singletracks leading off from both sides of the Power Line Trail. The trails to the east (right, as you head away from the parking lot) tend to roll up and down like a roller coaster—a very rewarding trip. The trails to the west of Power Line Trail (left as you head away from the parking lot) all either terminate at the West Coast Express Trail (see map) or continue on to the housing developments off in the distance. The western trails tend to be a bit sandier and slow, although taking the West Express is a qui-

eter alternative to the motorcycle traffic you may face on the Power Line Trail.

About five miles up the Power Line Trail, there's a fairly major intersection of doubletrack trails funneling from every direction into the Power Line Trail. If you look east, you'll notice that this intersection is northwest of Slant Mountain and looking at a saddle between Slant Mountain and the more distant Cholla Mountain (not on the map). The doubletrack called Stagecoach Trail heads east toward that saddle, giving you terrific access to several singletrack opportunities that wrap around the near mountains and head south back to the other side. The Stagecoach Trail used to be a major access road to Brown Ranch, which is now protected within the McDowell Sonoran Preserve.

Further north from the intersection mentioned above (and north of what our map describes), the Power Line Trail continues northeast until it hits Bartlett Dam Road, about eight miles north of the Pima and Dynamite corner as you ride up the Power Line Trail. On the way there, the Power Line Trail enters Tonto National Forest in about five miles, where many more trails wind around and over the mountains. The trails in the National Forest tend to be more difficult, both technically and aerobically, as the terrain becomes steeper and more rugged. You're also much further from help should you have a medical or mechanical emergency.

The total area encompassed by the "Pima and Dynamite" region is about eight miles north-south by four miles east-west. The northernmost edge is Bartlett Dam Road, and the easternmost edge is 136th Street.

If, after you've explored the trails in the southernmost end of Pima and Dynamite and are hungry for more, pick up Arizona Mapping Kompany's The Map: Trails of East Phoenix, which contains an excellent, comprehensive map of all of Pima and Dynamite's trails. The Map is available at most bike shops, and costs $13.50.

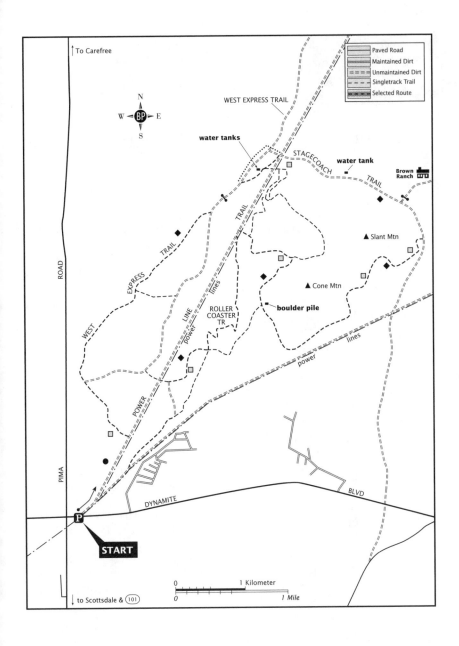

To Carefree

WEST EXPRESS TRAIL

	Paved Road
	Maintained Dirt
	Unmaintained Dirt
	Singletrack Trail
	Selected Route

N
W — BP — E
S

water tanks

STAGECOACH

water tank

Brown
Ranch

TRAIL

WEST

EXPRESS

TRAIL

▲ Slant Mtn

▲ Cone Mtn

LINE

power lines

ROLLER
COASTER
TR

boulder pile

POWER

power lines

ROAD

PIMA

DYNAMITE

BLVD

P

START

to Scottsdale & (101)

0   1 Kilometer

0   1 Mile

Trail 4 at Seven Springs

Ride Specs

Start: From Trail 4 trailhead at Seven Springs Campground
Length: 10.9-mile loop
Approximate Riding Time: 4-5 hours
Difficulty Rating: Extremely, mind-blowingly difficult, both physically and technically. Many of the descents are loose and scary, and the switchback climb out of Cave Creek is long, steep, and very slow.
Trail Surface: Singletrack and doubletrack (old mining roads and cow paths)
Lay of the Land: Rolling hills and canyons at the edge of the Sonoran Desert
Elevation Gain: 2,788 feet
Land Status: National forest
Nearest Town: Cave Creek/Carefree
Other Trail Users: Hikers and equestrians
Canine Compatibility: Dogs permitted
Wheels: Hardtail okay, full suspension strongly recommended

Getting There

From Phoenix: Take Scottsdale Road north until it turns into Carefree Road. Turn right heading north on Darlington Drive to Cave Creek Road. Turn right (east) on Cave Creek Road until it becomes FS 24, a dirt road that takes you into Tonto National Forest. Drive about 10 miles along FS 24 until you reach Seven Springs Campground. Entry fee is $4. Keep your eyes open for the trailhead parking lot on your left, about one mile past the campground entrance. *DeLorme: Arizona Atlas & Gazetteer:* Page 49 C/D6

The Seven Springs Campground is about a half-hour north of the artsy little town of Cave Creek. As the dirt road winds its way up the canyons feeding into the Humboldt and Cramm Mountains, cactus and yucca gives way to sycamore groves. Travelers may wonder if they're still in the middle of the desert. The road winds up into the mountains, passes over running water—an exotic treat for Arizonans—and eventually tops out at the tree-covered Seven Springs Campground.

At the Trail 4 trailhead, a large carved wooden map displays a network of trails in the area, and makes the region seem deceptively small: Each trail harbors many rugged miles for foot, hoof, or wheel.

More deceptive still is the sign's assessment of the various trails. Trail 4, for example, is noted as an "easy" trail. It isn't. Try *lethal*. In early March 2000, after some unexpected snowfall in the foothills, two hikers vanished somewhere off Trail 4. One of the hikers, a young woman, died of hypothermia; her brother, an experienced and fit hiker, barely made it out alive. But the unseasonable cold was just the nail in the coffin: What really killed her was getting lost in this vast, rugged, and remote part of the state.

This trail has killed, and will kill again. Cyclists should let somebody know where they are, and when they expect to be back. The time for this ride—four or five

hours—is no exaggeration. Yes, this means an average speed of about 2 MPH. Once riders have zoomed alongside the creek at a nice clip, the trail begins to ascend the canyon's edge, leaving Cave Creek a few hundred feet below. There's a fast bomb back down to the creek, then an extremely technical—remember, this is supposedly the "easy" trail—a few miles before crossing the creek again and heading up Skunk Ridge.

The singletrack switchbacks up Skunk Ridge (a "moderate" trail, according to the official map) are so narrow, rocky, and tight that many riders may not be able to get started again once stopped. Unless cyclists have mastered the uphill track stand,

expect to walk a bit of this trail. There are also several ultra-scary exposures into the canyon.

The climb up and out of the creek bed will take a couple hours all by itself. But, oh, the views! Looking west, the ominous dark ridge is Black Mesa. Due south, stands Skull Mesa; behind, to the north, is Cramm Mountain; and the big mountain, toward which the trail leads, Quien Sabe Peak.

MilesDirections

0.0 START from the Trail 4 trailhead. The trail is directly behind the large map carved into wood. Ride up the steep, rocky incline.

0.6 Trail intersects with FS 248 (a large dirt road). Pick up the singletrack on the other side (Trail 4), marked with an unsigned metal post.

0.7 The trail splits left and right. Continue on the main trail, to your right. The left is just a short side-trail that leads back down to the campground. Just past the split-off, there's a metal staircase that goes up and down over the barbed-wire fence. Go over the steps and continue. Shortly after, the trail splits left and right. To the left is the junction with the Skunk Creek Trail, from which you'll eventually exit. Stay right and continue on the Cave Creek Trail (Trail 4).

2.0 Arrive at a cattle gate. Open the gate, pass through, close the gate and continue ahead. Just past the gate you'll reach what may appear to be the "end" of the trail as it enters Cave Creek. No such luck! You have to get creative and pick your way across the rocky creek bed to pick up the trail on the other side. Look for the singletrack on the south side of the stream—it begins to go uphill pretty quickly.

3.1 Reach the bottom of a long, switchback descent and make another water crossing. Try to cross close to where a shallow waterfall runs—the crossing won't be as deep. The trail picks up on the other side of the creek and continues south.

4.2 The trail comes back down to Cave Creek. Cross the creek and look for the singletrack on the other side. It goes up a hike-a-bike rocky hill and continues.

4.4 Reach two wooden signs. The sign to your left points up the mountain and reads "Quien Sabe Trail 250 and Cottonwood Trail 247." The sign to your right points along Cave Creek and says "Skull Mesa, 5 miles." Turn left at the sign; you are now on the Skunk Creek Trail 246. Head up the mountain on the Skunk Creek Trail to the intersection with the Quien Sabe Trail. Up, up, up. Forever up.

5.9 Skunk Creek Tank, a large waterhole, is to your right and a barbed-wire gate is ahead of you. Go through and follow the sign pointing toward the "Cottonwood Trail" (you are still on the Skunk Creek Trail 246). Go through the gate, close it behind you, and continue up the singletrack to the left of the gate, up Trail 246.

6.4 Trail 246 splits left and right. Take the sin-

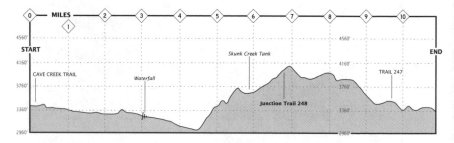

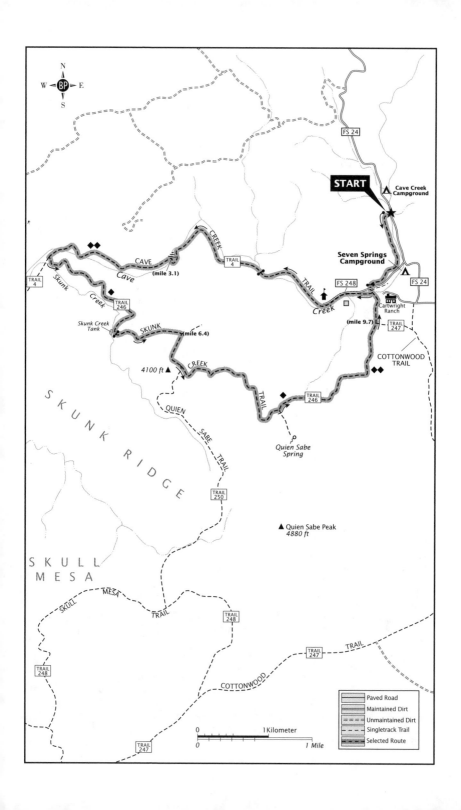

gletrack that goes up the hill, toward three large dark rocks. [**Note.** *The other trail dead-ends shortly.*]

6.8 Arrive at the top of a climb and a split in the trail. Two wooden signs point up and down the hill. The sign pointing up the hill says "To Skull Mesa Trail 248." The sign pointing down the hill says "To Cottonwood Trail 247." Head down the hill, still on Skunk Creek Trail 246, heading toward an intersection with the Cottonwood Trail. [**Side-trip.** *If you turn right, you'll get onto the Quien Sabe Trail 250 and climb for a mile before reaching the Skull Mesa Trail. These are all extremely difficult trails, arguably unbikeable although there are a few riders out there who live for this sort of thing. It's crazy-hard, and not in a fun way unless you know what you're getting into. Skull Mesa Trail is a two-mile long loop that starts and ends on the Cottonwood Trail. If you're not completely blown out at this point, Cottonwood Trail does eventually get you back to the Seven Springs Campground.*]

9.7 After a long descent and a short climb, you'll arrive at a split in the trail and two wooden signs. One indicates that Trail 246 turns to the left; the other indicates a junction with Trail 247. Turn left, continuing on Skunk Creek Trail 246 heading toward Cave Creek Trail 4.

10.0 After a descent with some steps the trail goes down to Cave Creek. Cross the rocky creek bed and pick up the singletrack again on the other side. As you enter the trees, just beyond the creek, you'll join with the Cave Creek Trail again. Turn right, onto FS 248, to head back to the parking lot, or continue across to pick up the Cave Creek Trail 4 and complete the ride on singletrack.

10.2 If you've been riding out on the dirt road, you'll reach a junction with FS 24. Turn left to continue back to the parking lot.

10.9 Return to the parking lot. Kiss the ground and be happy you're still alive.

At the "top" of Skunk Ridge, the trail starts climbing toward Quien Sabe Peak—another "moderate" climb of babyhead-littered, rutted doubletrack that was once used for ranching and mining. The roads up here in the highlands are rolling and fairly rugged, but cyclists will start making decent time again, now that climbing is mostly behind them.

The jeep roads that lead down from the mountains and back to the creek bed are roads only in the most academic sense. Keep eyes open for babyhead fields, ruts, and lots of other rugged badness. Much of the big, hard stuff cyclists would normally want to ride over is not actually attached to the ground. Taking it easy will lower the chances of becoming the trail's next victim.

This loop takes you on the Cave Creek Trail (Trail 4) to Skunk Creek Trail (Trail 246), Skunk Creek Trail to Cottonwood Trail (Trail 247), and then Cottonwood Trail back to Cave Creek Trail.

Ride Information

● Trail Contacts:
Tonto National Forest, Cave Creek District, Scottsdale, AZ (480) 595–3300

● Schedule:
Open year round

● Fees/Permits:
$4 per car

● Local Information:
Cave Creek/Carefree: *www.arizonaguide.com/destinations/cities/cavecreek.shtml*

● Local Events/Attractions:
Cave Creek Mistress Mine: (480) 488–0842 – *$1 entry fee to the mine museum gives you a look at the daily* operations of this working gold mine, established 1883 • **Taliesin West:** (480) 860–8810 or *www.franklloyd wright.org – the Arizona home and studio of famed architect Frank Lloyd Wright*

● Restaurants:
Crazy Ed's Satisfied Frog/Black Mountain Brewery, Cave Creek, AZ (480) 488–3317 or *www.satisfiedfrog.com* or *www.chilibeer.com*

● Local Bike Shops:
Cave Creek Bicycles (480) 488–5261 • **Spokesman Bicycle Shop** (480) 342–9200

● Maps:
USGS maps: New River Mesa, AZ; Humboldt Mountain, AZ

White Tank Sonoran Loop

Ride Specs

Start: From large parking lot at the end of dirt road (the tail end of Tank Mountain Road)

Length: 5.5-mile loop

Approximate Riding Time: 30–45 minutes

Difficulty Rating: Technically easy and aerobically moderate, with some moderate technical challenges in the "Technical Loop"

Trail Surface: Singletrack and a little bit of wider doubletrack

Lay of the Land: Lower Sonoran desert

Elevation Gain: 451 feet

Land Status: County park

Nearest City: Phoenix

Other Trail Users: Hikers and equestrians

Canine Compatibility: Dogs permitted

Wheels: Hardtails and hybrids are fine for this trail

Getting There

From Downtown Phoenix: Get on Dunlap Avenue/Olive Avenue and head west until it enters White Tank Mountain Park, somewhere around 140th Avenue. Pay the $3 entry fee and drive up White Tank Mountain Road until it ends about two miles into the park. Drive north up the dirt road and park in the large dirt lot.

From I-10 in Downtown Phoenix: Another quick way to get there from downtown Phoenix, depending on where you're coming from, is to take I-10 west to Loop 303 north (Exit 124). Travel north on Loop 303 (Estrella Freeway) to Dunlap/Olive Avenue. Turn left on Dunlap/Olive Avenue and head west until it enters White Tank Mountain Park, somewhere around 140th Avenue. Pay the $3 entry fee and drive up White Tank Mountain Road until it ends about two miles into the park. Drive north up the dirt road and park in the large dirt lot. **DeLorme: Arizona Atlas & Gazetteer:** Page 56 A3

The White Tank Mountains are a massive range, more in scale with the mighty Estrellas to the south than with the smaller North and South Mountain ranges. The mountains comprise the entire western border of the "Valley of the Sun" and host the White Tank Mountain Regional Park—the largest park in the Maricopa County park system at just over 41 square miles. Despite its size, the park is underdeveloped for mountain biking.

The good news is, cyclists never have to deal with Lycra-clad crowds of weekend warriors. There's also plenty of wildlife in the park, particularly the dangerous kind: Western diamondback rattlesnakes can get big and ornery. If you come across a diamondback on or near the trail, don't attempt to pass it. Toss rocks in its direction until it backs away, otherwise turn around. They can strike from a fair distance away.

The bad news is, the Sonoran Loop race course is the only practical mountain biking in that big, beautiful park. There are several loop variations, and riding them all might take three laps and a couple hours total. Because the Sonoran Loop is a race course, riders are expected to go fast. In what must be a dream to bikers everywhere who are sick of staring at those triangular signs telling bikes to yield to every-

thing on two or four legs, there is only one sign at this trailhead: "Slower yields to faster." Let 'er rip!

The Sonoran Loop itself is a nice ride, although not especially challenging. It begins along doubletrack wide enough to let bikes pass one another. The "Technical Loop," noted as requiring a "high level of skill" by the park flyers, is a fun mile-long twisty-turny passage closer to the mountain than the rest of the loop. Anyone who

Ride Information

○ Trail Contacts:
Maricopa County Parks & Recreation Dept, Phoenix, AZ (602) 506-2930 or *www.maricopa.gov/rec_svc*

○ Schedule:
Open year round

○ Fees/Permits:
$3 per car, or $50 for an annual pass

○ Local Information:
[See other rides in this section.]

○ Accommodations:
[See other rides in this section.]

○ Restaurants:
[See other rides in this section.]

○ Organizations:
The **MBAA** runs the White Tank Whirlwind race every year, late March.

○ Local Bike Shops:
Bicycle Corral, Youngtown, AZ (623) 933-9012

○ Maps:
USGS maps: White Tanks NE, AZ; White Tanks, AZ; Waddell, AZ

has not ridden this loop before should take care pedaling through this portion of the trail for their first time: Although the technical loop isn't particularly difficult, rocks and cacti are still very sharp when you land on top of them.

Once out of the Technical Loop, the race loop gets racy again: Wide doubletrack, with few climbs or dips, and the occasional arroyo. Take it easy the first couple times diving into the arroyos. They're rocky enough to mess up both cyclist and bike when things don't go as planned.

While the Sonoran Loop is the only bike-specific trail in the park, there are other multi-use trails to explore. The Ironwood and Ford Canyon Trails, just south and west of the race loop, are fair choices, because they're both in the outwash plain or *bajada* of the mountain. Once into Ford Canyon proper, however, the trail becomes too difficult to ride.

There are several excellent hiking trails in the White Tanks, notably the Waterfall and Black Rock Trails, south of the race loops. These lead about one mile into the range and to a cool water pool and ancient petroglyphs. You can find faint petroglyphs all over the White Tanks, particularly in an area called Petroglyph Plaza. According to the Arizona State Museum, the park area was inhabited by the Hohokam from 500 AD to 1100 AD. More recently, the main stagecoach route between Phoenix and Prescott ran along a string of water holes along the north end of the range.

The White Tanks are notorious for experiencing flash floods during rainy seasons. As the torrent builds speed and pours down ledges and chutes, they scour depressions—known as tanks, or *tinejas*—into the white granite. These white tanks are what give the range their name.

MilesDirections

START from the trailhead at the north end of the parking lot. Look for the big brown sign that says "Sonoran Loop Competitive Track." Head into the park along the trail, following the one-way trail signs. The trail is very well marked the entire way, making it almost impossible to get lost.

At the "Technical Loop" sign (1.1 miles), turn left to enjoy slightly more challenging fare than the rest of the "Competitive Track" loop.

The Technical Loop rejoins the main outer loop in 1.1 miles.

The entire loop is 5.5 miles long and extremely easy to follow. The map shows some interconnecting inner trails you can use to make your ride longer or shorter as you see fit. Remember, this is a one-way loop, traveling clockwise. If you see a sign that says "Wrong Way," pay attention and travel with traffic, not against it.

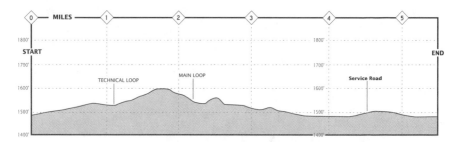

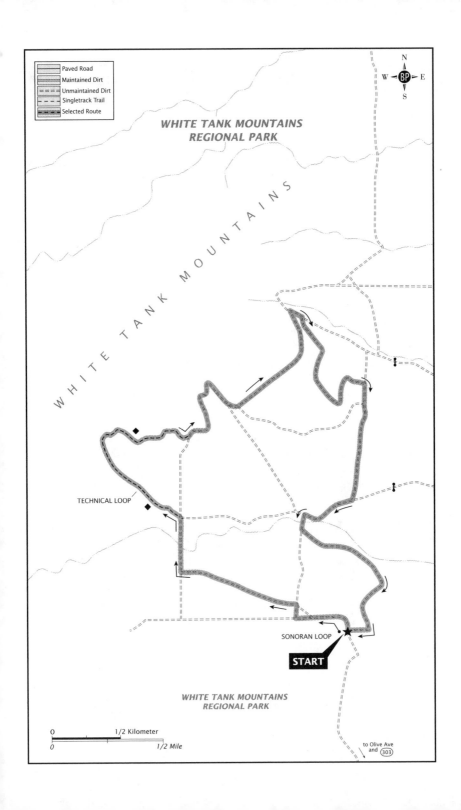

WHITE TANK MOUNTAINS REGIONAL PARK

W H I T E   T A N K   M O U N T A I N S

N
W — BP — E
S

Paved Road
Maintained Dirt
Unmaintained Dirt
Singletrack Trail
Selected Route

TECHNICAL LOOP

SONORAN LOOP

START

WHITE TANK MOUNTAINS
REGIONAL PARK

0   1/2 Kilometer
0   1/2 Mile

to Olive Ave
and (303)

Central Arizona

Compiled here is an index of great rides in Central Arizona that didn't make the A-list this time around but deserve recognition. Check them out and let us know what you think. You may decide that one or more of these rides deserves higher status in future editions or, perhaps, you may have a ride of your own that merits some attention.

(A) Usery Mountain Recreation Area

Usery Mountain is northeast of Mesa, connected diagonally to the Hawes Mountain rides (see *Ride 4: The Mine Loop*). There are several loop options within the recreation area. Blevins Loop and Moon Rock Loop are easy, fast three- to six-mile loops through the lowlands of the park, and are favorites for beginner riders. Pass Mountain, on the other hand, is a fairly difficult 7.5-mile singletrack loop around Usery Mountain with big exposures and no easy way to get back to civilization—the loop was closed to mountain bikers for a while after a rider died on the loop (he didn't bring enough water for a summer ride—avoid mistakes like this and you'll probably be fine). You'll have to walk parts of the Pass Mountain loop, especially at the end (assuming you ride it clockwise) where the trail enters a rocky wash. The views and much of the Pass Mountain riding is spectacular. There's a $5 fee to enter Usery Mountain Recreation Area.

Getting there: From Phoenix or pretty much anywhere east of Apache Junction, head east on the Superstition Freeway to the Ellsworth Road exit. Take Ellsworth Road north until it becomes Usery Pass Road. Turn right, enter the park, and drive to the equestrian staging area, which is also the trailhead. *DeLorme: Arizona Atlas & Gazetteer* Page 58 B1

(B) Papago Park

Its easy access from Arizona State University and Tempe's numerous call centers and offices makes Papago Park a popular escape for lunchtime bike rides. The park is an easy place to ride and there aren't many technical challenges—but it's dirt, and that's what we're looking for. Truth be told, there's a nice variety of technical and physical difficulties available in Papago Park; explore the desert on both sides of Galvin Parkway and you'll find some moderately difficult sections of trail.

The best loop isn't on any maps: Once you've parked at the Eliot Ramada at the end of Papago Park Drive, you'll want to cross the street going north toward the big mountain. A singletrack loop circles around the backside of the mountain, creating a cool little 1.5-mile loop. There's a high/low split on the north side, just east of a stone auditorium built into the side of the mountain. Do several laps if you're so inclined, clockwise or counterclockwise. For ASU students, this is a great off-road break from classes.

Getting there: From Tempe, go north on Mill Avenue until it turns westward and becomes Van Buren. Right where Mill Avenue ends, turn right on Galvin Parkway. Take the first left, Papago Park Drive, and follow it until it ends at the Eliot Ramada. Park here and go crazy. *DeLorme: Arizona Atlas & Gazetteer* Page 57 B6

Ⓒ McDowell Mountain Park

Once the crown jewel of the McDowell Mountains, county parks officials—in the interest of "safety"—recently plowed under the 15-mile Pemberton Loop. The loop is still there, but a six-foot-wide dirt road overlays the singletrack whoop-de-dos that were the hallmark of the ride. It's been so recently tilled that the ride is actually quite difficult and rugged. Just up the road a bit are the Cactus Cup Race Loops, three excellent, fast loops that were once the home of the Cactus Cup Race every February. There's a $5 fee to enter the park.

Getting there: From Phoenix, go to Shea and Saguaro boulevards in Fountain Hills and travel north on Saguaro Boulevard. After reaching Fountain Hills Boulevard, turn right (north). Drive eight miles, and look left for the turnoff to the McDowell Mountain Regional Park. There are ample brown park signs along the way to help guide you. About half a mile into the park, the Cactus Cup competitive tracks are to the left. Continue ahead on the park road. Three miles into the park, look right for a turnoff to the horse corrals; the road is called "Schallmo." Drive to the corrals and park. *DeLorme: Arizona Atlas & Gazetteer* Page 58 A1

(D) Sheep Bridge

This 27-mile out-and-back ride near Horseshoe Reservoir takes you to an old bridge once used by—wait for it—sheep herders to move their stock over the Verde River. There are some rocky stretches and, during the monsoon and winter rains, you'll have to portage your bike over some water. There's a $5 parking fee at Horseshoe Dam. Start by riding across the walkway that passes over the dam's spillway. In a couple miles, turn left on Chalk Mountain Road (FS 479). Just past that, you'll hit a T-intersection; keep left and remain on Chalk Mountain Road. Stay left again at the Davenport Road turnoff. You'll pass through several deep washes—some will have running water as mentioned above—and at 13.5 miles, you'll reach the Sheep Bridge, which is your turnaround point. Allow 3-4 hours to do the whole thing.

Getting there: From Carefree, go about five miles north on Cave Creek Road to Horseshoe Dam Road. Turn left where Horseshoe Dam Road splits with Bartlett Dam Road (FS 19) and drive six miles to Horseshoe Dam. *DeLorme: Arizona Atlas & Gazetteer* Page 50 C1

(E) Pyramid Mountain

This vast region of Arizona State Trust-managed desert (be sure to get a recreation pass) is a hidden jewel for west valley riders. The desert between Happy Valley Road and the CAP canal is crisscrossed with motorcycle and quad tracks, as well as various old dirt roads.

Once you get north of the canal, Pyramid Mountain stands pointy peaked directly ahead. Again, there are countless dirt roads and quad tracks all over the desert—keep aiming north, toward the mountain, and you won't get lost. There's a rather technical singletrack that encircles all of Pyramid Mountain and is about five miles long. Unfortunately, this singletrack is very hard to find and has no real "trailhead" to aim for. Your best bet is to simply keep your eyes peeled for singletrack cutting across wider doubletrack that you'll probably ride en route toward the mountain. There are also many other tracks, trails, and roads heading in all directions, so go explore!

It is possible that you could get lost here at Pyramid Mountain. Fortunately, however, you're never far from civilization. Keep heading east and eventually you'll hit the I-17 frontage road. Head west and you'll hit a neighborhood. Heading south takes you to more neighborhoods. And pedaling north is Lake Pleasant.

Pyramid Mountain has been the center of a biker-equestrian coalition called Hoofs, Wheels, and Heels. The Arizona State Horsemen's Association and the Saddleback Association started this event, and invited the Mountain Bike Association of Arizona (MBAA). The idea behind this coalition is to join the different user groups into supporting the preservation of land for outdoor recreation. HWH chose to initially focus on the Pyramid Mountain area because both mountain bikers and equestrians use it. They are also trying to involve more hikers, but so far, only Sierra Club has shown support.

Getting there: The riding area is accessible from various breaks in the fence along Happy Valley Road between 51st and 55th Avenues. The good stuff is to the north of the canal, which you can only cross at a bridge off 51st Avenue. 51st Avenue turns into a dirt road after turning north at Happy Valley Road. *DeLorme: Arizona Atlas & Gazetteer* Page 57 A5 and Page 49 D5

(F) Cave Creek Recreation Area

There are three singletrack loops within this relatively new park north of the Valley; assemble distance and difficulty to order. Gunsite Pass is fast, difficult, and very exposed. New River Road is a dirt road loop through flat desert below the mountains of the recreation area. The Apache Spring Loop is steep, rugged, and very difficult. The picnic areas are clean and new, but the trails are not yet well marked. Bring your full suspension for these rides and allow for a lot of time to get misplaced! There's a $3 weekend fee.

Getting there: From Phoenix, head north on Cave Creek Road to Carefree Road. Travel west on Carefree Road to 32nd Street, and then north on 32nd Street to the ranger station and the picnic area beyond. You can also slip into the park via Surry Pass Road; take Cave Creek Road past the Road and look for the left turn in about two miles. *DeLorme: Arizona Atlas & Gazetteer* Page 49 D 5-6

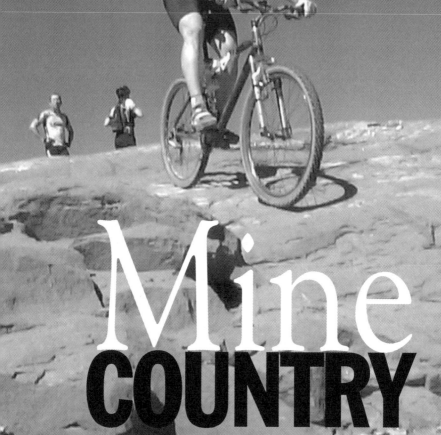

Mine
COUNTRY

Dropping down Chicken Point along the Oak Creek Trail system.

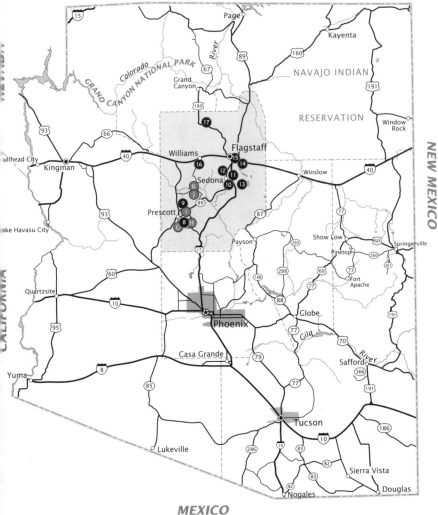

The Rides

Spruce Mountain **8.**
Granite Basin **9.**
Oak Creek Canyon Trails **10.**
Schnebly Hill to Seven Sacred Pools **11.**
Teacup Trail to the Cockscomb **12.**
Mormon Mountain **13.**
Walnut Canyon and Marshall Lake **14.**
Mount Elden **15.**
Bill Williams Mountain **16.**
Moqui Stage Route **17.**

Honorable Mentions

G. Yankee Doodle Trail
H. Crown King to Lake Pleasant
I. Peavine Trail
J. Mingus Mountain
K. Deadhorse Ranch

Mine Country

The trails around Prescott, Sedona, Williams, and Flagstaff are the spiritual heart of mountain biking in Arizona. This is the area that makes Arizona a destination for bikers from around the world. And it's here that cyclists can ride the awesome singletrack network around Mt. Elden in Flagstaff, the red rock majesty of Sedona, and the high pine forests of Prescott and Williams, each of which offer top-notch riding for intermediate and advanced riders of all kinds.

What's that? Where are the easy rides, you say? Well…the area *does* tend to have longer and more technically difficult rides at quite a bit of altitude (5,000–6,000 feet in Sedona; 7,000–9,000 feet in Flagstaff). The "easier" rides still involve climbing into ever-thinning air, and descending narrow, sometimes-dangerous trails that drop faster than you expect. Luckily, the area is crisscrossed with old dirt roads, all of which are a bit easier than the singletrack around here, while still providing a nice escape from the desert heat.

Besides the great trails in this region, the Mine Country (called such for its numerous old mining operations found throughout the area's mountain ranges) also features a very bike-friendly culture. You'll be hard-pressed to find cooler pro-bike towns than Flagstaff and Sedona, both of which feature some of the best bike shops in the west and terrific urban trail systems to boot.

Flagstaff is a funky hippie town, built entirely around its two most important businesses—Northern Arizona University and the railroad. Trains rumble through town so regularly that their deafening horns fade into the background after just a couple days' worth of exposure. NAU is a quiet, green campus that offers a lot of eco-oriented education (as well as a standard curriculum), such as forestry science. Just north of campus is "old town Flagstaff," a network of narrow streets and historic buildings filled with the hippest restaurants, great bike shops, outdoor gear stores, book stores, and clothing boutiques (true to the town's culture, these boutiques place a special emphasis on hemp clothing; hemp in all its forms is an important part of Flagstaff's eco-student/hippie/bike rat culture).

Prescott might be considered Flagstaff's right-wing alter ego. An attractive small town built around a central square (it used to be the territorial capital), Prescott is home to a strong religious community, the state's oldest rodeo, enormous mansions on acres of wooded land, and a wide range of outdoor sports. The local bike lobby is fairly strong, having negotiated a safe network of bike paths through town. Where Flagstaff has hippies, Prescott has cowboys—probably at a one-to-one ratio. The shops around Prescott's town square place an emphasis on cowboy art, hard drinking (especially along the infamous "Whiskey Row"), and western wear. Prescott is something of a hidden gem for mountain bikers—its trails rank among the best in the state—but nearby Flagstaff and Sedona draw so much of the limelight that its trails are rarely occupied ... with bikers, that is—emphasizing the town's cowboy culture, equestrians hit Prescott's trails with a vengeance.

Williams, about half an hour west of Flagstaff on I-40, bills itself as "The Gateway to the Grand Canyon." A railroad and a highway runs between Williams and Tusayan, on the Canyon's south rim, and the town is filled with motel rooms to hold the Canyon's many visitors. Before cashing in on the Grand Canyon, there was Route 66—Williams was an important stop along this famous cross-country highway. But when I-40 was built, sending people speeding past Williams instead of through it, the town began to falter. Today, Williams is all about tourism, both for those there to make the jump up to the Grand Canyon as well as for those taking in Route 66 memorabilia. For outdoors enthusiasts, The Bill Williams Mountain Trail, north of town, is another great draw.

Finally, there's Sedona. Red rocks, slickrock, amazing trails, Oak Creek Canyon, views—all superb. Local bike culture is very friendly, with two shops—the Bike & Bean and Mountain Bike Heaven—evenly splitting the town's business. The altitude is a little high for the desert dwellers but the climbs shouldn't leave you gasping for air like elsewhere in this region. Consequently, it's a bit warmer in the summer in Sedona than up in the pines—expect hot days to reach the high 90s by midday.

On the other hand, it's not just mountain bikers who are in love with Sedona. The town attracts as many as four million visitors each year. Some come for outdoor activities like hiking and rock climbing, while others come just for the shopping—Sedona is replete with tchochke shops, New Age crystal/fortune-telling stores, and overpriced boutiques—and the views from glass-enclosed, air-conditioned restaurants. With so many people coming to visit each year, the burden on the area and the environment is high. Because of this, there's now a "Red Rock Pass" program in place. If you want to park at any national forest parking lot, expect to cough up $5 at one of the Red Rock Pass kiosks around town. If not, you *will* get a fine, usually $30, from a ranger.

The Red Rock Pass is becoming big business in town, and it is not without controversy. As a cooperative effort between the U.S. Forest Service, Sedona Cultural Park, and the Sedona-Oak Creek Canyon Chamber of Commerce, one local bumper sticker sums things up nicely— "Can't see the forest for the fees."

If you can tolerate the crowds, the traffic, the white folks pretending to be Native Americans, the copper coyotes and kokopellis posing as southwestern "art", the pink/green/red jeep tours dragging countless tourists onto the rocks, the helicopters, and the infamous Red Rock Pass, then do not pass up an opportunity to visit Sedona's splendid mountain biking trails.

Is Sedona Arizona's very own Moab? It might be that Moab is Utah's very own Sedona.

Section Overview

Spruce Mountain

A favorite loop among locals and visitors alike, Spruce Mountain is a quintessential pine-covered downhill run, replete with roots, rocky drop-offs, and logs. But what goes down must first go up; the climb up Spruce Mountain is brutally steep near the end. The good news? It's longer going down than going up. (*See page 66.*)

Granite Basin

Set near the scenic and rocky Granite Mountain, Granite Basin Recreation Area has a large network of excellent singletrack loops. Except for the trails that head into the Granite Mountain Wilderness Area—off-limits for bikes—the trails are all rideable, fast, smooth, and very fun. Granite Basin is about a 15-minute drive from downtown Prescott. (*See page 70.*)

Oak Creek Canyon Trails

Whether you fancy an easy spin or a gut-busting epic, the gorgeous rides that comprise the southern trail network in Sedona/Oak Creek are what you're looking for. Set among the red rocks and pine forests that make Sedona so distinctive, these three loops offer rides for all skill and endurance levels. Bring a spare roll of film! (*See page 76.*)

Schnebly Hill to Seven Sacred Pools (East Sedona)

East Sedona's network of trails runs from the far eastern edge of town at Schnebly Hill Road, along red rock ledges with incredible views of the town, across Oak Creek and Midgley Bridge, and finally into the "Secret Trails" and two notable formations at the end. This loop is moderately difficult, not too long, and gives riders some great views as well as a complete mix of riding types—all within a mile or so of Sedona. (*See page 84.*)

Teacup Trail to the Cockscomb (West Sedona)

West Sedona's trails are a semi-secret network preferred by local riders. Winding around such striking landmarks as the Cockscomb, Chimney Rock, Coffee Pot Rock, and the mouth of Boynton Canyon, these trails are less traveled than the *Oak Creek Trails* or the trails of eastern Sedona (*see Ride 11: Schnebly Hill to Seven Sacred Pools*). If you've gotten your fill of the tourist-clogged mainstays, check out these west Sedona trails—and bring your trail-finding skills, because it's not always so easy to find your way! (*See page 90.*)

Mormon Mountain

This little-known gem of a ride is popular with northern Arizona riders. Mormon Mountain is virtually unknown outside the Flagstaff racing/downhill scene, but it's an easy drive from Phoenix and tacks on easily to a big tour of Sedona. The trail is like a miniature version of mighty Mount Elden in Flagstaff (*see Ride 15: Mount Elden*), featuring a shorter and less intense climb to the top followed by a fast romp all the way down to the bottom. Being less popular than other cycling gems in the area, you're guaranteed the run of the place. (*See page 98.*)

Walnut Canyon and Marshall Lake

The Flagstaff mountain biking success story doesn't end at Mt. Elden (*see Ride 15: Mount Elden*)—just to the south of town, there's a network of canyons that offer excellent singletrack, hard climbs, technical descents, and long miles. There are two options once you've gotten into the canyon network. One takes you up to the lip of Walnut Canyon and then across a high-forested plateau, the other takes you up a longer and less technical climb to Marshall Lake, a wetland for ducks and other migratory birds. Which one's harder? Depends on what you're looking for—Walnut Canyon is trickier, but once you're atop the canyon wall it's fairly flat and fast. The Marshall Lake arm of the ride is harder work all the way out, and a fast descent most of the way back. (*See page 104.*)

Mine Country

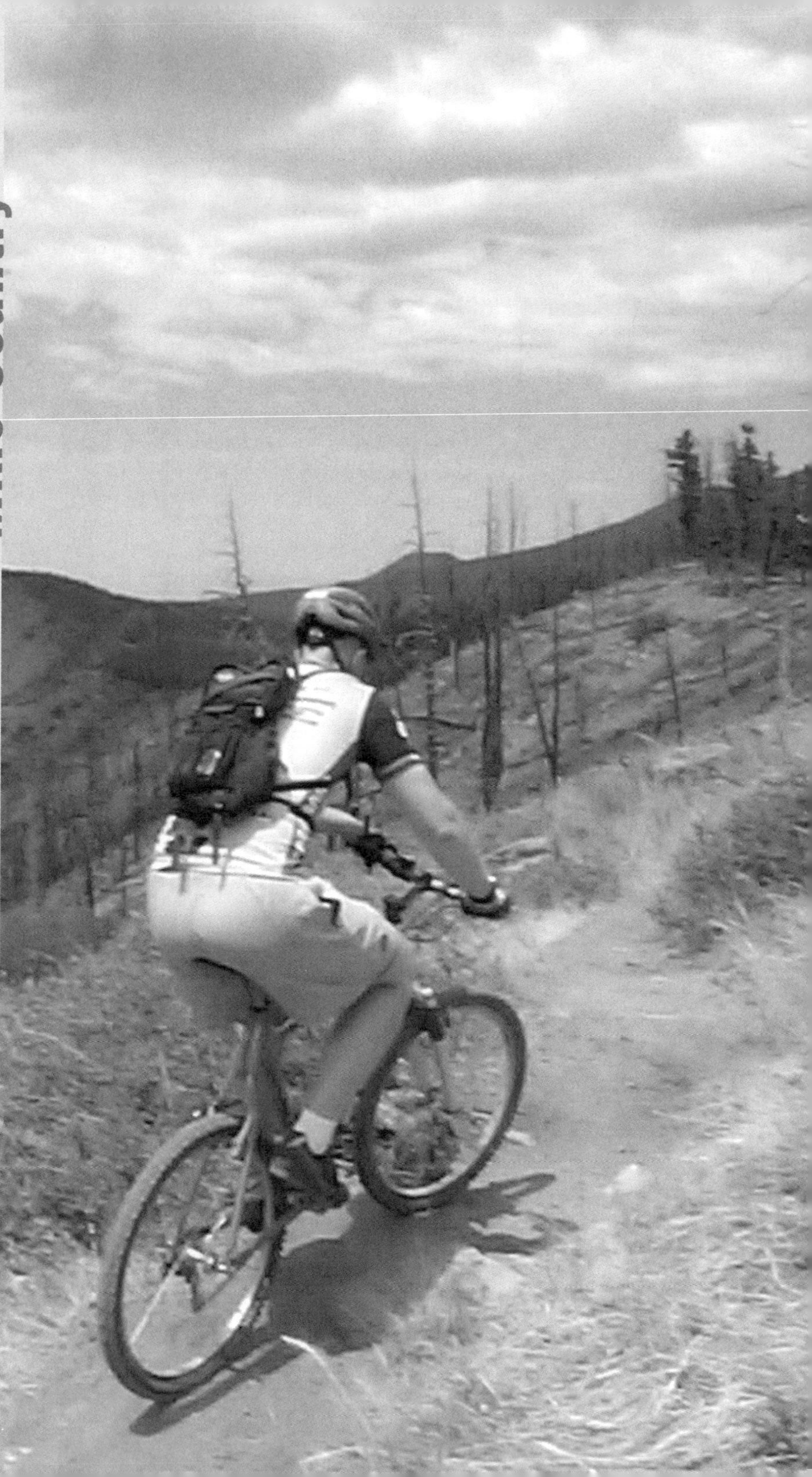

Mount Elden

Mount Elden is a destination for intermediate to advanced riders throughout Arizona and the entire Southwest. The radio tower-topped mountain, just north of Flagstaff, is covered with a network of world-class trails. For riders from the desert lowlands, the altitude is a kick in the pants—but the reward for the climb to the top of Elden makes it worthwhile. The higher trails are generally more technically difficult, while the lower ones offer fun, fast, rolling tracks through pine forests and high-desert juniper. *(See page 110.)*

Bill Williams Mountain

Just a half-hour west of Flagstaff, this ride gives you a big climb to the top of Bill Williams Mountain and dumps you back into a screaming descent down the north face. There are also numerous small trails near the ranger station (where the trailhead is located), providing opportunities of various lengths and difficulties. Although Bill Williams Mountain is a popular place to hike, it's still much less crowded with hikers than Mount Elden. *(See page 118.)*

Moqui Stage Route

If you've got the time, the endurance, and the courage to bite off a two-day cross-country epic, this is the ride for you. The Moqui Stage Route, named such because some of it follows an old stagecoach route, takes you from north of Flagstaff, across the vast lonesome plains of the Coconino Plateau, and into view of the Grand Canyon's south rim. You'll ride on gravel roads, jeep roads, forgotten doubletrack, and finally sweet singletrack. You'll go so fast your teeth will rattle loose. You'll go so slow you'd rather walk. You'll bonk—or come close. Sound like fun? Read on. *(See page 124.)*

8

Spruce Mountain

Ride Specs

Start: From Groom Creek trailhead, marked by brown Forest Service signs
Length: 9-mile loop
Approximate Riding Time: 1.5–2 hours
Difficulty Rating: Physically and technically moderate, with a difficult climb to the top and a few dangerous spots in the descent
Trail Surface: Singletrack
Lay of the Land: Pine forest in the foothills of the Bradshaw Mountains
Elevation Gain: 1,872 feet
Land Status: National forest
Nearest Town: Prescott
Other Trail Users: Equestrians, hikers, and more equestrians
Canine Compatibility: Dogs permitted, only if they're well mannered around horses

Wheels: Front suspension required, full suspension strongly recommended

Getting There

From Prescott: From Prescott's town square, head east on Gurley Street to Mount Vernon Avenue (the first right turn after leaving the square). Turn right (south) on Mount Vernon Avenue and continue driving until it becomes the Senator Highway. The Senator Highway will turn east after about one mile. At 6.6 miles, look for brown Forest Service signs for the Groom Creek Loop Trailhead on the left. Park here. *DeLorme: Arizona Atlas & Gazetteer:* Page 49 A4

Spruce Mountain is part of a favorite equestrian park in the middle of Prescott National Forest. The area is generally 15–20 degrees cooler than Phoenix and Tucson, and bikers from points south show up all summer in droves to escape the oven-like heat.

The ride begins at Groom Creek Trail, which is a singletrack loop running clockwise up and around Spruce Mountain to a lookout tower at the peak, then descending the other side. The trail begins with a mellow climb that gets progressively steeper as it approaches the top of the mountain. The trail is littered with roots and logs—unfamiliar obstacles for desert dwellers. Switchbacks add

Ride Information

🔵 Trail Contacts:
Prescott National Forest, Bradshaw Ranger District, Prescott, AZ (928) 771–4700 or *www.fs.fed.us/r3/prescott*

🕐 Schedule:
Open year round – The winters can be quite cold and snowy, and the summers can reach into the high 80s.

🟢 Fees/Permits:
$2 parking fee

❓ Local Information:
Prescott Chamber of Commerce, Prescott, AZ (928) 445–2000 or 1–800–266–7534 or *www.prescott.org* • **Prescott Convention & Visitor's Bureau,** Prescott, AZ: *http://mmm.arizonaguide.com/prescott/index2.html*

💡 Local Events/Attractions:
Prescott Frontier Days, Prescott, AZ (928) 445–2000 or *www.worldsoldestrodeo.com* – *Held during late June through July 4th weekend, this weeklong event is built around the Prescott Rodeo, the oldest rodeo in the world. Rides, food, music—very cool event, even if you aren't into watching cowboys getting kicked by bulls and horses* • **Prescott Bike Week,** Prescott, AZ (928) 445–2000 – *Primarily a promotion to get people to commute by bike more often, Bike Week is quite a festive event. Held the second week of May, it's a week's worth of road and mountain bike tours, races, swap meets, and other events.*

🛏️ Accommodations:
Apache Lodge Motel, Prescott, AZ (928) 445–1422

🍴 Restaurants:
El Chaparral, Prescott, AZ (928) 445–8447 – *Best Mexican fare in town—if you can find it; a local favorite*

🚴 Group Rides:
The Chain Gang Bicycle Club (see below) has weekly rides

🏢 Organizations:
Chain Gang Bicycle Club: *www.surf-ici.com/chaingang* – *The Chain Gang has weekly mountain and road rides all over the Prescott and Chino Valley area*

🔗 Other Resources:
Prescott Newspapers Online: *www.prescottaz.com*

🚲 Local Bike Shops:
Bikesmith, Prescott, AZ (928) 445–0280 or *www.pre-biz.com/bikesmithcycle* • **Mountain Sports,** Prescott, AZ (928) 445–8310 or 1–800–286–5156 or *www.mountainsport.com*

🅝 Maps:
USGS maps: Groom Creek, AZ

a little more spice to the climb. Add fields of loose rocks, and all but the strongest riders will find themselves walking the last half-mile or so of the climb to the Spruce Mountain lookout tower.

But we all know that the whole point of going up is to come down. Spruce Mountain is one of those blessed rarities: The uphill grind is shorter than the downhill back to your car. And what a downhill run it is! When it isn't pristinely groomed singletrack, the trail is crisscrossed with roots, rock outcroppings, some sand, and erosion-control logs so high and frequent the trail looks like a staircase. This roller-coaster ride continues for five-and-a-half miles, all of it demanding your utmost attention at all times.

The Groom Creek Trail is extremely popular with equestrians, somewhat less so for hikers. Control your speed and always be prepared to yield to the horses. There aren't many opportunities for anyone—hikers, horses, or bikes—to get off the narrow trail, either. On a busy weekend, cyclists could be faced with a real traffic jam for up to one mile. It doesn't happen often, but still go prepared to wait.

MilesDirections

0.0 START from the Groom Creek Loop Trail trailhead. The trail begins just past the bathrooms at the wooden sign. Head left, traveling along Groom Creek Loop Trail in a clockwise direction—the route up Spruce Mountain is steeper in this direction but the climb is shorter. Just past the turn about 100 yards, you'll cross over the dirt road that goes up to Wamatochick Camp. Pick up the singletrack on the other side and continue along Groom Creek Loop Trail. Follow the signs.

3.3 Arrive at a large picnic area very close to the top of Spruce Mountain. This is a popular equestrian area with lots of hitching posts and picnic tables. The lookout tower is up the trail to the left. Look to your right for a few wooden signs indicating the continuation of Groom Creek Loop Trail. Head for the climb to your right and keep riding up toward the radio tower.

3.4 Reach the radio tower. *[FYI. This is a good place to rest if you don't feel like being around horses down near the picnic area.]*

4.8 Go through a gate.

5.3 Reach a wooden sign indicating a turn to the Spruce Ridge Helispot. Continue ahead on the Groom Creek Loop Trail.

7.2 At a sitting log next to the trail, a second trail appears to split off to the left. This just goes down a bit to a camping area. Continue ahead on the main trail.

7.5 Reach a big brown sign indicating that the Groom Creek Loop Trail continues ahead. Cross over a doubletrack.

8.6 Cross over a dirt road and pick up the singletrack on the other side.

9.0 Reach the parking lot.

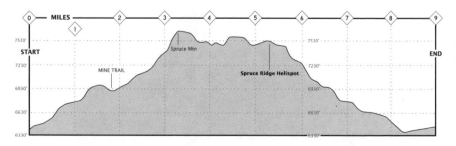

The Bradshaw Mountains, of which Spruce Mountain is a part, have a long and colorful history in Arizona's mining past. The mountains have produced millions of dollars in gold over the past 150 years, including $2 million out of the Crowned King Mine (outside the town of Crown King, perched atop the Bradshaw range). While there isn't any active mining in the range now, there are still hundreds of miles of rugged old mining roads crisscrossing the mountains.

Rising 4,000 feet from the surrounding desert, the Bradshaws stretch from Lake Pleasant to Prescott's southern edge. At the base of the mountains grow ponderosa pine, while the peaks are covered in white fir (which settlers commonly misidentified as spruce, hence the mountain's name) and hold onto their snow for weeks after it's melted in town. Riding from the top of the Bradshaws can transport cyclists from snow to hot desert in just a few hours—ride the infamous Crown King–Lake Pleasant epic for a prime example (*see Honorable Mentions H on page 133*).

Once upon a time, the Senator Highway was one of the main roads between Prescott—then the state capital—and Phoenix, via the various mining communities in the mountains and eventually Lake Pleasant. Today, this road, which you must traverse to reach the trailhead, ranges from poorly graded to outright rugged. While it *can* be driven, only 4x4s with serious clearance should attempt the drive. Biking the Senator Highway, and all the attached mining roads, can be a blast.

The area on the other side of the Senator Highway is called Wolf Creek, and is another popular biking area. The Wolf Creek area has a well-marked six-mile loop, used every year by the MBAA as part of its statewide race series. The trailhead is across the street from Groom Creek and fairly easy to spot.

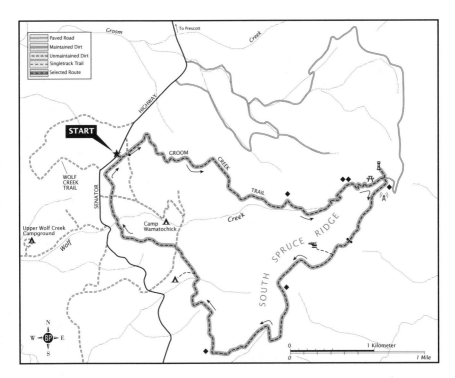

Granite Basin

Ride Specs

Start: From the Metate Trailhead
Length: 9-mile loop
Approximate Riding Time: 1 hour
Difficulty Rating: Technically and physically moderate, with some long, shallow climbs and one very technical section
Trail Surface: Singletrack
Lay of the Land: Granite boulders and pine forest
Elevation Gain: 1,053 feet
Land Status: National forest
Nearest Town: Prescott
Other Trail Users: Hikers and equestrians
Canine Compatibility: Dogs permitted
Wheels: Hardtail is enough, but full suspension will help with some of the more technical downhill segments

Getting There

From Prescott: Starting at the courthouse square, head north out of Prescott on Montezuma Road, which eventually becomes Whipple Street, then Iron Springs Road. After about 5 miles from where you began, look to your right on Iron Springs Road for the Prescott National Forest/Granite Basin Recreation Area sign. Turn right here on Granite Basin Road and drive 4 miles into the park. The Metate (pronounced muh-TAH-tay) Trailhead is just past the boat launch and the Playa Day-Use Area. Park here. **DeLorme: Arizona Atlas & Gazetteer:** Page 41 D4

G ranite Basin is Prescott's "urban" outdoors area. Just 15 minutes away from the town square, the area offers more than 20 miles of interlocking singletrack loops. It's a hidden gem for riding clubs from Phoenix and Flagstaff—while the neon Lycra crowd is swarming Sedona on the weekends, the smart ones are sneaking off to Granite Basin so they can have the trails to themselves.

Granite Basin's trails skirt perilously close to the Granite Mountain Wilderness Area, so pay attention to the Forest Service signs: If you see a post with a hiker and an equestrian but no bike, that means you're about to enter the wilderness. You'll probably see lots of bike treads on these trails, but don't add to the poaching problem. It's hard enough as it is to get the rangers to create and maintain bike-friendly trails.

The trail network winds its way around boulders and low hills, with Granite Mountain almost always in view. In the lower elevations, piñon pine and alligator juniper predominate—both are especially grabby on bike clothes. There's also quite a bit of manzanita and a variety of desert oaks. The wilderness area encompassing Granite Mountain exists in large part because the south face is an active nesting area for endangered peregrine falcons. The Granite Basin is also home to lots of other wildlife, aside from peregrine falcons, including several varieties of snake (they like to sun themselves on the trails, so stay alert—particularly during spring).

Much of the trail's surface is extremely well groomed, comprised of crushed granite, nice berms, and some sandbars perfect for jumping. Be careful to keep speeds in

check, though—Granite Basin is *very* popular with hikers and equestrians. There are also several blind turns that could be overshot if you're catching big air on the jumps.

The trail starts on the Metate Connector, a short climb to Trail 351 that is itself a connector between the Willow Creek Trail and the Balancing Rock Trail. The ride described here leads to Willow Creek, which has a mellow climb followed by miles of smooth singletrack descent interrupted only by the occasional root, rock outcropping, or hiker. The ride back up Mint Wash has a shallow climb, punctuated by some extremely steep, short little climbs and descents over dangerous rock outcroppings.

The Willow Spring-Mint Wash loop is a nice introduction to the area, but the really good stuff is hidden in the connector trails that crisscross this loop. Trail 352 (the Mint Wash Connector) is an exceptional mile-plus descent into Mint Wash from atop the trail's highest point. The trail is technically challenging punctuated with steep drops, roots, and a couple of switchbacks.

Balancing Rock Trail is another hidden pleasure also accessible via Trail 351 atop the Metate Connector. Balancing Rock Trail bobs and weaves through pine forest and eventually climbs to the top of a plateau. The descent back down to Trail 345 is fast and full of twists and turns.

Besides awesome biking, Granite Basin is known for its excellent technical bouldering opportunities. While riding on the weekends, try to spy climbers scampering up the sheer mountainsides. Those interested in climbing should be aware that the area is closed from February through July so the peregrine falcons can nest undisturbed.

MilesDirections

0.0 START from the Metate Trailhead on Granite Basin Road. The trailhead is right behind the bathrooms at the Metate Trailhead parking lot. For this loop, don't take the second trailhead, which is visible across Granite Basin Road. (It takes you to the Balancing Rock Trail.)

0.3 At the top of a short climb the Metate Trail Connector ends and intercepts Trail 351, which goes left and right here. Turn left, heading for Trail 348.

0.8 Cross over Granite Basin Road. Just beyond the road, Trail 351 connects with Trail 348, which goes left and right. Turn right on Trail 348, heading away from the lake.

1.0 The trail splits left and right. To the left is Trail 348; traveling to the right takes you toward the Willow Trail. Turn right, going around

the base of the hill toward the Willow Trail.

1.6 Arrive at the Cayuse Equestrian Center. Cut across the parking area and look for a "Road Closed" gate across what appears to be a dirt road. The dirt road immediately reverts to singletrack, which forks. Turn left, continuing on Trail 348. *[FYI. Turning right takes you to the Balancing Rock Trail 349.]*

2.0 Go through a gate. Just past this gate there's a split in the trail and a second gate. Turn left and go through the gate, heading toward Mint Wash. *[FYI. Turning right takes you to the Willow Trail Trailhead.]*

3.3 *[FYI. Pass a connector to Trail 348, which joins from the left. You'll probably miss this trail if you're rocketing down Willow Trail.]*

4.6 Arrive at some old corrals. The trail continues around to the left of the corrals.

5.6 The trail splits. To the right is Trail 309. To the left is Willow Trail 347. Continue left, heading toward Mint Wash Trail.

6.2 The trail splits. Turn left on Mint Wash Trail 345. Mint Wash Trail crosses over Mint Wash several times and can be very technically challenging. *[Side-trip. If you turn right at this split, continuing on Willow Trail 347 which goes through a gate, you will ride singletrack all the way back to a housing development north of Prescott, and Williamson Valley Road.]*

8.2 The Mint Wash Connector joins from the left. Continue straight ahead on Mint Wash Trail.

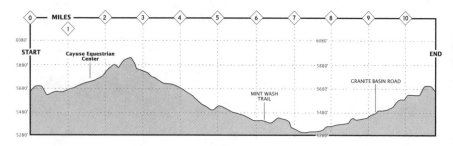

8.7 Go through a gate. Shortly after the gate, there is a potential water crossing (depending on the time of year).

9.2 Return to the split in the trail you hit back at 0.8 miles. Turn right onto Trail 351 and

cross Granite Basin Road.

10.5 Reach the Metate Trail Connector. Turn right and return to the parking lot.

10.8 Arrive at the parking lot.

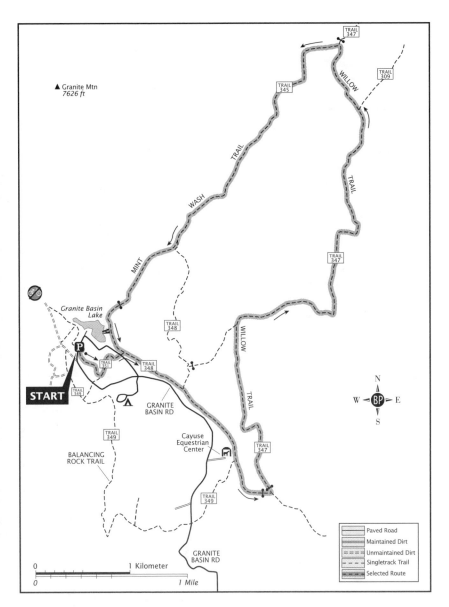

Ride Information

◷ Trail Contacts:
Prescott National Forest, Bradshaw Ranger District, Prescott, AZ (928) 771–4700 or *www.fs.fed.us/r3/prescott*

◷ Schedule:
Open year round – *can be hot in the summer (but nothing like how hot the Phoenix/Tucson area can get)*

⑤ Fees/Permits:
$2 parking fee

❓ Local Information:
[See Ride 08: Spruce Mountain]

● Accommodations:
Hotel Vendome, Prescott, AZ 1–888–468–3583 or *www.vendome hotel.com – A quaint, romantic little hotel with a dark secret: The Hotel Vendome is supposedly haunted. Good luck booking the haunted room—it's usually reserved.*

◉ Local Attractions:
Watson Lake/Granite Dells, near Prescott, AZ – *On the way into Prescott on AZ 69, turn north on AZ 89 and you'll get to scenic Watson Lake in about 5 miles. The Granite Dells are massive granite boulders jutting out of the lake.*

With strong legs and a little courage, you can leap from rock to rock and get way out into the water—and 60 feet up!

⑪ Restaurants:
Prescott Brewing Company, Prescott, AZ (928) 771–2795 or *www.prescottbrew ingcompany.com – If you like beer, you'll love PBC's award-winning brews. Also has excellent vegetarian fare that isn't just weeds and nuts.*

ⓑ Other Resources:
Mountain Sojourns (Castle Rock Publishing, 1994), by Ronald H. Smith. – *This book is considered a bible of outdoors adventuring around Prescott. Although currently out of print, Mountain Sojourns can still be found in many outdoor sporting stores.*

⚙ Local Bike Shops:
Ironclad Bicycles, Prescott, AZ (928) 776–1755 or *www.epfguzzi.com/iron clad* • **High Gear Bike Shop,** Prescott, AZ (928) 445–0636

Ⓝ Maps:
USGS maps: Jerome Canyon, AZ; Iron Springs, AZ

Red Rock Passes

Four and a half million visitors descend on the Sedona/Oak Creek area like a swarm of locusts every year, and they're starting to damage both the natural environment as well as the park facilities at each trailhead. The U.S. Forest Service, in partnership with the Sedona-Oak Creek Canyon Chamber of Commerce, Sedona Cultural Park, and the Arizona Natural History Association, recently began the Red Rock Pass program to recoup the costs of maintaining this "Red Rock" area of the national forest. All the national forest trailheads now require that visitors have a $5 Red Rock Pass; one pass lasts the day, and can be used at any of the forest parking lots. There is also a $15 pass that lasts for a week, a $20 pass for the year, and a Super Annual Pass for $40 (it also gets you into the national parks, which are concession-operated, five times).

The Red Rock Pass is available at any visitors center, ranger station, and even some local businesses (such as the all-important Circle K right next to the Bell Rock parking lot). When you see the green ranger truck parked in the lot, you'll know the pass is being enforced. Any car not displaying a Red Rock Pass may be fined $30.

Don't want to pay? You'll have to park elsewhere and ride to the trailhead. However, this too is frowned upon both by the Forest Service (the shoulders of the roads into Sedona are getting trashed worse than the parking lots) and the local merchants. Best bet for overnight visitors is to rent a room near the trailhead and ride from the hotel.

The Red Rock Pass program will be in effect until 2004. Read all about it at *www.redrockpass.com*.

Oak Creek Canyon Trails

Ride Specs

Start: From Bell Rock Pathway parking lot
Length: Varies (three loops described)
Approximate Riding Time: 1.5–4 hours
Difficulty Rating: Easy to Difficult—you pick! These rides are all at around 6,000 feet, so beware of the air if you're used to lower altitudes.
Trail Surface: Singletrack, doubletrack, some road connectors, and slickrock!
Lay of the Land: Sedona's red rocks set among juniper and pine forests
Land Status: National forest
Nearest Town: Oak Creek
Other Trail Users: Hikers, equestrians
Canine Compatibility: Dog permitted
Wheels: Hardtail is fine; full suspension will be nice for some of the crazier stuff on the Little Horse and Broken Arrow trails. A hybrid will be able to handle much of the Bell Rock Loop.

Getting There

From Oak Creek: Driving north toward Sedona on U.S. 179, drive through the light at Bell Rock Road (there's a Circle K convenience store there) and turn right immediately into the parking lot for the Bell Rock Pathway. All three trails start here. ***DeLorme: Arizona Atlas & Gazetteer:*** Page 42 C1

Sedona is a city besieged by tourists. Like any city under siege, Sedona has brought out heavy equipment to deal with the invaders: a fleet of helicopters, prop planes, and pink jeeps swarm Sedona every day of the year, carrying hordes of international tourists up and around the area's distinctive red rock formations.

The red trails of Sedona are a mountain biking mecca known worldwide in much the same way as Moab, Utah or Fruita, Colorado. Like those other meccas, Sedona has its share of slickrock, epic daylong rides, and mind-blowing scenery.

There are essentially three "networks" of trails in and around Sedona. This chapter covers the southern network, comprised of three separate loops: *Bell Rock Loop, Chicken Point* and *Submarine Rock,* and *Cathedral Rock.*

Bell Rock Loop

The Bell Rock Loop is the easiest of the three rides in the network. The trail runs along the base of Bell Rock and Courthouse Butte, the two big outcroppings visible due north of the Bell Rock Pathway parking lot. The smaller of the two red blobs is Bell Rock, considered a "vortex" by the New Age crowd that sort of defines Sedona's culture. The meaning of "vortex" depends on whom you ask—some say there's a spaceship buried under the rock, others say it's a natural bubbling-up of Earth's ener-

gies. Whichever; Sedona is rich in vortexes. You'll definitely get a good vibe from riding near them.

After riding up the Bell Rock Pathway a short bit, you'll turn and ride along the base of the two big red mountains. The trail doesn't climb or descend much, but it's twisty and fast—a great introduction to what Sedona has to offer. There are also

numerous cut-across trails you can use to shorten or lengthen the time you spend on the Bell Rock Loops.

Be mindful of the various wilderness areas around these trails. In particular, you'll end up in wilderness if you take a left instead of a right and find yourself on the north side of Courthouse Butte. Although there's only 0.7 miles of wilderness back there, it's best not to risk getting caught riding through it.

MilesDirections: Bell Rock Loop

0.0 START from the Bell Rock Pathway parking lot. Look for a wide singletrack that heads due east past the map kiosk next to the parking lot. There's also a little connector that goes north out of the lot—both trails end up connecting to the pathway, which is more of a gravel walking path.

0.5 Reach a wooden sign that reads "Courthouse Butte Loop" and points to a singletrack splitting off to the right. Turn right at the split and head down the trail.

0.9 A singletrack cuts across the trail. Continue ahead (it's marked with another "Courthouse Butte Loop" sign). *[Side-trip. Turn right here and cut across to the other side of the loop. Rejoin the loop at the 2.9-mile notation; this mini-loop is 1.3 miles long.]*

1.1 Another singletrack joins from the right. Continue ahead. *[Side-trip. Turn right here and cut across to the other side. Rejoin the loop at the 2.4-mile notation; this connector is 0.3 miles long.]*

1.5 Enter a slickrock wash that goes north-south. The trail picks up a little south (right) and climbs out of the wash. *[Side-trip. Turn left and go north, up the wash. A singletrack climbs out of the wash. Ride down this little trail 0.7 miles until you reach Spaceship Rock, which looks either like a flying saucer or— if you've been on the trail a few hours and you're running low on fuel— a hamburger bun. Turn around at the rock and head back, because the trail beyond Spaceship Rock enters Munds Mountain Wilderness (there's no sign as you approach the wilderness area from this direction, but if you've gone through*

a gate you've entered the wilderness area).]

1.9 The trail splits. The right is marked with a brown Forest Service sign; turn right and continue. *[Side-trip. Turning left takes you to the Lee Mountain Loops, which are more difficult than the Bell Rock Loops. Lee Mountain will take you about six miles out of the way and eventually deposit you onto Jacks Canyon Road, south of the Bell Rock Pathway parking lot.]*

2.1 As the trail narrows, there's a split. Take the right split, following the brown Forest Service sign. *[Bailout. The left trail takes you to a neighborhood in about 0.3 miles. From there you can ride Bell Rock Road back to the start.]*

2.4 The trail splits. The crossover trail described in the side-trip at mile 1.1 connects from the right. Continue ahead. *[Side-trip. Turn right here and you'll end up back at mile 1.1. This crossover is 0.3 miles long.]*

2.7 The trail splits. The left trail goes out to a neighborhood in about 0.3 miles. Go right.

2.9 Singletrack cuts across the path; this is the side-trip trail from mile 0.9. Continue ahead, toward the parking lot. *[Side-trip. Turn right at the singletrack to rejoin the Courthouse Butte Loop at mile 0.9; this trail is 1.3 miles long.]*

3.1 Return to the parking lot.

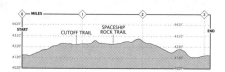

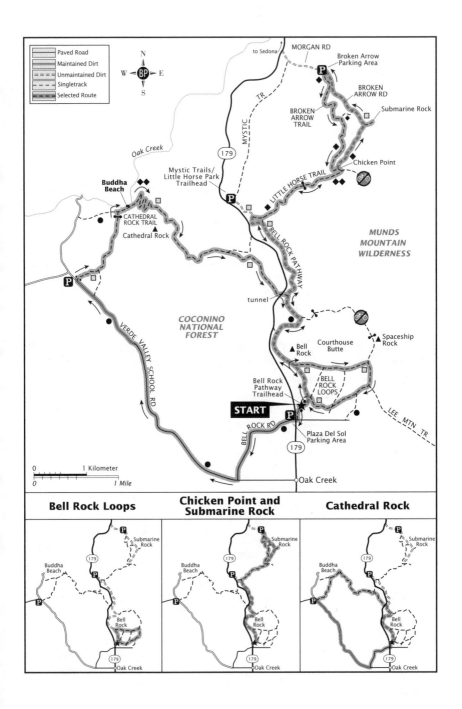

Legend:
- Paved Road
- Maintained Dirt
- Unmaintained Dirt
- Singletrack
- Selected Route

to Sedona · MORGAN RD

Broken Arrow Parking Area

MYSTIC TR

179

Oak Creek

Mystic Trails/
Little Horse Park
Trailhead

Buddha Beach

CATHEDRAL ROCK TRAIL

Cathedral Rock

BROKEN ARROW TRAIL

BROKEN ARROW RD

Submarine Rock

Chicken Point

LITTLE HORSE TRAIL

BELL ROCK PATHWAY

MUNDS MOUNTAIN WILDERNESS

COCONINO NATIONAL FOREST

tunnel

VERDE VALLEY SCHOOL RD

Bell Rock

Courthouse Butte

Spaceship Rock

Bell Rock Pathway Trailhead

BELL ROCK LOOPS

START

BELL ROCK RD

LEE MTN TR

179

Plaza Del Sol Parking Area

0 — 1 Kilometer
0 — 1 Mile

Oak Creek

Bell Rock Loops

Buddha Beach

179

Submarine Rock

Bell Rock

179

Oak Creek

Chicken Point and Submarine Rock

Buddha Beach

179

Submarine Rock

Bell Rock

179

Oak Creek

Cathedral Rock

Buddha Beach

179

Submarine Rock

Bell Rock

179

Oak Creek

Chicken Point and Submarine Rock

These are two slickrock destinations much loved by hardcore bikers throughout the state. Chicken Point is visible from the highway—a pair of rock spires that look like a chicken's beak. The base of Chicken Point is a slickrock playground overlooking an incredible vista. Most of Sedona is visible from atop Chicken Point.

The climb up to Chicken Point via the Little Horse Trail is tricky in spots but very do-able. You'll probably have to walk a couple big staircase-like formations, but otherwise it's a tame climb through juniper and pine as you catch peeks of red rocks between the trees. The Chapel of the Holy Cross, built directly into the side of the mountain north of the Little Horse Trail, is visible for most of the climb.

When you're done playing on Chicken Point, point your bike down either the jeep road or the tough-and-scary Broken Arrow Trail. Be careful of the pink jeeps that swarm the area! The bottom of either the gnarly jeep road—don't be fooled into thinking it's "just a road"—and the Broken Arrow Trail both will deposit you at Submarine Rock. This slickrock formation, named such because it's shaped a little (very little) like a sub, is another great place to fool around. Strong downhillers will enjoy bombing the eastern face of Submarine Rock.

The climb up the Broken Arrow Trail is long, tough, and not entirely rideable. There's at least one spot where you'll have to portage the bike up a rock face. The ride down is great if your technical skills are up to snuff, and if you're the type who enjoys unannounced four-foot drops.

MilesDirections: Chicken Point and Submarine Rock

0.0 START from the Bell Rock Pathway parking lot. Look for a wide singletrack that heads due east past the map kiosk next to the parking lot. There's also a little connector that goes north out of the lot—both trails end up connecting on the pathway, which is more of a gravel walking path.

0.5 Reach a wooden sign that reads "Courthouse Butte Loop" and points to a singletrack splitting off to the right. Continue straight ahead.

1.0 Reach a sign that reads "Curve, Keep Right." An equestrian access trail joins from the left. As you make the right turn, there are a number of rock cairns pointing the way along the slickrock.

1.4 Arrive at a crossroads. A singletrack splits off to the right taking you to Courthouse Butte Loop (and into the wilderness area—no bikes allowed). The main doubletrack bends to the left and continues north. [*FYI. There's anoth-*

er singletrack between the main doubletrack and the Courthouse Butte Loop trails; disregard this and take the furthest-left trail. Look for the rock cairn marking the main trail.]

1.8 Reach a brown Forest Service sign the reads "Trail" off to the left. Pass this, staying right on the Bell Rock Pathway.

2.2 Cross over a stone bridge.

2.4 Pass a sign indicating that Bell Rock Pathway goes north and south. The connector trail to Cathedral Rock goes left and passes under U.S. 179. Continue north.

3.0 An unmarked singletrack splits off to the right. This trail is a shortcut to Little Horse Trail. If you take it, deduct 0.2 miles from the rest of the distances. Continue on the main trail. Just beyond that split, another little trail (marked with a Forest Service "trail" sign) splits off to the left just before you reach a wooden bridge. Again, continue on the main trail.

3.3 A wooden sign indicates the Little Horse Trail splits off to the right. Turn right. Just beyond the trail, there's a sign-in post. Write the names of everyone in the party and continue ahead. *[Bailout. The Bell Rock Pathway continues ahead and ends at the Mystic Trails/Little Horse Park trailhead in 0.3 miles.]*

3.4 The Little Horse Trail enters a rocky wash. Look to the left, down the wash, and pick up the singletrack climbing out of the wash. Another singletrack connects in the wash from the right (this is the end of the shortcut at 3.0 miles).

4.6 Pass through an open gate.

4.8 Just past a steep hike-a-bike staircase, you'll top out on some slickrock. The trail splits left and right. Continue following Little Horse Trail, which splits off to the left; an unmarked trail goes right and into the Munds Mountain Wilderness.

4.9 Arrive at Chicken Point. After you play around on the slickrock for a while (careful of the pink jeeps!), you have a couple choices on how to get down to Submarine Rock. There's a wide, rocky jeep road to the north of Chicken Point that leads almost directly down to Submarine Rock. You can also look for the Broken Arrow Trail just north of the jeep road (look for a rock cairn). These directions follow the rocky jeep road to Submarine Rock.

5.3 Reach the bottom of the jeep road, which splits. Take the right split 0.5 miles to reach Submarine Rock.

5.8 Arrive at Submarine Rock. Pass between the signs that say, "closed to motorized vehicles" and ride up the staircase to the slickrock. Enjoy! When you're done, get back out onto the jeep road and turn right (north) to ride the 2.0 miles north to the Broken Arrow Trailhead parking area.

6.0 Pass by a super-steep jeep road to your left that says "Exit Only."

6.1 Pass by a wooden post and cairn that marks an unrideable descent into a wash to your right.

6.3 Arrive on some slickrock. Two jeep roads join here. A painted white arrow points up the right trail; actually it doesn't matter, as both jeep roads rejoin on the other side of the hill.

6.9 Arrive at the Broken Arrow parking area. Broken Arrow Road picks up where Morgan Road ends. When you leave the Broken Arrow parking area, look for the hike/bike sign for Broken Arrow Trail just to the left of the big tri-panel map kiosk and head up the singletrack. The trail cuts across the road and picks up immediately on the other side. *[Option: If you want to make a day trip of just playing on Submarine Rock, consider parking at the Broken Arrow parking lot. It is then a five-mile round trip, excluding time spent on the slickrock.]*

8.1 The trail splits; the sign says Submarine Rock to the left, Chicken Point to the right. Go right and continue to Chicken Point. Follow the rock cairns to follow the trail across the slickrock.

8.4 After a little hike-a-bike, come out onto a wide area of slickrock. Look for the cairns to guide your way along Broken Arrow Trail; don't jump onto the jeep road.

8.7 Come out onto some more slickrock. Again, follow the cairns across the rock until you find the singletrack again.

8.9 Arrive at Chicken Point. Head down Little Horse Trail to the Bell Rock Pathway (1.6 miles), and return to the Bell Rock Pathway trailhead (3.3 more miles) the way you came.

13.8 Return to the Bell Rock Pathway trailhead. also a little connector that goes north out of the lot—both trails end up connecting to the pathway, which is more of a gravel walking path.

Cathedral Rock

Cathedral Rock, the massive formation to the west of the Bell Rock Pathway parking lot, is another vortex similar to Bell Rock. Accessing the Cathedral Rock Trail involves several miles of road riding, but it's mostly an easy downhill roll to the trailhead.

Cathedral Rock Trail takes you down to the shore of Oak Creek, where you can kick off your shoes and soak while sitting on the sands of Buddha Beach. Hiking/biking opportunities near running water are painfully rare in Arizona; take your time on this one because it's just about the prettiest trail near water you'll ever ride along in the state of Arizona.

Just past Buddha Beach, the trail suddenly ascends at an unrideable angle. Locals have been building an alternate trail a few yards back from this ascent—you'll know it when you get to it—that involves switchbacks up to the same point. The switchbacks are certainly much more rideable going up; they're also a lot of fun going down.

Once you've climbed up and out of the canyon, the trail follows along the slickrock face of Cathedral Rock itself. There are a few climbs along the way, but mostly you'll descend back down to the highway and hook up with the Bell Rock Pathway again. Big fun.

MilesDirections: Cathedral Rock

0.0 START from the Plaza Del Sol parking lot (across the street from the Bell Rock Pathway parking lot, at the corner of U.S. 179 and Bell Rock Road). Head west on Bell Rock Road.

1.1 Take a right on Verde Valley School Road. The pavement will end in 2.2 miles. Continue on the dirt road.

4.4 Just past the "dip" sign, look for a singletrack that splits off to the right, passing

between some big rocks. There's a parking area off the road to the right just past the singletrack, should you be interested in parking at the very beginning of the trail and riding the road back in.

5.5 Pass through gate. A doubletrack joins from the left. Continue ahead, turning right and following the singletrack.

5.8 Arrive at Buddha Beach, on the shore of Oak Creek. Check out the swimming hole and the tire swing! Continue west on Cathedral Rock Trail.

6.0 Look to your right for a switchback up the hill. Start climbing!

6.4 At the top of the switchbacks, the Cathedral Rock Trail continues south, winding its way around the slickrock shelves. As you traverse the slickrock, follow the rock cairns to find the trail.

7.1 At the bottom of the descent, you'll reach AZ 179. Pass under AZ 179 through the tunnel.

9.3 Connect with Bell Rock Pathway. Turn right to head back to the parking area.

11.2 Arrive at the Plaza Del Sol parking lot.

Ride Information

🕐 Trail Contacts:
Coconino National Forest, Sedona Ranger District, Sedona, AZ (928) 282–4119 or www.fs.fed.us/r3/coconino

🕐 Schedule:
Open year round – Sedona gets surprisingly hot in the summer, so ride before noon from June-September.

🅢 Fees/Permits:
Each national forest parking lot requires that you have a $5 Red Rock Pass • (See State Land Recreation Permits sidebar on page 221)

❓ Local Information:
City of Sedona, Sedona AZ: www.city.sedona.net • **Sedona-Oak Creek Chamber of Commerce,** Sedona, AZ 1–800–288–7336 or www.sedona chamber.com • **Sedona website:** www. sedona.net – Looking for something in Sedona? This extensive web directory can probably help you out!

🅠 Local Events/Attractions:
Sedona Film Festival, Sedona, AZ 1–800–780–ARTS or www.sedonafilm festival.com – Held every March, the film festival features early releases of mainstream movies as well as smaller art films. Many of the celebrities who keep homes in Sedona show up at the film festival as well • **Sedona Heritage Museum,** Jordan Historical Park, Sedona, AZ (928) 282–7038 or www.sedonamuseum.org – Learn everything you could ever want to know about Sedona

🍴 Accommodations:
Bell Rock Inn, Sedona, AZ (928) 282–4161 or www.bellrockinn.com – Pricey but nice; just down the street from the Bell Rock Pathway parking lot • **Wildflower Inn,** Sedona AZ (928) 284–3937 or 1–888–494–5335 or www.sedonawildflowerinn.com – Cheaper and close to the trails

🍴 Restaurants:
Red Planet Diner, Sedona, AZ (928) 282–6070 or www.redplanetdiner.com – This goofy theme restaurant is a cross between a '50s truck stop diner and a sci-fi convention.

🚴 Mountain Bike Tours:
Sedona Bike & Bean, Sedona, AZ (928) 284–0210 or www.bike-bean.com – Bike & Bean offers a three-hour tour for $65.

🕐 Other Resources:
Sedona Vortex Map: www.sedona.net/fun/vortex/index.html – Get zapped by some of that healthy vortex energy!

🅖 Local Bike Shops:
Sedona Bike & Bean, Sedona, AZ (928) 284–0210 or www.bike-bean.com – Terrific bike shop and coffee bar across the street from the Bell Rock parking lot. Extremely knowledgeable staff, and a cool 3D model of all of Sedona with the trails painted on it. They even have a bed & breakfast room available.

🅝 Maps:
USGS maps: Sedona, AZ; Munds Mountain, AZ

11

Schnebly Hill to Seven Sacred Pools (East Sedona)

Ride Specs

Start: From Huckaby Trailhead on Schnebly Hill Road, less than one mile north of the AZ 179 bridge over Oak Creek.
Length: 13-mile loop
Approximate Riding Time: 2–3 hours
Difficulty Rating: Moderate with some difficult climbs and a dangerous section called "the stairs." Otherwise the trail is well groomed, with quick bailouts back to town.
Trail Surface: A mix of singletrack, doubletrack, gravel road, and a long paved return to the trailhead to create a loop.
Lay of the Land: Sedona's red rocks, juniper, and piñon pine forests.
Elevation Gain: 2,194 feet
Land Status: National forest
Nearest Town: Sedona
Other Trail Users: Hikers, equestrians, cars (on the scary-dangerous return on AZ 89A and AZ 179)

Canine Compatibility: Dogs permitted, as long as you keep the dog leashed during the pavement portion of the ride.
Wheels: Hardtail is fine, but a full suspension is suggested for some of the rockier parts.

Getting There

From Sedona: Get to the intersection of Schnebly Hill Road and AZ 179; Schnebly Hill Road turns due north just east of where AZ 179 crosses over Oak Creek. Drive up Schnebly Hill Road to just before the pavement ends (less than one mile). Look to your left for the Huckaby Trail/Marg's Trail trailhead parking area; it's marked with a big brown Forest Service sign. Park here and ride.
DeLorme: Arizona Atlas & Gazetteer: Page 42 C1

Theodore Schnebly, who built a post office in the valley and christened his new town "Sedona" after his wife, founded Sedona in 1902. Schnebly Hill Road, which winds up a canyon and eventually onto the Mogollon Rim, was the passage he took to sell vegetables and livestock in Flagstaff some 30 miles away. This road still exists, although it's awfully rugged for all but high-clearance vehicles—and mountain bikes.

This tour of the eastern Sedona trails begins on Schnebly Hill Road, heading north out of Sedona en route to Flagstaff the old-fashioned way. The trailhead, about a mile north of the Schnebly Hill Road turnoff just right next to the bridge over Oak Creek, overlooks Oak Creek Canyon winding its way north and south, a ribbon of brilliant green among Sedona's famous red rocks. The trip starts out with a bang, as the Huckaby Trail quickly descends into a side canyon, followed by a fairly short, steep climb back out.

Within three miles of the start, you'll be good and warmed up from the big climb that puts you on the edge of Oak Creek Canyon. The view is just about the best you'll get in Sedona; you can see every "named" rock from the overlook. The Huckaby Trail continues along this high ledge, and it's hard to stay focused on the ride when there's so much spectacular scenery to take in. Take your time and enjoy the ride.

Eventually, the Huckaby Trail descends into Oak Creek Canyon via "the stairs," a 30-foot descent down a staircase-like set of erosion controls. Then it leads to the shore of Oak Creek and a wide stream. This portage will be impossible during high waters; call the Forest Service before attempting this ride. Even at its normal height, the waters of Oak Creek run swiftly over a boulder-strewn streambed. A twisted ankle or knee will be no fun down here.

The climb up to Midgely Bridge, which carries FS 89A over Oak Creek, is mellow doubletrack that ends at the touristy overlook. Go ahead, be a tourist—the views are, again, great from the overlook just below the bridgeworks.

From Midgely Bridge, the trail skirts the Red Rock Secret Mountain Wilderness, which encompasses Wilson Mountain to the north. You're cool as long as you stay on the Wilson Canyon Trail, which starts at the Midgely Bridge parking lot. Wilson Canyon ends at an entrance to the wilderness, but the Jim Thompson Trail starts there and carries cyclists all the way to its trailhead, on Park Road (off Jordan Road; it's the same trailhead for Brins Canyon—a wilderness hiking trail—and the Jordan Trail, which is an entry into the Secret Trails network).

The Secret Trails are infamous among visitors for being impossible to navigate, and among locals for being terrific singletrack. It's a network of trails that bob and weave their way behind the ever-encroaching houses, constantly changing and disappearing as disgruntled homeowners and developers modify the trails. The Jordan Trail, which starts at the Brins Canyon/Jim Thompson parking lot, is the only trail through the area officially recognized by the Forest Service. If you go anywhere else, you run the risk of

MilesDirections

0.0 START from the Huckaby Trail trailhead. Marg's Trail begins in the same place, but it immediately enters wilderness—no bikes allowed! Just beyond the trailhead, Marg's Trail splits off to the left (there's a sign). Continue along Huckaby Trail as it turns to the right.

0.7 Top out on a lengthy climb. There's a park bench at the top of the climb. Check out the views! Continue ahead on Huckaby Trail, overlooking the edge of Oak Creek Canyon.

1.7 As you come around a hairpin turn, arrive at "the stairs" (a rock staircase about 30' down). If you like (and are good at stairs), enjoy riding the descent. If you're not up for it, then don't even try it. The exposure on your right is pretty extreme and a false move can prove ugly. At the bottom of the stairs, make a right hairpin and continue along the floor of Oak Creek Canyon toward the big water portage ahead.

2.4 Trail arrives at the edge of Oak Creek. Carefully pick your way across the creek, ride across the little island, and cross the creek again in about a hundred yards. At the end of the second portage, ride up the wide doubletrack to the Midgley Bridge overlook just above you. *[FYI. This portage may not be possible during high waters, so you may want to call the Forest Service for water levels before attempting this ride.]*

2.7 As you ride up the doubletrack, there's a wooden sign that says "trail" and points back the way you came. Continue up the trail, turning left toward the bridge.

3.0 Reach the Midgely Bridge overlook. *[FYI. To take in the views, hike the bike up to the parking lot behind you, climbing up the rock stairs.]* From the parking lot, look to your left (north) for a map kiosk and the beginning of the Wilson Canyon Trail, which starts as a wide doubletrack running along the base of Wilson Mountain *[FYI. Wilson Mountain is within the Secret Mountain Wilderness; so don't take any of the singletracks that split off to the right].* Head down the Wilson Canyon Trail.

3.3 Look to your left for a little pull-off that used to be a bridge across Wilson Canyon. Check out the view down the canyon and continue ahead. Cross the wash to pick up the trail on the other side. The trail will cross the wash once more.

3.6 Hit the end of Wilson Canyon Trail as it enters the Red Rock Secret Mountain Wilderness. The trail continues, but bikes have to make a hairpin turn to the left and pick up the Jim Thompson Trail, which quickly ascends the wall of Wilson Canyon.

3.8 At the top of the climb out of Wilson Canyon, the trail splits. The left trail takes you on a short (0.1 miles) loop around a hill and provides a nice overlook of Sedona. Take either trail; they get you to the same place. Follow the rock cairns on the other side.

5.8 Pass through a gate.

6.3 Reach the beginning of the Jim Thompson Trail as it splits off Brins Mesa Trail (a gravel road that goes into the Secret Mountain Wilderness). Look behind you and you'll see

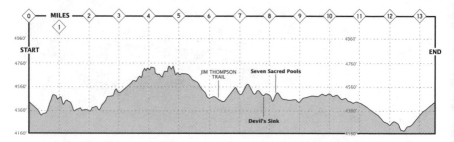

wandering onto private property or, more likely, upsetting homeowners who feel protective of "their" access to the hiking trails. You can spend hours in the Secret Trails area and never be more than half a mile away from civilization. Enjoy!

If you take the Jordan Trail to its end, you end up on a large sheet of slickrock. There are several ledges that bikers like to jump as well as one quite unjumpable "ledge"—Devil's Sink, a more than 100-foot-deep sinkhole that collapsed near the end of the nineteenth century. The sinkhole is marked with stone cairns and a few black diamond markers indicating the danger.

From Devil's Sink, you can either jump onto the Teacup Trail and continue westward (*see Ride 12: Teacup to Cockscomb*), or turn north on Soldier Pass Trail, a buttery smooth bit of trail that winds along a slickrock ledge and bobs into and out of the trees. Finally it arrives at the Seven Sacred Pools, a series of shallow pools carved into the slickrock that always seem to have water in them. Soldier Pass Trail continues north from here, but in about a mile it hits a gate and enters wilderness. This is a good place to turn around, hook onto Soldier Pass Road (a gnarly jeep road that tour companies use to haul sightseers to the sinkhole and pools), and take the road back to the trailhead.

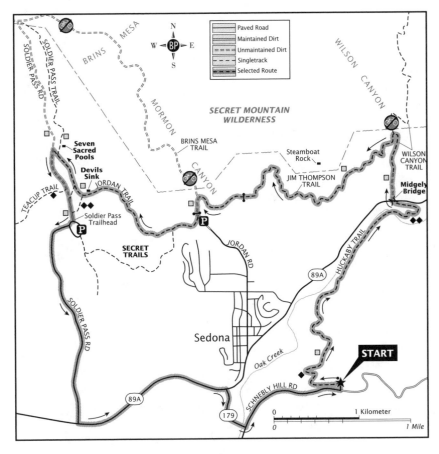

Rock Cairns

Many of the major Sedona trails are marked with cairns, which look like upside-down waste baskets filled with stones. These cairns are usually placed on slickrock or other areas where wooden signposts can't be placed. If you get lost on an open stretch of slickrock, keep your eyes open for a string of cairns to indicate the trail's actual pathway.

that "Jim Thompson Trail" is painted on a rock, pointing back to where you came. Turn left and head toward a closed gate. Ride around the gate and into a parking area with a map kiosk. Continue south toward the Jordan Trail trailhead. [*Bailout. Head south on Jordan Road out of the parking area to get back to AZ 89A and downtown Sedona (about one mile).*]

6.5 Turn out of the parking area and onto the Jordan Trail, going up a quick hill.

6.8 The Jordan Trail follows a power line up a hill. At the top of the hill, look to your left for a paint-marked tree indicating that the trail goes down the hill. Turn left (south) away from the power line. Follow the cairns to stay on the Jordan Trail; this area is also known as the Secret Trails area, and many undocumented singletracks zip around on and near the slickrock.

7.8 Arrive at a slickrock playground and Devil's Sink, a big sinkhole. Continue riding around the sinkhole, heading north. The singletrack stays to the right, close to the sinkhole. [*Bailout: As you head north and around the sinkhole, a gnarly, steppy jeep road splits off to the left. This is the beginning of the Teacup Trail, and hooks up with Soldier Pass Road in a few yards. The Soldier Pass parking lot is 0.4 miles south.*] [*Another bailout. Look to the southern edge of the slickrock playground, and you'll see a cairn-marked single-*

track heading southeast. This is Soldier Pass Trail, which gets back to the Soldier Pass parking lot in 0.5 miles.] [*Side-trip. Due west of the sinkhole is the beginning of the Teacup Trail (see Ride 12: Teacup to Cockscomb).*]

8.2 Arrive at the Seven Sacred Pools. The jeep road that hooks up with Soldier Pass Road is atop the ledge to the northwest of the Seven Sacred Pools. Jump onto the double-track; turn left when it hits Soldier Pass Road, and bike back to the Soldier Pass parking lot. [*Side-trip. Look for a narrow singletrack that continues north out of the Seven Sacred Pools area. This trail continues ahead for another mile or so, until it hits the edge of the wilderness area. Turn around and head back when you're done.*]

8.8 Arrive at the Soldier Pass parking lot. The return to the Schnebly Hill parking area is easy to get to from here. Simply head south to the cul-de-sac, turn right, and you're at Soldier Pass Road (the paved neighborhood road, not the jeep road that heads into the Secret Mountain Wilderness). Soldier Pass Road hooks into AZ 89A in less than two miles; keep your eye peeled for an urban trail to the east of Soldier Pass Road, which you can ride if the pavement isn't to your liking. Turn left and head down the hill to the Schnebly Hill turnoff. Turn left on Schnebly Hill Road and head up the hill back to the parking area

13.5 Return to the Huckaby Trail parking lot.

Ride Information

Trail Contacts:

Coconino National Forest, Sedona Ranger District, Sedona, AZ (928) 282–4119 or *www.fs.fed.us/r3/coconino*
• **Sedona Parks & Recreation,** Sedona, AZ (928) 282–7098

Schedule:

Open year round – Summers get quite warm in Sedona, and winters can bring snow. Call the Forest Service for water levels on Oak Creek, which may block your trail if levels are high.

Fees/Permits:

Each national forest parking lot requires that you have a $5 Red Rock Pass • *(See State Land Recreation Permits sidebar on page 221)*

Local Information:

(See Ride 10: Oak Creek Canyon Trails.)

Local Events/Attractions:

Jazz on the Rocks, Usually late September, Sedona, AZ (928) 282–1985 or *www.sedonajazz.com* – *annual jazz festival featuring some big-name draws as well as non-jazz events* • **Sedona Chamber Music Festival,** in mid-May, Sedona, AZ (928) 204–2415 or *www.chambermusicsedona.org* – *The other major music event in Sedona, the Chamber Music Festival brings classical music to the red rocks. The Sedona Chamber Music Society also offers performances year-round.*

Accommodations:

Desert Quail Inn, Sedona, AZ (928) 284–1433 or 1-800-385-0927 – *Extremely friendly hotel; gives $10 off if you mention you'll be mountain biking.*

You can also get discounted bike rentals from Mountain Bike Heaven when you stay here.

Restaurants:

Javelina Cantina, Sedona, AZ (928) 203–9514 or *www.shugrues.com/javelina_cantina.html* – *pricey but yummy Mexican fare; spectacular margaritas made with exotic tequilas. It's in the "Hillside" shopping complex about half a mile south of the "Y"* • **Oak Creek Brewing Company,** Sedona, AZ (928) 204–1300 – *Biker-friendly microbrewery, live music, and it's just yards away from the Sugarloaf Mountain trailhead.*

Group Rides:

Mountain Bike Heaven, Sedona, AZ (928) 282–1312 or *www.mountainbikeheaven.com* – *Mountain Bike Heaven runs group rides almost every day of the week. Each day is scaled to a different level of rider, from beginner to post-extreme.*

Organizations:

T.R.A.C.S. (Trail Resource Access Coalition of Sedona) – *A local non-profit multi-user trail access group. They put out a cool map of local trails, including lots of "hidden gems." The map is available at Mountain Bike Heaven. Contact TRACS at 50 Yucca Street, Sedona, AZ.*

Local Bike Shops:

Mountain Bike Heaven, Sedona, AZ (928) 282–1312 or *www.mountainbikeheaven.com*

Maps:

USGS maps: Wilson Mountain, AZ; Munds Mountain, AZ; Sedona, AZ; Munds Park, AZ

Teacup Trail to the Cockscomb (West Sedona)

Ride Specs

Start: There are several good starting points for this region of Sedona's trail network—the Soldier Pass parking lot, a dirt lot off FS 152 to Vultee Arch, and the Boynton Canyon Trailhead parking lot.

Length: Varies with route taken

Approximate Riding Time: 1–5 hours

Difficulty Rating: Moderate difficulty, both technically and aerobically. There are some tricky spots on the Teacup Trail, and some downright hard technical challenges on the Lost Watch Trail. If you go all the way to the Cockscomb, you'll be a few miles away from civilization, so be sure you're in good enough shape to ride *or* walk out.

Trail Surface: A mix of singletrack over dirt and slickrock, dirt roads, and old doubletrack. There are also numerous opportunities to bail out onto pavement.

Lay of the Land: Juniper and a few pine trees. Much of this area is in "Grasshopper Flat," a rolling juniper forest that leaves you very exposed for most of the ride. A large portion of the Teacup Trail also places you directly against the southern face of Coffee Pot Rock, on a narrow rock ledge. Bring plenty of sunscreen!

Land Status: National forest

Nearest Town: Sedona

Other Trail Users: Equestrians, pink jeeps, and hikers

Canine Compatibility: Dogs permitted

Wheels: Hardtail is adequate for everything on these trails. A hybrid could handle the dirt road portions of Boynton Pass Road and FS 152 (to Vultee Arch).

Getting There

From Sedona: All of the West Sedona rides start west of the Y-intersection at AZ 89 and AZ 179 in the middle of Sedona. Whether you're coming from Phoenix (south) or Flagstaff (north), you will have to pass through Sedona and this Y-intersection. From this intersection, travel west on AZ 89, then follow the respective directions for each of the four trailheads listed below. *DeLorme: Arizona Atlas & Gazetteer:* Page 42 C1

Soldier Pass Trailhead: From the Y-intersection in Sedona, travel five miles west on AZ 89 to Soldier Pass Road. Turn right on Soldier Pass Road, traveling north to Rim Shadow Drive. Turn right (east) on Rim Shadow Drive and take the first right. Look for the Soldier Pass Trailhead parking lot and gate. Park here. This parking lot gives you access to the Teacup Trail (described in this chapter), as well as Soldier Pass Trail, Jordan Trail, and the "secret trails" *(see Ride 11).*

FS 152 Parking Area (turnoff to Vultee Arch): From the Y-intersection in Sedona, travel six miles west on AZ 89 to Dry Creek Road. Turn right (north) on Dry Creek Road. At 1.9 miles, look to the right for a brown Forest Service sign reading "Vultee Arch 5 Miles," as well as distances to some other areas in the Secret Mountain Wilderness. FS 152 is just past this sign. Turn right on FS 152 and pull in about 20 yards, looking to the right (south) for a parking area. This parking area gives you access to the Lost Watch Trail, the Cockscomb Loop, and (if your eyes are sharp) a connector trail over to Thunder Mountain Trail (around the south end of Chimney Rock) called by locals "My Own Private Idaho."

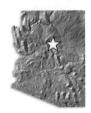

Long Canyon Trailhead:
From the Y-intersection in Sedona, travel six miles west on AZ 89 to Dry Creek Road. Turn right (north) on Dry Creek Road and head north until Dry Creek Road splits about half a mile past FS 152 (the turnoff to Vultee Arch). Turn right at this split onto Long Canyon Road. In about 1.5 miles, look to the left (northwest) for a

parking area and the trailhead for Long Canyon Trail. Use this trailhead to reach Deadman's Pass and Lost Watch Trail.

Boynton Canyon Trailhead: From the Y-intersection in Sedona, travel six miles west on AZ 89 to Dry Creek Road. Turn right (north) on Dry Creek Road and head north until Dry Creek Road splits about half a mile past FS 152 (the turnoff to Vultee Arch). Turning right takes you to Long Canyon Road (and the route to the Long Canyon Trailhead); to the left is Boynton Pass Road. Turn left, onto Boynton Pass Road. You'll reach the Boynton Canyon Trailhead in about 3.5 miles, just a few yards up the turnoff to Enchantment Resort; it's past the turnoff where Boynton Pass Road becomes dirt. Stay on the pavement, heading toward Enchantment Resort, and look for the trailhead on the right. This trailhead is a good place to start for Deadman's Pass, or to reach the Cockscomb via Boynton Pass Road.

Tourists often don't see west Sedona, the city and natural formations that lie west of the intersection of AZ 89 and AZ 179 at the center of town (also called "The Y" by pretty much everyone who knows Sedona). While tourists swarm like locusts to Oak Creek and east Sedona, west Sedona attractions like Boynton Canyon, the western end of Red Rock Secret Mountain Wilderness, and the Cockscomb remain relatively unvisited.

West Sedona's under-use may not last long, because many of the city's newest and most extravagant houses are popping up along Dry Creek Road and points west. Consequently, trails frequently change as new houses come in and fence off their personal piece of the desert.

The rock formations in this part of town become progressively less red as you head west toward the Cockscomb, as the distinctive red layers of the Supai Formation give way to gray layers of Coconino Sandstone and Kaibab Limestone. Secret Mountain dominates the landscape, rising quickly from the desert and creating a border between the city and the wilderness. The plant life in this area, known as Grasshopper Flat, is generally juniper and piñon pine—low, scrubby, and not a lot of cover from the sun.

Teacup Trail and Thunder Mountain Trail: This pair of trails connects the trails of east Sedona (*see Ride 11: Schnebly Hill to Seven Sacred Pools*) to the rest of the trails in west Sedona. Starting at the Soldier's Pass trailhead parking lot, the Teacup Trail winds up to a slickrock ledge at the base of Coffee Pot Rock and Capitol Butte. This is a fairly new addition to the National Forest's trail inventory; signs of unauthorized side routes that evolved during the creation of the Teacup Trail are abundant. Teacup Trail ends on the western face of Sugarloaf Mountain, a small hump of a hill, where another new network of trails winds around the hill. It also connects to the Thunder Mountain Trail, which is a very difficult trek across the northern edge of Sedona to the base of Chimney Rock. Riding westward, Thunder Mountain Trail enters progressively deeper and more difficult arroyos.

Long Canyon Trail and Deadman's Pass Trail: This pair of trails goes behind Mescal Mountain and leads to the mouth of Boynton Canyon, another of Sedona's famous vortexes. The Enchantment Resort is up the road in Boynton Canyon, strategically positioned to soak up the vortex's healing energies. Long Canyon Trail eventually enters wilderness (and just happens to be a great hike if you're up for it), but you have to ride the first (non-wilderness) bit of it to reach Deadman's Pass Trail. Deadman's Pass is a lot of fun going either direction, and features some old ranching ruins at the far western end of the trail (where it joins Boynton Pass Road).

Cockscomb Trail and Power Line Trail: Visible from most of Sedona once you head west of the Y-intersection, the Cockscomb is a distinctive rock formation and an excellent landmark. The Cockscomb Trail is, like many of the trails of west Sedona, a little hard to find but worth the work to get there. Starting from the FS 152 parking area, the trail starts on the other side of the paved road without much fanfare. Once you're on the trail, always keep the Cockscomb formation in view—it's the best way to make sure you're headed the right direction. Luckily, this is a safe place to get lost; the juniper forest's boundaries are Boynton Pass Road to the north, Dry Creek Road to the east, and AZ 89A to the south.

Another landmark in the area is Doe Mountain, a modest mesa just north of the Cockscomb. Legends of Sedona, a very nice resort, takes up the area between Doe Mountain and the Cockscomb. Although relations between Legends' jeep tour operators and local mountain bikers can be sometimes strained, treat the drivers with respect and they'll usually do the same in return.

The Power Line Trail is a quick access into the Cockscomb Loop Trails via Boynton Pass Road. There are a couple access points to this trail from Boynton Pass Road. Heading south on the Power Line Trail is much more fun than going north.

Lost Watch Trail: This hard-to-find trail cuts across the swath of desert between FS 152 and Long Canyon Road. There are many, many undocumented trails in this area, much like the Secret Trails a few miles east (*see Ride 11: Schnebly Hill to Seven Sacred Pools*). It's much more fun going north, toward the Long Canyon/Deadman's Pass trailhead up on Long Canyon Road, featuring one segment of wicked descents that will either have you behind your seat, on your feet walking down, or flying over your bars. There's also a portage over Dry Creek, with a find-the-trail scavenger hunt on the other side. Just keep heading north and you'll be fine.

MilesDirections: **Teacup to Thunder Mountain**

0.0 START from the Soldier Pass Trailhead *(see Getting There for directions to the trailhead)*. Go north on the jeep road (FS 9904).

0.1 To the right is Teacup Trail's short jeep-road access to Devil's Sink (the big sinkhole). About 20 yards past this is the beginning of the Teacup Trail (singletrack). Turn left onto the Teacup Trail and head uphill. Stick to the main trail, which is marked with rock cairns. The Teacup Trail tops out in about half a mile and follows along a slickrock ledge at the base of Coffee Pot Rock.

1.1 At the top of a climb, the trail splits left and right. Turn right to continue on Teacup Trail. *[**Side-trip.** Turning left takes you along Sugarloaf Loop, which is 0.3 miles long and comes out at mile 1.4 (below).]*

1.4 Reach a wooden sign indicating the Teacup Trail continues ahead; Sugarloaf Loop begins here and loops back up the mountain to the south. Continue following the rock cairns for the Teacup Trail. *[**Side-trip.** Take Sugarloaf Loop back to the Teacup Trail, as described above.]*

2.3 At the bottom of the hill, there's a sign indicating that Thunder Mountain Trail is ahead and Sugarloaf Trailhead is to your left. Continue ahead on Thunder Mountain Trail, which drops into a wash and comes back out on the other side (both trails that come out on the other side get to the same place, but the left is much harder than the right). Several unmarked singletracks will intersect with Thunder Mountain Trail; just stick to the main trail, marked with brown signs. *[**Bailout.** Turn left to get to the Sugarloaf Trailhead at the corner of Caswell and Buena Vista in 0.3 miles.]*

3.8 Arrive at the intersection of Thunder Mountain Trail and Chimney Rock Trail, which splits off to the right (west). The parking lot is just a few yards ahead. *[**Side-trip.** Follow Chimney Rock Trail north and look for a connector trail that takes you nearly two miles to the Vultee Arch access road (Dry Creek Road).]* Turn around and head back to the Soldier Pass Trailhead.

7.2 Return to the Soldier Pass Trailhead.

MilesDirections: **Deadman's Pass Loop** (north of Boynton)

0.0 START at the FS 152 parking area *(see Getting There for directions to the trailhead)*. Cut across the paved Dry Creek Road and pick up a singletrack trail on the other side behind a rock barricade.

0.1 Shortly after you turn onto the singletrack, there will be two left turns in quick succession. Pass by the first left (this takes you to the Cockscomb Loop; see *Cockscomb Loop* above) and continue along the trail as it bears left around the corner. You'll pass by a couple of other unmarked singletracks; keep right each time until you hit the doubletrack.

1.9 Join up with another doubletrack. Bear left, heading west. *[**Bailout.** There's a pair of metal poles creating a gate in the barbed-wire fence. Turn right at this gate and hit Boynton Pass Road in 0.1 miles.]* There's an endless network of old ranch roads and semi-legal singletrack in here. Keep bearing right at the various turnoff options, keeping the Cockscomb ahead of you at all times. If you get lost, don't forget Boynton Pass Road is to your right. Good luck!

2.7 The doubletrack hits the Power Line Trail, so named because it follows a power line up

MilesDirections: **Deadman's Pass Loop** (north of Boynton)

to Boynton Pass Road to the right and down to the Cockscomb to the left. Bear right to return to Boynton Pass Road. *[Note. There are a couple killer-deep drainages that cut across this trail. They're all navigable if you look for the perfect line, otherwise be prepared to walk a little.]*

3.2 Pass through a green gate. Bear right past the gate and continue north.

3.6 Come out on Boynton Pass Road, about 150 yards east of where the power line crosses the dirt road. Turn right onto Boynton Pass Road.

3.8 To your left is the Fay Canyon parking lot, which enters the wilderness area (no bikes!). Continue east.

4.1 To your right is FS 9587, which hooks into the rest of the network. *[FYI. This road is right next to a power line but is NOT the "Power Line Trail."]*

4.5 Arrive at the end of Boynton Pass Road (FS 152C). Turn left, heading toward Enchantment Resort. Shortly after the turn, look to your right for a cable gate and a doubletrack trail heading east. This is the Deadman's Pass trailhead. If you miss it, you can get onto Deadman's Pass Trail at Boynton Canyon Trailhead just up the road a bit (look south from the Boynton Canyon Trailhead parking lot for a trail heading into trees). You'll pass the ruins of an old corral to your right. There are little rock piles all along Deadman's Pass, marking the trail.

5.7 Heading east on Deadman's Pass, Long Canyon Trail splits off to the left and enters the wilderness area. Turn right and head south on Deadman's Pass. Looking from the other direction, there's a metal sign marking the split in the trail.

6.1 Pass through a barbed-wire gate.

6.7 At the bottom of the descent down the Long Canyon Trail heading toward Long Canyon Road, arrive at the Long Canyon trailhead. Cross Long Canyon Road to pick up the

Lost Watch Trail to the right (southwest) about 20 yards. Look for a "Natural Gas Pipeline: Danger!" marker for the beginning of the trail. There are a couple other accesses from the road; look for brown Forest Service "no motorized vehicles" signs.

7.3 Portage across Dry Creek. It's in fact a dry creek and fairly rocky. Be careful! Keep a sharp lookout for the singletrack that continues on the other side, heading south. You'll have to cross over a second wash once you're across Dry Creek.

8.2 Reach a slickrock area. Follow the contour of the shelf the trail starts on. As the trail is about to leave the slickrock area, it splits off to the right. It's unmarked and easy to miss – look out for it! Take the right. The left continues into the slickrock area and other trails. When the trail hits a jeep road, turn right onto it and head back to Dry Creek Road (FS 152).

8.6 Arrive on the Vultee Arch access road. The parking area is down the road a few yards. The "My Own Private Idaho" trail that connects to the Lower Chimney Rock Trail has an access directly across the road from where the Lost Watch Trail singletrack exits. It also starts at the parking area (look next to the "No Vehicles in Wilderness" sign). It's about three miles long before it connects to Lower Chimney Rock Trail.

MilesDirections: **Cockscomb Loop** (south of Boynton)

0.0 START from the FS 152 parking area *(see Getting There for directions to this trailhead)*, and head west across Dry Creek Road. Pick up a singletrack on the other side, behind a rock barricade. Shortly after you turn onto the singletrack, there will be two left turns in quick succession – take the first left, which is the beginning of the Cockscomb Trail. *[Side-trip. If you take the second left, you'll end up on an unnamed trail that eventually takes you to the Power Line Trail in 0.8 miles.]*

1.3 Pass through a dry wash and continue on the other side.

1.7 Top out on a hill. As you hit the top, you can see the Cockscomb in the distance. Drop down the hill, where doubletrack (which has been blocked off by rocks) joins from the left. The trail, now doubletrack, continues ahead, to the right. *[Side-trip. That doubletrack that joined from the right is an old, old jeep road that's a blast to ride...until it hits the back of new housing developments in 1.5 miles. Other unnamed, unofficial singletrack also splits off here and there – there's plenty to explore back here.]*

2.0 The Cockscomb Trail enters a dry riverbed. Walk or ride across, then pick up the trail as it goes up a steep hill on the other side.

2.5 At the top of a climb, a doubletrack trail splits left and right. Turn left and head up the

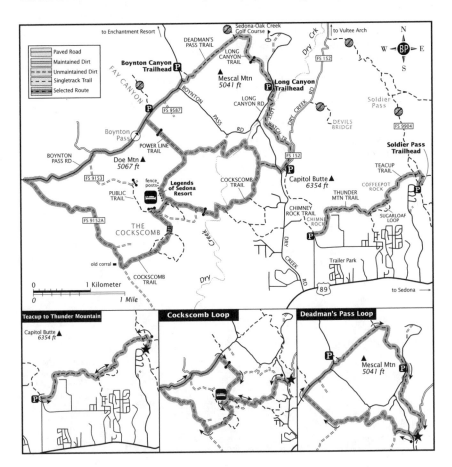

95

Vultee Arch

The Vultee Arch Trail is a hiker-only footpath into the Secret Mountain Wilderness, starting at the end of FS 152 (the Vultee Arch road from which many of west Sedona's trails start). It's an easy hike, about 1.7 miles up a gradual ascent. The arch itself, and the view from the end of the trail looking back down Sterling Canyon, is quite beautiful. The entire hike is under a heavy canopy of trees, and is cool even during the hottest summer days. Vultee Arch was named after the Vultee couple who, in 1938, crashed their private plane near the arch. There's a plaque commemorating them at the end of the trail.

hill. At the top of the climb, there's a barbed-wire gate you'll have to pass through. Shortly after passing through the gate, the trail splits left and right. The left drops down the hill, the right continues ahead, up a climb, toward the Cockscomb. Take the right.

2.7 At the top of the climb, the trail splits. Old fence posts stand where a ranch fence once stood. Turn left. *[Side-trip. Turning right takes you to the Power Line Trail in less than a mile. The Power Line Trail is fun and fast, featuring deep dips and sudden washes – be careful and watch your speed! The Power Line Trail exits at Boynton Pass Road in about 3 miles.]*

3.5 The trail comes out onto a jeep road that comes up the hill from the left. To the right is a gate with private property signs all over it; this is the Legends of Sedona resort. Look around and you'll see the singletrack you're on has a "public trail" sign. Pick up the "public trail" on the other side of the jeep road, as it follows just outside the fence surrounding the Legends of Sedona Resort.

4.2 The "public trail" ends at a dirt road (FS 9153). You have to go straight here and follow FS 9153 out to Boynton Pass Road.

4.9 Cross over a cattleguard. A doubletrack joins from the left, before the fence. Continue ahead on the dirt road. It eventually winds north, passing by an old corral in about one mile.

7.4 Arrive at Boynton Pass Road. Turn left.

8.2 Look for the "Limited Use Road" sign marking the beginning of FS 9152A. Turn left on FS 9152A and head south.

10.8 Arrive at a cattle chute. Look for doubletrack heading left (east), toward the base of the Cockscombs, and take this trail.

11.0 Arrive at the bottom of FS 9153, which heads left and goes uphill to the Legends of Sedona gate. Turn left and head up the hill.

11.6 Arrive at the Legends of Sedona gate. Turn right on the singletrack you came in on and follow it out.

15.1 Return to the trailhead at FS 152.

Cryptobiotic Soil

The desert ecosystem throughout Arizona—and especially around Sedona—is tied together with a living organism called cryptobiotic soil. This layer of lichen, blue-green algae, fungi, and mosses holds the sandy soil in place and produces a nitrogen-rich bed for seeds. Riding or hiking off-trail easily destroys the crust, and the soil dies almost instantly. It can take a century or longer to regrow; in the meantime, a strong rain can erode away the soil in an instant.

The singletrack that crisscrosses the desert isn't just there as an amusement source for trail-users—it's there to help limit cross-country travel and protect the cryptobiotic soil. Stay on the trails. Period. You'll know if you've found cryptobiotic soil by the walking-on-eggshells sound your shoes and tires make. As the locals say, "Don't bust the crust!"

Ride Information

● Trail Contacts:

(See Ride 11: Schnebly Hill to Seven Sacred Pools)

● Schedule:

Open year round – Summers get hot, so bring plenty of water and sunscreen.

● Fees/Permits:

Each national forest parking lot requires you have a $5 Red Rock Pass (see page 75.)

● Local Information:

(See Ride 11: Schnebly Hill to Seven Sacred Pools)

● Restaurants:

Oak Creek Brewing Company, Sedona, AZ (928) 204–1300 • Heartline Café, Sedona, AZ (928) 282–0785 – If you're wondering where Sedona's celebrity population hangs out, and you have $50 burning a hole in your pocket, check out the Heartline Café. This award-winning restaurant has received the highest possible ranks from culinary groups around the world. Don't expect to carbo-load here after a hard day's riding, though—Heartline is about quality, not quantity.

● Group Rides:

Mountain Bike Heaven, Sedona, AZ (928) 282–1312 or www.mountainbike-heaven.com – Mountain Bike Heaven runs group rides almost every day of the week. Call to check which days suit your riding ability.

● Other Resources:

Sedona by Trail, a crazy-looking, large-format, two-sided hand-drawn map of darned near every trail in Sedona, is available at Mountain Bike Heaven. It's super-useful for finding trailheads and connections, but far from GPS-accurate. The map also features lots of ads and local tidbits. A worthy $10 investment • The Original Sedona Mountain Bike Trail Map and Field Guide, a hand-drawn map similar to Sedona by Trail, is also available at Mountain Bike Heaven—it's their own creation, and costs $5.

● Local Bike Shops:

Mountain Bike Heaven, Sedona, AZ (928) 282–1312 or www.mountainbike-heaven.com

● Maps:

USGS maps: Page Springs, AZ; Sedona, AZ; Wilson Mountain, AZ; Loy Butte, AZ

13

Mormon Mountain

Ride Specs

Start: From the turnoff to Munds Park (FS 240) off Mormon Lake Road

Length: 12.6-mile loop with additional side-trips

Approximate Riding Time: 2.5–3 hours.

Difficulty Rating: Technically easy, except for a few spots on the Mormon Mountain descent that involve loose rocks and tight switchbacks. Aerobically moderate; the climb up Mormon Mountain is very tame, and can be done in the middle ring by most moderately fit cyclists.

Trail Surface: The ride is along well-graded dirt roads all the way up to the top of the mountain, then singletrack all the way back down. A bit of pavement finishes up the ride.

Lay of the Land: The trail winds through ponderosa pine forest and areas of lush fern along the singletrack descent.

Elevation Gain: 1,600 feet

Land Status: National forest

Nearest City: Flagstaff

Other Trail Users: Theoretically, hikers and equestrians. The hikers typically stick to the side routes at the lower end of the trail (Dairy Springs Loop and Ledges Trail), as the climb to the top of Mormon Mountain is fairly steep.

Canine Compatibility: Dogs permitted, if the dog can handle the distance

Wheels: Hardtails are fine for this trail

Getting There

From Flagstaff: Heading south on I-40 toward I-17 southbound, turn right at the light on Forest Meadows Road; there's a Denny's and a Texaco on the opposite corner. At this corner, there's a big green sign that reads "To Lake Mary Road." Just follow the signs to Lake Mary Road southbound. Take the immediate left onto Beulah Road, continuing to follow the signs to Lake Mary Road. Once on Lake Mary Road, drive south. Exactly 21 miles south of the I-40 overpass turn right at the sign for Mormon Lake Village onto Mormon Lake Road. Pass the Dairy Springs Campground on your right. Keep driving toward the next right turn, one mile past the Dairy Springs Campground, to Munds Park (FS 240; it's marked with a trailhead sign for "Mormon Mountain Trail North"). Turn right onto FS 240 (a dirt road) and park off to the side of the road—there's a handy parking spot on the left.

From Phoenix and points south: On I-17 north, look for the Stoneman Lake Road turnoff (Exit 306) north of Camp Verde (it's the next turnoff after the exit to Sedona). Turn east onto Stoneman Lake Road. The road changes to dirt and reaches a T-intersection in 6.7 miles. Turn left onto FS 213 (still Stoneman Lake Road), heading toward Stoneman Lake. Reach Lake Mary Road (which is paved) in 7.7 miles, and turn left (north), heading toward Mormon Lake. Just past mile marker 317, there's a paved road that splits off to the left. This is Mormon Lake Road; take it to Mormon Lake. The Munds Park turnoff (FS 240) is 3 miles past the village, on your left. ***DeLorme: Arizona Atlas & Gazetteer:*** Page 42 B-C 2-3

Mormon Lake is officially the largest natural lake in Arizona. Most of the year, though, the "lake" is little more than a grassy basin or wetland. According to the owner of the Mormon Lake Lodge, who has lived here since 1963, the last time he saw the lake completely full was back in 1990. He blames a shift in local weather patterns. Still, the monsoons roll through every summer and the snow runs off every spring, and Mormon Lake does get a bit of water in it. But even completely full, the deepest part of the lake is only about six feet and a strong wind can evaporate a foot off the top of the lake in just a couple days.

This lake is one of a dozen or so lakes scattered across the high plateau area of Coconino National Forest, which spreads south of Flagstaff across the Colorado Plateau (the plateau starts at the Mogollon Rim to the south). Lake Mary Road cuts directly across the plateau, connecting Payson with Flagstaff and providing access to all the various lakes and volcanic mountains along the way.

The area's first European settlers were Mormons, who began building ranches and working the land in the area in 1873. Arizona's first dairy farm was also established in 1873, near Lake Mary, to supply Mormons traveling to California. News of the lake soon spread, and it became a popular escape from Phoenix and Tucson. The Mormon Lake Lodge was built in 1924, and became a famous steakhouse and saloon popular with ranchers who worked the plateau. Although the original lodge burned down in 1974 during a Fourth of July celebration, it was quickly rebuilt in what was later called the largest barn-raising event in Arizona history. The ranchers who got togeth-

MilesDirections

0.0 START from the parking pull-off on FS 240. Pedal up the dirt road toward Munds Park.

2.1 Turn right onto FS 132A. There's a sign that says "Mormon Mountain." You can't miss it.

4.2 Turn right onto FS 648 and head up the mountain. *[Side-trip. If you continue ahead on FS 132A, you'll end up going down quite quickly and then reach a split in the road in two miles. From there, you can turn left heading toward Antelope Park and Lake Mary Road, or right to explore the forest roads north of Mormon Mountain.]*

7.5 Reach a "Road Closed to Vehicle Traffic" gate across the road. Bike around the gate and continue.

7.7 There's a brown sign pointing to the right that reads "Mormon Mountain Trail Parking." Turn right here and head down to the parking area. *[Side-trip. Continue ahead to reach the radio towers in 0.6 miles. Unfortunately, you don't get any good views from up here—the forest is so dense that all you can see is trees and towers.]* The doubletrack that goes down to the parking area turns right and continues south. Look to your right about 10 yards down the trail, and you'll see a trailhead sign for Mormon Mountain Trail. Turn right onto the singletrack and begin the romp down!

10.5 Arrive at a gate. Lift the bike over and continue down the trail, which now turns into doubletrack.

10.7 A sign to your left indicates the top of the Dairy Springs Loop. Continue ahead.

[Side-trip. Turn left here and enjoy an extra mile of singletrack winding around and eventually back down to the Mormon Mountain Trail. Add 0.8 miles to the ride total.]

10.9 A sign to your left indicates the bottom of the Dairy Springs Loop. Continue ahead.

11.1 Reach the end of the Mormon Mountain Trail. The trail terminates at a dirt road cutting left and right. Turn left and head back down to Mormon Lake Road. *[Side-trip. If you turn right, you can ride 0.6 miles up and check out some private cabins. Add 1.2 miles to your total.]*

11.2 There's a cable gate to your left and a little trail that connects over to the Dairy Springs Campground. Continue ahead on the dirt road toward Mormon Lake Road. *[Side-trip. If you turn left here and left again once you're in the campground, you can reach Ledges Trail in 0.3 miles. The trailhead is 0.3 miles into the campground. The trail winds its way toward Ledges Vista, which overlooks the "lake" in 0.6 miles. Add 1.7 total miles if you take this side-trip.]*

11.4 Arrive at Mormon Lake Road. Turn right and head toward FS 240 (the Munds Park road).

11.6 Check out the Mormon Dairy historic site to your right. Continue ahead.

12.6 Arrive back at your vehicle.

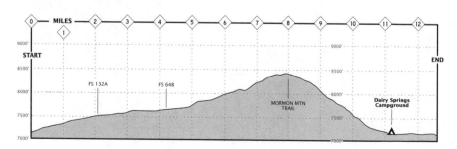

er to rebuild the lodge branded the building, and today you can still see hundreds of different brands burned forever into the lodge's walls.

Mormon Mountain stands west of the lake, rising quickly from the plateau like other volcanic mountains in the area. The road up Mormon Mountain is comprised almost entirely of crushed volcanic rock. The mountain is covered with ponderosa pine, mixed conifers, and aspen—so covered, in fact, that you get only brief glimpses of the lake while descending the eastern face of the mountain. One of the lower spur trails, the Ledges Trail, descends into juniper and Gambel oaks. Elk and mule deer are common sights along the trail.

Riding-wise, Mormon Mountain consists of a fairly tame, if long, middle-ring climb up to 8,500 feet, and a singletrack switchback that almost anyone can blast down with some speed. The upper reaches of the trail aren't often maintained, so expect the occasional deadfall and loose rubble to keep things interesting. The descent is moderately technical singletrack, featuring some small drops and lots of loose stuff—depending on the time of year, either leaves or post-monsoon debris. The top of Mormon Mountain is totally shrouded in trees, so there's not much of a view as you careen between trees along the top en route to the descent. The further down the mountain you go, the shallower and more maintained the descent—expect more hikers as you go down. Near the bottom of the descent, you'll have an opportunity to climb again out to a lookout by taking the Ledges Trail out of the campground. Although a little tiring after the climb, the trip out to the ledge to views of the lakebed is well worth your time.

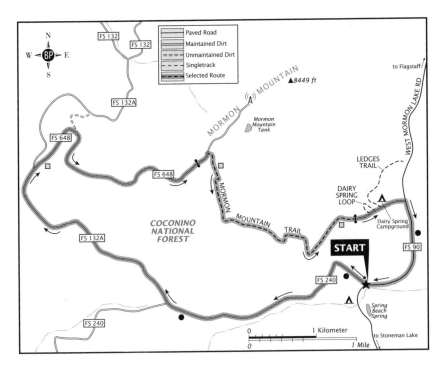

Ride Information

Trail Contacts:

Coconino National Forest, Mormon Lake Ranger District, Flagstaff, AZ (928) 774–1147 or *www.fs.fed.us/r3/coconino/rec_plateau.html*

Schedule:

Open year round – May be snowed in November-March, so call first.

Fees/Permits:

No fees or permits required

Local Information:

Great Outdoor Recreation Pages: *www.gorp.com/dow/southwst/cocoinfo.htm*

Local Events/Attractions:

Mormon Lake Ski Center, Flagstaff, AZ (928) 354–2240 – *The Center provides more than 30 kilometers of groomed trail for novice, intermediate, and advanced cross-country skiers. It's open daily, snow permitting, with a trail fee of $5 per adult or $15 per family, rental ski sets for $11, and instruction at $15 for 90 minutes in a small group.*

Accommodations:

Mormon Lake Lodge, Mormon Lake, AZ (928) 354–2227 or *www.foreverresorts.com/mormon.html* • **Montezuma Lodge,** Mormon Lake, Arizona (928) 354–2220 or *www.arizonamountainresort.com/* – *You can bike the Mormon Mountain trail right out of the lodge's front door, which is next to the Dairy Spring campground* • **Motel In The Pines,** Munds Park, AZ (928) 286–9699

– To get to the trailhead from Munds Park, take Mormon Lake Road 10 miles east toward Mormon Lake—it's the same road you'll be riding en route to Mormon Mountain. There's plenty of signage in town to find your way. Munds Park has also had more than its fair share of UFO sightings. Maybe you'll luck into an abduction!

Restaurants:

Mormon Lake Lodge, Mormon Lake, AZ (928) 354–2227 – *The Lodge's steakhouse and saloon is worth the trip. If red meat's not your thing, there's a decent chicken sandwich. Don't expect a plate of greens, though. Located three miles south of the trailhead in Mormon Lake Village.*

Mountain Bike Tours:

Backroads, Berkeley, CA 1–800–462–2848 or *www.backroads.com/trips/BAZI.html* – *runs a tour around Mormon Lake, as well as Flagstaff and Sedona*

Local Bike Shops:

Sinagua Cycles, Flagstaff, AZ (928) 779–9969 – *Nobody is more knowledgeable about northern Arizona biking than the folks at Sinagua. Full-service shop with a broad selection.*

Maps:

USGS maps: Mormon Mountain, AZ; Mormon Lake, AZ

Arizona Trail Project

In Addition

If you like your bike rides long—really, really long—cast an eye toward the Arizona Trail. The Arizona Trail is a 780-mile long network of nonmotorized singletrack and doubletrack trails, both historic and newly constructed, that stretches between the Mexican and Utah borders. Envisioned first in 1985 by Dale Shewalter during a 24-day hike from Nogales to the Utah border, the mission of the Arizona Trail is to provide nonmotorized access across the state for everyone. Some portions of the trail's current pathway pass through national parks and wilderness areas, where bikes are restricted from trail use. In those cases, alternate routes are currently being developed.

The Arizona Trail Association (ATA) is responsible for coordinating the complex partnership between state and federal landowners, private landowners ranging from ranchers to corporate mining operations, the National Park Service, the U.S. Forest Service, cities, counties, unincorporated communities, and organizations like the Sierra Club. Hundreds of volunteers have worked together to complete the trail by 2000.

The Arizona Trail is divided into 42 passages. Each passage makes up a portion of the trail that can be traversed by foot, horse, or bike in one to three days and has easy access and exit points. Several of these passages are covered in this book. Your best bet for detailed information about the Arizona Trail's passages is to buy *On the Arizona Trail* by Kelly Tighe and Susan Moran (1998, Pruett Publishing). This excellent book provides good descriptions of all the passages along the trail, and notes which ones are bike-accessible for those of us looking for two-wheeled adventures.

When traveling along the Arizona Trail, you'll see distinctive Arizona Trail markers every mile or so. If you ever think you've wandered off the trail, backtrack until you find the last trail marker you passed. If you're thinking about biking your way up the Arizona Trail, there are several alternate passages that follow highways. Get the book for details.

The ATA is always looking for volunteers! If you want to join, volunteer, or buy a T-shirt, contact the ATA at P.O. Box 36736, Phoenix, AZ 85067, or call (602) 202-4794, or visit the website at *aztrail.org*.

14

Walnut Canyon and Marshall Lake

Ride Specs

Start: From the parking area off Lone Tree Road and Zuni Road, south of old town Flagstaff—one main doubletrack/gravel road feeds into the canyons south of Flagstaff, which then splits off into two distinct trails.

Length: The ride along the lip of Walnut Canyon is 23.6 miles round-trip, with an option to continue along the Arizona Trail for a total 32 mile out-and-back. The ride out to Marshall Lake and back is 19.6 miles round-trip.

Approximate Riding Time: Both rides are 3.5–5 hours long, depending on the strength of the rider.

Difficulty Rating: Moderate to Difficult. Walnut Canyon demands more technique than Marshall Lake, due to some technically difficult descents and ascents. The climb out of the canyon is both technically and aerobically difficult on both rides. Once out of the canyon, Walnut Canyon becomes a fairly flat, fast ride atop the canyon ledge. Marshall Lake is a fairly consistent grind upward all the way to the lake, but doesn't demand any special technical skill.

Trail Surface: Both trails begin on the same old logging road, heading south away from Flagstaff into the canyons. Both trails later become singletrack. Some of the track atop Walnut Canyon is doubletrack and forest road; it's all well marked with Arizona Trail signs, as both trails are part of this statewide network.

Lay of the Land: The land south of Flagstaff is riddled with canyons both large and small—sort of an inversion of the mountains to the north. Both rides pass through deep, dark ponderosa pine forests.

Land Status: National forest

Nearest Town: Flagstaff

Other Trail Users: Hikers are quite common on both trails. Equestrians are allowed, but are rarely seen. Expect an occasional truck on the forest road portions of Walnut Canyon.

Canine Compatibility: Dogs permitted, but both trails are fairly long and strenuous for dogs. Some of the doubletrack and logging road loops in the immediate vicinity of Lone Tree Road are perfect dog-assisted rides, though.

Wheels: Hardtails are adequate for either ride, but full suspension is nice to have on the descent both out of Walnut Canyon and on the return from Marshall Lake.

Getting There

From Flagstaff: Follow I-40/Route 66 as it goes eastbound through the middle of Flagstaff. Turn south on Mt. Humphreys Street, and shortly after that turn, turn left (east) on Butler Road. Very shortly—less than a mile after the turn onto Butler road—turn right (south) at the Lone Tree Road stoplight (look for the Flagstaff Saddlery building at the corner) and drive about two miles, past the I-40 overpass, until Lone Tree Road turns to dirt and Zuni Road turns to the right. Coconino Community College is at this corner as well. Continue past the Zuni Road turnoff and drive up Lone Tree Road a few yards (now a dirt road) and park anywhere.

Second Trailhead: Just south of the I-40 overpass heading southbound on Lone Tree Road, turn right (west) onto Lake Mary Road and drive 2.7 miles. Look for the first dirt road to your left, south of the water treatment plant. If you reach Chisholm Street, you've gone too far. This dirt road eventually feeds into the Skunk Canyon Trail, and then connects to the Walnut Canyon/Marshall Lake trails (see the map). **DeLorme: Arizona Atlas & Gazetteer:** Page 42 A2

A ccording to ceramic dating and tree circles, there are signs that Sinagua Indian tribes have inhabited the Flagstaff area for 800 years. Just south of Flagstaff, though, there are signs of human habitation of caves along the walls of Walnut Canyon that are at least 2,000 years old. The "houses" built into the sides of the canyon help fill in many anthropological details, providing a look at the transitional centuries between year 0 and the years of flourishing Sinagua civilization.

Walnut Creek has carved a canyon out of Kaibab Limestone as it flows seasonally toward the Little Colorado River, eastward, and eventually to the Grand Canyon. The walls of Walnut Canyon occur in various layers, some harder than others, resulting in shallow caves at different levels. At its farthest eastern end, Walnut Canyon is 600-feet deep, its walls protected from both the heat of the summer sun and harsh winter snows. At Walnut Canyon National Monument (founded 1915), you can take a mile-or-so walk along the Island Trail, which takes you around an "island" in the middle of the canyon dotted with caves. Some of the caves are quite deep, and you can see caves all along the walls of the canyon from the Island Trail.

There is some speculation that the Sinagua tribes ended up in Walnut Canyon (as well as Verde Valley and the Wupatki village, now a popular ruin to visit) because they were forced to move during the eruption at Sunset Crater in 1064. The canyon was a natural fortress, impenetrable by attackers. The caves were easy to enclose with primitive masonry, providing cool quarters in the summer and protection during the winter.

The sweep of singletrack from Marshall Lake, down to the canyon floor, and back up to Fisher Point and the lip of Walnut Canyon is all part of the Arizona Trail (see *Arizona Trail Project sidebar on page 103*)—actually, a part of an "equestrian bypass" that will be less strenuous on pack horses than the standard route. It just so happens it's less strenuous for mountain biking as well. And despite its appellation as an equestrian trail, horses are a very rare sight on the trail.

The vegetation changes noticeably in different parts of the canyon. The north facing walls have fir and pine trees, while some of the sunny, south-facing slopes have

MilesDirections

0.0 START from where you've parked on Lone Tree Road. Look due south and you'll see a gate. A singletrack winds around the left of the gate. Get around the gate and take the doubletrack beyond the gate going south.

0.6 The doubletrack splits here. Both splits take you to the same place around the hill. Take the left this time. *[Option. If you take the right, take every left at every split you're offered. Add + 0.7 miles to the total distance.]*

1.4 A doubletrack joins from the right—this is the doubletrack that split off back at 0.6 miles. Continue ahead (east). Just past the split, you'll go around a gate and a sign that says "Walnut Recreation Area, No Motor Vehicles."

2.1 Pass a "Trail Not Regularly Maintained, Use At Your Own Risk" signpost at a trailhead to your left. Continue ahead on the main trail. *[Side-trip. Take the left beyond the ominous warnings and you'll ride very gradually downhill across some open meadows. Take the first right you hit (0.9 miles) to pick up some singletrack and rejoin with the Marshall Lake Trail in 0.3 miles (at mile 3.5), or continue straight and end up on a portion of the Arizona Trail that dumps you off very close to NAU in 2.4 miles. Check the map for an*

option that takes you along logging roads below I-40 and returns you to Lone Tree Road.]

3.0 The singletrack comes to a T-intersection. To the left is an "Area Closed" sign. Turn right at this T-intersection. *[Option. The left is the singletrack that split off back at mile 2.1. Check the map to see where you'll end up.]*

3.3 A singletrack joins from the right. Continue ahead. *[Side-trip. This singletrack winds its way up into Skunk Canyon, a narrow, dark fern-filled canyon, eventually exiting onto a meadow and dumping you out onto Lake Mary Road in 3.0 miles. This is a very cool, fairly technical trail, especially coming at it from the other direction and starting from the second trailhead.]*

3.9 Reach a wooden sign indicating Marshall Lake is 5.6 miles ahead. This is the intersection where you need to decide whether to follow Walnut Canyon Trail, to the left, or Marshall Lake Trail, straight ahead. Both of these trails are part of the Arizona Trail.

Cues continuing along the Walnut Canyon Trail and the Marshall Lake Trail are found on pages 108–109.

agaves and several species of cactus—typical of the Upper Sonoran desert. The canyon floor has many examples of the walnut trees from which the canyon and creek were named.

There are several nice overlooks available along the Walnut Canyon trail. The first and most prominent is Fisher Point, which gives a great view not only into the canyon but also across the plateaus south of Flagstaff. There are three more overlooks along the way, each marked with a sign. None is longer than 0.6 miles long; so take the time to check them out.

Going due south, the Arizona Trail equestrian bypass heads up to Marshall Lake. The climb out of the canyon is longer but less technical than the climb up to Fisher Point. Once you've made the climb, though, the work isn't over—the trail rolls up and down as it passes through ponderosa forest. Marshall Lake is a worthy destination, though, so pack a lunch and relax at the side of the "lake." (Marshall Lake isn't really a lake at all, but a marshy wetland for most of the year.) Co-sponsored by Ducks Unlimited, a national duck preservation/hunting group, Marshall Lake is home to great blue herons, bald eagles, and of course, ducks.

Arizona Trail

The Arizona Trail is, in a manner of speaking, "superimposed" on other local trails throughout the state (see Arizona Trail Project sidebar on page 103). On the map for this particular ride, The Arizona Trail starts at Marshall Lake, travels west to the trail intersection near Fisher Point (mile 3.9), goes up to Fisher Point, and then continues past the large parking lot and trailhead on FS 303 at the end of the Walnut Canyon Trail.

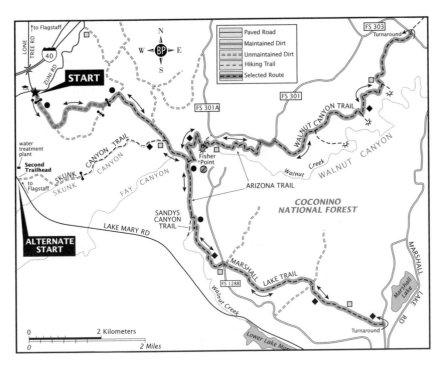

MilesDirections Walnut Canyon Trail (The Arizona Trail)

3.9 Turn left at the sign, heading toward the rocky cliff face of Fisher Point. You'll know you're in the right place because a shallow cave is visible at the foot of Fisher Point. A little past the turnoff, you'll turn left again at an Arizona Trail sign (to Fisher Point Vista) and begin the tricky ascent up to the lip of the canyon along Walnut Canyon Trail. *[Side-trip. Ride 0.1 miles down to the cave and check it out. Turn around at the cave, because the singletrack beyond the cave enters a wilderness area.]*

5.0 Arrive at the split-off to Fisher Point Vista. Turn left and continue along Walnut Canyon Trail (the Arizona Trail). There's a gate a few yards up from the turn; be sure to close it behind you when you go through. *[Side-trip. Turn right here and check out the vista. Awesome views of Walnut Canyon! Add 0.2 miles to the trip distance.]*

5.2 A singletrack joins from the left, and goes to FS 301A in 0.3 miles. *[Bailout. Take this bailout to reach FS 301A. From the forest road, you can work your way back to town and eventually your vehicle on an easy route— it's all downhill from here!]*

7.1 The trail intersects with FS 301. Look for the Arizona Trail sign on a doubletrack that heads off to the right (east). Continue following these signs.

7.6 A doubletrack trail splits off to the right and is marked with an Arizona Trail sign. Turn right, following the sign.

8.2 A wooden sign indicates an unnamed viewpoint to the right. Continue ahead. *[Side-trip. The vista is 0.6 miles in; add 1.2 miles to the trip distance. Check out the work being done to convert the old doubletrack into singletrack, by building up one of the ruts with branches and rocks.]*

9.5 As you come down a slightly steppy, rocky descent, look for a sign indicating that Walnut Canyon Trail (the Arizona Trail) turns sharply to the left and heads down into a canyon. *[Side-trip. Walnut Canyon Vista is ahead 0.2 miles. Add 0.4 miles to the trip.]*

10.4 Top out on the hard climb out of the canyon. There's a game water tank to the left. Walnut Canyon Trail (the Arizona Trail) turns left here and becomes doubletrack; follow the Arizona Trail signs and you can't get lost. *[FYI. Just past the sign, a singletrack splits off to the right and parallels the doubletrack for a bit before splitting off. Again, just continue following the Arizona Trail signs.]*

11.8 Arrive at a large parking lot and trailhead, off FS 303. This is an excellent turnaround spot, and an easy place to designate a pickup or drop-off if you're making this a shuttle ride. The total distance as an out-and-back is 23.6 total miles, including trips to all the vista points along the way. *[Option. From this parking lot and trailhead, pick up the Arizona Trail across the road and continue heading east. You'll reach the frontage road at the Cosnino exit in 4.2 miles, from which you could loop back via frontage roads along I-40. This option is quite long; the ride along the highway back to the Lone Tree Road trailhead is another 10 miles or so.]*

23.6 Return to your car on Lone Tree Road.

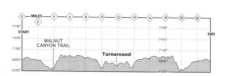

MilesDirections **Marshall Lake Trail**

3.9 Turn right at the split in the Arizona Trail, following the Marshall Lake Trail.

4.8 The trail splits. Straight ahead is the Sandys Canyon Trail; the Marshall Lake Trail splits to the left. Turn left on the Marshall Lake Trail and head toward the cliff face. *[Side-trip. Sandys Canyon is unrideable after about a quarter mile, but you can hike in more deeply onto this verdant, narrow trail.]*

6.3 There's a very old wooden sign for the Arizona Trail to your right. An unnamed doubletrack—most likely an old logging road—cuts across the trail. Pick up the singletrack on the other side.

8.2 Cross over some unmarked doubletrack and pick up the singletrack on the other side. Just past the little gully you dip into, a game tank is to the right, behind a fence. Continue ahead.

9.1 Pick up your bike and walk around the cattle-proofed gate.

9.8 Arrive at Marshall Lake. *[Side-trip. A singletrack picks up way, way across the road around Marshall Lake, over by the national forest sign explaining the wetland's importance as a duck preserve. Go explore if you choose!] [Bailout. Take the gravel road around the lake over to the national forest sign. Turn right at the gravel road and this will get you back to Lake Mary Road in about eight miles. The ride back to town is long, but at least it's all along a paved road. This would also make a decent shuttle ride (presumably going downhill back to Lone Tree Road— shuttling from the top of the ride would be a drag!).]*

19.6 Return to your car on Lone Tree Road.

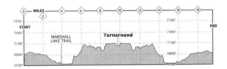

Ride Information

Trail Contacts:
[See Ride 15: Mt. Elden]

Schedule:
Open year round – best riding May-November

Fees/Permits:
No fees or permits required

Local Information:
[See Ride 15: Mt. Elden]

Local Events/Attractions:
Walnut Canyon Visitors Center, Flagstaff, AZ (928) 526–3367 or *www.nps.gov/waca – There's a $3 individual fee to enter the visitors center. You can get to the Walnut Canyon Visitors Center via bike by riding south* on FS 303 from the far east turnaround point of the Walnut Canyon ride. If you drive, turn south on exit 204 off the I-40 and drive south for 3 miles on Walnut Canyon Monument Road.

Organizations:
The Arizona Trail Association, Phoenix, AZ (602) 252–4794 or *www.aztrail.org – ATA manages this segment of the Arizona Trail in partnership with Coconino National Forest* • **Ducks Unlimited:** *www.ducks.org – read everything you'd ever want to know about ducks, duck hunting, and wetland preservation.*

Maps:
USGS maps: Flagstaff East, AZ; Lower Lake Mary, AZ

15

Mount Elden

Ride Specs

Start: From one of several trailheads, depending on the type and length of ride you want.

Length: 5-30 miles (depending on the loop)

Approximate Riding Time: 1–7 hours (depending on the loop)

Difficulty Rating: Varies. Any climb to the top of Mt. Elden involves a 2,000-foot climb to more than 9,000 feet in six miles, so it is aerobically demanding. The loop around the base of the mountain is a long haul; much of it exposed, and is therefore also physically demanding. Several of the trails (specifically Rocky Ridge, Upper Oldham, Heart, and portions of Sunset and Brookbank) feature significant technical challenges as well—rocky drops, tight switchbacks, and other challenges. These more difficult trails are popular practice runs with local pro downhill racers.

Trail Surface: Except for the wide gravel road up to the top of Mt. Elden, everything in the Elden Trail Network is singletrack on fairly well groomed pine forest floor.

Lay of the Land: Pine forest, high desert at the base of the mountain

Elevation Gain: 4,508 feet

Land Status: National forest

Nearest Town: Flagstaff

Other Trail Users: Many hikers on the weekend

Canine Compatibility: Dogs permitted, and many of the shorter loops are dog friendly, but don't take a dog on long loops such as 'Round the Mountain.

Wheels: Depending on the trail, any bike from a rigid to a full-suspension is advisable. Schultz Creek Trail is smooth in both directions, for example, while portions of the Sunset, Brookbank, and Upper Oldham Trails are very rocky. As previously noted, many Mt. Elden downhill runs are popular with pro racers—bring all the suspension you have, because you'll find a way to use it!

Getting There

From Flagstaff: There are several trailheads and parking opportunities all around the mountain (see the route map on page 113).

To Buffalo Park Trailhead: From the corner of Milton (U.S. 66/89) and Humphreys Street (U.S. 180), head north on Humphreys. Turn right on Cedar Street, about a mile north of the junction with U.S. 89. Going east on Cedar, look for Gemini Drive to your left (north) about 2 miles from the turn off U.S. 180. Turn left on Gemini less than one mile, just past a USGS field office. The Buffalo Park parking lot is just past the field office. Use this trailhead to access the Lower Oldham and Pipeline trails. Buffalo Park was originally developed to hold a small herd of buffalo. *DeLorme: Arizona Atlas & Gazetteer:* Page 42 A2

A rizona features every bio-zone in the world but two: rain forest and coastline. Flagstaff and its surrounding mountains contain all the high-altitude zones, providing a stark contrast to the desert lowlands to the south. From the tundra atop Mt. Humphreys (12,633 feet) to the Ponderosa forest that surrounds the city, Flagstaff offers welcome relief from the searing heat of Phoenix and Tucson.

Founded in 1876 by a sheepherder from California, Flagstaff was named after a flagpole erected during the centennial celebration held by travelers passing through

en route to California. Several groups of settlers attempted to farm and mine the area, with little success. The railroad reached Flagstaff in 1882 and forever changed the town's identity. Flagstaff became an important link for cross-country transportation, growing again with the construction of Route 66, which passed through the town in the 1930s. As motorists constantly traveled between Chicago and the Pacific Coast via Route 66, motels cropped up along the road for miles in every direction. The main drag through Flagstaff still features the neon signs of these motels (which today make for extremely affordable lodging). Route 66 was entirely replaced with modern highways by 1984, but the road—as well as the rail lines that continue to run into town—will forever be a part of Flagstaff's character.

Flagstaff is a great base of operations to visit seven noteworthy attractions, all within 100 miles of town: Wupatki National Monument, Sunset Crater, Meteor Crater, Oak Creek Canyon (*see Ride 11: Schnebly Hill to Seven Sacred Pools*), Mt. Humphreys, Walnut Canyon (*see Ride 14: Walnut Canyon & Marshall Lake*), and the Grand Canyon (*see Ride 17: Moqui Stage Route and Ride 18: North Rim: Rainbow Rim Trail*).

Flagstaff is the acknowledged champion of mountain biking in Arizona. It's a destination for riders from around the world, who come to sample its fast singletrack as well as its technical challenges. Professional cross-country and downhill riders live in Flagstaff, enjoying the competitive advantage of the challenging local trails and the altitude. And the white-hot core of Flagstaff's mountain biking scene is Mount Elden.

Mount Elden is an extremely popular destination for hikers, mountain bikers, equestrians, and even dirt bikers on its lowest trails. Any day of the week, hundreds of outdoors enthusiasts take to its slopes. Despite the heavy use of Mount Elden,

wildlife sightings are still quite common on its trails. The mountain is covered with ponderosa pines, with aspen stands and verdant fern forests interspersed across the mountain. The southeast corner of Mount Elden, however, still shows the signs of the Radio Fire, which burned much of the mountainside in 1977. Aspens are now repopulating the burned areas.

The area commonly referred to as "Mount Elden" is a series of volcanic mountains—Mount Elden, Little Elden Mountain, and Dry Lake Hills—just south of Arizona's highest peak, Mt. Humphreys. These mountains range from 7,000 to 9,400 feet, and virtually every ride worth doing involves climbing to the tippy-top of Elden and bombing back down some singletrack. Surrounded by trailheads and crisscrossed with singletrack, it could take weeks to ride all the trails in all their various combinations. Unless you live in the area or are willing to make the pilgrimage every weekend for a summer, chances are you won't have a lot of opportunities to explore all of Elden's mysteries. Some popular loop options are described under Miles/Directions.

MilesDirections 'Round the Mountain

0.0 START from the Buffalo Park parking area. Following the Lower Oldham Trail north along the wide gravel trail past the "gateway" building.

0.5 Go through a gate just past a water tank. There's a map kiosk here.

0.7 The trail splits left and right. The right is a rocky, dangerous descent down to the Pipeline Trail. Bear left onto the singletrack. *[Side-trip. If you go right and down to the Pipeline Trail, bear left at the Pipeline Trail and continue north until you reach signs for the Lower Oldham Trail, about 0.6 miles away.]*

0.9 The trail splits; both get you to the same place. Pass through a wide doubletrack just a few yards ahead continuing on Lower Oldham Trail.

1.3 Cut across the Pipeline Trail, a broad doubletrack going northwest and marked with

several "Danger: Pipeline" signs. The Lower Oldham Trail picks up on the other side of the Pipeline Trail (marked with a trail sign).

2.4 At the bottom of a long, twisty descent, the trail splits. The sign indicates the Rocky Ridge Trail is to the right 0.8 miles; bear right here. *[Side-trip. The left is the Rocky Ridge Access Trail, which cuts through some woods and eventually drops you out on the Elden Lookout Road about half a mile down from the other trail's exit point.]*

3.3 Reach Elden Lookout Road. Rocky Ridge Trail is on the other side of the road. Cross Elden Lookout Road and continue along Rocky Ridge Trail.

3.6 A singletrack splits off to the left and hooks into Elden Lookout Road (this is the Rocky Ridge Access Trail you passed before. Continue ahead. *[Bailout. Take this trail over*

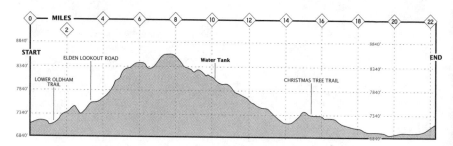

to Elden Lookout Road if you're not up for the technical challenges of the Rocky Ridge Trail. You'll know if you can handle Rocky Ridge Trail within this 0.3-mile stretch from the original turn-off. Add +0.3 miles if you opt to take the Elden Lookout Road to the Schultz Creek Trailhead bailout option.]

5.7 Arrive at the Schultz Creek Trailhead. There's a sign-in roster at the trailhead to the Rocky Ridge Trail. In the Schultz Creek parking lot, look to your right, just past the map kiosk, for the start of the Schultz Creek Trail. Take this trail, heading north.

9.4 Reach a gate across Schultz Creek Trail. Around the gate, a singletrack trail crosses to the left and right. Go around the gate and continue straight on Schultz Creek Trail. *[Side-trip. Turning right takes you up Little Gnarly Trail and eventually to Dry Lake Hills Overlook (1.9 miles) and Brookbank Trail (1.3 miles;*

the unmarked singletrack that splits off to the left at the top of the big climb up Little Gnarly Trail).] [**Bailout.** Turning left dumps you onto Schultz Pass Road. You will then have a three-mile downhill cruise back to Schultz Creek Trailhead.]

9.6 Arrive at the Sunset Trailhead. Follow the singletrack marked Sunset Trail just to the left of the map kiosk.

10.0 Reach a wooden trail sign. Little Elden Trail splits off to the left; the Sunset Trail continues straight ahead. Bear left, following Little Elden Trail. *[Side-trip/loop options. The Sunset Trail continues to climb rather quickly until it connects with the Brookbank Trail in 1.3 miles. Turn left at the U-turn where the Brookbank Trail intersects and, in less than a mile, you'll hit the top of the Little Bear Trail. Little Bear Trail down to Little Elden Trail and back to Schultz Creek Trail is a popular loop.]*

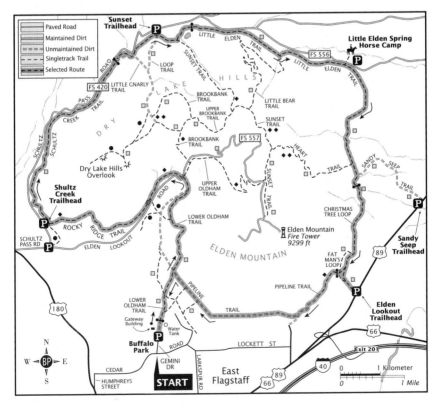

10.2 Pass a water tank enclosed in barbed wire on your left. *[FYI. A doubletrack heads off to the left, connecting to Schultz Pass Road.]* Continue ahead.

10.4 Pass through a gate. There are several water tanks enclosed in barbed wire.

11.9 Little Bear Trail connects from the right. Continue straight on Little Elden Trail. *[Side-trip. Turn right and head up Little Bear Trail to join with Sunset Trail in 3.7 miles. This is a tame climb and a great way to get high up into the Dry Lake Hills without grinding up the difficult Elden Lookout Road.]*

12.6 Horse Camp Trail splits off to the left, reaching the Little Elden Spring Horse Camp in one mile. Continue ahead on Little Elden Trail.

13.3 Pass a parking area and an old concrete water tank to your left. Continue ahead.

15.3 Heart Trail joins in from the left. Continue ahead. *[Side-trip. The Heart Trail is an extraordinarily difficult climb nearly to the top of Sunset Trail. If you really want to try it, it's 2.4 miles straight up.]*

15.4 Little Elden Trail splits. Sandy Seep Trail is to your left and the Christmas Tree Trail goes to your right. Turn right onto Christmas Tree Trail and continue making your way around the mountain. Pass through a gate shortly after. *[Side-trip/Bailout. Sandy Seep Trail, on the left, is a nice doubletrack descent through the charred remains of the Radio Fire. It reaches its trailhead on U.S. Route 89 in 1.5 miles. Even if you just want to ride it just to ride it, Sandy Seep Trail is a tame ascent on the way back and won't be too demanding.]*

16.6 Fat Man's Loop joins from the right. Continue ahead. *[Side-trip. Fat Man's Loop features a steep, difficult ascent and connects with the Pipeline Trail in about 0.8 miles.]*

17.0 The beginning of Fat Man's Loop, which splits off to the right. Turn right here and head back up the hill. *[Bailout. Continue ahead to reach the Elden Lookout Trail trailhead on U.S. 89 in 0.5 miles. Just past the split-off, there's a gate you'll have to carry your bike over.]*

17.3 Pass through a wooden gate. A single-track splits off to the right and reconnects with Fat Man's Pass in 0.3 miles. Continue ahead.

17.8 Pass a wooden trail sign indicating the beginning of the Pipeline Trail, a singletrack that splits off to the left. Fat Man's Loop continues ahead. Turn left onto the Pipeline Trail.

18.0 Another split-off to the left. Continue ahead, going up the switchback. Shortly after this split-off, the trail will split again and is marked with a sign. The Spring Trail continues ahead and the Pipeline Trail splits to the left. Take the left and head down the hill. At the bottom of the hill, take the doubletrack and head up the hill to your right. *[Side-trip. The Spring Trail is 0.7 miles long, and reconnects with the Pipeline Trail.]*

21.0 Lower Oldham Trail cuts across the Pipeline Trail. Turn left onto Lower Oldham Trail and head back to Buffalo Park.

22.3 Reach Buffalo Park.

Various Options Down the Mountain

While riding around Mt. Elden is a worthy epic, it's the descent down its various prime singletrack trails that makes it a world-class mountain biking destination. Here are some of the more popular combinations (see the map for details). All of them involve riding up Elden Lookout Road, generally from the Schultz Creek trailhead.

Perhaps the most popular route is to ride Sunset Trail to Schultz Creek. Get to the top of Elden via the Elden Lookout Road, which is a 6.3-mile climb. The Sunset Trail begins at "The Catwalk," a narrow slice of singletrack with some fairly scary exposure. After The Catwalk, pass the Heart Trail turnoff and continue ahead. The Sunset Trail then becomes a very difficult, boulder-ridden stretch that will challenge even

the most skilled technical rider. As the Sunset Trail drops into a valley, there will be options to turn right onto the Little Bear Trail or left onto the Brookbank Trail—both excellent options, but for this ride stick to the Sunset Trail. At the bottom of the Sunset Trail, hook up with Schultz Creek Trail—one of the best pieces of singletrack in all of Arizona—and return to the Schultz Creek trailhead. Total loop is 14.2 miles, and 2-2.5 hours.

Another great ride is to turn right onto Little Bear Trail when the Sunset Trail enters its first valley. This is a great, fast, smooth switchbacking descent down the north face of Mt. Elden. At the bottom of Little Bear, turn left on Little Elden Trail, climb a bit to the Sunset Trailhead, and then hook up again with the Schultz Creek Trail. This version is 17.6 miles and about 3.5 hours long.

The Brookbank Trail is another option not to be missed. As the Sunset Trail begins to climb out of its first valley, the Brookbank Trail will split to the left. Take the left, follow the Brookbank as it switchbacks down the inner valley of Mt. Elden and spits you back out onto Elden Lookout Road. For a good technical challenge, try the Rocky Ridge Trail back to the Schultz Creek Trailhead; the turnoff for Rocky Ridge is just a few yards down the road, so keep your eyes open. This route, with the Rocky Road option, is 14.6 miles and about 3 hours long.

There are many, many other loop options. Mt. Elden deserves multiple visits so you can put together your own favorite version.

Getting There from Flagstaff:

Elden Lookout Road/Schultz Creek Trailhead: From Flagstaff from the corner of Milton Road (U.S. 66/89) and Humphreys Street (U.S. 180), go north on Humphreys Street to Fort Valley Road, which is also marked with a sign indicating that U.S. 180 goes this way. Drive three miles north to Schultz Pass Road and turn right. Drive 0.4 miles, around the bend, to where Schultz Creek Road and Elden Lookout Road split apart. There's parking at the split (the parking area for Elden Lookout Road). If you turn left at the split and go up Schultz Creek Road, there's a steep descent along a dirt road to the Schultz Creek Trailhead on your right. Use this trailhead to immediately access Schultz Creek and Rocky Ridge trails.

Ride Information

Trail Contacts:

Coconino National Forest, Peaks Ranger District, Flagstaff, AZ (928) 526–0866 or www.fs.fed.us/r3/coco nino

Schedule:

Open year round – However, snow becomes an issue from December until as late as March some years. Also, summer monsoons (June-August) can make the trails unrideable. Call the Forest Service or any of the excellent local bike shops first.

Fees/Permits:

No fees or permits required

Local Information:

Flagstaff Chamber of Commerce, Flagstaff, AZ (928) 774–4505 or www.flagstaffchamber.com • **Flagstaff Visitor's Center,** Flagstaff, AZ (928) 774-9541 or 1–800–842–7293

Local Events/Attractions:

Lowell Observatory, Flagstaff, AZ (928) 774-3358 or www.lowell.edu – Take a tour of Arizona's oldest observatory, built in 1894. This is where astronomers decided Mars was crisscrossed with an intricate canal system—a sure sign of alien civilizations! • **Museum of Northern Arizona,** Flagstaff, AZ (928) 774-5211 or www.musnaz.org – Check out their collection of Native American artifacts and dinosaur bones • **Wupatki National Monument,** Flagstaff, AZ (928) 679-2365 or www.nps.gov/wupa – Extensive pueblo ruins across 35,000 acres of lava fields. From Flagstaff, take U.S. 89 north for 12 miles; turn right at a sign for Sunset Crater Volcano/ Wupatki National Monuments. The Visitor Center is 21 miles from this junc-

tion. While you're there, visit Sunset Crater, a 1000-foot high volcanic cone • **Cosmic Soulstice Race,** Cosmic Cycles (928) 779–1092 – This two-day, non-NORBA event is always a great time. Advanced riders do a hill race up Mt. Elden on the first day, and then everyone does a 40+ -mile loop on forest roads around the base of the San Francisco Peaks. Held in mid-September.

Accommodations:

Any of the motels along Route 66 will have adequate, cheap rooms most times of the year.

Restaurants:

Café Express, Flagstaff, AZ (928) 774–0541 – Great healthy food and coffee bar, lots of vegetarian cuisine, very pro-mountain biker place. Highest possible recommendation • **Salsa Brava,** Flagstaff, AZ (928) 774–1083 or www.flagguide.com/salsa – Authentic Guadalajaran-style Mexican food. If you eat only one meal before you die, it has to be Salsa Brava's baja tacos.

Group Rides:

Absolute Bicycles runs a group ride every Tuesday morning at 6 A.M. • **Sinagua Cycles** has group rides that leave their store around 4:30 P.M. every Thursday; sometimes they go up to Mt. Elden (and sometimes they don't!).

Organizations:

Coconino Cycling Club, Flagstaff, AZ: www.coconinocyclingclub.com – has been riding bikes off-road since 1893, pretty much putting the lie to claims that mountain biking was "invented" in Marin County or postwar France. Club meetings are the third Tuesday of the month.

Back in the late 1890s (no, that's not a typo) members of the Coconino Cycling Club rode the Moqui Stage Route in eight to twelve hours—on singlespeeds! Bicycles of this era were heavy, painful contraptions, mind you, and nothing like the ultralight creatures beloved by modern singlespeed fanatics. Maybe we're softer today than a century ago, but this ride is extremely strenuous even with all the comforts of modern bike design.

Day One:

The first day's ride begins north of Flagstaff, west of Mt. Humphreys in the San Francisco Peaks. There'll be snow atop the mountains much of the year, even well into spring. The beginning of the ride is a lengthy, gentle ascent for about 15 miles,

with a few short drops. Overall the climb ascends nearly 1,000 feet. The forest roads wind through pine forests and cross open fields.

At nine miles, the road narrows to doubletrack as it passes through a swath of burned forest. Fires plague the forests of northern Arizona every year, until the monsoons arrive mid-July. This was the result of one such fire.

After you make the vital turnoff at around 16 miles, you'll turn north on a segment of the Arizona Trail (*see Arizona Trail Project sidebar on page 103*) and stay on it until you reach camp. The road begins as fairly rugged doubletrack, but in a mile or so the ruts in the road become so deep and distinct that it's really two parallel slots—practically a dual-slalom racetrack, in fact. These ruts are deadly; one miscalculation and your front wheel will turn and grab the side of the rut. Unless you're a master of the sideways bunny hop, you're going to crash. Keep your speed under control and stay off the back seat, particularly as the dual-slalom track passes west of Missouri Bill Hill and quickly descends to a plain.

The rest of the day's ride crosses open plains. About a mile out from the campsite, there's a pretty big sign indicating you're about to enter Babbitt Ranch via the Arizona Trail. The ranchlands are big-sky country, open plains as far as the eye can see. Camp off the main road and enjoy a night of perfect starlight.

Day Two:

Babbitt Ranch is one of the biggest in Arizona, even though it is substantially smaller than it once was. Spending the first 25 miles traversing the property offers an appreciation of just how big Arizona's ranches can be. The road crosses vast prairies and offers absolutely no technical challenge at all. In fact, if you're traveling with a support vehicle, you might consider hopping into the truck and driving to the Moqui

Stage Stop. Although remember, all bragging rights of completing the heralded trek are relinquished if you shuttle to the singletrack.

The ranch roads and doubletrack are bane to bike tires. The weeds that grow up in the median between the tracks are covered in goat heads. Another caveat: you will get a flat, guaranteed, unless you run a tire liner or tube sealant.

The Moqui Stage Stop has a large brown Forest Service sign explaining the history of the stagecoach route. One interesting footnote it won't tell you is that two sheep ranchers got into a fisticuffs that turned deadly here: One shot the other, and the authorities chased the shooter all the way to New Mexico. The ruins of the Stage Stop are interesting but mostly gone, little more than a foundation and the remains of a concrete water tank.

Day two's ride gets interesting upon arrival at the Moqui Stage Stop. The trail is a combination of singletrack and doubletrack, following the stagecoach route itself at this point. The portion from the Stage Stop to Russell Tank is a moderate climb; the further north/up you go, the greener and more lush the surroundings. Within five miles, you're into pine forest.

And then, finally, you reach the singletrack of the Coconino Rim Trail. This primo singletrack zips up and down and around trees as it works its way along the rim of the Coconino Plateau (that big expanse of ranch land you just spent the last two days riding across). As the trail tops out, the Grand Canyon plays peek-a-boo through the trees to your right. At some spots, even the Painted Desert (the region, not the park) becomes visible far to the east.

Traditionally, the ride isn't considered complete until you've ascended the Grandview Lookout Tower. This 70-foot tower is a fire lookout that anyone can climb up into. Although the public can't enter the shack atop the tower, the view of the South Rim from the steps is breathtaking by itself. Bonked or no, take the time to make the climb.

MilesDirections **Day One**

0.0 START from the parking area off FS 151. Head northeast on FS 151, away from the freeway.

7.6 FS 151 splits to the left, and FS 418B heads right. Continue left (north) on FS 151. [*Side-trip. This is the turnoff to Little Spring. Turn right onto 418B to visit the spring (+0.6 miles up 418B to the spring, +1.2 miles total)].*

8.4 Reach a split in the road, with FS 418 going to the right and FS 151 continuing ahead and a bit to the left. U.S. 89 is about 12 miles to the right. Bear left, remaining on FS 151.

9.1 The trail splits. The main dirt road splits off to the left; a doubletrack splits off to the right and enters a burned forest. Turn right here, entering the burned forest.

10.2 Go through a large gate and come out into a very large meadow (Kendrick Park). Continue ahead.

10.9 Arrive at a crossroads. The road directly ahead is marked 514B. There's a large main dirt road (FS 514A) that cuts directly across your path and passes east and west through Kendrick Park. Turn right onto this dirt road, FS 514A.

13.0 Pass Kelly Tank on your right.

15.9 As you travel northeast, look for a painted sign to your right that says "Summertree." This is a critical turn, and you'll be going very fast at this point, so keep your eyes open! A dirt road joins from the left, opposite of the

"Summertree" sign; turn left here and start riding northwest, up FS 523.

16.6 A doubletrack turns to the right. Look for a signpost indicating that this doubletrack is FS 416. It will be the second right turn after making that critical turn back at mile marker 15.9. Ride over the cattleguard and continue north.

18.5 The trail splits left and right. Look for the Arizona Trail sign to the left. Split left and continue on FS 416 [*FYI. The Arizona Trail is the statewide trail that runs from Mexico to Utah; see page 103 for more information*].

18.9 Go through a gate.

19.6 Cross over a doubletrack and pick up the Arizona Trail on the other side.

21.2 The trail splits left and right. To the left is 9005B, and to the right is the Arizona Trail. Continue ahead (right), following the Arizona Trail signs.

23.8 The trail joins with FS 417. Continue following the Arizona Trail signs, indicating that you go left, heading west up FS 417. [*FYI. FS 417 also heads east from here, reaching U.S. 89 in about 15 miles.]*

26.9 The trail stops at a very wide dirt road, the head of Cedar Ranch Road. Look to your right and find the "Arizona Trail: Babbitt Ranch" sign. Turn right and head for the Babbitt Ranch.

27.6 Look for the first right turn past the Babbitt Ranch sign and pull into the campsite for the night.

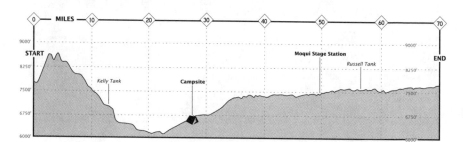

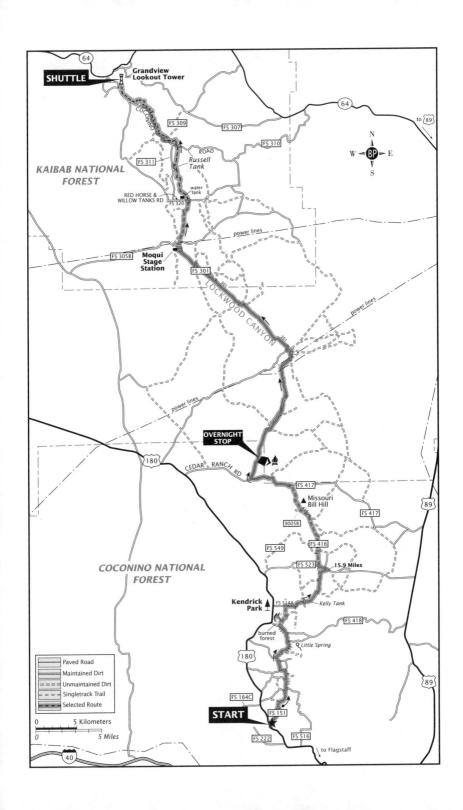

MilesDirections **Day Two**

27.6 From the campsite, head north on the big dirt road, toward the Grand Canyon.

29.9 Go through an open gate.

30.9 Go through a gate. Just past the gate, the road splits. Turn right. The Arizona Trail sign indicates the trail goes to the left. However, you're now getting off the Arizona Trail and taking the gentler grade north through Lockwood Canyon.

37.1 As you run alongside some power lines, the trail splits. Turn left, go through a gate, and pass under the power lines. To the right, a doubletrack heads off into the prairie.

39.2 En route through Lockwood Canyon, go through a gate and continue ahead.

45.1 Cross over a cattleguard.

49.7 Arrive at the Kaibab National Forest sign for the Moqui Stage Station. Turn right and visit the Station. The doubletrack (the Moqui Stage Route proper) travels southeast briefly from the Stage Station ruins, then goes east, and eventually winds north. Pick up this doubletrack, sort of to the right as you're looking at the Moqui Stage Station from the road, and continue.

49.9 Pass a couple wooden signs. Several have the Arizona Trail symbol. Turn right and continue along the Stage Route toward the Russell Tank trailhead.

50.5 Cross over the doubletrack.

52.6 The trail splits. The Arizona Trail splits off to the left and goes through a gate. Turn left, getting back on the Arizona Trail, and go up the hill.

53.4 Pass through the barbed wire gate. Just past the gate the doubletrack splits. Each will get you to a dirt road just beyond the hill; take either one and continue on the Arizona Trail.

53.8 Cross over Red Horse Road and Willows Tanks Road, a wide dirt road. Pick up the Arizona Trail on the other side. This is the beginning of the super-cool singletrack reward waiting for you at the end of your journey.

54.1 Pass by a water-filled tank to your left.

56.8 Pass through a gate and aim for the wooden sign visible to your right. Russell Tank, a small artificial lake surrounded by a fence, is to your right. There's a parking lot in view to your left. The singletrack runs alongside Russell Tank and then drops into a wash; the doubletrack has been torn up to keep cars and trucks from driving on it. Follow the singletrack north, passing through a gate.

58.6 Cross over Coconino Road, a wide, well used gravel road. Pick up the trail on the other side.

60.1 The trail splits. A wooden sign that reads "bike route" points to the left; stick to this route, heading up on the ridge. *Do not go down the singletrack going to the stand of trees.* There's a gate just past the left turn. Pass through and continue.

60.6 Join up with doubletrack. An Arizona Trail sign here reads "bike route" and points back the way you came. Look carefully for the singletrack that comes into the doubletrack from your left. This is the trail! Do not continue on the doubletrack (FS 309); it bombs down and takes you way off-course. Turn left at the "bike route" sign and look for the Arizona Trail signage just past the turn. The trail is obvious and well marked from here all the way to the end.

70.3 Arrive at Grandview Lookout, where (hopefully) your shuttle awaits.

Ride Information

Trail Contacts:

Coconino National Forest, Peaks Ranger District, Flagstaff, AZ (928) 526–0866 or *www.fs.fed.us/r3/coco nino* • **Coconino National Forest,** Supervisor's Office, Flagstaff, AZ (928) 527–3600 or *www.fs.fed.us/r3/coconino* • **Kaibab National Forest,** Tusayan District, Tusayan, AZ (928) 638–2443 • **Kaibab National Forest,** Supervisor's Office, Williams, AZ (928) 635–8200 or *www.fs.fed.us/r3/kai* • **Arizona Trail Association,** Phoenix, AZ (602) 252–4794 or *www.aztrail.org*

Schedule:

Open year round – *Because of the strenuous nature of the ride, try to do this in mid-spring (April–May) or early fall (September–October). Too close to winter, and you'll have to deal with snow and freezing winter nights. Too close to summer, and you'll bake on the open road.*

Fees/Permits:

No fees or permits required. If your shuttle vehicle enters Grand Canyon National Park to pick you up at Grandview Lookout, there is a $6 entry fee. If you're clever and can follow a map, ride forest roads from the south to enter the park without paying the fee.

Local Information:

City of Flagstaff: *www.flagstaff.az.us* • **Flagstaff Chamber of Commerce,** Flagstaff, AZ (928) 774–4505 or *www.flagstaffchamber.com* • **Flagstaff Convention & Visitor's Bureau** 1–800–217–2367 or *www.flagstaff arizona.org* • **Grand Canyon Chamber of Commerce,** Grand Canyon, AZ (928) 638–2901 or *www.grandcanyon chamber.org* • **Grand Canyon Tourism website:** *www.thecanyon.com*

Accommodations:

None: You'll be sleeping under the stars for this ride!

Mountain Bike Tours:

Arizona White-Knuckle Adventures, Scottsdale, AZ (602) 684–8833 or *http://arizonaadventures.com – dialed in this ride, and takes individuals and groups for $245 a pop. Given the excellent food and outdoor expertise of the staff, it's worth every penny. Visit them or call them for more information.*

Organizations:

The Arizona Trail Association: (602) 252–4794 or *www.aztrail.org – responsible for the passages the Arizona Trail takes between Flagstaff and the South Rim. The passage numbers are 35 (Babbitt Ranches) and 36 (Coconino Rim). Call the Arizona Trail Association or visit for more information about the trail, trail conditions, and upcoming events.*

Local Bike Shops:

Loose Spoke, Flagstaff, AZ (928) 774–7428 • **Mountain Sports,** Flagstaff, AZ (928) 779–5156 or 1–800–286–5156

Maps:

USGS maps: Wing Mountain, AZ; Humphrey's Peak, AZ; White Horse Hills, AZ; SP Mountain, AZ; Chapel Mountain, AZ; Additional Hill, AZ; Lockwood Canyon, AZ; Peterson Flat, AZ; Harbison Tank, AZ; Grandview Point NE, AZ; Grandview Point, AZ.

Mine Country

Compiled here is an index of great rides in Mine Country that didn't make the A-list this time around but deserve recognition. Check them out and let us know what you think. You may decide that one or more of these rides deserves higher status in future editions or, perhaps, you may have a ride of your own that merits some attention.

G Yankee Doodle Trail

South of Prescott in the Bradshaw Mountains, the Yankee Doodle Trail is a rugged mix of doubletrack and singletrack that loops around Mount Union. The trail is pretty remote, and at 15.5-miles long and as much as 6,000 feet up, it's a worthy and dangerous challenge.

Starting from the intersection of Old Senator Highway (FS 52) and Hassayampa Lake (FS 197), head south on FS 52. At the first available left (Mount Union Lookout Road, also called FS 261), turn left and begin the climb toward Mount Union. Mount Union is about 8,000 feet high—the climb is hard, and the views are worth it. At the top of Mount Union, take the spur up to the lookout. After you return from the lookout, turn left (west) on FS 261 and keep your eyes peeled for the Yankee Doodle Trail, a somewhat technical singletrack that will bomb down the mountain until reaching the Orofino Mine. At the mine, turn right to rejoin Old Senator Highway, and begin climbing up Crooks Canyon, back to the intersection where you parked the car. Check out the old Palace Station House, a historic cabin built in 1874, a mile west of the mine.

Getting there: Head south out of Prescott on Mount Vernon Road, which will turn into Old Senator Highway. Continue south on Old Senator Highway until you reach the intersection with Wolf Creek Road (also called FS 97). At this point, Old Senator Highway turns into dirt. You can either begin your ride here, or continue another three miles south on Old Senator Highway to shorten the overall ride length. The second starting point is at the intersection with FS 197 at Hassayampa Lake—deduct six miles from the total loop if you park here. *DeLorme: Arizona Atlas & Gazetteer:* Page 49 A4

(H) Crown King to Lake Pleasant

The ride down Old Senator Highway from the little tourist town of Crown King atop the Bradshaw Mountains, all the way down to the shores of Lake Pleasant, is a must-do epic ride, best ridden in mid-spring or late fall. This is a long, long ride, and despite its appearance it's not all downhill. The first five miles or so climb upward out of Crown King to the top of the Bradshaws, followed by 12 miles of fast, somewhat dangerous downhill into the desert at the range's base. The middle ten miles is a beautiful cruise beneath a canopy of trees, featuring some very nice water crossings (don't drink the water—extensive mining in the Bradshaws has contaminated the water with cyanide!) and a fairly smooth path. The final miles of the course involve steep—really steep, like hike-a-bike steep—climbs, and some long, fast segments on ranch roads as you close in on Lake Pleasant.

Plan on taking at least six hours to ride the 32-mile course. Bring as much water as you can carry—100 oz. bladders and several bottles in cages. If you travel on the weekend, you can get more water from the various 4x4 clubs that drive from the lake up to Crown King every weekend (rendering assistance is in the clubs' bylaws). Don't attempt this ride alone, and always make sure somebody knows where you are before you begin the trip; if something goes wrong, you're a long way away from help. The most vital part of a successful run from Crown King down to Lake Pleasant is the shuttle setup. See Getting There directions for the details.

Getting there: This ride is a shuttle. First, everyone drives to Lake Pleasant: Heading north on I-17 out of Phoenix, turn left (west) on Exit 223 onto Carefree Road. There is a sign for Lake Pleasant and the Ben Avery Shooting Range. Drive about 15 miles west, past the first signs for the marinas, to the major road that goes along the west coast of Lake Pleasant. I strongly recommend you drive to the end of the pavement, about seven more miles north, and pay to park in the guarded lot—your car will be left alone for many hours, and it's reassuring to have a human being nearby. Alternately, you can greatly reduce the stress of the trip by driving further up the dirt road. Another good spot to stop would be the campground near the bridge that crosses over a small tributary of the lake. The northernmost spot I'd recommend taking a passenger car would be the intersection of Cow Creek Road and Castle Hot Springs Road, about 11 miles north of the end of the pavement. There are plenty of signs, so you shouldn't get lost.

Once you've dropped off the shuttle car, head back to I-17 and travel north. From I-17, turn left (west) on either Exit 248 or Exit 259; both have signs that say "To Crown King," and both eventually merge to become Crown King Road (also called FS 259 on maps). Crown King is at the end of Crown King Road. Park at the convenience store in town and disembark. The road you want to take heads due west out of town. *DeLorme: Arizona Atlas & Gazetteer:* Page 49 B4–D4

Ⓘ Peavine Trail

In 1994, the city of Prescott applied for a grant of nearly $200,000 from the U.S. Department of Transportation to purchase about 6.6 miles of railway along Watson Lake that once belonged to the Santa Fe Railroad. Five years later, after extensive wrangling with various federal and state agencies, the City of Prescott inaugurated a new rails-to-trails conversion, now called the Peavine Trail.

The Peavine Trail is a 5.7-mile-long stretch of old railway that runs at an extremely flat grade along scenic Watson Lake. While the trail offers no technical or aerobic challenges, it is quite beautiful, as well as a very good choice for a "date ride" with spouse or significant other who prefers a casual ride rather than a gonzo grind. The trail surface is crushed cinder, an excellent surface both for biking as well as a leisurely hike if you're so inclined. The trail begins next to a sewage plant but gets less stinky as you head northward along the rail grade. There are numerous little side trails along the way that take you down to the lake's edge. Continue heading north until you hit AZ 89A, then turn around and head back.

The most interesting part of the Peavine Trail is the view of the Granite Dells, mighty boulders and other rock formations that jut out of Watson Lake. The dells make for an excellent hiking/climbing trip, although you'll have to get to them from the other side of the lake.

Getting there: From downtown Prescott, drive east on Gurley Street to the AZ 89/AZ 69 intersection. Turn north on AZ 89 for 1.1 miles to a bridge crossing Granite Creek at Sun Dog Ranch Road. Continue east, passing under the railroad overpass, and turn left onto Sun Dog Ranch Road. Continue north for another 1.5 miles to where the road turns left, opposite the Animal Control headquarters. This is the main trailhead for the Peavine Trail. The trail is just a few yards west of the locked gate. *DeLorme: Arizona Atlas & Gazetteer:* Page 41 D4

Ⓙ Mingus Mountain

There are numerous biking opportunities on Mingus Mountain, but all of them are hard to find, not maintained, and considered generally difficult and dangerous. There are three trails and two roads to look for on USGS quads (Hickey Mountain and Cottonwood, AZ quads). The trails are Trail 110 (Gaddes Canyon), Trail 108 (Coleman Trail), and Trail 114 (Black Canyon Trail). The two roads are FS 413 (Mescal Gulch Road, a dirt road to Jerome) and FS 493 (Allen Springs Road, an 18-mile descent off Mescal Gulch Road directly into Cottonwood).

The easiest-to-find route on Mingus Mountain involves three forest roads that will take you from the tourist/art community of Jerome back down to Cottonwood. Starting from Jerome, head south on Mescal Gulch Road (FS 413). After a 500-foot climb, Mescal Gulch Road will follow alongside the mountains. Head south on the super-twisty Mescal Gulch Road for about 22 miles until you hit the intersection with Allen Springs Road (FS 493). Take Allen Springs Road due east all the way

back into Cottonwood, about 18 miles later. You'll hit one split in the road; take the right and keep heading east. The total mileage is about 40 miles. Although mostly all downhill, it's still a long day on the saddle. Be sure to bring lots of water and food, and always let someone know where you are.

Getting there: A good place to start exploring is the campground at the intersection of AZ 89A and FS 104. From Jerome, head south on AZ 89A and keep an eye out for a campground, about six miles south of town. You can also get there from Prescott by heading north on AZ 89A (not AZ 89, which will take you way, way north to Ash Fork). The campground is a couple miles north of the Yaeger Canyon Ranger Station. For more details, stop in at Mingus Mountain Bicycles in Cottonwood, 418 N. 15th Street (15th and Main), or call them at (928) 634–7113. *DeLorme: Arizona Atlas & Gazetteer:* Page 41 D6

Ⓚ Deadhorse Ranch

This eight-mile loop was constructed through a partnership with the U.S. Forest Service and local mountain bikers. The Dead Horse Park Loop in Cottonwood consists of three trails, all of which pass through the Verde Botanical Area. Due to the delicate natural of the plants in the botanical area riders must be extra careful to stay on the designated trail. In addition, some parts of the trail may be closed during the nesting season, so check in with the ranger station before heading out.

The recommended loop begins at the gate and heads north on Raptor Hill Trail, a rough doubletrack ascent. Raptor Hill Trail intercepts Thumper Trail, a singletrack trail, in 2.9 miles. Turn right on Thumper Trail, pass through a gate, and then head downhill for 2.3 miles. Thumper then intersects with Lime Kiln Trail, also singletrack. Turn right on Lime Kiln Trail and head back to the campgrounds.

Getting into Deadhorse Ranch State Park costs $1 for bikes to roll in, $4 for cars, and $10 to camp ($15 with hookups). Check out the Verde River Greenway, a riparian wildlife area, south of the state park campgrounds.

Getting there: From Cottonwood, head northwest on Main Street to 10th Street. Turn north on 10th Street and drive over the Verde River across the bridge. The park entrance is just past the bridge. Turn into the campgrounds and head north to find the well-marked trailhead. *DeLorme: Arizona Atlas & Gazetteer:* Page 41 C6

Grand Canyon
COUNTRY

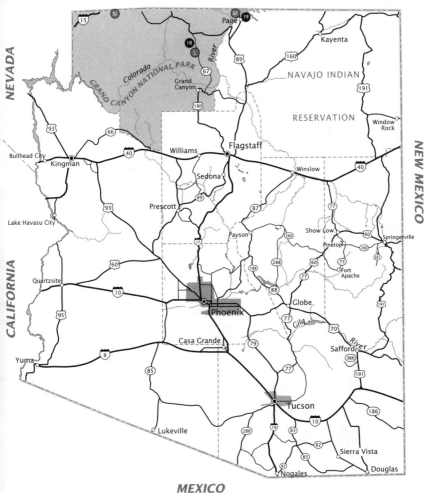

The Rides
North Rim Loop **18.**
Page Rimview Trail **19.**

Honorable Mentions
L. Point Sublime
M. Greene Haven Slickrock
N. Arizona Strip

Grand Canyon Country

The Grand Canyon, a vast rift torn across the northernmost reaches of the state, is worthy of all the hype and attention it receives. It's much more than a giant hole half a mile deep and a dozen miles across—it's a statement, by nature, by the Earth, by God, by whatever you want to call it. The Grand Canyon is the surest reminder of awesome forces that have been around, and will be around, longer than anyone can imagine.

The views from each rim, the tourist-swarmed south and the isolated north, show two different canyons. From the south rim, it's an endless valley of gold and orange, filled most of the year with a hint of summer's warmth. It's also quite busy on the south rim, being an achievable goal of tourists coming up from Flagstaff and Williams for a day trip.

The north rim is something else entirely. The Kaibab Plateau (Kaibab means "mountain laying down" in one of the native tongues) rises quickly up from the hot desert floor even further north than the canyon, then gently slopes back down to the edge of the canyon and suddenly drops away. It's a couple thousand feet higher than the south rim, so north rim flora and fauna hark to alpine conditions, including unimaginably harsh winters. The views from the north rim are, in my opinion, so much more spectacular than those from the south that visiting the south rim will always pale in comparison. The valleys are deeper, the vistas more dramatic, the colors deeper.

North of the Grand Canyon lies the Arizona Strip, a desolate stretch of desert and low mountains that comprises the border with Utah. Lake Powell neatly bisects the northern border, with the Arizona Strip stretching westward and the Navajo Nation heading east into New Mexico. This is high Sonoran desert, between 4,000-5,000 feet and a bit cooler than the lowest deserts in the state. Some of the views are amazing; so is the sense of isolation.

Surrounding Lake Powell, the desert gives way to the soft curves and dramatic spires of Navajo sandstone. Page, the only major town in this part of the state, is poised atop a mesa overlooking Lake Powell and Glen Canyon, the vermilion ravine that extends south of Glen Canyon Dam—the big cork responsible for Lake Powell's existence.

Other than the small towns that support a booming eco-tourism industry, there's hardly any Arizona civilization north of Flagstaff. If you're going to be riding the Rimview Trail around Page or the Rainbow Rim Trail along the North Rim, bring everything you may need—the closest bike shop is five hours away.

Getting to these rides is a major time commitment, even for those lucky souls in Flagstaff. Both the North Rim and Page are about five hours from Flagstaff, meaning it's an eight-hour journey from Phoenix and ten or more (depending on in-town traffic) for Tucsonians. The good news is, if you're into camping there's hardly any better place to go than the North Rim in the summer: At 7,000+ feet, temperatures hover in the mid-70s during the day and drop to the low 50s, or lower, at night. Page is a bit more exposed, being both lower and less vegetated: Expect mid to high 80s in the dead of summer, with a few days spiking above 90°F. If you're not into camping, both the North Rim and Page have motel rooms available—call in advance to the motels in Jacob Lake, because they're always in high demand.

Grand Canyon Country

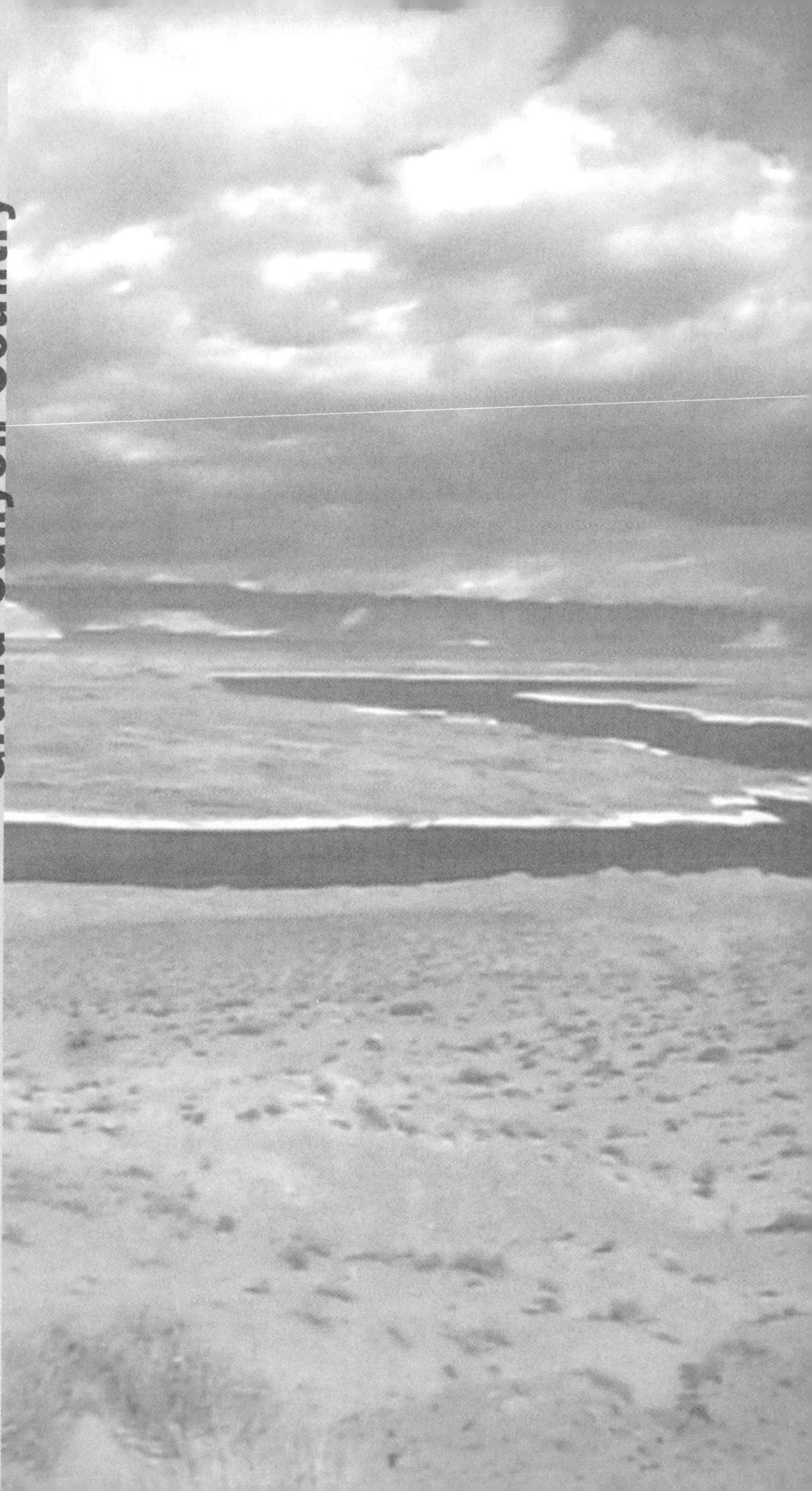

Section Overview

North Rim Loop

Nineteen miles of singletrack overlooking one of the greatest natural wonders of the world. Moderate mid-70s weather—when it isn't raining—in the heat of the summer. Numerous loop options. Endless camping options. Clean, thin air. Mountain biking the North Rim is a spectacular adventure suitable for everyone from rank amateurs to hardcore endurance riders. *(See page 142.)*

Page Rimview Trail

Visitors passing through Page shouldn't miss out on this cool little singletrack loop that bounds the entire city of Page. The views of Lake Powell, the Navajo Generating Station, the Vermilion Cliffs, and Glen Canyon Dam are spectacular and can be seen while pedaling around Arizona's northernmost outpost. *(See page 148.)*

Grand Canyon Country

18

North Rim Loop

Ride Specs

Start: From the Parissawampitts parking lot
Length: 36.3 miles
Approximate Riding Time: 6–7 hours
Difficulty Rating: Moderate to Difficult. The loop down Rainbow Rim Trail and back up forest roads is technically easy-to-moderate (a couple climbs and some switchbacks keep things interesting) but physically challenging, due to both the length of the rides and the altitude.
Trail Surface: The Rainbow Rim Trail is fresh, narrow singletrack along the very top of the Grand Canyon. Everything else on the Kaibab Plateau is forest road.
Lay of the Land: The Kaibab Plateau is covered in ponderosa forest and stands of aspen. The plateau gradually slopes downward toward the edge of the canyon, meaning all rides are generally downhill as you head toward the lip and uphill as you head away. Rainbow Rim follows five "fingers" or ridges that poke out into the canyon.
Elevation Gain: 3,223 feet
Land Status: National forest
Nearest Town: Jacob Lake
Other Trail Users: Hikers are fairly common on the Rainbow Rim Trail. While on forest roads, car traffic is quite common. Given the length of the ride, this is a good thing, as you can often wave down a ride, or at least some additional water, from passersby if needed.
Canine Compatibility: Dogs permitted, but unless you're planning on doing a short out-and-back between a couple of the points (Locust Point north to Fence or Parissawampitts, or south to North Timp or Timp, are both popular), all the rides are too strenuous for dogs.

Wheels: Any non-road bike is adequate for this ride. In fact, given the distances involved, a non-suspended bike may be your best option. If you're running full suspension, lock out the rear or otherwise preload it—you probably won't need much more than a slight softening.

Getting There

From Jacob Lake: Head south on AZ 67 (a.k.a. the North Rim Parkway) until you pass by the Kaibab Lodge about 15 miles south of Jacob Lake. Go 0.8 miles past Kaibab Lodge and look for the turnoff onto FS 22, which is well marked. Turn right (west) onto FS 22 and reset your odometer to zero—the rest of the directions are in relation to this turnoff

At 3.1 miles past the turn onto FS 22, turn left (south) on FS 270 (there's a sign). At 4.1 miles, just past a snowmobile play area sign, turn right (west again) on FS 222—look for a narrow, vertical Forest Service sign (it's easy to miss, so keep your eyes peeled). At 6.1 miles, FS 231 splits off to the left; continue ahead on FS 222. At 9.2 miles, FS 226 splits off to the right; continue ahead. Just past this turn, at 9.4 miles, there's a sign indicating that turning left takes you to Timp Point. Turn right (north) here onto FS 206, following the sign to Parissawampitts Point. Turn left on FS 214 and follow it all the way to the trailhead (follow the signs). *DeLorme: Arizona Atlas & Gazetteer:* Page 23 C5

Completed in the late 1990s, the Rainbow Rim Trail is a 19-mile-long epic singletrack journey along the very edge of the North Rim of the Grand Canyon. This is a view of the mighty Canyon not often enjoyed by the typical tourist crowd: It's a long, long way to get to the North Rim from pretty much anywhere (5 hours from both Flagstaff and Las Vegas), and you have to know your way around the back roads to see anything interesting. The roads leading to this ride are all well marked, and should provide good guidance to the various trailheads.

The Rainbow Rim Trail runs between five "points," long fingers of land sticking deep into the canyon. The northernmost, Parissawampitts Point, is a good place to start if you intend on riding the entire trail in one shot. From there, the points (from north to south) are:

Fence Point. There are some terrific overlooks along a singletrack opposite the parking lot; keep your eyes open for the vista signs. From Fence Point, you can see numerous amphitheaters and mountain ranges within the canyon. The largest, to the south, is Steamboat Mountain.

Locust Point, named such for the nasty locust bushes that grow all around the point. Wear a long jersey if you own one. Locust Point makes an excellent campground from which the trail can be explored over a couple of days. There are several spots along the forest roads, and at the parking lots of the points themselves, that are adequate for a tent or RV.

North Timp Point. Mostly a rest stop before the final push to the end, the views are, as always, spectacular from here.

And finally, Timp Point. The vista trail from the Timp Point parking lot is 0.3 miles long, mostly rideable, and presents a great end-of-ride view of the canyon. Either rest a while here or get going, because the return trip is long.

The North Rim of the Grand Canyon is also the rim of the Kaibab Plateau, sitting between 7,000 to 8,500 feet. The various roads and trails all start high on the plateau and generally travel downward toward the rim. The Kaibab Plateau has a very broad array of wildlife, all of which will be visible any day of the year—mule deer, elk, porcupines, bears, raccoons, innumerable birds, and the Kaibab Squirrel. The squirrels of the South Rim and the North Rim share a common ancestor, but over the past 10,000 years, the two species have diverged and become distinctly different critters. The Kaibab Squirrel is distinct for its bright white tail standing out in stark contrast against its dark belly and limbs. Its southern cousin, the Abert Squirrel, is more uniformly gray with a white belly.

There are other important differences between the flora and fauna of the North and South Rims. For example, the North Rim is quite wet, and a bit higher than the South Rim, so the dominant North Rim plant life is ponderosa pine and white aspens. The South Rim still has some cacti and yuccas. The North Rim is also quite a bit cooler, as much as 5–8 degrees on average.

The Grand Canyon is considered one of the seven natural wonders of the world. It's 277 miles long from Lee's Ferry to the Grand Wash Cliffs of Lake Mead. The average elevation of the south rim is around 6,800 feet; the average elevation of the north rim is about 8,000 feet. (Be aware of this when planning your trip—you'll feel the elevation.) The depth of the Grand Canyon from Grand Canyon Village (south rim) is almost a vertical mile. The width of the canyon averages around 10 miles. Its narrowest point is five miles across and the widest is 18 miles. The distance from the Rainbow Rim Trail across to the South Rim is about 12 miles.

It took Europeans more than 200 years to visit the North Rim after reaching the South Rim. In 1776, Father Escalante became the first European to visit the North Rim. Ownership of the North Rim remained in question until well into the twentieth century; the territories of Utah and Arizona both laid claim to the area, and it took the creation of Arizona as a state in 1912 before the issue was settled.

Ride Information

🕓 Trail Contacts:
Kaibab National Forest, North Kaibab District, Fredonia, AZ (520) 643–7395 or *www.fs.fed.us/r3/kai* • **Kaibab Plateau Visitors Center,** Jacob Lake, AZ (520) 643–7298

🕓 Schedule:
May 15-October 15 – *The gates close in the off-season due to snow. Also, the monsoon season (June to August) brings a lot of rain to the rim. Check the weather forecasts and prepare for a downpour in any case.*

💲 Fees/Permits:
There are no fees to access the forest roads of the Kaibab National Forest. If you want to enter the North Rim Village by car, there's a $20 charge.

🛏 Accommodations:
Jacob Lake Inn, Jacob Lake, AZ (520) 643–7232 or *www.jacoblake.com* • **Kaibab Lodge,** 27 miles south of Jacob Lake (and just one mile off the turn-off to Parissawampitts Point) (520) 638–2389

or *www.kaibab.org/gc/serv/gc_ol_xl.htm* or preseason reservations may be made January-April by calling (520) 526–0924 or 1–800–525–0924

🍴 Restaurants:
There are restaurants at both the Jacob Lake Inn and Kaibab Lodge, as well as general stores.

🚲 Mountain Bike Tours:
Arizona White-Knuckle Adventures- *Several tour companies offer multi-day tours of the North Rim.* Operates out of Phoenix and offers a combination tour of the North Rim and Flagstaff (602) 684–8833 or *www.arizona-adventures.com*

🌐 Other Resources:
Grand Canyon Explorer: *www.kaibab.org* • **Insiders' Guide to Southwestern Utah:** *www.insiders.com/utah/*

🇳 Maps:
USGS maps: Timp Point, AZ; De Motte Park, AZ

MilesDirections

0.0 START from the Parissawampitts Point trailhead. The Rainbow Rim Trail is clearly marked at the far western end of the parking lot. Drop onto the trail and begin! A few yards into the ride, you'll notice a doubletrack that's been blocked off just as the Rainbow Rim Trail turns to the left. Disregard this and all other blocked-off logging roads, trails, etc. as you follow signs for the Rainbow Rim Trail. If you do this, you shouldn't get lost.

5.9 Reach Fence Point. The viewpoint marker to your right takes you out to a great view and camping spot right on the rim. Just past the viewpoint marker, a singletrack joins the main trail from the left. This is the connector to the Fence Point parking area. *[**Bailout.** The connector gets you to the lot in 0.1 miles. From there, you can take FS 293 back to FS 250, returning to FS 214 and eventually Parissawampitts Point in about 5 miles.]*

9.0 The viewpoint marker to your right takes you out to Locust Point Lookout. The Locust Point parking lot is visible to the left. *[**Bailout.** Take FS 294 back out to FS 250, and back to FS 214 and Parissawampitts Point in about 7 miles.]*

15.6 The viewpoint marker to your right indicates North Timp Point Lookout. The parking lot is visible to the left. From this point, the trail closely follows FS 271A for about a mile before diverging. *[**Bailout.** From the North Timp Point parking lot, take FS 271A out to FS 271, then to FS 250, back up to FS 214 and Parissawampitts Point in about 9 miles.]*

18.7 Arrive at Timp Point. Rest up, because you've got a big return trip either back along the Rainbow Rim Trail (another 19 miles!), or by way of the forest road network. *[**FYI.** The rest of the directions assume you're taking the forest roads. Take FS 271 east as it climbs up the side of Parissawampitts Canyon.] [Side-trip. The Timp Point lookout is 0.3 miles one way out onto the point, and is bikeable (but difficult).]*

21.6 FS 271A joins from the left and goes back to North Timp Point. Continue ahead on FS 271.

22.7 FS 250 splits to the left. Continue ahead to take additional forest roads and add another 7 miles to your ride. *[**Bailout.** Turn here and head back to FS 214 and Parissawampitts Point in about 8 miles.]*

26.9 Arrive at the junction with FS 294 (to Locust Point and Fence Point). Just beyond this junction the road splits again. Take the left, which is FS 206, heading north. *[**FYI:** The right is FS 222, which eventually takes you back out to AZ 67].*

28.3 Arrive at the turn onto FS 214 to Parissawampitts Point. Turn left here. If you continue ahead on FS 272, you'll end up at Crazy Jug Point in about 9 miles.

32.7 Join with FS 250 from the left (the shorter route back from Timp Point). Continue ahead on FS 214. *[**Side-trip.** FS 250 cuts through FS 214 and continues north. Take this to join up with FS 272 if you want to visit Crazy Jug Point, about 11 miles from this intersection]*

36.3 Arrive at Parissawampitts Point.

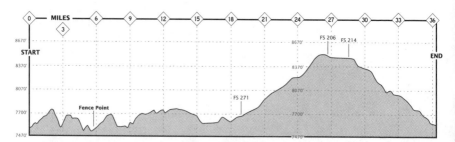

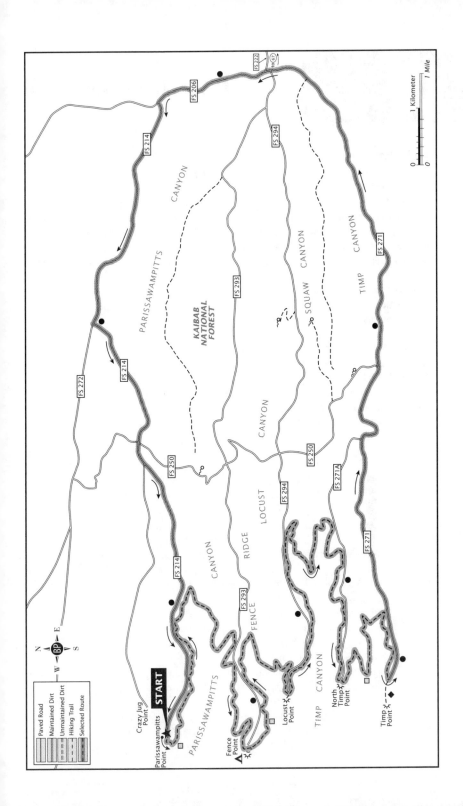

19

Page Rimview Trail

Ride Specs

Start: From the McDonald's parking lot near the intersection of U.S. 89A and Lake Powell Road
Length: 10.3-mile loop
Approximate Riding Time: 1–2 hours
Difficulty Rating: Physically and technically easy, with a little sand and some hard-to-find transitions. Finding trails is the only real challenge on this ride. Luckily, you're very close to civilization for most of the ride.
Trail Surface: Singletrack
Lay of the Land: Red sandstone, high desert plain
Elevation Gain: 887 feet
Land Status: City of Page property
Nearest Town: Page
Other Trail Users: Hikers
Canine Compatibility: Dogs permitted
Wheels: Hardtails and hybrids are fine

Getting There

From Page: Near the intersection of U.S. 89 and U.S. 89 Loop (Lake Powell Road), look for a McDonald's. Park along the road either north or south of the McDonald's parking lot. The trailhead is at the northeast corner of the parking lot, and the trail goes up the side of the mesa from here. *DeLorme: Arizona Atlas & Gazetteer:* Page 24 A 2–3

L ake Powell is a massive artificial lake, created by the damming of the Colorado River at the mouth of Glen Canyon. Most of the lake's 1,960 miles of shoreline lie in Utah, but some of the most spectacular views of the reservoir are in Arizona. The lake—named after Major John Wesley Powell, a one-armed Civil War veteran who led the first Colorado River expedition through the Grand Canyon in 1869—is a recent creation; Glen Canyon Dam was completed in 1963, and it took until 1980 before the lake completely filled. Today, the dam generates electricity for cities in Arizona, Colorado, Utah, Wyoming, New Mexico, and Nevada.

The city of Page was constructed to house the workers who built Glen Canyon Dam. It started as a small construction camp, built on a mesa the Navajo warned was "the place where the trees died of fear." It was named after John C. Page, Commissioner of Reclamation in the late 1930s. The city now has a population of about 8,500 and hosts millions of visitors annually. Adjacent to Page is the Navajo Nation, home of the largest Native American tribe in the country.

The Page Rimview Trail was recently created through a partnership between the city's government and its schools. The city paid for the initial construction of the trail, which encircles the city and all of Manson Mesa. And in a rather unique agreement, Page's school children now volunteer to maintain it.

The view during the ride is stellar, offering a panorama of water, rock formations, and mountains. To the north is Lake Powell, stretching off into the horizon. The large island directly offshore is Antelope Island. Across the water, rising out of the lake, is Castle Rock.

To the east rise the massive mountains of the Navajo Nation. The largest mountain in the distance is aptly named Navajo Mountain. A large, constant flume of rising steam comes from the Navajo Generating Station. Visible from about half the Rimview Trail and all of Page, the generating station is the largest coal-powered electric generating station in Arizona. It's about five miles southeast of Page on the Navajo Reservation.

To the south is the Colorado Plateau, stretching as far as the eyes can see. In fact, most of the land seen from here belongs to the Navajo Nation.

To the west are the Vermilion Cliffs—known for their distinctive red-purple hue. Major Powell originally called them the "Passion Cliffs," probably for their color but possibly for the role these cliffs also played in the area's Mormon polygamist history. During the late 1800s, Mormon polygamists traveling from St. George, Utah, to Arizona would take the "Honeymoon Trail" (now Highway ALT-89). The Vermilion Cliffs are a completely impassable obstacle to entering the state, so the Mormons would

MilesDirections

0.0 START near the McDonald's on Lake Powell Road (U.S. 89 Loop), just east of the turnoff from U.S. 89. The trailhead is at the northeast corner of the McDonald's parking lot; look for the switchbacks that take you up to the mesa's edge.

1.0 There's an information sign to your left that describes the various landmarks visible from this vista.

1.7 A line of boulders and a U.S. Forest Service sign indicates that no motorized vehicles are allowed beyond this point. Ride through the line of boulders and be extra careful to stay on the singletrack.

2.9 Keep your eyes peeled for a Rimview Trail sign indicating that a singletrack splits off to the left. Turn left at the sign and go down the switchback. *[Side-trip. If you continue ahead, the trail becomes doubletrack and eventually connects to the Lake View Elementary School.]*

4.4 The trail begins to bend south, following the edge of the mesa. There is an overlook point here where you may want to take a second to check out Antelope Canyon directly below you.

4.7 The trail forks. A brown signpost at the split indicates the Rimview Trail continues on the left, along the mesa's edge. Veer left. *[Side-trip. The right takes you back to the top of the mesa.]*

6.0 A small trail splits off to the left and heads down onto the slickrock just below the mesa's edge. Check it out!

7.0 Cross over a little metal bridge. You'll end up in

a very torn-up area with lots of ruts and tire markings obscuring the trail just ahead of the bridge. Stay to the far left of this area and pick up the singletrack as it rises. You may get caught in some silt here. Look for the trail marker a few yards south.

7.3 The Rimview Trail finally turns away from the rim and heads west toward a power line tower. Look for the brown trail sign. The trail crosses over a doubletrack and continues ahead. Look for another brown trail sign beyond the doubletrack.

7.6 The trail intersects with AZ 98. To reach the road, turn left and head down a shallow hill. Pick up the Rimview Trail about 10 yards north of AZ 98, on the other side. Continue following the Rimview Trail signs.

8.6 Cross U.S. 89 Loop. Look for the Rimview Trail sign on the other side of the highway.

9.3 Cross over a golf cart pathway. Follow the edge of the Lake Powell National Golf Course. The trail continues alongside the edge of the golf course, but does not enter the greens. There are numerous signs indicating that bikes are not allowed to ride on the golf cart pathways—please respect them. Quickly cross over the golf cart path and back onto the singletrack. Occasionally the trail crosses over a bit of slickrock, which is marked with black paint to show the path of the trail.

10.2 At the base of the mesa (the Ramada Inn is above you), the singletrack crosses over the golf cart path and makes one switchback up the mesa. The trail will actually split left and right; take the left, heading toward U.S. 89 Loop.

10.3 Cross over U.S. 89 Loop (Lake Powell Road). Head down the hill and return to your vehicle.

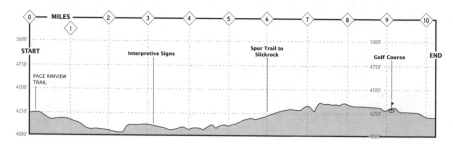

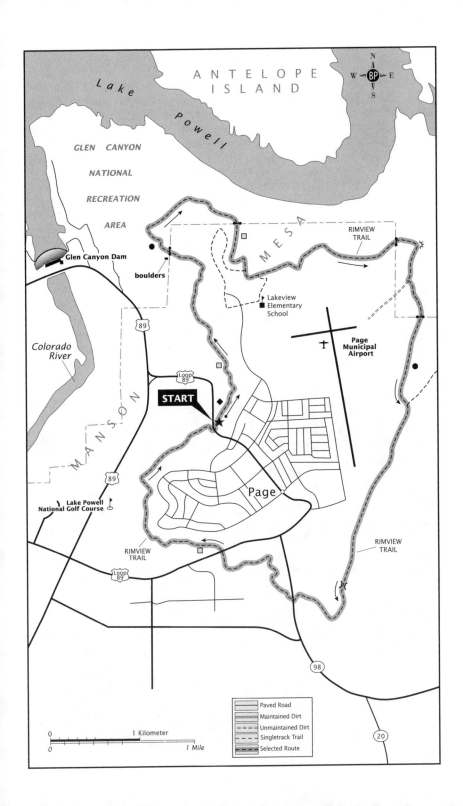

shuttle their new brides into Arizona via Lee's Ferry at the mouth of Glen Canyon, the only crossing over the Colorado River for hundreds of miles. The village was named after John D. Lee, a Mormon settler with 17 wives who established the ferry in 1871 while in exile following his alleged role in the massacre of 70 emigrants near St. George, Utah. Lee's Ferry is now an extremely popular fishing area. Also visible to the west is Glen Canyon Dam. At 710 feet high, it's just 16 feet shy of Hoover Dam.

The Glen Canyon National Recreation Area includes all of Lake Powell and much of the land surrounding it. The NRA does not allow mountain biking anywhere except on dirt roads. In addition, there are no areas that allow riding along or from the shoreline of Lake Powell. On a more positive note, the Glen Canyon NRA offices provide an excellent list of rideable roads that includes distances and trail notes.

Ride Information

📞 Trail Contacts:

City of Page: (520) 645–8861 or www.page-lakepowell.com • **Glen Canyon National Recreation Area and Rainbow Bridge National Monument,** Page, AZ (520) 608–6404 or www.nps.gov/glca

🕐 Schedule:

Open year round

💲 Fees/Permits:

No fees or permits required.

❓ Local Information:

Page/Lake Powell Chamber of Commerce: (520) 645–2741 or www.pagelakepowellchamber.org • **John Wesley Powell Museum,** Page, AZ (520) 645–9496

💡 Local Events/Attractions:

Carl Hayden Visitor Center at Glen Canyon Dam: (520) 608–6404 • **Antelope Canyon,** Navajo Parks and Recreation: (520) 698–3347 – *Several miles east of Page, Antelope Canyon is a regular subject of Arizona Highways's photo essays—so much, in fact, that time-delayed images of Antelope Canyon are something of a cliché in that magazine. To visit the canyon, you'll need to take a tour with an authorized guide* • **Grand Staircase Escalante National Monument,** Kanab, UT (435) 644–4300 or www.ut.blm.gov/monument – *President Clinton designated this vast area a national monument in 1996. Located just north of the Utah border, you can access this 1.7-million-square-mile wilderness area (no bikes, except on designated roads) between Utah mileposts 17 and 18 on U.S. Route 89.*

➖ Accommodations:

Warm Creek Motel, Big Water, UT (801) 675–9119 or www.az.net/lodging/warm-cree.htm • **Lake Powell Resorts and Marinas,** Wahweap Lodge, Page, AZ (520) 645–2433 or 1–800–528–6154 or www.visitlakepowell.com

🍴 Restaurants:

Zapata's, Page, AZ (520) 645–9006

🅝 Maps:

USGS maps: Page, AZ

Honorable Mentions

Grand Canyon Country

Compiled here is an index of great rides in Grand Canyon Country that didn't make the A-list this time around but deserve recognition. Check them out and let us know what you think. You may decide that one or more of these rides deserves higher status in future editions or, perhaps, you may have a ride of your own that merits some attention.

(L) Point Sublime

The rugged dirt road to Point Sublime is one of the few roads in Grand Canyon National Park that is still open to vehicles, including bicycles. The 18-mile (one way) road is much too rugged for passenger vehicles, but for a bike with suspension and a strong rider, it's a great trip out to one of the Grand Canyon's greatest vistas.

Getting there: Enter Grand Canyon National Park ($20 entrance fee for cars) from AZ 89 heading south from Jacob Lake. Turn west at the sign for Wildforss Trail, three miles north of the Grand Canyon Lodge; there's a parking area about a mile further where the ride begins. If you park outside the national park and ride in, there is no entrance fee but it adds about five miles each way (total +10 miles to the 36 mile out-and-back). *Delorme: Arizona Atlas & Gazetteer:* Page 23 D5–D6

(M) Greene Haven Slickrock

North of Lake Powell, heading toward Utah on AZ 89, there's a big stretch of slickrock off the west side of the road at around mile marker 553 south of the town of Greene Haven. Look for a wide dirt road that heads directly into the hills following an old power line. This power line takes you two miles to a seismic sensor bunker that once operated at the base of this slickrock area, but is now a burned-out hangout for quads, trucks, and motorcycles.

The Bureau of Land Management doesn't have any specific policies against riding on the slickrock, but it is extremely remote and potentially very dangerous. The slickrock, starting from the seismic bunker, heads northeast toward the Utah border for about five miles. You'll have to lift the bike over some barbed-wire fence less than a mile away from the bunker. The higher you go on the slickrock, the steeper the descent—you can get very high and in a lot of trouble if your bike handling skills aren't up to the task. However, the views of massive rock amphitheaters and Mars-like wastes as you work your way around the finger of Navajo sandstone are unforgettable.

There are no marked trails in the area. The dirt roads are popular with the motorized crowd, but the sand is so silty and soft that it's nearly impossible to bike on. Stick to the rock and you can't lose your way. In a pinch, keep heading down off the rock until you get to the old ranching roads at the base of the slickrock, and they'll take you either back to the bunker, or to the road leading to the bunker.
Delorme: Arizona Atlas & Gazetteer: Page 24 A2

Ⓝ Arizona Strip

The Bureau of Land Management has designated two mountain bike trails—Sunshine Loop and Dutchman—on the Arizona Strip, a five-million-acre chunk of land along the state's northernmost border. Ironically, these two Arizona bike trails can only be reached from Utah.

The Sunshine Loop, a moderately difficult 8.5-mile loop, starts on the main road heading north out of the parking lot. Cross Fort Pearce Wash and take the first road to the right (east). Follow the bicycle trail markers through a gate and across Fort Pearce Wash again. From there, the trail works its way south to a fence. Go through the gate and turn right. Follow the trail as it heads northwest to the main road and back to the trailhead parking area.

The Dutchman Trail is a nine-mile loop, with a half-mile side trip to Little Black Mountain Petroglyph Site. From the trail parking lot, the Dutchman Trail starts on the road heading west along the fence, and is well marked with bicycle trail markers. To visit Little Black Mountain Petroglyph Site, stay right at the junction marked with a two-headed arrow (leave your bike outside the fence at the site). To ride the entire loop, take the trail that heads left (south). This trail heads south to the power line road. Turn left (east) on the power line road and stay on the main road as it turns to the north and back to the trailhead parking area.

Flooding is possible on either of these trails, and they are quite remote. Be careful on water crossings during the rainy season.

Getting there: The trailhead for both rides is 10 miles southeast of St. George, Utah. Take Sunshine Trail Road to a parking area just south of the Arizona state line. **DeLorme: *Arizona Atlas & Gazetteer:*** Page 21 A3

Colorado River
COUNTRY

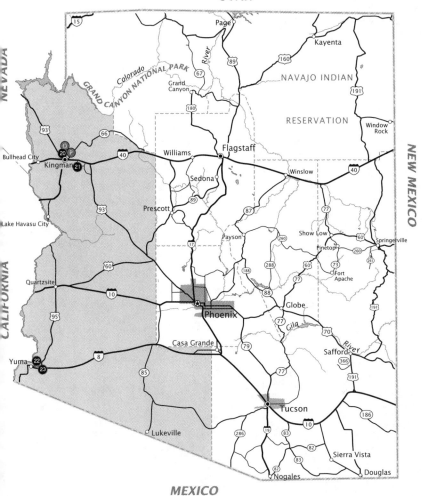

 UTAH

Colorado River Country

The Rides
Camp Beale Loop **20.**
Moss Wash Mines **21.**
Gila Mountain **22.**
Marty's Ridge to Liberty Bell **23.**

Honorable Mentions
O. Badger Trail
P. Slaughterhouse Canyon

Colorado River Country

For the most part, the western edge of Arizona is sandy, dusty, and generally bike-unfriendly. The Colorado River winds down out of the Grand Canyon and then heads due south to the Sea of Cortez, gradually losing steam the further south it goes as it feeds crop fields along both shores. In its wake, the river leaves behind vast shores of sand and grit.

There are big stretches in this area that are unsuitable for bikes: The Kofa National Wildlife Refuge, the Colorado River Indian Reservation, Lake Mead National Recreation Area—in all these circumstances, riding is limited to whatever roads you can find passing through them (although rumors abound of game trails and secret singletrack, particularly in the mountains surrounding historic Oatman). And then there are also numerous wilderness areas along the western edge of the state, within which bikes are strictly prohibited.

Motorized off-roading is quite popular along the Colorado River. This is because motorcycles, quads, and trucks are the only vehicles that can stay aloft on the endless tracts of sand and gravel present along most of the river. Unfortunately, what attempts have been made to carve decent singletrack in the area have been undermined—*literally*—by motorcyclists who discover these trails. I heard more than one sob story from local bike shop owners (who are supported largely by the local roadie scene) about years of trail-building ruined in just a couple of weekends by motorcycles and quads.

Despite all of this, however, there are several bikeable mountain ranges in the western reaches of the state. Kingman is nestled in a valley between the Hualapai Mountains and the Black Mountains, with biking opportunities—albeit of the mine/forest road variety—in both. The rich mining history and plentiful supply of old west-era ruins makes these rides interesting. If you're passing through the area, definitely take the time to check out the local riding for a change of pace. Good news for mountain bikers: There's a concerted effort going on in Kingman to build a network of singletrack trails west of town, in the Cerbat Foothills Recreation Area. Two trails have been completed—the Camp Beale Loop and the Badger Trail. With a little luck, the town will enjoy many more miles of good biking trails in the future.

At the southernmost end of the Colorado River you find the city of Yuma, a surprisingly busy town supported both by the nearby farms and visiting tourists. The fields spread out across the flat plains surrounding the city (elevation around 40 feet), while the Gila and Laguna Mountain ranges suddenly sprout from the desert floor. They're not high enough to create their own ecosystems (like the Sky Islands— see page 212), but provide some interesting contrast to the flat plains of the river. The mountains around Yuma are largely decomposing granite, and like their counterparts to the north are dotted with old mines and ruins. East of Yuma, you'll find the Yuma Proving Grounds, which would provide some sweet riding through the Laguna

Mountains if it weren't for, well, the undetonated bombs that litter the countryside (and the military police charged with guarding them).

Summers along the Colorado River are hot—oftentimes it's the hottest place in the nation. Winters are mild, even bringing a bit of snow into the Kingman area. Because of its very mild winters, Yuma makes for an interesting biking weekend—stop in at one of the local bike shops and ask about the trails in the mountains just past the state border, in California.

Section Overview

Camp Beale Loop

This sweet little loop is the first of many trails the city of Kingman plans on building in the Camp Beale Recreation Area. The loop is made up of wide single-track that loops up and around some of the low hills on the west side of town, providing a great view of Kingman and of the distant Hualapai Mountains. Although cyclists may have to share the trail with cattle, odds are slim they'll bump into other trail users on this loop. Camp Beale Loop is a favorite of local mountain bike racers, who enjoy taking multiple laps along the trail for training on its lengthy climbs as well as its speedy descents. *(See page 162.)*

Moss Wash Mines

This tour of the eastern face of the Hualapais takes cyclists on doubletrack and dirt roads deep into a protected canyon. The trail leads to the ruins of two gold mines and a remote, green valley in the middle of one of Arizona's less-explored mountain ranges. The climbs are all very do-able (if long), and the setting is unparalleled for exploring and picnicking. *(See page 168.)*

Gila Mountain

For cyclists who want to train for the mountain biking race circuit, look no further than the Gila Mountain Loop. The pros can do this up-and-down-and-up-and-down jeep road, followed by 10 miles of canal road along the old Butterfield Stage line, in a couple hours. The ride finishes with a grinding climb up I-8 through Telegraph Pass—and because of the pass's persistent winds, cyclists will even have to pedal hard coming down! *(See page 172.)*

Marty's Ridge to Liberty Bell

Mountain biking is alive and well in Yuma. The Laguna Mountains, also known as Sugarloaf Mountain, is a hilly area partially within the Yuma Proving Grounds that provides ample opportunity to practice climbing up loose, relentless ridges, sketchy descents, and twisty new singletrack. Hook up with the local club and have the members show off their latest trail-maintenance projects. *(See page 178.)*

Camp Beale Loop

Ride Specs

Start: From the trailhead at the end of Black Mesa Pipeline Road

Length: 3.3-mile loop

Approximate Riding Time: 30 minutes–1 hour

Difficulty Rating: Physically and technically moderate with some long climbs that will get you breathing pretty hard

Trail Surface: Singletrack

Lay of the Land: High Sonoran desert

Elevation Gain: 576 feet

Land Status: City of Kingman land

Nearest Town: Kingman

Other Trail Users: Equestrians and livestock

Canine Compatibility: Dogs permitted

Wheels: Hardtail is fine

Getting There

From Kingman: From downtown Kingman, follow I-40/U.S. 93 west out of town. Take Exit 48 to Fort Beale Road. Travel along Fort Beale Road 2 miles to Black Mesa Pipeline Road, the official trailhead for the Camp Beale Loop (Black Mesa Pipeline Road is the first paved left turn you can make as you drive along Fort Beale Road). *[Option. You can also park along Fort Beale Road directly opposite the first large bluff to your right. See the map to follow the trail from this secondary parking area to a second, minor trailhead.]* **DeLorme: Arizona Atlas & Gazetteer:** Page 36 A3

The Cerbat Foothills Recreation Area is at the west end of Kingman, just north of U.S. Route 93. There's not much to see there, yet; the Camp Beale Loop Trail is the first effort to apply any sort of planning to the area.

The Camp Beale Loop is a recreation project jointly managed by the city of Kingman and the Bureau of Land Management. Camp Beale was an Army outpost named after the Army Topographical Corps officer who was charged both with building a road to California across the 35th parallel, and with testing the feasibility of camels as pack animals in the southwest.

Camp Beale, fed by the Beale Road that ran from New Mexico to the Colorado River, became a hub of activity in northwest Arizona. The camp served as a trading outpost between the settlers and the Hualapai tribe. The tribe was eventually forced southward to La Paz, north of Yuma, but they broke out of the reservation and returned to their homelands in and around the Hualapai Mountains. A railroad eventually paralleled the Beale Road, and Route 66 in turn overlapped the railroad.

Camp Beale was built here because of the numerous springs in the area. These springs are still active, although they are becoming polluted. An offshoot from the trail at 0.5 miles leads visitors to the Grapevine Spring. While visiting this spring, you will probably spot a few blue crawdads in the spring's water. Just be careful not to touch the water, as the crawdads living in the spring are considered endangered and may be affected by even the slightest shift in their environment.

The trails of the Cerbat Foothills are being built largely by juvenile delinquents who are part of the Mohave County Shock Program. These kids are put in a boot

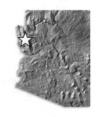

camp-like environment in an effort to help steer their lives back on track and away from trouble. The result is good news for mountain bikers: two singletrack routes with more planned over the next few years.

Camp Beale Loop can be ridden clockwise or counterclockwise. Clockwise, the climb up to the top of the hill is longer but less brutally steep; but the reward is many switchbacks and a shorter, but steeper, descent. Riding the loop counterclockwise means facing some steep climbing right from the outset.

The top of the ride provides two views: Kingman's skyline with the Hualapais and the Black Mountains in the distance, and cows—lots of cows. The Cerbat Foothills Recreation Area resides on leased grazing land, so cyclists may find themselves sharing the trail with a single bovine or a large herd of calves, protected by bulls. Cows usually get out of the way in a peaceful manner if you ride toward them slowly. But if you come rocketing toward a cow, you may look like a predator to them and risk sending them off in a stampede. Take it easy around the cattle and ride slowly.

MilesDirections

0.0 START from the Camp Beale Loop trailhead on Black Mesa Pipeline Road. The Camp Beale Loop trail starts out from behind the kiosk heading northwest from the parking area. Just past the start of the trail, the singletrack passes into a wash and exits in two places. Take the left-most exit and ride this loop in a clockwise direction [*FYI. Riding this loop in a counterclockwise direction is an option but is much steeper and therefore more difficult*].

0.5 As you begin to arc around the southern end of the loop, you'll pass a second brown BLM sign. This is the second "trailhead," used mostly by local cyclists, which passes just a few yards from a jeep road traveling from Fort Beale Road to Grapevine Spring and points westward. Stay on the trail and begin

climbing. [*Option. If you want to visit Grapevine Spring, hop onto the jeep road and ride 0.4 miles due west; the spring is to your left off the road. If you take this option, be sure to add 0.8 miles total distance to the rest of your mileage cues hereafter.*]

1.2 The trail tops out in a saddle between two hills. [*FYI. If you look straight ahead, you'll see a faint, abandoned doubletrack heading up the hill. This is not the trail!*] The trail turns immediately right and drops down over the saddle onto the east face of the hill. Begin your descent. [*FYI. The BLM has considered putting a sign here. It's possible that, by the time of this book's printing, they may already have done so.*]

3.3 Return to the trailhead on Black Mesa Pipeline Road.

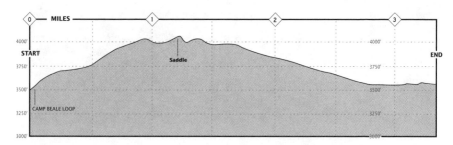

The city of Kingman and the BLM have big plans for the Cerbat Foothills Recreation Area. They've just completed a second trail in the area (the Badger Trail; *see the Honorable Mentions for this region on page 184*), and plan to build a five-mile connector trail between this and the Camp Beale Loop. As long as Kingman and the BLM keep scoring development grants, the Cerbat Foothills will continue growing as an outdoor recreation center for all of northwestern Arizona.

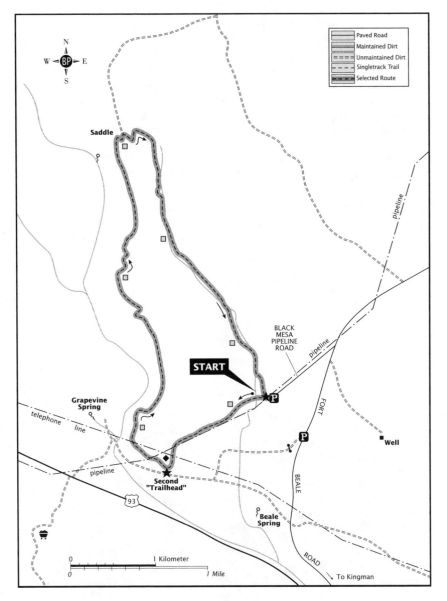

Hi Jolly and the Army Camel Corps

In 1856, Lieutenant Edward Beale, an officer in the Army Topographical Corps, received two orders. The first was to survey and build a road along the 35th parallel to join New Mexico to the Colorado River. His second: Participate in the feasibility test of camels as pack animals. Jefferson Davis, then the Secretary of War, believed camels could solve the Army's transport problems in the arid southwest, so he imported more than 60 animals and a full complement of drivers from the Middle East. One of these drivers was Hadji Ali, later nicknamed "Hi Jolly" by Army officers.

Hi Jolly, a mixed Syrian-Greek, became a sort of figurehead for the Arizona camel movement at the turn of the century. Nobody knows his real name (Hadji Ali was his name after converting to Islam), but he was an adventurer and dreamer of the first order.

Although camels can carry 600 lbs. and travel 60 miles a day without water, the Army pulled the plug on the project. Hi Jolly sold some of the animals; others escaped into the desert. He kept a few himself, operating a freight line between Yuma and Tucson.

Hi Jolly died in 1902. According to the legends that survive him, Ali perished when he went out into the desert to find a wild camel. When they found his body, he had one arm wrapped around a dead beast of burden. Nobody can substantiate the story, but it is repeated in an account of his life published by The Arizona Capitol Times *in 1995.*

To learn more about Hi Jolly and the Army Camel Corps, visit the town of Quartzsite north of Yuma. Camelmania is a celebration of the humped creatures, featuring a parade, memorabilia show, and other activities. Tourists can also visit Hi Jolly's grave, marked with a stone pyramid and a silhouette of a camel. Call the Quartzsite Chamber at (928) 927–5600.

Ride Information

(i) Trail Contacts:

Bureau of Land Management, Kingman Field Office, Kingman, AZ (928) 692–4400 or *azwww.az.blm.gov* • **City of Kingman,** Community Planning Office (928) 753–8133

(i) Schedule:

Open year round

(S) Fees/Permits:

No fees or permits required

(?) Local Information:

[See Ride 21: Moss Wash Mines]

(i) Local Events/Attractions:

Chloride, AZ - *Four miles east of U.S. 93 en route to Las Vegas off mile marker 53, Chloride is Arizona's oldest silver mine. It never quite became a ghost town, instead becoming a retirement community and tourist attraction. The Immortal Gunfighters of Chloride perform at high noon on the first and third Saturdays of each month* • **Oatman, AZ:** (928) 768–6222 or *www.ghosttowns.com* – *This ghost town has become a major tourist attraction, with a mix of Old West gunfighter/mining history and burros. Oatman is home to the largest herd of wild burros in North America. 25 miles southwest of Kingman on Oatman Road (the historic Route 66).*

(—) Accommodations:

[See Ride 21: Moss Wash Mines]

(i) Other Resources:

Mohave County Museum of History and Arts: *www.ctaz.com/~mocohist/museum/index.htm*

(i) Local Bike Shops:

Cactus Cyclery, Kingman, AZ (928) 718–8800

(N) Maps:

USGS maps: Kingman, AZ

Moss Wash Mines

Ride Specs

Start: From the trailhead at Moss Creek Trail and Blake Ranch Road

Length: 9.6-mile loop

Approximate Riding Time: 2–2.5 hours

Difficulty Rating: Moderate, with some loose climbs and a couple hike-a-bike sections

Trail Surface: Doubletrack and dirt road

Lay of the Land: High Sonoran desert, transitioning to pine forest

Elevation Gain: 1,487 feet

Land Status: Bureau of Land Management land

Nearest Town: Kingman

Other Trail Users: Off-road vehicles

Canine Compatibility: Dogs permitted

Wheels: Hardtail is fine; although full suspension will let you really rip on the long downhills

Getting There

From Kingman: Head east on I-40 to Exit 66, a Petro truck stop. Turn right on Blake Ranch Road and drive ten miles on a well-graded dirt road to the Moss Creek Trail. There are numerous little turn-offs along Blake Ranch Road, including the abandoned airstrip at Laughlin Ranch, but stick to the main, obvious road. After about ten miles along Blake Ranch Road, look for a jeep road off to your right marked with a brown BLM sign. The sign is about 100 feet down this road (this jeep road is very easy to miss, so keep your eyes pealed). If you pass down into a very deep wash (marked with a "Moss Wash" sign), you've gone a bit too far. Park along the side of the road at the Moss Creek trailhead and start biking from here. **DeLorme: Atlas & Gazetteer:** Page 37 B4–5

In their native tongue, the Hualapai tribe calls itself the "Pine Tree Folk." They lived in the Hualapai Mountains, a long range of peaks towering 3,000 feet above the high Sonoran plains below. The western face of the mountains is steep and forbidding, while the eastern face is comprised of more gentle slopes, intercut with canyons and valleys. This eastern face captures rain and funnels it down into its valleys sending running water flowing eastward out of the Hualapais much of the year. Pine trees begin about halfway up the mountain, filling out until the peaks are covered.

In more recent history, the Hualapai Mountains have been home to dozens of working gold mines. Going up any canyon cyclists are likely to find a prospecting hole, cyanide-stained tailing remnants, even complete mining operations. Most of the gold mining in the Hualapais came to a sudden end during the Great Depression; wealthy owners simply abandoned the mines and their workers before taking any greater losses than they already were.

This ride leads to the ruins of two such mines: The Gold King Mine and the Merlo Mine. The Gold King Mine, and its abandoned two-story "mansion," is now on the Arizona State Preservation Office's register.

Gold King is just 1.7 miles in from the trailhead, making it an excellent picnic destination. About halfway to the mansion, the trail enters a streambed; expect running water at all times of the year, with a small danger of flash flooding during the

monsoon season. For the rest of the year, riders will just get their wheels wet while working their way up Moss Creek.

The mansion itself is impressive, and is one of the first—if not *the* first—slip-form concrete buildings in Arizona. Built just before the Great Depression in the early 1920s, the large two-story house overlooking the Gold King Mine was lavishly appointed in its day: delicate moldings along the ceilings and floors, polished wood floors, imported furniture. The mine owners would bring investors to the mine to impress them with the operation; the manag-

er lorded over his minions from atop the mine like a captain commanding a ship. But the Depression came and the Gold King Mining Company quickly folded. Today, the mansion is covered in arcane graffiti, its guts long burned out. Its solid concrete walls and floors are still very stable, and crawling around inside and atop the mansion seems quite safe. Nevertheless, you should still be careful if you decide to poke around.

There is a faint trail that leads up from the western side of the mansion to the top of the yellowing tailings. A short hike brings visitors to the rusted remains of old mining equipment left behind when the mine was abandoned.

The ride between the Gold King Mine and the Merlo Mine is mostly a steady climb up dirt road and doubletrack. The trail gains several hundred feet over the course of a couple miles. Once past the ruins of an old cor-ral, the climb becomes steeper, but drops a bit before arriving at the Merlo Mine.

The Merlo Mine appears to be much older than Gold King. Now a tangle of timber and concrete, Merlo in its heyday extracted gold from mica; there's a massive pile of paper-thin mica sheets stacked up behind the mine ruins. Tread carefully, especially around the timber—locals have noted the building is in a state of collapse, and looks different every time they visit.

The return trip out of the Merlo Mine descends a different valley, following Cedar Creek. The views down the valley of the distant Aquarius Mountains are stunning. Take a little time to enjoy the views while bombing down the doubletrack and dirt roads that lead back to Blake Ranch Road.

This is just an introduction to the network of roads and trails that crisscross the hidden valleys at the base of the Hualapai Mountains. Once finished with this loop, there are dozens of other roads, tracks, and game trails to explore in the area.

MilesDirections

0.0 START at the Moss Wash OHV Trail sign and head due west into the Hualapai Mountains.

0.2 A doubletrack enters in from the right. *[FYI. This doubletrack connects back to Blake Ranch Road.]* Just ahead and around the corner, yet another connector joins in from the right. Continue straight on Moss Wash OHV Trail, heading toward the mountains.

1.7 Arrive at the ruins of the Gold King Mine and Mansion. The trail continues behind the "mansion," heading due west. Continue following the streambed.

2.6 After a difficult climb, the trail splits off to the left as the wash continues on the right. Get out of the wash and continue left on the doubletrack as it exits out of the wash.

2.9 The doubletrack splits left and right, with a camp area to the far right. Turn left here. *[Side-trip. Turning right will take you into the mountain for about half-a-mile, and then dead-ends at the Mica Grant Mine.]*

3.5 Arrive at an abandoned corral on your left. A dirt road forks to the left here (you'll be coming back to this later). For now, pedal straight ahead, continuing toward the mountains.

4.4 Arrive at the Merlo Mine ruins. After you've had a chance to look around (carefully!), turn back and return along the trail on which you came.

5.3 Reach the abandoned corral. This time, turn to the right and take the doubletrack that heads south.

6.1 The doubletrack bends to the left. Another doubletrack joins in from the right. Continue leftward and ahead on the main doubletrack.

6.3 At the top of a short, steep climb, a doubletrack joins in from the right. *[FYI. This trail eventually reaches the top of the saddle visible from here (and it's a very long, steep climb)].* Continue ahead on the main road.

8.7 As you come down a hill, you'll come across a metal signpost painted green (no sign though). The trail forks at this signpost. Continue around the corner going leftward and down the hill. *[Side-trip. If you turn right here, you can ride about four hundred yards and reach a hidden area called the "Blue Tanks." These "tanks," which are greenish-blue in color, earn their moniker from the natural water chutes cut into the rock.]*

9.3 Reach Blake Ranch Road. Turn left on this wide dirt road and head north, back to Moss Creek trailhead.

9.6 Reach your car.

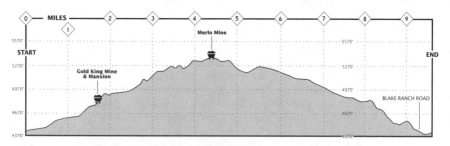

Ride Information

◑ Trail Contacts:
Bureau of Land Management, Kingman, AZ (928) 692–4400 or *azwww.az.blm.gov*

◐ Schedule:
Open year round – *chance of snow through late spring.*

⑤ Fees/Permits:
No fees or permits required

❓ Local Information:
Kingman Area Chamber of Commerce/ Powerhouse Visitor's Center, Kingman, AZ (928) 753–6106 or *www.arizonaguide.com /cities/kingman/index.html*

⬤ Local Events/Attractions:
Hualapai Mountain Park, Mohave County Parks Department, Kingman, AZ (928) 757–0915 or 1–877–757–0915 or *www.hualapaimountainpark.com* – *Beautiful hiking, but the singletrack is all off-limits to bikes* • **Mohave Museum of History and Arts,** Kingman, Arizona (928) 753–3195 or *www.ctaz.com/ ~mocohist/museum/index.htm*

⬤ Accommodations:
High Desert Inn, Kingman, AZ (928) 753–2935

🍴 Restaurants:
El Palacio of Kingman, Kingman, AZ (928) 718–0018 – *Excellent Mexican fare by a local family. They also have restaurants in Bullhead and Mohave Valley.*

🚴 Group Rides:
Bicycle World: (928) 757–5730 – *Call Phil about the group mountain biking rides every Sunday.*

ⓛ Other Resources:
The Historic Route 66 Association of Arizona, Kingman, AZ (928) 753–5001 or *www.azrt66.com*

🚲 Local Bike Shops:
Bicycle World, Kingman, AZ (928) 757–5730

Ⓝ Maps:
USGS maps: Dean Peak, AZ

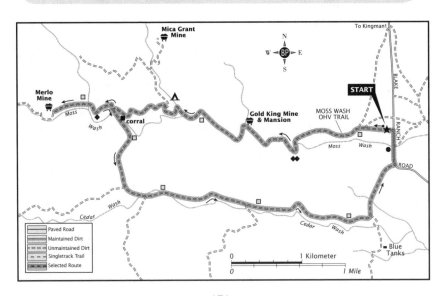

Gila Mountain

Ride Specs

Start: From Foothills Plaza parking lot
Length: 27.6-mile loop
Approximate Riding Time: 2.5-3.5 hours
Difficulty Rating: Technically and aerobically moderate, with some long climbs. It's a long ride, so riders need strong endurance
Trail Surface: Jeep roads, canal roads, and pavement
Lay of the Land: Old mining country and agricultural fields
Elevation Gain: 2,163 feet
Land Status: Bureau of Land Management
Nearest Cities: Yuma and Ligurta
Other Trail Users: Cars and OHVs
Canine Compatibility: It's an awfully long way to bring a dog. Leave the pooch at home.
Wheels: Hardtails and hybrids are fine

Getting There

From Yuma: Take I-8 east (toward Phoenix) to the Foothills Boulevard (Exit 14). Go south (right) and park in the Foothills Plaza parking lot. Start from here. *DeLorme: Arizona Atlas & Gazetteer:* Page 62 B1

A map of southwestern Arizona reveals several large mountain ranges cutting diagonally across the desert: The Mohawk Mountains, the Sierra Pinta, the Cabeza Prieta, and the Tinajas Atlas. The westernmost of these slashes is the Gila Mountains, which chop off Yuma's little corner of the world from the rest of Arizona.

The Gilas are entirely on BLM land, all the way south until they enter the Barry M. Goldwater Air Force Range. Miners have worked the Gilas for 150 years, and continue working them to this day. From the jeep roads through the Gila's foothills, cyclists can see holes dug into the sides of canyons and the mountain itself. While the bulk of the profitable gold has already been dry-panned out of the mountains by the Yuma Gold Mine, solo prospectors and rock hounds alike still scour the mountain in search of nuggets or quartz geodes.

The beginning of this ride rolls across slate-flat desert, destined to someday be developed into subdivisions. Foothills Boulevard abruptly becomes a gravel road and continues north for some distance, closing in on the railroad tracks that go around the north end of the mountain. When the ride finally turns east and heads into the foothills, the climbs and descents get interesting.

At the northernmost end of the ride, the trail passes the ruins of the Yuma Gold Mine. There's not much left here except for some scaffolding and a concrete foundation; the water tank that used to tower over the ruins was pushed over several years

ago, and crashed down into the wash below. This area is sometimes referred to as the "Train Wreck" ride.

The bulk of the ride shows what happens when greed is allowed to exist in a world without regulations. Many miles of the Gila Mountains have been mined out,

stripped, and abandoned when they became unprofitable. The hills are nothing but gravel now, an occasional mine pit alongside the trail or against the hillside.

Soon after the abandoned pits, the trail rounds a corner and heads south, following the Southern Pacific Railroad line for several miles. The rail traces exactly the old Butterfield Stage Route, one of the first transcontinental stagecoach lines. Back in the day, Butterfield would trundle along at about five miles per hour all day, every day, taking 27 days to bring passengers from St. Louis to Los Angeles. The Butterfield Stage, named after the engineer who created the route, began service in Arizona in 1857, building 26 stations along 437 miles of trail. Fort Yuma was one such station.

Today, the trail is like a ghost town that is hundreds of miles long and several centuries old. The "Butterfield Overland Trail" has become a generic name for a route that consisted of many trails over a long period of time. Its history stretches from Spanish explorers of the 1500s to the coming of the Southern Pacific railroad in the late 1870s.

The stage route was active until 1880, when rail lines made the operation unprofitable and forced it closure. However, during its operation, stage masters often hid bags of loot away from the station, rather than give it up to robbers—some of these stage masters died before they could retrieve their loot, which remains buried in the desert to this day.

Gila Mountain is now a favorite training loop for mountain bike racers, triathlon soldiers, and adventure cyclists of all stripe. At 27 miles long, it's a multi-hour grind guaranteed to keep your heart rate up while providing ample opportunity to hammer extremely hard along the railroad and canal. During "snow bird" season, keep eyes open for cars and RVs that use the train and canal roads as a shortcut between Dome

and Ligurta. This is also a main access for farmers who work Dome Valley, the stretch of farmland between the Gila Mountains and Muggins Mountains.

Besides this particular loop around the Gilas, cyclists can also check out the old and new versions of the "Blaisdell Blowout" racecourse. For several years, Yuma played host to a mountain bike race event by this name. The race was way, way out of the way for most racers, so the event eventually shut down a few years back. The loops, though, remain—one to the north of I-8, one to the south. They're not especially long or difficult, but they provide a nice change of pace from the marathon-length loop around the Gila Mountain.

Ride Information

🄲 Trail Contacts:
Bureau of Land Management Yuma Office, Yuma, AZ (928) 317-3200 or www.az.blm.gov/yfo/index.htm

🄾 Schedule:
Open year round

🄢 Fees/Permits:
No fees or permits required

🄿 Local Information:
Yuma Proving Ground Heritage Center: www.yuma.army.mil – Take AZ 95 north to Imperial Dam Road and turn left. The Heritage Center is a collection of uniforms, munitions, and old military equipment that has been tested at the Yuma Proving Ground. Open every day from 10:00 A.M. to 4:00 P.M.

🄾 Local Events/Attractions:
Yuma Territorial Prison, Yuma, AZ (928) 783-4771 – This prison once held stagecoach robbers, gunslingers, cattle rustlers, and gangsters. As you drive through old town Yuma on 4th Avenue (the main drag through town), turn right (east) on Harold Giss Parkway. Pass under I-8 and make an immediate left turn on Prison Hill • **Yuma Crossing, Yuma,** AZ (928) 329-0471 or www.pr.state.az.us – Yuma Crossing is the site of the Yuma Quartermaster Depot and Fort Yuma, used by the US Army to store and distribute supplies to military posts throughout the southwest. It was the only easy crossing into California until the Southern Pacific Railroad built the Ocean-to-Ocean bridge in 1877, bringing an end to Fort Yuma • **Imperial National Wildlife Refuge** (928) 783-3371 – View 15,000 acres of pristine Colorado River coastline, just 35 miles north of Yuma. Go north on AZ 95 to Martinez Lake Road, and take that until it hits the Visitor Center.

🄽 Maps:
USGS maps: Laguna Dam, AZ; Dome, AZ; Fortuna, AZ; Ligurta, AZ

MilesDirections

0.0 START from the Foothills Plaza parking lot. Head back over I-8 on Foothills Boulevard going north. Foothills Boulevard will eventually turn into a dirt road (at about 0.4 miles). Continue heading north.

2.3 A dirt road turns off to the right. Continue ahead, going due north.

3.3 The road splits left and right. Stay to the left, heading toward the distant grain silos.

3.6 Arrive at a five-way intersection of dirt road, paved road, and railroad tracks. Look for Gowan Milling Parkway (it's well signed) and head east on it, toward the Gila Mountains.

4.1 Just past the entrance to the Gowan Milling plant to the left, look for a dirt road that runs in front of a low block wall fence to your left. Turn left and follow this dirt road.

4.6 A gravel road splits to the right. Continue ahead, heading toward the railroad tracks.

5.0 Trail splits left and right. Take the road to the left, heading toward the train tracks.

5.5 The trail turns due east, heading toward the Gila Mountains. Trail forks left and right; stay on the wide gravel road on the right and head toward the mountains. Just past that last fork in the road, take another right, still heading toward the mountains. The trail gradually narrows down to doubletrack and winds into the hills.

5.8 One more fork in the road. Take the left this time, which takes you around the north side of the mountain rather than directly toward the mountain face.

6.4 As you pass through a valley, there's a fork in the trail. Take the right, staying close to the side of the mountain. There's a wooden post with a bullet-ridden mannequin's head nailed to the top of it.

7.7 Near the top of a descent, a doubletrack splits off to the right, closely following the mountainside. Disregard it and head down the hill, away from the mountains for now.

8.0 At the bottom of the descent down a reddish-orange hill, you enter a camp area. As you bike across a wash, look for a road that splits off to the right and up a hill. Turn right here, going up the hill and back toward the mountains.

8.6 At the top of a climb, the road suddenly stops at a washed-out canyon. It's a hike-a-bike down and back up out of the gully, and you're back on the road.

9.3 Arrive at the bottom of a long, shallow hill. There's a train bridge ahead of you. Before you get to the bridge, you'll pass by a grove of salt cedar. Turn right just past the grove and head up the hill, before you go under the bridge, and head up the hill toward the Yuma Gold Mine. After you reach the top of the climb to the Yuma Gold Mine (the mine is to the right of the road), take a break to check out the ruins. Return to the road and head up the widest, most obvious gravel road heading up the hill ahead.

9.9 A doubletrack splits off to the right; stay to the left. As you head toward the train tracks, the trail will wind through some washes and over hills. As long as you end up on

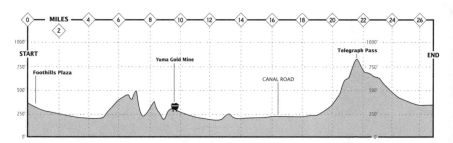

the dirt road parallel to the train tracks (the Butterfield Stage Route), you'll be okay.

11.9 An underpass is to the right. Continue ahead. *[**Side-trip.** Cross under the train tracks, pass by a rusted out old car and climb up a loose, gravelly hill. The trail splits left and right; go right, following the mountain's edge. This is a side route that loops up closer to the mountain and then goes back down toward the railroad. Add 1.2 miles.]*

16.1 The road splits left and right. *[**FYI.** The left goes toward the pump station on the canal, which is a nice rest spot.]* Past the pump station, stick to the canal road until you hit pavement. Make sure you stay on the west side of the canal.

19.0 The canal road intersects with Dome Valley Road. Turn right (south) onto the road. After a few hundred yards, the road turns to the left. Go straight ahead, off the road, and catch the doubletrack that goes straight toward the highway. In about half a mile, enter the Ligurta Station Adult RV Park and head for the stop sign. At the stop sign, the road goes left and right. Turn right, heading toward I-8.

20.0 Enter the town of Ligurta. Take a break at the Ligurta Station store. There's a ramada with tables and chairs, and the store should be open (unless there's a bingo day or square dance at the adjacent barn). When rested up, head west up I-8 and over Telegraph Pass.

27.6 Go up the turnoff to Foothills Boulevard, turn left, and return to your vehicle parked at Foothills Plaza.

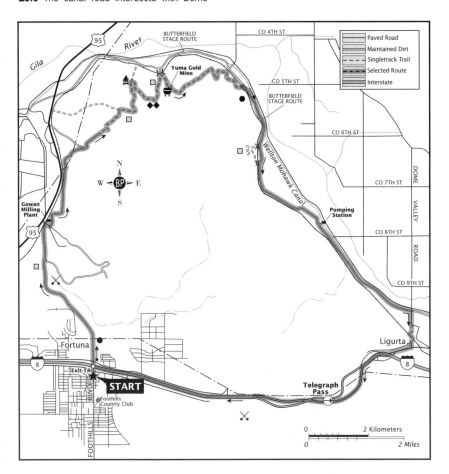

Marty's Ridge to Liberty Bell

Ride Specs

Start: From the parking area outside the dump, just on the other side of the Gila Main Canal

Length: 9.9-mile loop

Approximate Riding Time: 2 hours

Difficulty Rating: Aerobically and technically moderate, with some difficult climbs up loose, gravelly hills. The hardest part of the trail is just finding your way around.

Trail Surface: Doubletrack and jeep road

Lay of the Land: Desert pavement (baked, black granite)

Elevation Gain: 1,194 feet

Land Status: Bureau of Land Management land

Nearest City: Yuma

Other Trail Users: Off-road vehicles

Canine Compatibility: Dogs permitted

Wheels: Hardtail

Getting There

From Yuma: Take U.S. 95 North (which actually travels east) and follow the signs to Mittry Lake. At the sign, turn left (due north) on 7E (Laguna Dam Road). Drive past the Yuma Lake sign about one mile down the road and keep your eyes pealed for the power line that crosses the road. At this point you should see a blue sign that reads "Solid Waste Transfer Site 1 Mile." Turn right at the sign on County 5th Street. Travel over the bridge that crosses Gila Main Canal. You can either park in the lot on the other side of the bridge or take an immediate left onto the dirt road that runs alongside the canal and park about a hundred yards up the road in another lot. *DeLorme: Arizona Atlas & Gazetteer:* Page 62 A1

R iding through the Laguna Mountains is like riding across one of the more unpleasant circles of Dante's *Inferno*. The landscape is bleak and barren, yet starkly beautiful. Single blooming ocotillos sprout here and there, orange blossoms standing in contrast with the "desert pavement." This desert pavement is the result of Yuma's geography and weather: Wind has blown away the topsoil, leaving behind ore-rich granite that has subsequently been baked black and shiny by countless millennia under the Arizona sun. Turning over any rock reveals its original color on the underside.

Surprisingly, wildlife is abundant in this wasteland during the cooler winter months. The Gila Canal, which runs along the western edge of the Lagunas, provides ample water for coyotes and deer.

More abundant than the wildlife are the "desert rats," folks who have made a home of the barren hills. Mine claims pepper the hills, marked with lonely white pipes or painted wooden posts upended in piles of rocks. This trail hosts a seasonal camp for the "Wishful Thinking Mine Company" in Tabletop Valley; their colorful signs warn away other miners from their claims. Non-miners should also heed this warning—don't assume everyone who lives in the desert is friendly (or even sane).

When one thinks of Yuma, images of nearby sand dunes (a misnomer created during the filming of Tatooine scenes from *Star Wars*, which was credited to the city, yet filmed in nearby California) and endless flat farmland may come to mind. The area's rides, however, are surprisingly brutal, comprised of nothing but climbs and descents. For such a "flat" part of the state, there are few level portions on the ride. In the

Lagunas especially, the surface also tends toward loose and gravelly. Bring wide tires to deal with the surface conditions.

While warnings about water and sunscreen apply universally in Arizona, they are especially critical in Yuma. The air is no dryer anywhere else in the world, despite the vast irrigated fields that follow the canals snaking from the Colorado River. It's very hard to stay hydrated, even with bottles and hydration packs to help you. The sun is no help either; because the desert pavement doesn't have any topsoil for plants to hold on to, shade is a rare treat. Therefore, the highest SPF sunblock is recommended. Alternatively, cyclists can opt for what the locals wear—thin, long-sleeve shirts.

The ride itself starts out along the Gila Canal, and then leads into the network of jeep roads in the hills. Climbing begins as soon the trail leaves the canal road, and with a few exceptions it is relentless until reaching the top of "Marty's Ridge" (named after a local rider who has been riding this ridge for many years). At the top of Marty's Ridge, cyclists can climb to the top of the hill. From here, the view includes Mittry Lake, Colorado River, and Imperial Dam to the north, the Muggins Mountains and Castle Dome Mountains to the east, the Gila Mountains to the south, and endless fields of lettuce and other crops to the west.

As the trail travels east into the Laguna Mountains, it gets increasingly closer to the Yuma Proving Grounds. This is one of the Army's test beds for tanks, personnel carriers, NASA prototype aircraft, and pretty much anything else that rolls, flies, or trundles in the name of national security. While the proving ground area is well-

marked at its eastern reaches, it is less so coming in from the west. There are supposed to be signs, but they get knocked down all the time. Riding on the Yuma Proving Grounds is both illegal and dangerous (due to the presence of live munitions that have littered the proving grounds since WWII), and the MPs may escort you off the grounds if they find you there. How to know if you've gone too far? If you can see a series of 100-foot concrete ramps, used to test climbing abilities of various wheeled and treaded vehicles, you've gone too far east. Although the base tends to turn a blind eye toward cyclists, hunters, quad drivers, and others who wander onto their base, it's still against the rules.

Ride Information

🕐 Trail Contacts:
Bureau of Land Management Yuma Office, Yuma, AZ (928) 317-3200 or www.az.blm.gov/yfo/index.htm

🕐 Schedule:
Open year round – But the summers are unbearably brutal.

💲 Fees/Permits:
None

❓ Local Information:
Yuma Convention & Visitors Bureau: (928) 783-0071, 1-800-293-0071 or www.visityuma.com • **Yuma County Chamber of Commerce,** Yuma, AZ (928) 782-2567 or www.yumachamber.org

💡 Local Events/Attractions:
Yuma Proving Ground Heritage Center: www.yuma.army.mil – Take AZ 95 north to Imperial Dam Road and turn left. The Heritage Center is a collection of uniforms, munitions, and old military equipment that has been tested at the Yuma Proving Ground. Open every day from 10:00 A.M. to 4:00 P.M.

🛏 Accommodations:
Best Western Coronado, Yuma, AZ (928) 783-4453 or www.bwcoronado.com – located in Yuma's historic district • **Shilo Inn,** Yuma, AZ (928) 782-9511 or 1-800-222-2244 or www.shiloinn.com

🍴 Restaurants:
Mi Rancho Restaurant, Yuma, AZ (928) 344-6903

🕐 Other Resources:
City of Yuma On-line: www.ci.yuma.az.us

🚴 Group Rides:
Contact DuWayne Fritz: (928) 726-5794 or **Bart Hatcher:** (928) 341-4896 for information – Yuma has a small but dedicated cadre of mountain bikers that regularly hit the Laguna Mountains, the Gila Mountains, and the old and new Blaisdell Blowout race courses.

🚲 Local Bike Shops:
Mr. B's Bicycles & Mopeds, Yuma, AZ (928) 783-2916

N Maps:
USGS maps: Laguna Dam, AZ; Fortuna, AZ

MilesDirections

0.0 START from the parking area off the canal. Cross over the bridge, turn left, and head north alongside the canal on the dirt road.

0.4 The trail crosses over a concrete drainage overflow structure. This is the first road that turns into the mountain range. For this particular route, pick up the dirt road on the other side and continue north, along the canal.

0.9 Reach the second dirt road that turns in toward the Laguna Mountains, again at a concrete overflow structure. Turn right on this road and ride into the mountains.

2.1 A doubletrack joins the trail from behind you, on the right. Continue ahead, toward the hill.

2.3 The trail comes to a fork. Turning left takes you toward Sugarloaf Mountain. Continue right, up Marty's Ridge.

2.4 The trail splits off to the left and down the hill. Continue right, up Marty's Ridge.

3.3 Reach the top of Marty's Ridge. From here, look down at the network of roads winding all over the blackened hills. You'll see three intersections. The first is a dead end to the right; go left. Then, for this loop, take the next two right turns and drop into the valley below. The hill is pretty steep, so you'll just have to know to make the turns.

4.2 At the top of a lengthy, fairly steep climb, the trail splits left and right. To the left, you can see a hint of some new singletrack that

locals are developing. For this loop, continue right.

4.6 At the bottom of a steep descent, you enter a valley filled with "desert pavement," or sun-blackened granite. This is "Steam Shovel Valley," named after the abandoned yellow steam shovel at the end of the valley. The road splits left and right here; go left. The right turn takes you back to the parking area.

4.9 You'll pass two large, painted mining claim signs for the Wishful Thinking Mining Company. At the second sign, a dirt road splits off to the right from the gravel road, which continues west. Turn right onto the dirt road and head up the hill.

5.0 Top out at the end of a very steep and loose climb. Faint singletrack splits off left and right from the main road, which continues due south. Stay on the main road and descend the hill into Picnic Table Valley.

5.1 At the bottom of the hill into Picnic Table Valley there's another mining claim sign from the Wishful Thinking Mining Company. Take the dogleg that goes east.

5.3 Just beyond a massive pile of cut wood, the semi-permanent camp of the Wishful Thinking Mining Company—a truck with a camper, and a tan trailer—is visible ahead. Step back from the hill and look for the faint singletrack that ascends the hill on your right, switches back, goes left, and continues eastward up the ridge that defines the southern edge of Picnic Table Valley. This is

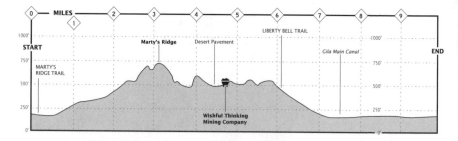

the beginning of the Liberty Bell Trail, called such for a nearby old mine claim signpost with a liberty bell embossed on the top of it.

5.5 At the top of the climb out of Picnic Table Valley, the singletrack splits left and right. To the left, the singletrack continues deeper into the Laguna Hills and eventually takes you to the Adair Shooting Range. For this trip, go right on the main and most obvious singletrack, eventually heading south/southwest toward the Gila Mountains.

6.9 The singletrack ends at a steep, loose climb up to a gravel road. The gravel road splits left and right; take the right and head down the hill. Both roads lead you back to the canal, but the right puts you closer to the parking area.

7.5 The trail exits onto the canal road. Go right, north along the canal. Stay on this road until you get back to your vehicle.

9.9 Pass by the bridge and return to the parking area.

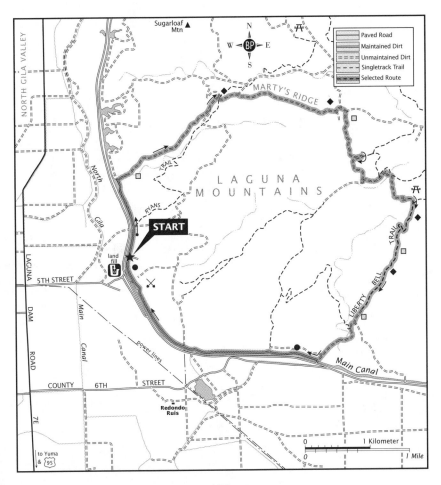

Colorado River Country

Compiled here is an index of great rides in Colorado River Country that didn't make the A-list this time around but deserve recognition. Check them out and let us know what you think. You may decide that one or more of these rides deserves higher status in future editions or, perhaps, you may have a ride of your own that merits some attention.

(O) Badger Trail

This four-mile (one way) trail was finished spring 2000, and is still a relatively undiscovered gem. Locals consider this the most challenging trail in the area, both technically and aerobically. The Badger Trail is the second trail built in the Cerbat Foothills Recreation Area; the first is the Camp Beale Loop (*see Ride 20: Camp Beale Loop*). Next up on the Kingman BLM office's wish list is a five-mile singletrack connector between the Camp Beale Loop and the Badger Trail.

Getting there: En route to Las Vegas on U.S. 93, go a quarter-mile north of the intersection with AZ 68. Badger Trail is the first right after the intersection. *DeLorme: Arizona Atlas & Gazetteer:* Page 36 A3.

(P) Slaughterhouse Canyon

Once the location of an old NORBA race that was cancelled after 1998, this area, bounded by train tracks and Hualapai Mountain Road, is a nice, but complicated, mix of doubletrack and singletrack. There's little chance that mapping would be possible or even useful in this complex network of trails. Go a little further south than Slaughterhouse Canyon proper (the first deep gorge) to find the trails that have not yet been shredded by 4x4s.

Getting there: At the corner of Andy Devine and Stockton Hill, go east on Stockton Hill, as it becomes Hualapai Mountain Road. Look for the radio station on your right; start riding on the first dirt road east of the radio station. *DeLorme: Arizona Atlas & Gazetteer:* Page 37 A4.

Sky
ISLANDS

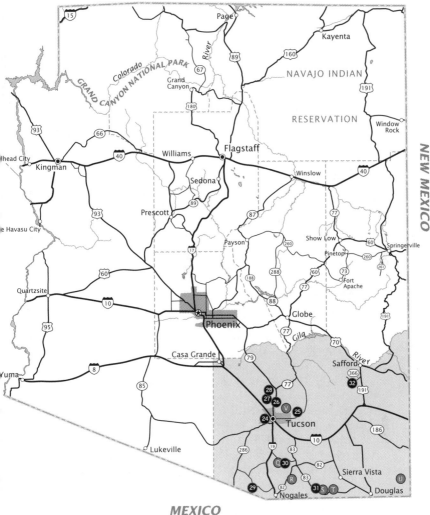

The Rides

Starr Pass–Yetman Wash **24.**
Chiva Falls **25.**
Mount Lemmon Top to Bottom **26.**
50 Year Trail **27.**
The Tortolitas **28.**
Cobre Ridge **29.**
Gold Country **30.**
Brown Canyon **31.**
Mount Graham **32.**

Honorable Mentions

Q. Elephant Head
R. Patagonia
S. Sierra Vista
T. San Pedro River
U. Chiracahua Mountains
V. Santa Catalina Mountains

Sky Islands

South of Phoenix, the Arizona desert spreads out toward the Mexican border. Erupting from the desert floor are isolated, super-tall mountains that tower thousands of feet above the valley floor. These "sky islands" are so tall that each has its own unique ecosystem—some even have their own weather. While it's sunny and hot in Tucson, you might experience cold rain up on Mount Lemmon.

These sky island mountains are all part of the Coronado National Forest, making this forest unusual in that, if you look at a map, the forest boundaries aren't contiguous. Some of the mountains are open, some are wilderness. The largest of the islands—the Santa Catalina Mountains, north of Tucson, and the Santa Rita Mountains, south of Tucson—are a mix of both wilderness and non-wilderness areas.

Tucson is ground zero for southern Arizona mountain biking. Whereas Phoenix's bike population is so spread out and diverse that nobody can seem to even get a bike club together, Tucson's underlying vibe is so pro-activist that the town sports not one but *two* large bike clubs—Sonoran Desert Mountain Bikers (SDMB) and the Southern Arizona Mountain Bike Association (SAMBA). The University of Arizona, in the middle of Tucson, dominates the city's smallish population, which houses huge numbers of young, super-fit off-road cyclists. Combined with a nice selection of bike shops, including some very elite boutiques, and a fairly safe bike-commuting network, it's clear that Tucson is Arizona's largest bike-friendly town.

There are some very nice desert rides around Tucson: in the Tucson Mountain Park to the west, "Fantasy Island," a stretch of Arizona State Trust land to the east, and the non-wilderness areas of the Rincon Mountains to the east. However, the real center of mountain biking attention in Tucson is Mount Lemmon, the central peak of the Santa Catalina Mountains that dominate the city's north edge. World-class, technically difficult singletrack winds up and down the mountaintop, while the 50 Year Trail takes up the foothills north of the mountain range. To get to the 50 Year Trail, you have to drive *around* the Santa Catalinas; many Tucson riders don't bother making the trek, but it's worth it nonetheless. Riders in the East Valley of metro Phoenix can actually get to the 50 Year Trail in just a little more time than it takes to reach it from downtown Tucson—a surprisingly central location!

The Santa Rita Mountains south of Tucson are an often-overlooked riding resource. Much of the riding in the foothills is on old mine roads, but hidden in these foothills lie some terrific singletrack following the Arizona Trail as well as some interesting old mining ruins. Most of the riding is a bit higher than Tucson, so you get a nice 5–10 degree temperature break throughout the year. There's not much civilization in this part of the state; Patagonia, a little artist's colony that was once the site of Cannondale's spring training camp, is the main base of operations.

There are other sky islands as well, each with some really great high-altitude rides. Mount Graham, east of Tucson, features two loops that make for a nice day of moderately difficult riding. Down in the Huachuca Mountains near Sierra Vista, there are a couple nice, short loops that are a welcome break from the difficult riding elsewhere around here; check with the Dawn to Dust mountain bike club, based in Sierra Vista, for information about group rides. Way, way south, the backroads and forgotten doubletrack west of Nogales are hiding years' worth of exploration.

Weather down in the desert in this part of the state tends to be almost as hot as in Phoenix during the summer. But because there are so many good rides above 7,000 feet, it's easy to ride year-round here. Winters open up all the low desert rides, but shut down the sky islands with snow.

Section Overview

Starr Pass–Yetman Wash

The Starr Pass–Yetman Wash loop, a classic Tucson
fast-but-fun ride, is great for teaching technique to
beginners but is still fast and challenging for experienced riders. This is an ideal ride to squeeze in over the
lunch hour. A strong rider could probably hammer
through this trail in 45 minutes and be back in time for
a quick shower and a bag lunch before the boss catches you slacking. *(See page 194.)*

Chiva Falls

This technically challenging, daunting area is a hotbed
of hardcore mountain biking in Tucson. Chiva Falls,
the most popular trail in the Rincons, affords a beautiful introduction to the Rincon Mountains and
Coronado National Park, and some great practice for
honing technical skills. There are many opportunities
to jump off the main trail and explore after you've mastered the Chiva Falls portion of the Rincons. *(See page
200.)*

Mount Lemmon Top to Bottom

Mount Lemmon Top to Bottom is constructed from
pieces of several trails, and will give you an overview of
what the highest parts of the Santa Catalinas have to
offer. This is a difficult, epic ride: Plan for both a long
and technically challenging journey. This pseudo-loop
takes cyclists to the top of Mount Lemmon via paved
road, drops down very technical singletrack featuring
tight switchbacks and drops (and sometimes both at
the same time), and then to the beautiful-but-difficult

Crystal Springs Trail, which takes riders back to the beginning of the route. Much of this last
portion of the trail is frighteningly exposed on one side, with steep but nonvertical drops to
one side of the trail that go down a hundred feet or more before anything would stop a falling
body. Given sufficient preparation and ability, Mount Lemmon Top to Bottom is one of the
most rewarding rides in all the state. *(See page 204.)*

50 Year Trail

The 50 Year Trail is a two-hour adventure along the little-traveled but mighty northwestern face of the Santa Catalinas. Portions of the trail pass through prickly cactus gardens, others drop into rocky arroyos and climb steep hills. At times sandy, rocky, and smooth, the 50 Year Trail is always scenic. It's also just the backbone to a network of trails across this area that's never been adequately mapped but, according to locals, encompasses a couple hundred miles of mixed singletrack and doubletrack. *(See page 210.)*

The Tortolitas

This little-explored gem of property, north of Tucson by about 20 minutes, offers miles of doubletrack and jeep roads twisting among hills, valleys, washes, and the occasional ruins of forgotten ranches. *(See page 216.)*

Cobre Ridge

This isolated doubletrack loop, just minutes away from the Mexican border, leads through long forgotten mining country and into the depths of California Gulch. It's a long descent for the first half of the ride, and a hot, dry grind to get back out of the gulch. But along the way, you'll pass the ruins of old mines, see the old ghost town of Ruby, and have a chance to enjoy the rocky beauty of the Atascosa Mountains. *(See page 222.)*

Gold Country

What a combination: Cooler temperatures within an hour of Tucson, some terrific non-brutal singletrack, and a history lesson—all in one ride! This mongrel of a loop, with two out-and-backs acting as bookends, zips along some of the best singletrack the Arizona Trail has to offer as well as some rugged jeep roads and graded dirt roads. It's also a good introduction to the vast network of trails and jeep roads that crisscross the eastern face of the Santa Ritas. *(See page 228.)*

Brown Canyon

Sierra Vista is a semi-secret little hotbed of mountain biking. The Dust to Dawn Mountain Bike Club calls Sierra Vista home, and MBAA has started running races in the area. The Brown Canyon Trail is probably the sweetest ride in the Huachuca Mountains—it's a beautiful combination of mid-altitude climbing and a very fun semi-technical descent along water. This trail is a cool, shady alternative to the low-altitude desert rides so common throughout the southern half of the state. *(See page 234.)*

Mount Graham

Okay, so Mount Graham is out of the way no matter where you live. Given the serpentine paved crawl up to the top, it's even out of the way if you live in nearby Safford or Willcox. *Make the effort.* The loops atop Mount Graham won't disappoint. At 8,000 feet to 9,000 feet up, both rides will require you bring spare lungs as well as a fair bit of technical skill—and don't forget the camera, because you'll get an endless supply of views from the trail down to the desert, 6,000 feet or more straight down. There are two loops, both built specifically for mountain bikers, atop the mountain and you should be able to do them both in one day. If you want to poke around a while and give yourself time to take in the amazing views, there's even a great little campground within a mile of the trailhead. Hardly anyone ever goes up Mount Graham, so you're probably going to get the trail all to yourself even in the middle of the summer. *(See page 240.)*

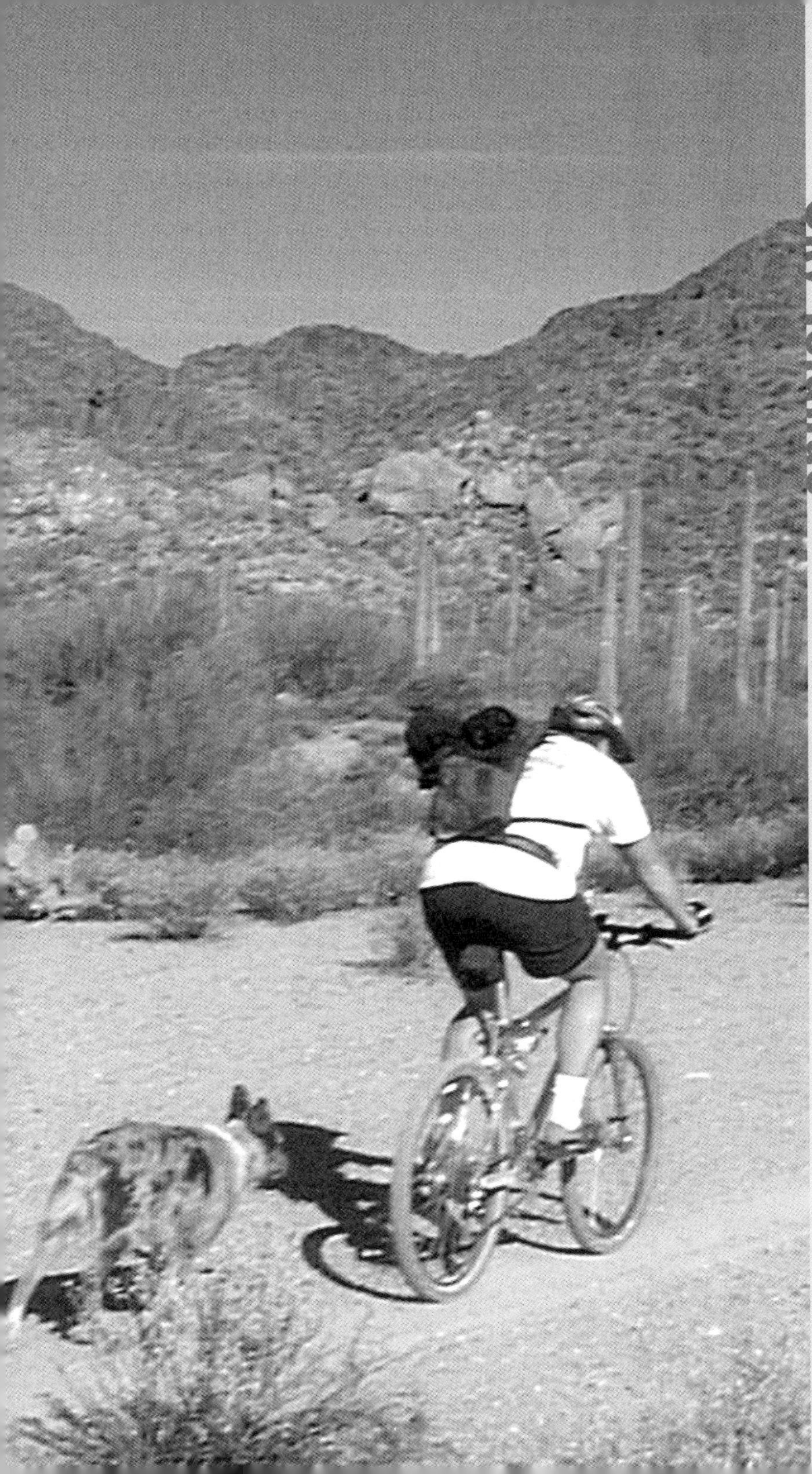

Sky Islands

24

Starr Pass–Yetman Wash

Ride Specs

Start: From the parking lot outside Tucson Mountain Park's north entrance
Length: 7.8-mile loop
Approximate Riding Time: 1 hour
Difficulty Rating: Moderately difficult, both technically and aerobically. There are a couple steep climbs, and the passage through Starr Pass itself is tricky the first time you try it (poorly lit, some unexpected steps).
Trail Surface: Singletrack, with one double-track passage
Lay of the Land: Lower Sonoran Desert
Elevation Gain: 673 feet
Land Status: State park
Nearest City: Tucson
Other Trail Users: Hikers and equestrians
Canine Compatibility: Dogs permitted
Wheels: Hardtail (front suspension) okay

Getting There

From Tucson: Take Speedway Boulevard west past I-10 to Greasewood Road. Turn left on Greasewood Road and drive until you reach Anklam Road. Turn right on Anklam Road, and keep your eyes pealed for a major housing development sign that says "Starr Pass." This road, Daystone Mountain, weaves through the Starr Pass master-planned golf community. It terminates at Player's Club; go left and, in about 30 yards, there will be a dirt road to your right that heads toward Tucson Mountain Park. This road is across from Deer Meadow Loop. Turn on this road. You can either park here or in the next parking lot a few yards down the road. All mileage directions are given from this second parking lot. There are a total of five trailheads into Tucson Mountain Park. *DeLorme: Arizona Atlas & Gazetteer:* Page 67 D3–D4

Founded in 1928, Tucson Mountain Park is a favorite among Tucson's mountain biking community. The Starr Pass–Yetman Wash loop is arguably the best set of trails through the park, and an excellent course on which novice riders can build their bike handling skills.

Starr Pass is a narrow canyon strewn with boulders that passes through the saddle of Cat Mountain. As cyclists approach the pass, they can see the endless sweep of housing developments and golf resorts across the desert on the other side of the mountain. The western side of this trail passes back and forth between Tucson Mountain Park and the beginnings of various housing developments—so ride it while you can.

The David Yetman Trail, named after a former County Supervisor and conservation advocate, is the only asterisk on this otherwise excellent trail. It's a long passage of soft sand with just a few rocky punctuations (*see the Sailing Through Sand tip on page 198*). Luckily, riding the loop in a clockwise direction means you'll be riding slightly downhill for the entirety of the wash. Consider this portion of the trail good practice for other soft-sand conditions.

Starr Pass once served as the main wagon route connecting the silver mines at Quijotoa, on the Papago Indian Reservation to the south and west, with the rail line

at Tucson. There's no indication of that now, and the pass itself has become one of the more technically challenging parts of the trail. Other parts of the park's history smack of the Old West as well. For example, a legendary figure named El Tejano supposedly hid treasure somewhere in Cat Mountain, the distinctive peak at the southern end of the park, past which Starr Pass itself goes.

The Old West vibe in the Tucson Mountains proved so strong to film producers that Old Tucson Studios was founded in the park in 1939. Columbia Pictures chose the location to build a 50-building replica of 1860s Tucson for the movie *Arizona*. Many other Westerns were filmed at Old Tucson over its lifetime: *Gunfight at the OK Corral*, *Mclintock!*, *Mark of Zorro*, *The Outlaw Josey Wales*, and *Tombstone* are just a few notable examples.

Twenty years after its creation, Old Tucson Studios became a combination theme park and movie set. Each movie filmed there added new buildings to the set, and Old Tucson grew and grew. Eventually, more than 300 movies and television episodes were filmed there.

Old Tucson Studios still exists, but sadly not in its most glorious form. An arson fire destroyed 40 percent of the studio in 1995, which reopened 18 months afterward.

MilesDirections

0.0 START from the Tucson Mountain Park north parking lot. Look for the gravelly doubletrack heading southwest out of the parking lot. This doubletrack will drop into a couple washes and eventually head up a hill.

0.8 At the top of a rocky climb veer left and you'll see the gate into Tucson Mountain Park. It's a bike-proofed gate, so you'll have to get off and carry the bike over the metal bar. Continue up the hill. *[FYI. You can also park at this higher clearing if you have a high-clearance vehicle that can navigate the climb.]* Just past the gate are wooden signs that are often marred with shotgun blasts. Follow the arrow that says "Starr Pass Trail, 1.5 miles," pointing down the hill.

1.2 The trail will split several times in the next few hundred yards, but if you continue heading southwest you'll eventually reach Starr Pass Trail. Keep the pass in your view and you can't go wrong.

2.1 At the top of a sandy climb, there's a large clearing before you enter Starr Pass itself, a rocky, technically tricky cataract through the mountain. On the other side of the pass, continue ahead. *[Side-trip. At the top of the pass, there's also a trail that splits off to the right. This is Walser's Wall Trail, a technically diffi-*

cult route around the north side of the hill. This trail takes you to the same place as Starr Pass on the other side of the hills.]

2.7 Pass through the gate and exit the park. You'll ride alongside the park on doubletrack that parallels the park's fence.

3.0 Pass a gate on your right. This is the exit point of Walser's Wall Trail.

3.4 Pass through a gate and re-enter Tucson Mountain Park. Just on the other side of this gate there is a poorly marked singletrack; the park has marked it restricted, so stay off. Continue straight ahead on the obvious trail.

3.7 Stop at the large gate, pass your bike through the gate, and continue forward. There will be numerous faint and little-used trails splitting off in various directions. Stick to the main, well used trail and you can't get lost.

4.1 Ride onto the new asphalt that is the outermost reach of new housing developments around the southern side of Starr Pass. Just past the intersection of Tucson Estate Parkway and Triangle Drive, to your right and hidden behind some mesquite, you'll find the gate back into Tucson Mountain Park. Go through the gate and continue ahead.

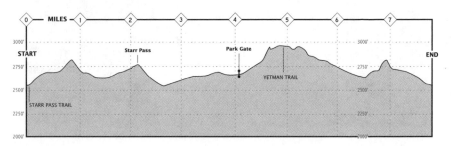

Once you've explored and mastered the Starr Pass-Yetman Wash loop, consider exploring the rest of the network of trails within the Tucson Mountain Park. The John Krein Trail, an offshoot of the Yetman Wash, is a challenging climb up the mountain and ends with spectacular views of the park and the city beyond. This trail is highly recommended for those who are gluttons for punishment.

4.9 To your right, at the top of a rocky climb, you'll see a wooden sign that reads "John Krein Trail." Continue straight ahead; do not take John Krein unless you know what you're doing. You're about to enter Yetman Wash. *[Side-trip. Okay, go ahead and ride John Krein Trail. Don't say I didn't warn you. It's a hard trail that dead-ends at a nice overlook, and it's about half a mile long. Check it out, but expect to walk a lot of it.]*

5.8 Exit Yetman Wash, a mile-long corridor of sand, gravel, and boulders.

6.3 Reach a split in the road. There's a pair of wooden signs; one reads "Starr Pass Trail" and the other reads "David Yetman Trail." Go on the Yetman arm, to your left.

6.3 About a hundred yards past the last pair of signs, you come across another wooden sign pointing to the Starr Pass Trail to the right. Continue left, past the sign.

6.3 Rejoin with the original trail; go left.

7.0 Pass through the first gate you came through. Head down the hill and back to the parking lot.

7.8 Return to the parking lot.

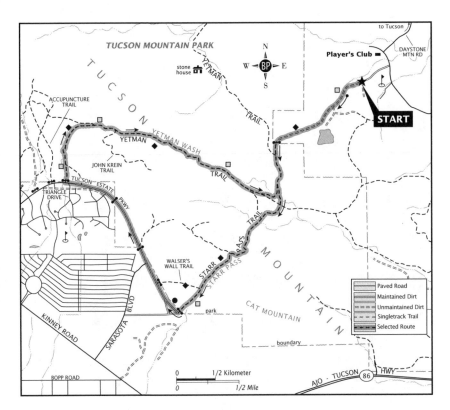

Sailing Through Sand

In Tucson, many trails feature short—or, in the case of the Yetman Wash portion of Starr Pass-Yetman Wash, quite extended—sandy passages. The grit varies from gravelly to silt-like, but in all cases it's a royal pain to pedal through. For cyclists who'd rather spend more time pedaling than walking, try these tips for handling the sand.

The secret to getting through sand is to shift your weight back by sliding your posterior over your back tire, and put as little weight on the front tire as possible. This will help the rear tire cut down into the sand and give you more traction, while keeping the bike from diving forward and down. Steer with your hips, rather than your handlebars, when possible.

Pedal in a lower gear than you think you need to avoid putting too much pressure on the pedals and driving it into the sand. Next, aim for whatever negotiable rocky areas you can get to. These will give you more traction than the sand. If the sand is still getting you down, consider changing to a wider tire, like a 2.35-inch tread.

Finally, don't be too proud to walk. It's often impossible to restart in the sand after stopping, anyway.

Ride Information

📞 Trail Contacts:
Pima County Parks and Recreation Department, Tucson, AZ (520) 740–2690

🕐 Schedule:
Open year round

💲 Fees/Permits:
No fees or permits required

❓ Local Information:
Tucson Metropolitan Chamber of Commerce, Tucson, AZ (520) 792–1212 or *www.tucsonchamber.org* • **Metropolitan Tucson Convention & Visitors Bureau,** Tucson, Arizona (520)–624–1817 or 1–800–638–8350 or *www.visittucson.org*

🚌 Public Transportation:
Sun Tran, Tucson, AZ (520) 792–9222 or *www.suntran.com – Route 23 serves Kennedy Park on Mission Road, which is* adjacent to the southeast corner of Tucson Mountain Park

🎡 Local Events/Attractions:
Old Tucson Studios, Tucson, AZ (520) 883–0100 or *www.oldtucson.com - Take Speedway or Ajo Way west and follow the signs* • **Arizona-Sonora Desert Museum,** Tucson, AZ (520) 883–1380 or *www.desertmuseum.org – Like Old Tucson Studios, this world-famous zoo, botanical garden, and museum resides in Tucson Mountain Park.*

🚲 Local Bike Shops:
Full Spectrum Schwinn Cycling & Fitness, Tucson, Arizona (520) 327–3232 • **Arizona Bicycle Experts** (ABE), Tucson, AZ (520) 881–2279

🗺 Maps:
USGS maps: Cat Mountain, AZ; Brown Mountain, AZ; Jaynes, AZ; Avra, AZ

Chiva Falls

Ride Specs

Start: From the parking lot across from the cattle tanks, about 4.5 miles up Redington Road after it turns to dirt
Length: 7.8-mile out-and-back
Approximate Riding Time: 1-2 hours
Difficulty Rating: Physically moderate with some very difficult, dangerous technical sections. A couple hike-a-bike sections that are too hard to climb but fun to bomb down
Trail Surface: Mixed doubletrack and singletrack
Lay of the Land: High Sonoran desert, with mesquite and cottonwoods. The Rincon Mountains are rockier and lower than the Santa Catalinas to the north, and feature a lot more sun exposure during long portions of the ride.
Elevation Gain: 1,005 feet
Land Status: National park
Nearest City: Tucson
Other Trail Users: ATV, motorcycle, and equestrians
Canine Compatibility: Dogs permitted
Wheels: Full suspension recommended

Getting There

From Tucson: From downtown Tucson, take Tanque Verde east until it becomes Redington Road. As Redington Road heads up into the Rincon Mountains, it's surface changes to dirt. Travel up this dirt road for about 4.5 miles *[Note. This is best done in a vehicle with high clearance, although cars can make it without too much trouble]*, until you cross over a cattle guard. A green-painted metal corral is to your left, and parking is to the right. Park here. ***DeLorme: Arizona Atlas & Gazetteer:*** Page 67 D6

T he Rincon Mountains rise over Tucson's easternmost marches. Not as well publicized as the impressive Catalina Mountains to the north, the Rincons are a rolling, rugged range laced with a network of roads, trails, and rocky singletrack.

Most of the Rincon Mountains are part of the Rincon Mountain District, and all of the mountains are part of Coronado National Park (which also includes the Santa Catalina Mountains on the north side of town; check out the *Butterfly/Crystal Spring* trail elsewhere in this region: *see Ride 26: Mt. Lemmon Top to Bottom*).

Much of the Rincons have been designated wilderness, and with good reason: The amount and variety of plant life present in the mountains is mind-boggling, with more than 900 plant species identified to date in the 98,520-acre wilderness, established back in 1984. The base of the wilderness is a desert scrub community consisting of vast Saguaro cactus forests, colla, prickly pear cactus, ocotillo, mesquite, and paloverde. At the highest reaches of the Rincons, ponderosa pine and Douglas firs

create a cool, moist forest. The wilderness offers examples of every life zone from Lower Sonoran to Canadian.

The Rincon Mountain Wilderness encompasses most of the southern and eastern portions of the range and surround three sides of the Saguaro National Monument, where bikes are not allowed.

The Chiva Falls route passes through many of the Rincon's life zones while threading down from Redington Road into the valleys of the Rincons. Atop Redington Road, expect high winds year round; by the time this route has dropped a few hundred feet into Tanque Verde Canyon those winds become relatively nonexistent. The mountain bike trails, north of the wilderness area, are at the 4,000-foot level, populated mostly by lone junipers and shrub live oaks. This area has been used for cattle ranching for more than a century, and you may still see cattle in the distance—and on the trail! Approach slowly and the cattle will usually move out of the way. If there's a bull or calves in the herd, don't do anything to upset either of them because the whole herd will start a fight. Wait for them to leave or simply turn around.

The highlight of the trail is a short hike at the far end of the trail to Chiva Falls itself, a sometimes-magnificent waterfall more than a hundred feet high. The fall is little more than a drizzle in the winter, but during the summer monsoons and spring thaw they really open up.

Riding in the Rincons can be dangerous in the summer, because the area is mostly exposed and nearly as hot as Tucson itself. If visitors want to see the falls, leave very early in the morning to avoid the hottest part of the day. You might get lucky and catch the waterfall in full form during the winter as well, if it's a wet season and not a white one (rare but not unheard of in Tucson). If this is the case, riding in the Rincons is quite a bit safer and less exposed. Still, be sure to bring plenty of water—you're a long way from civilization.

Redington Road is a primary access into the Rincon Mountains. Originally a Pony Express route linking Tucson to the towns of Redington and Mammoth, and ultimately Globe, Redington Road is a fairly well-maintained dirt road that passes through the saddle between the highest portions of the Santa Catalinas and the Rincons.

Besides offering great mountain biking, the Rincons are also a favorite for off-road vehicle play, particularly motorcycles and Jeeps. Some of the major trails, such as the Chiva Falls route, are being eroded by this use. Watch out for sandy washouts in corners.

Ride Information

🕿 Trail Contacts:
Coronado National Forest, Santa Catalina Ranger District, Tucson, AZ (520) 749–8700 or *www.fs.fed.us/r3/coronado/scrd*

🕐 Schedule:
Open year-round

💲 Fees/Permits:
No Fee or permits required

❓ Local Information:
Metropolitan Tucson Convention & Visitors Bureau, Tucson, AZ 1–800–638–8350 or (520) 624–1817 or *www.visittucson.org*

📍 Local Events/Attractions:
El Tour de Tucson, the Saturday before Thanksgiving, Tuscon, AZ (520) 745–2033 – *111-mile roadbike race* • **Tucson Rodeo & La Fiesta de Los Vaqueros,** Late February, Tuscon, AZ (520) 741–2233 or *www.tucson rodeo.com*

🚴 Group Rides:
The Sonoran Desert Mountain Bicyclists

(SDMB), Tucson, AZ: *www.sdmb.org – holds regular group rides in the Redington Pass area and throughout metro Tucson* • **The Southern AZ Mountain Bike Association** (SAMBA), Tucson, AZ (520) 320–9195 – *also hosts group rides every weekend.*

🏢 Organizations:
Perimeter Bicycling Association of America, Inc. (520) 745–2033 – *As well as sponsoring the El Tour de Tucson, Perimeter organizes weely rides* • **Pima Trails Association,** Tucson, AZ (520) 577–7919 or *www.pimatrails.org*

🕮 Other Resources:
Southern Arizona Trails Resource Guide by John Dell and Steve Anderson (Pima Trails Association, 1998)

🚲 Local Bike Shops:
Sabino Cycles, Tucson, AZ (520) 885–3666

Ⓝ Maps:
USGS maps: Agua Caliente Hill, AZ; Piety Hill, AZ

MilesDirections

0.0 START from parking lot across Redington Road opposite the corrals. Look for the rocky descent heading northeast out of the parking lot. This is called "The Chute" and is how you begin your ride. *[Note. This can be a scary descent. Study it carefully the first time, or just walk it until you feel comfortable.]*

2.3 Pass a waterhole to your left (Chiva Tank). The doubletrack appears to go due east and a singletrack splits off to the right. Take either. These cues lead you along the singletrack that heads south toward the Rincon Mountains. *[Option. FS 4426 is the doubletrack that continues east. In about a quarter*

mile, FS 4417 will split to the left as FS 4426 turns and heads south. Take the south option and you'll rejoin the trail.]

2.6 Rejoin the doubletrack (FS 4426) you split from earlier. Cross over the cattleguard.

2.7 The singletrack comes to a fork. Turn right, down FS 4405 (marked with a metal sign).

3.6 The trail splits at the top of a technical little climb. Take the trail to the left continuing toward Chiva Falls. *[Option. The trail to the right is FS 4405, which climbs for less than a mile and then joins the extremely difficult FS 4426. The loop that goes northeast on FS*

4426 and passes above Chiva Falls is locally known as the High Chiva Loop.]

3.9 At the bottom of a descent, you'll enter a grove of trees. Take the higher trail, to the right, until you feel like you can't ride any further. This is the walking path back to Chiva Falls. Soak your feet (if there's water), and then turn back the way you came to the start of the ride.

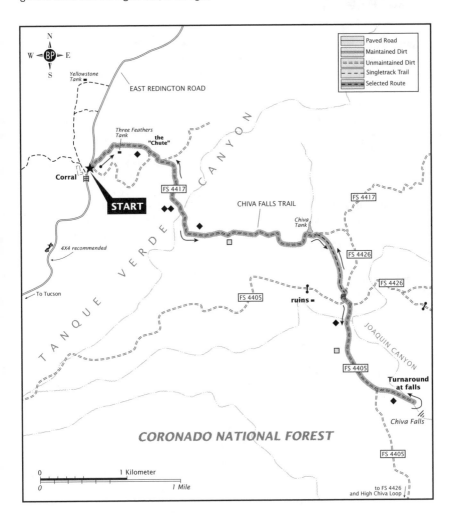

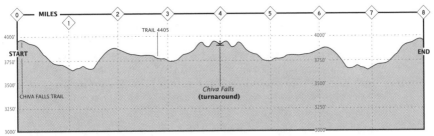

Mount Lemmon Top to Bottom

Ride Specs

Start: From the parking lot across from Crystal Springs trailhead on Oracle Control Road.
Length: 17.5-mile loop
Approximate Riding Time: 5-6 hours
Difficulty Rating: Somewhere between difficult and brutal. Seven miles and 3,000 feet of climbing, morale-bruising drop-offs, and hike-a-bikes abound
Trail Surface: Mixed pavement, dirt road, doubletrack, and singletrack
Lay of the Land: Everything from ponderosa pine forest to pine-oak woodland
Elevation Gain: 4,510 feet
Land Status: National forest
Nearest City: Tucson
Other Trail Users: Hikers
Canine Compatibility: Dogs permitted
Wheels: Full suspension strongly advised

Getting There

From Tucson: Take the Sky Island Parkway up toward Summerhaven. Around mile marker 23, you'll see a sign indicating the Oracle Control Road, also called FS 38, to your right. This is where the Summerhaven fire station is. Turn onto the Oracle Control Road and drive onto the graded dirt road. Drive about 2.9 miles, and keep a lookout for a metal Crystal Springs Trail trailhead sign on the right of the road. The sign is a little off the road, so go slowly. Parking for this trailhead is up an incline just *before* you get to the trailhead sign, so be prepared to back up a little the first time you go looking to park here. *[FYI. There's a tight dogleg in the road just past the parking area and the trailhead sign. If you find yourself making a switchback after about three and a half miles, you've gone too far.] **DeLorme: Arizona Atlas & Gazetteer:** Page 67 C5

The Santa Catalina Mountains, rising nearly 7,000 feet over the Sonoran Desert, have been a rich resource for human settlers for thousands of years. The Hohokam, and later the Apache, hunted and gathered food in the mountains. Later, Mexican and Anglo settlers established mines all over the range; "Buffalo Bill" Cody worked the mines near Oracle, on the western end of the range, until his death in 1917.

For outdoor enthusiasts, Mount Lemmon is the crown jewel of outdoor adventure in the Santa Catalina Mountains, just north of Tucson. The drive from the base of the mountain to the summit traverses seven of the world's nine life zones—it's like driving from Canada to Mexico in 20 minutes. The summit town of Summerhaven is cool in the summer and quite pleasant even into late fall. The Mount Lemmon Ski Valley, a couple miles up the road from Summerhaven, is a popular ski area during winters when there's snow.

Mount Lemmon is named in honor of botanist Sara Lemmon who, with her husband John, journeyed to the top of the Santa Catalinas during their honeymoon in 1881. Since then, Tucson residents have continued to escape the summer heat by traveling to the top of Mt. Lemmon. This journey was made easier at the turn of the twentieth century, back when the city was the state's largest community, and trails up

to the range's peaks continually improved. The highway to Summerhaven, built largely by federal prisoners, opened in 1949.

"Top to Bottom" is an amalgam of several challenging trails that takes cyclists from the very top of Mount Lemmon down 3,000 feet to the canyons and ridges of the lower Santa Catalinas. The topmost trail is called the Aspen Draw Trail, and descends alongside a ski slope near Ski Valley. The trail twists and turns as it quickly loses altitude, passing over slippery roots and around super-tight switchbacks the whole way. This is a very technically challenging trail, sure to amuse even the hardest-core trick riders. Watching an accomplished local rocket down Aspen Draw is a sight to behold.

The next section, down the Sky Island Parkway a short spell, is the Butterfly Trail, named after Butterfly Mountain within the Santa Catalinas. Butterfly Trail is less steep and stepped than Aspen Draw, but is longer and has more opportunities to go *too* fast. It's also a popular hiking trail, so check your speed and be mindful of other trail users.

The final portion of the ride is the Crystal Springs Trail, which crosses over a year-round spring and goes up and down several ridges. The turn onto Crystal Springs off the Butterfly Trail is easy to miss, so keep your eyes wide open for a trail marker just a couple miles down Butterfly Trail. Crystal Springs Trail repeatedly dives down into drainages against the mountain, and then climbs back out to wonderful overlooks with views eastward to the horizon. Much of this portion of the trail is very exposed, with long, steep drops to the cyclists' right. Near the end of the trail, you'll have to climb up a rocky waterfall (at Crystal Spring proper) to continue ahead. The good news is it's just a mile to the end of the trail after this climb.

Aspen Draw and Butterfly are well-traveled hiking trails all year long, but Crystal Spring—the most dangerous part of the ride—is quite remote. Cellular phone service is spotty at best, so take extra precautions to be as self-sufficient as possible (extra tubes, spokes, first aid kit, water, food, etc.).

As an added reminder: The Santa Catalinas are largely taken up by wilderness designation. As a rule of thumb, the trails to the east of Sky Island Parkway (to your right as you head up the mountain) are open to bikes, and the ones to the west (the left) are in the Pusch Ridge Wilderness and are closed to mountain bikes.

Mount Lemmon is a great biking resource, offering dozens of trails, in addition to the ones described here, which are open to bikes. Most of these trails are somewhat-to-very technical, and all of them require some amount of climbing.

MilesDirections

0.0 START across from the Crystal Springs trailhead on Oracle Control Road (a.k.a. the Old Mount Lemmon Road, a.k.a. FS 38). Start pedaling up the mountain. Take it easy—you've got a long, long climb ahead of you.

2.4 Reach a junction with Oracle Ridge Trail, behind you to the right as you cross over the cattleguard. Stay on Oracle Control Road. Keep going up.

2.9 Exit Oracle Control Road, turn right, and ride on the shoulder of a paved road into Summerhaven. This is your only downhill, so enjoy it.

3.9 Enter the town of Summerhaven. Look for Turkey Run Road, to your right. Turn right onto Turkey Run Road and head up, up, up. *[Option. Turkey Run Road will soon terminate, become doubletrack, and eventually become singletrack. The climb is somewhat difficult. For a longer, but paved and somewhat less difficult, version of this climb, turn right where the highway splits off to Summerhaven, and continue up to Ski Valley, and then past Ski Valley up to the top of the mountain. This route adds about*

half a mile, but the climb isn't so tough.]

4.3 The pavement ends; continue up the doubletrack.

4.4 Go around a gate. The trail shortly turns into singletrack. You're now on the Upper Sabino Canyon Trail. Still going up.

5.0 Reach a junction with Aspen Draw Trail, to your left. Go straight, toward the ski lift area ahead, and turn right. Head up the singletrack that parallels the paved road.

5.2 Reach the Ski Valley ski area. Lift your bike over the guardrail and continue up the paved road ahead.

7.0 Reach the top of Mount Lemmon. There are radio towers to your left and right. The singletrack to your right leads you onto the Meadow Trail, a very nice loop. However, you will be going to the left, toward the nearer radio towers.

7.2 Just as you pass the radio towers on your left, there will be a wide seating area and the top of the ski lift area. Look to your left for the

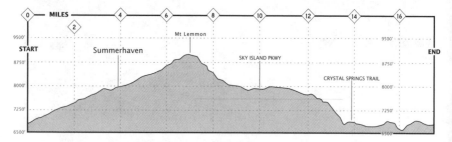

metal Forest Service sign indicating the top of the Aspen Draw Trail. Head down the trail. [**Note.** *Be careful that you do not go straight across the seating area and head down the south face of the mountain—it's wilderness area, and no bikes are allowed!*]

8.8 Reach the intersection with Upper Sabino Canyon Trail, where the Aspen Draw Trail ends. Turn right and head down the hill, back to Turkey Run Road and back into town.

10.0 Exit Turkey Run Road onto Sabino Canyon Road. Take a break in Summerhaven, or turn left and head back toward Sky Island Parkway.

12.8 Blast down Sky Island Parkway and look for the Butterfly Trail trailhead to your left. It's marked with a large trailhead sign on the high-

way. Mile marker 22.8. Go around the gate at the north end of the parking lot and head down the hill on the doubletrack. Stay left.

13.9 Reach a junction with Crystal Springs Trail. This is easy to miss—look for the metal sign. Turn left and hold onto your helmet!

17.5 Exit Crystal Springs Trail and ride onto Oracle Control Road. Your vehicle is hopefully still parked across the road.

The Tohono O'odham tribe's name for the Santa Catalinas is "Babad Do'ag," which means "Frog Mountain." If you use your imagination the mountain range, from downtown Tucson, looks like a giant frog.

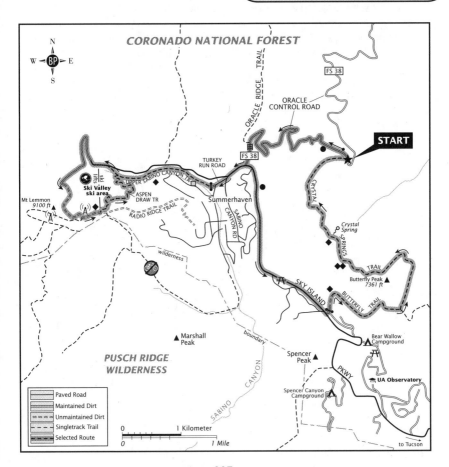

Ride Information

Trail Contacts:

Santa Catalina Ranger District, Coronado National Forest, Tucson, AZ (520) 749–8700 or *www.fs.fed.us/r3/corona-do/scrd/*

Schedule:

Open year round—*snows in January–March make this trail inaccessible.*

Fees/Permits:

$5 day pass to enter the Santa Catalina Mountains if you are stopping at vista points, restrooms, trailheads, undeveloped areas, parking areas, roadside pull offs, picnic areas, or campgrounds. If you park at the parking lot in Summerhaven or Ski Valley, there is no fee. You can also buy a weekly pass for $10, or an annual pass for $20.

Local Information:

www.mt-lemmon.com

Accommodations:

Cabins & Cookies, Mt. Lemmon, AZ (520) 576–1542 or *www.mt-lemmon.com/cabins.htm* • **Mt. Lemmon Summerhaven Suites,** Mt. Lemmon, AZ (520) 576–1542

Restaurants:

Mt. Lemmon Café, Summerhaven, AZ (520) 576–1234

Local Bike Shops:

Sabino Cycles, Tucson, AZ (520) 885–3666 – *Sabino Cycles is about a mile west of the Catalina Highway turnoff off Tanque Verde.*

Maps:

USGS maps: Mt. Lemmon, AZ and Mount Bigelow, AZ • *The Map: Trails of the Tucson Area* by Chris Guibert & Rob Reed, Arizona Mapping Kompany

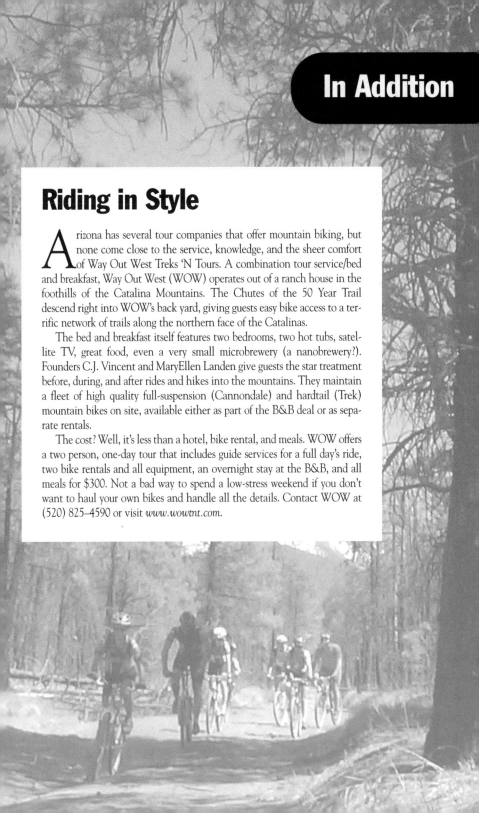

Riding in Style

Arizona has several tour companies that offer mountain biking, but none come close to the service, knowledge, and the sheer comfort of Way Out West Treks 'N Tours. A combination tour service/bed and breakfast, Way Out West (WOW) operates out of a ranch house in the foothills of the Catalina Mountains. The Chutes of the 50 Year Trail descend right into WOW's back yard, giving guests easy bike access to a terrific network of trails along the northern face of the Catalinas.

The bed and breakfast itself features two bedrooms, two hot tubs, satellite TV, great food, even a very small microbrewery (a nanobrewery?). Founders C.J. Vincent and MaryEllen Landen give guests the star treatment before, during, and after rides and hikes into the mountains. They maintain a fleet of high quality full-suspension (Cannondale) and hardtail (Trek) mountain bikes on site, available either as part of the B&B deal or as separate rentals.

The cost? Well, it's less than a hotel, bike rental, and meals. WOW offers a two person, one-day tour that includes guide services for a full day's ride, two bike rentals and all equipment, an overnight stay at the B&B, and all meals for $300. Not a bad way to spend a low-stress weekend if you don't want to haul your own bikes and handle all the details. Contact WOW at (520) 825–4590 or visit *www.wowtnt.com.*

50 Year Trail

Ride Specs

Start: There are a couple good starting points. Catalina State Park's equestrian center is a good jumping-off spot for the southernmost trails, while the end of Golder Ranch Road (just over the cattleguard after it turns to dirt) starts you out midway up the trail network, giving you quick access to The Chutes and other more technically interesting trails to the north.

Length: Varies depending on route taken

Approximate Riding Time: As long as you want to ride

Difficulty Rating: Varies from easy to difficult.

Trail Surface: Mixed singletrack, doubletrack, and a few dirt roads. There's some sand, some sharp rocks, and lots of opportunities to roll over fallen cacti. Bring sealed or thorn-resistant tires.

Lay of the Land: Sonoran desert uplands

Land Status: State trust and state park lands

Nearest Town: Oro Valley

Other Trail Users: Hikers and equestrians

Canine Compatibility: Dogs permitted

Wheels: Hardtail okay, full suspension recommended

Getting There

From Tucson: Head north on Oracle Road (AZ 77) to the turnoff to Catalina State Park, about five miles north of Oro Valley. The turnoff is to the right (east) toward the Catalina Mountains, and is marked with an unmistakable brown recreation sign. Follow the signs in to the equestrian center and park there.

For a shorter ride and more immediate access to the best trails, continue north—instead of turning in to Catalina State Park—on AZ 77 to Golder Ranch Road, another two miles north of the Catalina State Park entrance. There's a Texaco and a stoplight at the turn. Turn right on Golder Ranch Road and drive in three miles. At the top of the hill, the road crosses over a cattleguard and turns to dirt. There's a convenient parking area just inside the fence. Park here; the 50 Year Trail passes through here and is prominently marked with signs. *DeLorme: Arizona Atlas & Gazetteer:* Page 67 C4

The 50 Year Trail is called such because the area is on a 50-year public lease for bikers, equestrians, and hikers. This means that the annual recreation pass fee of $15 normally required to access state land is waived in this area through 2039. Only half the 50 Year Trail is on state land—about halfway through, the trail passes through a gate, and you find yourself in Catalina State Park. The park does not have an entry fee if you enter by bike; it's $3 if you drive in by car. The 50 Year Trail itself follows an old horse trail once commonly used by the local ranchers. The trail is generally sandy, but well packed, and follows a fairly easy grade either north or south.

The state trust land upon which the 50 Year Trail resides is historic ranching property that has been worked for more than a century. But the land around Oracle has another, more peculiar history. UFOlogist and fringe scientist Wilhelm Reich claims to have fought a "galactic Valley Forge" with flying saucers over the skies of Oracle in 1954. In his final book, *Contact With Space*, Reich recounts using "orgone"—ambi-

ent life energy he claimed to have found and harnessed—to interfere with the flying saucers as they flew over the Catalina foothills. Reich, convinced the aliens were waging their "war" against Earth by poisoning its orgone and creating deserts, decided to test his orgone-powered spacegun in the drought-wracked wastelands north of Tucson. According to *Contact With Space*, it had not rained in Tucson for five years, making the desert a perfect proving ground for both orgone's rainmaking and UFO-weakening abilities. Reich claims to have both defeated the marauding aliens as well as bringing rain to the desert and transforming the Oracle area into a verdant valley.

UFO sightings aside, the northern foothills of the Santa Catalinas are a bird-watching paradise. Any given morning will bring roadrunners, quail, red tailed hawks, gray cardinals, red cardinals, woodpeckers, Harris hawks...more than 100 species of birds are abundant in the area. One notable bird in the area is the endangered Cactus ferruginous pygmy-owl; in 1998, only 32 pygmy-owls were found in southern Arizona. The once common owl, measuring only seven inches from beak to tail and the second smallest owl in North America, is on the verge of extinction in Arizona because it is losing its nesting habitat, the saguaro cactus. Although cacti are seemingly plentiful around Tucson, pygmy-owls get out-competed by other animals that nest in the cacti's cavities, such as Gila woodpeckers and the non-native European starling. Now that pygmy-owls are on the endangered list, permits for new developments around Tucson have slowed until a regional study is completed to determine the impact on these owls and other endangered species.

Sky Islands

The various mountains that spring up from the Sonoran Desert throughout Southern Arizona are known as "Sky Islands," because they are large enough to have their own high-altitude eco-systems and separated from one another by a gulf of open desert. The Santa Catalina Mountains are one such island. The various districts of the Coronado National Forest are each their own Sky Island, and each has a slightly different, but distinct, set of species of birds and other wildlife. Threats to these distinct micro-species, such as the Mt. Graham red squirrel, have halted major developments in these areas.

Besides birds, the 50 Year Trail area is also home to javelina, coyote, gila monsters, bobcats, deer, mountain lions, and the ubiquitous cattle that graze the state lands. This trail presents an incredibly lush version of the Arizona Uplands of the Sonoran Desert, a transitional zone just a few hundred feet below the tree line.

Ride Information

◐ Trail Contacts:
Arizona State Land Department, Tucson, AZ (520) 628–5480 or *www.land.state.az.us*

◐ Schedule:
Open year round – *low desert gets dangerously hot in the summer, so plan accordingly*

Ⓢ Fees/Permits:
There are no fees or permits required to ride the 50 Year Trail, but an annual $15 recreation permit is required from the State Trust Land department if you want to explore some of the spur trails. Also, there's a $3 fee if you enter Catalina State Park by car.

◉ Local Information:
Town of Oro Valley, Oro Valley, AZ: *www.ci.oro-valley.az.us* • **Northwest Pima County Chamber of Commerce,** Tucson, AZ (520) 297–2191 or *www.the-chamber.com*

◉ Local Events/Attractions:
Great Pumpkin Fat Tire Race and Festival, Catalina State Park – *held in late October; contact SAMBA, Tucson, AZ (520) 320–9195 for more information*

◉ Accommodations:
Way Out West Trailside B&B, Tucson, Arizona (520) 907–TREK or *www.wowt-nt.com – This charming bed & breakfast, run by CJ Vincent and MaryEllen Landen, is right in the middle of the Catalina foothills. Accommodations include hot tubs and a continental breakfast. For not much more than the cost of a simple* rental, *you can take one of their high-performance full-suspension rigs and be guided by CJ on a journey calibrated to your skill and fitness level.*

◉ Group Rides:
The Sonoran Desert Mountain Bicyclists (SDMB), Tucson, AZ: *www.sdmb.org – holds regular group rides on the 50 Year Trail and throughout the metro Tucson area* • **The Southern Arizona Mountain Bike Association** (SAMBA), Tucson, AZ (520) 320–9195 – *also hosts group rides every weekend*

◉ Mountain Bike Tours:
Way Out West Treks & Tours (see Accommodations)

◉ Organizations:
Pima Trails Association, Tucson, AZ (520) 577–7919

◉ Other Resources:
Catalina State Park websites: *www.pr.state.az.us/parkhtml/catalina.html* and *www.desertusa.com/azcatalina/azcatalina.html*

◉ Local Bike Shops:
R&R Oracle Road Schwinn Bicycle, Tucson, AZ (520) 575–5594 – *This well-equipped full-service bike shop is about 12 miles away from the 50 Year Trail trailhead, next door to Fry's, at the southwest corner of Magee and Oracle Road in far-northern Tucson.*

Ⓝ Maps:
USGS maps: Oro Valley, AZ, Oracle Junction, AZ, and Oracle, AZ

MilesDirections

The 50 Year Trail area is an extensive network of horse trails, old ranch roads, and game trails that have evolved into singletrack. There's no specific route to be followed here, but there are three noteworthy areas to explore. Throughout all areas, the 50 Year Trail is well marked with Forest Service signs at every turnoff. You can't get lost if you follow the signs.

Catalina State Park is the southernmost reach of the 50 Year Trail. Starting from the equestrian center at the farthest southern end of the trail (see map), the 50 Year Trail climbs up a sandy hill and begins a long ascent toward the foothills of the Catalina Mountains. You'll pass through a gate to get out of the park; once past the gate, you're on Arizona State Trust land.

The southern half of the 50 Year Trail is generally flat and fast, with a few rock gardens and a slight incline as you head north. If you plan on riding the 50 Year Trail from Catalina State Park to the other end, north of The Chutes (see below), and back, it's about 17 miles total; allow 2–3 hours for this ride.

The Chutes are a collection of super-fast whoop-de-dos and, well, chutes, at the far northern end of the riding area. The Chutes themselves all descend sharply out of the foothills and end up onto the shores of the Canada del Oro, a stream that often has water in it. During the spring, the Canada del Oro can get quite high, although not dangerous for portaging your bike across.

The 50 Year Trail continues north through the Chutes and ends at a Forest Service gate. Through the gate, the Upper 50 Year Trail continues and loops around to connect to the Deer Camp Loop. Be warned: The Upper 50 is a *hard* trail, both technically and aerobically. The Deer Camp Loop (reachable by heading east away from the Chutes) is a very cool, sometimes difficult, but always fun series of super-steep climbs and descents featuring lots of water crossings and shade—a must-ride when it gets warm. A popular route is to park at Golder Ranch Road, head north on the 50 Year Trail, turn onto the Deer Camp Loop (just south of The Chutes), loop around to The Cottonwoods, and follow the 50 Year Trail signs back to Golder Ranch Road. This route is about 10 miles and can be ridden in about 2–2.5 hours (you may have to hike a bit of the Deer Camp Loop).

Finally, there's the Baby Jesus Trail. It's hard. It's really hard. Pick a definition of "difficult" and the Baby Jesus Trail fulfills it. For starters, trail finding is often difficult along the Baby Jesus Trail because it so rarely receives any sort of maintenance. Second, it's technically hard because it's an amazingly steep grind up to the top—and God forbid you try to descend FS 636 at the end of the trail, which is one of the rockiest, most dangerous "jeep roads" you'll ever experience. In every measure, Baby Jesus Trail is brutal. Great news if you're into that sort of thing.

To get to the start of the Baby Jesus Trail, find your way to the grove of cottonwoods along the Sutherland Wash (see the map) and head south on the main road through the cottonwoods. Where the road crosses the wash, the Baby Jesus Trail splits off to the left while the road continues to the right. Give yourself 4–6 hours to ride all of the Baby Jesus Trail (16 miles), generally started from the Golder Ranch Road lot and heading down toward The Cottonwoods.

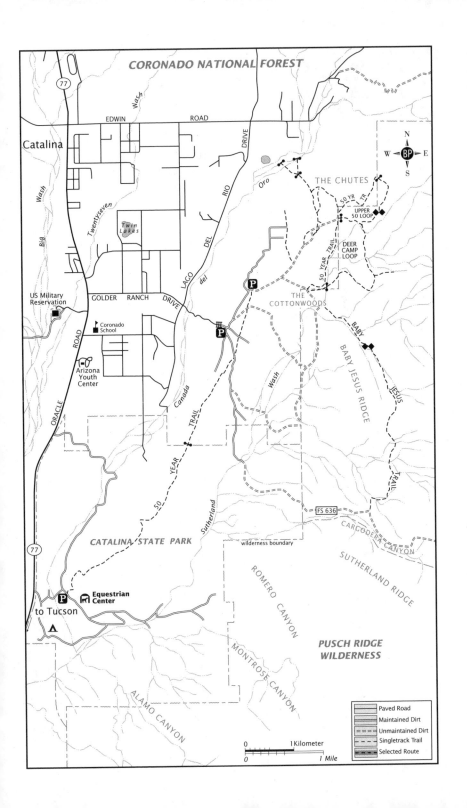

CORONADO NATIONAL FOREST

77

Catalina

EDWIN ROAD

RIO DEL DRIVE

Oro

Wash

Wash

Twentyseven

Twin Lakes

Big Wash

US Military Reservation

GOLDER RANCH DRIVE

LAGO del

Coronado School

Arizona Youth Center

ORACLE ROAD

Canada

TRAIL

50 YEAR

Sutherland

THE CHUTES

BP

N
W   E
S

50 YR TR

UPPER 50 LOOP

DEER CAMP LOOP

50 YEAR TRAIL

P

THE COTTONWOODS

Wash

BABY JESUS RIDGE

BABY JESUS TRAIL

FS 636

CARGODERA CANYON

SUTHERLAND RIDGE

CATALINA STATE PARK

wilderness boundary

77

P   Equestrian Center

to Tucson

ROMERO CANYON

MONTROSE CANYON

ALAMO CANYON

PUSCH RIDGE WILDERNESS

0   1 Kilometer
0   1 Mile

Paved Road
Maintained Dirt
Unmaintained Dirt
Singletrack Trail
Selected Route

The Tortolitas

Ride Specs

Start: From the parking area off Rail X Ranch Road

Length: 8.6-mile out-and-back

Approximate Riding Time: 1.5 hours

Difficulty Rating: Physically and technically easy, with some moderately difficult hills and sandy washes. Trail finding can be challenging, although you're never in much danger of getting lost.

Trail Surface: Doubletrack

Lay of the Land: Low Sonoran desert

Elevation Gain: 948 feet

Land Status: State land

Nearest Town: Catalina

Other Trail Users: Off-road vehicles, equestrians, and hunters

Canine Compatibility: Dogs permitted

Wheels: No suspension required; anything from hardtail to hybrid should be fine

Getting There

From Tucson: Take Oracle Road (AZ 77) north past the town of Catalina to Pinto Lane. Turn left (west) on Rail X Ranch Road – look for a sign just past Sanchez Nursery & Irrigation Supply. Set your vehicle's odometer as you cross over the cattle guard. At 4.2 miles, there is a parking area (well, a wide spot next to the road) to the left (south) of Rail X Ranch Road. It's unmarked; look for doubletrack on the north side of Rail X Ranch Road directly opposite the parking area. *DeLorme: Arizona Atlas & Gazetteer:* Page 67 B4

State land in Arizona, which requires a $15 annual recreation pass in order to ride here, often hides great mountain biking gems. The Tortolita Mountains, nestled in the space between Oracle Road (FS 77) and I-10 heading north out of Tucson, is one such secret.

The Tortolitas have been ranched for a hundred years. While much of the ranching has disappeared, the Martin Ranch Company still operates near the Tortolitas although Rail X Ranch, the namesake of the road that accesses the Tortolitas, is defunct.

Today, the fate of the Tortolita Mountains is uncertain. Development continues encroaching on the south side of the mountains. Meanwhile, much of the range is planned to become Tortolita Mountain Park, a 21,000-acre county park accessible from both the town of Oro Valley and metro Tucson. The park's master plan, adopted in 1997 by the Pima County Board of Supervisors, overlaps planned golf courses, resorts, and housing developments. Because of strong pro-development sentiments in local government, plans for the park are uncertain at best. Preservation in the Tortolitas is further complicated because much of the range is in Pinal County, which has to coordinate its efforts with Pima County if the entire range is to be protected. To date, Pima County owns less than 3,500 acres of the planned park area; more than half of the master plan is on Arizona State Trust land and continues to be available for development. Explore the Tortolitas while you still can.

The ride through the Tortolitas goes entirely through State Trust holdings. There are a few private acres here and there in the Tortolitas, generally ranches—both abandoned and operating—but they're not well documented. This ride climbs to the top of a saddle overlooking several private areas; for those wanting to go down the other side of the saddle and explore the inner reaches of the mountain range, be aware that parts of the trail may cross private property. Look for and respect "No Trespassing" signs, especially at cattleguard crossings.

The best time to enjoy this seldom-visited range is fall through spring; the summertime temperatures are no better here than in downtown Tucson. Expect summer temperatures to sit in the high 90s, and consistently break 100 degrees. And because the Tortolitas are a very open stretch of desert, not unlike Tucson Mountain Park (see Ride 24: Starr Pass–Yetman Wash), the summer sun is brutal.

From the top of the climb that marks the halfway point of this ride, cyclists can see many different mountain ranges rising from the flat desert. Look for the Picacho Mountains to the northwest, the Tortilla Mountains to the north, the Galiuro Mountains to the northeast, the Silver Bell Mountains to the west, and of course the mighty Santa Catalinas to the southwest.

MilesDirections

0.0 START from parking area just off Rail X Ranch Road, 4.2 miles from the Oracle Road turnoff.

0.2 After passing through some sandy washes, you'll reach a T-intersection in the road. Turn left, toward the foothills of the Tortolita Mountains.

0.6 Enter a three-way intersection. Some narrow, unmaintained doubletrack heads off to the left. Stay forward and slightly to the right, around a little island of cactuses.

1.5 Cross over a cattle guard. To the left, you can see the remains of the Black Tank Corrals, which were part of the old Rail X Ranch.

1.7 Cross over another cattle guard.

2.1 The doubletrack comes to a fork. Take the right fork.

2.8 Join with Cochie Springs Road, a doubletrack. Turn left and head toward the hills.

2.9 A doubletrack joins in from the right. Continue straight ahead toward the hills.

3.2 The trail intersects with a wash going left and right. Turn left, continuing toward the hills.

4.3 Reach the top of a big climb. The trail splits left and right. Turn right toward a rocky rest area with views of several mountain ranges. This is the turnaround spot. Retrace your steps back to the starting area and Rail X Ranch Road.

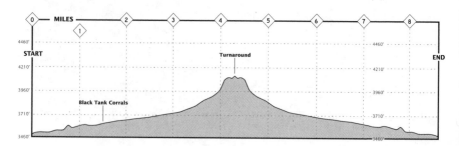

Foliage in the low Sonoran desert includes mesquite, cholla, prickly pear and saguaro cacti, and the dreaded hackberry bush. Avoid falling anywhere near the hackberry, which is covered with sharp little claws and hooks. Because the Tortolitas are still quite untouched, visitors may also see a remarkable array of wildlife: hawks, mountain lions, and even a herd of feral horses, which has been spotted in the park.

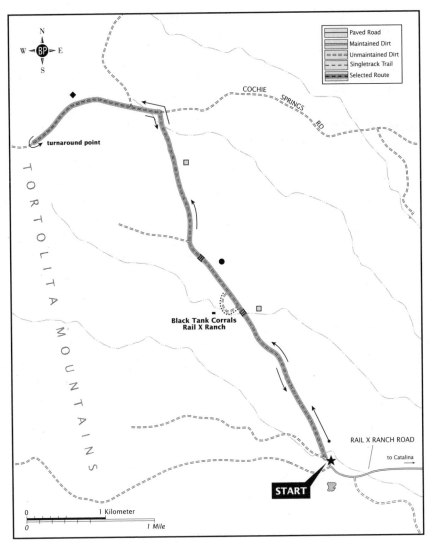

Ride Information

📞 Trail Contacts:

Arizona State Land Department, Tucson, AZ (520) 628-5480 or *www.land.state.az.us*

🕐 Schedule:

Open year round – *but watch out for summer temperatures!*

💲 Fees/Permits:

$15 annual recreation pass required

❓ Local Information:

Town of Oro Valley, Oro Valley: *www.ci.orovalley.az.us/HOME/* • **Greater Oro Valley Chamber of Commerce,** Tucson, AZ: *www.arizonaguide.com/cities/orovalley*

💡 Local Events/Attractions:

Biosphere 2, Oracle, AZ (520) 896-6400 or *www.bio2.com* – *This controversial experiment in creating a sealed, self-sustaining living space was opened to the public several years ago. You can now explore inside the quarters of the original scientists, who locked themselves inside Biosphere 2 for two years. Biosphere 2 also recently added a space observatory to its facility* • **Oracle** (520) 896-6400 or *www.bio2.com*

🍴 Restaurants:

Mi Tierra Restaurant, Catalina, AZ (520) 825-3040

🔧 Local Bike Shops:

R&R Bicycles: Oracle Road Schwinn Bicycle, Tucson, Arizona (520) 575-5594

🧭 Maps:

USGS maps: Tortolita Mountains, AZ; Oracle Junction, AZ

State Land Recreation Permits

The State Land Trust, a management agency charged with getting top dollar for this land through leases and sales, ties up almost ten million acres of Arizona's land. State Trust profits go into Arizona's public education system and 13 other beneficiaries.

Most state land is already leased to ranchers, farmers, and miners to create an ongoing income for both the state and the leaseholder. However, it is still publicly owned and, in most cases, mountain bikers and other recreational users can enter this leased land. If you ride on state land, keep in mind that someone is trying to make a living there. Leave gates the way you find them, camp away from established watering places, stay on established roadways, and obey all posted signs.

To legally ride on state land, you must have either a hunting/fishing license, or a recreation permit. Individual recreation permits cost $15 and family permits cost $20. Both are good for one year from the date of purchase. To get a permit in person, you have to go to the State Land Department at 1616 West Adams in Phoenix. You can also get a permit by phone, by calling (602) 542–4631.

Not all state land is open for public use, even with a recreation pass or hunting license in hand. State land on military bases, and land closed for public safety purposes, is always closed to recreational activities. Not all activities are allowed with a pass either: Paintball, fireworks, extended camping, archaeological digging, metal detecting, and removing/harvesting natural products are strictly prohibited.

Not sure if you're riding on state land? Big "State Land: No Trespassing" signs are a good first hint. Check out the *DeLorme: Arizona Atlas & Gazetteer* for more information.

Cobre Ridge

Ride Specs

Start: From the parking area on FS 39 (Ruby Road) heading south out of Arivaca, just past FS 217

Length: 14-mile loop

Approximate Riding Time: 2–3 hours

Difficulty Rating: Physically and technically moderate, due to some long climbs and a couple sketchy descents. The greatest risks on this ride are the great distances you are from help if you get in trouble. You'll more likely get found by illegal immigrants or coyotes before other trail users. Don't travel this trail by yourself, and make sure somebody knows where you are before you leave.

Trail Surface: Doubletrack

Lay of the Land: High Sonoran desert and grasslands

Elevation Gain: 2,064 feet

Land Status: National forest

Nearest City: Tucson

Other Trail Users: Equestrians, hunters, and off-road vehicles

Canine Compatibility: Dogs permitted, except during the hunting season

Wheels: Hardtail

Getting There

From Tucson: Head south on I-19 about 25 miles to Arivaca Junction. Take Exit 48 at Arivaca Junction and head west on Arivaca Road. *[FYI. Look for the Cow Palace, an old restaurant with enormous steer horns. Arivaca Road passes between the Amado Market and the Amado Giftshop, directly across from the Cow Palace.]* Travel along Arivaca Road for 23 miles to the town of Arivaca. Once in Arivaca, the Arivaca Road comes to a fork. Go left at the fork onto FS 39 (Ruby Road), following the brown Forest Service road sign that reads "To Arivaca Lake." Drive about 12 miles on FS 39, which eventually changes to a washboarded gravel surface. After crossing over two cattleguards you'll enter the Coronado National Forest; look for the big brown sign. Turn right (south) on FS 217, just past a marker for FS 39. Park under the trees. ***DeLorme: Arizona Atlas & Gazetteer:*** Page 72 D3

W ay, way south, just minutes north of the Mexican border, there's an endless maze of old mining roads, active and inactive mines, and ghost towns from the days before our national borders were so well defended. A hundred years ago, travelers would never have known when they had left Arizona and entered Mexico. Today, armed Border Patrol officers touring the length of the border will let everyone know when they've strayed too far—especially along Cobre Ridge.

Coronado National Forest is a fragmented forest, each fragment corresponding to one of the many "sky island" mountain ranges of southern Arizona. The mountains just west of Nogales, comprised of the Pajaritos, the Atascosas, and Cobre Ridge, have been home to countless mines over the past century and a half. One of the most significant mines in the area was the Montana Mine, which was started in the 1870s and became a boom by 1910. The nearby Montana Camp became the town of Ruby, named after the postmaster's wife.

Ruby is now a crumbling ghost town, a collection of adobe walls, rusted tin roofs, and collapsing wood frames. The ghost town was purchased in 1961 by investors who had an eye on the excellent fishing ponds on the property. Ruby was named to the National Historic Register in 1975, and is now slowly being renovated as a tourist attraction. A tour of the town costs $12, and the caretaker is very protective of "his" town. He's been known to threaten trespassers—including those who didn't know they were trespassing—with a shotgun. Is the tour worth $12? Maybe. Not being peppered with birdshot? Priceless.

The ride through this portion of Coronado National Forest is as much a history lesson as it is a great bike ride in a little-used corner of the state. The forest roads once served the many small mines scattered throughout the mountain range—they still serve some mines, in fact, as squatters have claimed several mined-out holes throughout the area as their own. At about four miles into the ride, the trailer homes of these latter-day prospectors can be seen camped on the side of the road.

While it's all doubletrack, some of the downhills throughout the ride are fairly rugged and long. Don't let your speed get away from you: You're far away from everything in this corner of the state. There's no cell phone service, no water, and not much to eat that won't want to eat you first.

Just past 10 miles, before the trail rejoins Ruby Road, there is a massive dam built into a gulch to the right. The dam is one of three built in the 1920s (this one's dated 1928) that created reservoirs to provide water to the mines. Nobody swam in or drank from these reservoirs when the mine was in operation, because the miners dumped the tailings directly into the water.

At about 4,500 feet, the Cobre Ridge ride is a great escape from the summer heat in Tucson, but in the summer it's dry, hot, and very isolated. By contrast, most winters bring random rainstorms and running water across the ride's many washes. That makes the spring and fall as ideal times to ride here.

MilesDirections

0.0 START from the parking area off FS 39 and ride south along FS 217 (Warsaw Canyon Road).

2.7 Cross over a cattleguard.

3.5 FS 217 splits just past Warsaw Tank. Bear to the left, staying on FS 217. There will be a Forest Service sign indicating the road number.

4.9 Look for ruins of an old smelter to your left down in Warsaw Gulch.

5.1 Reach a crossroads with Company Gulch Road. Stay on the main road (FS 217) and pass straight through the crossing. As you come down the hill at the crossroads, you'll look down into California Gulch.

6.4 FS 217 splits at the bottom of a downhill and comes to a fork; take the left fork, continuing on FS 217.

6.6 Cross a cattleguard.

7.3 The road splits; stay to the left, on FS 217. The road is marked with a Forest Service road sign.

8.6 Join with Company Gulch Road. Continue ahead on the marked doubletrack.

8.8 A road to your left goes up to the Oro Blanco Mine. Continue ahead and over the yellow cattleguard.

10.1 The road forks. Turn left.

10.2 Reach a crossroads. To the left is FS 4162. Turn right, continuing on FS 217. *[Side-trip. FS 4161 is straight ahead—there's a difficult climb along this road, but it'll take you back to Ruby Road nonetheless.]*

11.1 To your right you'll come across an old dam. Continue around the bend.

12.5 Rejoin with Ruby Road. Turn left (west) on Ruby Road (FS 39).

14.0 Come down the hill and over the cattleguard. Your car should be on your left.

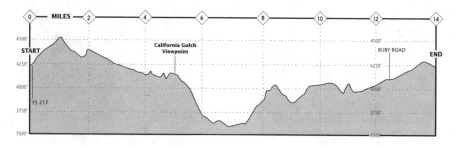

224

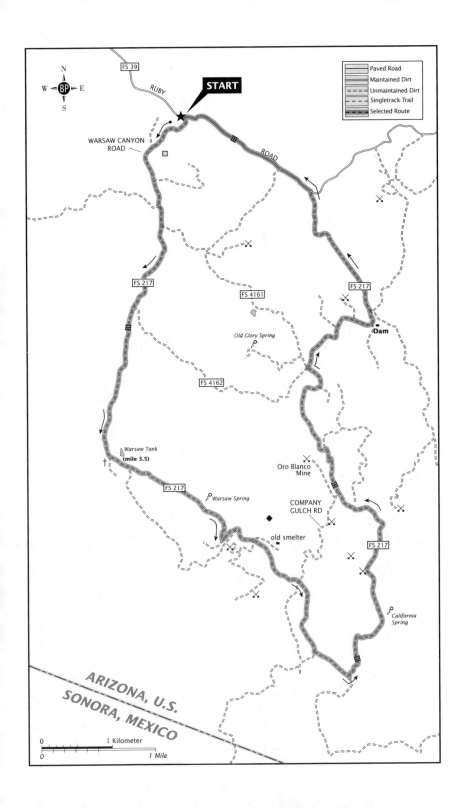

Baboquivari

In the Tohono O'odham creation story, the reproductive powers of the universe gave birth to the Papagueria (the Papago Indians) and the world thanks to I'itoi, the god who was born in Wawkiwalik, or Baboquivari Peak. The peak is the navel of the world, the opening in the earth from which the tribe emerged after the world flood. This incredibly tall, steep finger of rock continues to be a focal point of contemporary Tohono O'Odham religious practice. Baboquivari Peak is visible from the road to Arivaca, en route to the Cobre Ridge ride. Look for the looming, dark peak due west.

Baboquivari Peak is the only major peak in Arizona that requires technical climbing ability to reach its summit. It's also the only climb with grade 6 aid routes in the entire state.

Although Baboquivari is a sacred site, it is available for climbing. For more information about access and directions, contact the Bureau of Land Management Tucson Field Office at (520) 722–4289.

Ride Information

📞 Trail Contacts:

Coronado National Forest, Nogales, Arizona (520) 281–2296 or *http:// www.gorp.com/gorp/resource/ US_National_Forest/az_coron.HTM*

🕐 Schedule:

Open year round

💲 Fees/Permits:

None for the ride. $12 for a tour of Ruby

❓ Local Information:

Tubac Chamber of Commerce: (520) 398–2704 or *www.tubacaz.com*

👁 Local Events/Attractions:

Ghost Town of Ruby – *about 8 miles west of the trailhead, on Ruby Road headed toward I-19; $12 per person, $8 per person in groups of 12 or more* • **Tumacacori National Historic Park,** Tumacacori, AZ (520) 398–2341 – *A stone's throw from Tubac, the Tumacacori National Historic Park preserves the ruins of three early Spanish colonial missions on 47 acres. The oldest and best preserved of the three, San Jose de Tumacacori, was built on the site of a Pima Indian village.*

🆖 Maps:

USGS maps: Bartlett Mountain, AZ; Ruby, AZ

Gold Country

Ride Specs

Start: From the parking lot at the end of Gardner Canyon Road (FS 92)

Length: 18.5-mile loop, with out-and-back spurs

Approximate Riding Time: 3 hours

Difficulty Rating: Moderate due to altitude and overall technical difficulty, with some technically tricky passages and one hike-a-bike ascent (and possible descent, depending on your skills)

Trail Surface: Mixed jeep road, doubletrack, and singletrack.

Lay of the Land: High desert chaparral; grassy plains dotted by juniper and mesquite

Elevation Gain: 2,045 feet

Land Status: National forest

Nearest City: Tucson

Other Trail Users: Hikers, equestrians, and off-road vehicles (only on dirt roads)

Canine Compatibility: Dogs permitted, but not recommended because of the length of the trail

Wheels: Front suspension is advised

Getting There

From Tucson: Take I-10 south (toward El Paso) to the AZ 83 junction (Exit 281) going south (toward Sonoita), about 10 miles past the city limits. About 22 miles south of the I-10/AZ 83 junction you'll see a sign for Gardner Canyon Road (FS 92) to your right. Turn here and drive onto the dirt road. Head straight down this road, making no turns. At 4.4 miles down the dirt road, you'll see a sign that says "Apache Springs Ranch" and "Gardner Canyon Road;" follow the right-pointing arrow for Gardner Canyon Road. Just past that sign, you'll see another sign pointing to four different trailheads. Follow the forward-pointing arrow for Gardner Canyon Road along the clearly established dirt road; don't make any turns onto forest roads. Five and a half miles down Gardner Canyon Road you'll reach a large, obvious parking area. There are several new signs at one end of the parking area describing the Santa Rita trail system, and the Arizona Trail in particular. Park anywhere and disembark. *DeLorme: Arizona Atlas & Gazetteer:* Page 73 C5

South of Tucson, the Santa Rita Mountains rise from the desert like the other "sky islands" of the Coronado National Forest. This range separates Tucson from the rest of southern Arizona, and historic old towns like Patagonia, Sonoita (the center of Arizona's small "wine country"), and Tumacacori dot the foothills and savannahs of the Santa Ritas.

The tallest peak in the Santa Ritas is Mt. Wrightson, also known as Old Baldy because its peak is devoid of tree cover. At 9,453 feet, it's actually a little higher than Mt. Lemmon in the Santa Catalinas, north of Tucson. The Super and Old Baldy hiking trails provide access through the wilderness area and up to the Mt. Wrightson's peak. Because of its great height, weather can change unexpectedly on Mt. Wrightson; as one example in 1958 three Boy Scouts died at Josephine Saddle, en route to the top of Mt. Wrightson, during a sudden snowstorm.

The first singletrack arm of the trail is part of the Arizona Trail, and follows along and within the bed of an old aqueduct. This aqueduct, designed and built by James Stetson in 1903, was the linchpin of the Kentucky Camp mining operation. Until

the aqueduct was created, Kentucky Camp hauled water into its dry gulch via mules and Mexican workers. Stetson's plan was to pump water to Kentucky Gulch, which had been mined out, and flush hidden gold out of the hillside by shooting water at it. This was leading-edge mining technology at the time, borrowed from similar operations in California that had also revitalized dead mines.

Stetson's lust for all things Californian continued in his tastes at Kentucky Camp. He constructed the buildings out of the finest materials, including doors and windows imported from California, and equipped his facilities with telephone lines fed through

MilesDirections

0.0 START from the Gardner Canyon Trail parking lot. Head southwest down the dirt FS 92, also called Gardner Canyon Trail. Continue along this trail in the same direction as you drove in to the parking lot.

0.2 The Arizona Trail intersects on the left. Continue up the dirt road.

0.7 Just beyond a cattleguard, a sign indicates several trail turnoffs. Cross over the cattleguard and make an immediate left on FS 785.

1.0 FS 785 intersects with the Arizona Trail. Continue straight ahead on FS 785.

1.4 FS 4111 splits off to the left. Disregard this road and continue straight ahead.

2.2 After crossing a stream and climbing the hill on the other side, continue ahead on FS 785. *[FYI. There's a rusted metal sign inscribed with "Arizona Trail" and mileage indicators for several trails. A doubletrack trail drops off to the right. Remember this sign: You'll be turning at this sign later.]*

2.8 At the split, continue straight, heading toward Mt. Wrightson.

3.4 Arrive at a barbed-wire gate. Go through the gate, close it behind you, and look for the singletrack ahead marked with a metal Arizona Trail sign. Head up the singletrack, leaving the doubletrack.

3.6 At the top of the hill, there's another gate. Go through the gate and continue down the hill. This area makes an excellent picnic area.

3.8 At the bottom of a treacherous descent,

look for a sign explaining the aqueduct and the tunnel it passes through. Check out the tunnel, then continue along the singletrack that follows the bed of the old aqueduct.

5.0 The singletrack enters a designated wilderness area. Despite the obvious tire treads going in the wilderness area, do the responsible thing and turn around here, heading back the way you came.

6.4 After climbing the steep hill past Tunnel Spring return to the gate atop the hill.

6.6 Return to the barbed-wire gate and rejoin the doubletrack. Go through the gate and head back the way you came.

7.8 As you descend the shallow hill you climbed earlier (FS 785), keep your eyes open for the backside of the rusted Arizona Trail sign you saw earlier (mile 2.2). Turn left here and head down into the wash.

9.2 At the bottom of the hill, you'll rejoin with FS 785. Turn left onto the dirt road.

9.5 Return to the intersection of FS 785 and Gardner Canyon Road. Cross the cattleguard, and make a hard left immediately past the cattleguard onto doubletrack FS 4084. Cross the creek at the bottom of the hill.

9.7 After crossing the creek bed and climbing the hill on the other side, come across a parking area and a campground. Head down the hill continuing on FS 4084 that turns to the right (or left if you're looking down the hill) off the hill you just climbed. *[Side-trip. There's a faint singletrack trail straight ahead, wrapping*

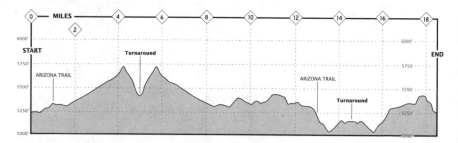

underground pipes. Kentucky Camp hosted many visiting stockholders, impressing them with beautiful gardens watered by the same aqueduct used to blast the hillsides.

Shortly after the aqueduct to Kentucky Camp was completed, Stetson died by falling three stories from a Tucson hotel. The mine failed, and the aqueduct languished. One mine's death, however, turned out to be a mountain bike trail's birth. Today, the bed along which the aqueduct was built is fast, winding singletrack. Racing down the bermed, narrow ditch, you'll feel like a slot car zipping along at top speed. The century-old aqueduct pipe is still visible at several points along the singletrack, poking out of the ground like a massive iron water bar.

After Kentucky Camp died as a mine operation, it was purchased by a Tucson lawyer and turned into a ranch. This ranch operated until 1965. Between then and now, the Kentucky Camp buildings have been scavenged for most of their useful or valuable materials. They've also hosted S.W.A.T. team training sessions (look for the spray-painted human outlines peppered with shotgun blasts), and most recently, they've been under rehabilitation. There's even a volunteer organization, The Friends of Kentucky Gulch, who come in once a month to help rebuild and maintain

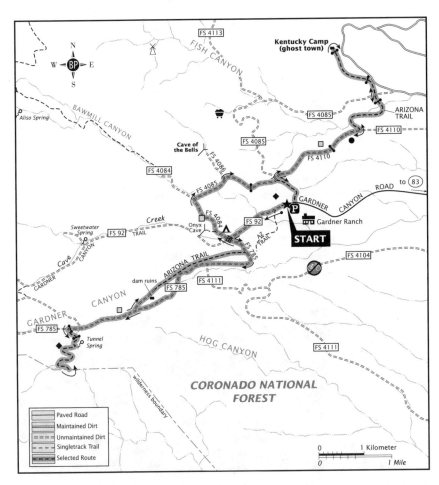

around the hill ahead of you. This is the trail to Onyx Cave, about a quarter mile away.]

10.2 The road splits. FS 4084 goes to the left, and FS 4085 goes to the right. Turn right and head down FS 4085.

10.7 The road splits again. Turn right and continue down the hill. FS 4086 goes left.

11.4 After almost topping out on the hill, the road intersects with several trails. Continue up the hill. About 100 yards up the hill, you will come upon a split in the road to the right, onto FS 4110. Turn onto FS 4110 and head down the hill. *[Bailout. Note that the single-track that splits off to the extreme right is the shortcut trail you'll eventually take to get back to your vehicle. If you don't want to make the trek out to Kentucky Camp, turn here.]*

11.8 Another barbed-wire gate. Pass through and continue. Just beyond the gate, a sign for FS 4110 points you to the left.

One of the original buildings at Kentucky Camp is in the process of being rehabilitated and may soon be rented out for about $40 a night. This original adobe building has since been patched up and wired for electricity, and will be able to hold a half-dozen people comfortably. Call Coronado National Forest, Nogales Ranger District (see Ride Information) for information about renting this building.

13.0 As you come down some rocky double-track, keep your eyes open for an exit onto the Arizona Trail to your left. Don't go all the way down the hill or you'll miss it! Turn onto the Arizona Trail and head down the singletrack.

13.6 Pass through another gate.

13.8 After crossing over a large, grassy meadow, a doubletrack road intersects with the singletrack. Continue on the Arizona Trail, across the doubletrack.

14.1 Go through the gate.

14.6 Cross through another gate. Visible ahead is the caretaker's trailer for Kentucky Camp.

14.6 Enter Kentucky Camp. Park the bikes and check it out. When you're done, turn around and head back the way you came.

15.4 Pass through the gate.

15.4 Cross over the doubletrack again.

16.4 Rejoin the doubletrack trail. Turn right as you exit the Arizona Trail segment.

17.5 Almost all the way up a climb, watch to your left for an Arizona Trail sign. Turn left at the sign and head down the singletrack.

17.8 Go through the gate.

18.1 The Arizona Trail rejoins with doubletrack. Go left, and then *immediately right* up a rocky doubletrack that takes you to the top of a ridge. You should be able to see the parking lot from up here. Head carefully down the precarious descent.

18.5 Return to the parking lot.

the facilities.

Today, Kentucky Camp is a fascinating look back at the gold mining business during the turn of the twentieth century. The caretaker is extremely knowledgeable and will often give visitors extensive tours of the area.

Once done with the walking tour, cyclists can pedal across the grassy slopes of Santa Rita's eastern reaches, across rolling foothills, into and out of stream beds, and into forests of oak and juniper, mostly on old mining roads (now very popular with the 4x4 crowd). There is also riding on singletrack, specifically on the portions that are designated as part of the Arizona Trail. Opportunities for exploration of these old mining roads are almost endless, and it's fairly easy to get lost in the foothills. When in doubt, head east (away from the mountains). Worst-case scenario, you'll end up back at the highway. From there, you can ride established roads back to the parking area.

Ride Information

🌐 Trail Contacts:

Coronado National Forest, Tucson, AZ (520) 670–4552 or *www.fs.fed.us/ r3/coronado/staffs/natres/kcamp/inde x.htm*

🕐 Schedule:

Open year round

💲 Fees/Permits:

No fees or permits required

❓ Local Information:

Sonoita Community Homepage: *www.sonoitaaz.com* • **Patagonia, Sonoita, and Elgin Visitor's Guide:** *www.theriver.com/Public/patagoniaaz* • **Coronado National Forest,** Nogales Ranger District, Nogales, AZ (520) 281–2296 or *www.fs.fed.us/r3/coronado/ nrd/nogo.htm*

◎ Local Events/Attractions:

Callaghan Vineyards, Sonoita, AZ (520) 455–5322 or *www.callaghanvineyards.com*

• **Patagonia-Sonoita Creek Sanctuary,** Patagonia, AZ (520) 394–2400 – *300- plus acres of wildlife preserve, maintained by the Nature Conservancy* • **Patagonia Fall Festival,** late October, Patagonia, AZ (520) 394–0060

🛏 Accommodations:

Stage Stop Inn, Patagonia, AZ (520) 394–2211 • **Circle Z Ranch,** Patagonia, AZ (520) 394–2525 or *www.circlez.com – Arizona's longest-operating dude ranch*

🍴 Restaurants:

Velvet Elvis Pizza Co., Patagonia, AZ (520) 394–2102

🚲 Local Bike Shops:

Patagonia Cyclery, Patagonia, AZ (520) 394–2794

🅝 Maps:

USGS maps: Mt. Wrightson, AZ; Sonoita, AZ

31

Brown Canyon

Ride Specs

Start: From the Brown Canyon Trail trailhead, off Ramsey Canyon Road south of Sierra Vista

Length: 5.3-mile loop (do more than one!)

Approximate Riding Time: 1–1.5 hours each lap

Difficulty Rating: Technically moderate, with some difficult climbs and a couple rocky patches. Aerobically moderate, with a difficult climb at the beginning and at the end. Also note the ride is at 5,000-5,500 feet.

Trail Surface: A mix of pavement, gravel road, doubletrack, rugged jeep road, and singletrack.

Lay of the Land: The Brown Canyon Trail passes through lush piñon-juniper forests, and is mostly shaded.

Elevation Gain: 802 feet

Land Status: National forest

Nearest Town: Sierra Vista

Other Trail Users: Hikers, equestrians. Some cars share the paved portion of the ride at the very beginning

Canine Compatibility: Dogs permitted—it's a short-ish ride with some water for them to play in!

Wheels: Any mountain bike or hybrid will be adequate for this ride

Getting There

From Sierra Vista: Head six miles south on AZ 92 heading toward Bisbee. Turn right (west) on Ramsey Canyon Road and head toward the Huachuca Mountains (the road is called Ramsey Road as it heads away from the mountains on the east side of AZ 92). Drive two miles and look for a parking area and trailhead for Brown Canyon Trail 115 to the right. Park here. *DeLorme: Arizona Atlas & Gazetteer:* Page 74 D1

S ierra Vista is a fast-growing city within 30 minutes of the Mexican border. The heart of the city is Fort Huachuca, one of the U.S. Army's most important and most heavily guarded intelligence bases in the country. To the south of town, the Huachuca Mountains, one of the southernmost sky islands of Coronado National Forest, dominate the skyline and extend into Mexico.

Miller Peak, at 9,466 feet in the middle of the Huachuca Mountains, is the highest southernmost peak in the United States. Once covered by a pine and fir forest, forest fires have altered the area's growth primarily to grasslands and evergreen oak woodlands. There are several excellent hiking trails that will take you to the peak and throughout the Huachucas, including Brown Canyon Trail 115—the bottom of which is *not* in wilderness, and is the heart of this trail ride.

The Brown Canyon Trail is a local cycling favorite. Not deadly hard but not a creampuff ride either, Brown Canyon Trail begins with a fairly steep grind up a

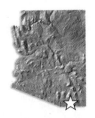

MilesDirections

0.0 START from the Brown Canyon Trail trail-head parking lot. Get back onto Ramsey Canyon Road and follow the shoulder southwest toward the Huachuca Mountains. *[Note. Be careful— it's a narrow road and fairly well traveled both by tourists and locals.]*

0.5 Brown Canyon Road, a maintained dirt road, splits off to the right, down a short hill. Head down the hill, heading due west. There will be several opportunities to turn right or left off the main road; these all go to private residences. Stick to the main dirt road. The road is also marked with a "Discovery Ranch" sign. *[FYI. There are lots of "No Trespassing— Private Road" signs, but locals insist this is just to keep away solicitors and drunk teenagers. The home owners down Brown Canyon Road are very biker-friendly.]*

0.8 Pass a "Keep Right" sign. If you follow the sign, you'll end up at a private residence. Bear left and continue ahead, as the road becomes a bit more rugged and difficult.

1.2 A narrow jeep road splits off to the left. Continue on the main jeep road as it goes right. *[Side-trip. The singletrack at this split takes you up a very steep climb just 0.2 miles (round trip) to a water tank and an old cabin foundation.]*

1.5 At the top of the climb, go through a barbed-wire gate, close it, and continue ahead.

2.4 The doubletrack stops at the Brown Canyon Trail 115. There's a short, shallow water crossing and a concrete trough. The trail goes left and right; take the right. *[FYI. The left is also Brown Canyon Trail, but it enters the Miller Peak Wilderness—no bikes!*

It's marked with a wooden sign.]

2.6 A short bit past the water trough and stream crossing, the Pomona Mine Trail 116 splits to the left and climbs very, very steeply up the side of the mountain. Continue on the main singletrack. *[Side-trip. If you enjoy climbing— really enjoy it—then go poking around up the Pomona Mine Trail. Did I mention it's steep? The sign says it's 1.5 miles. Also look for an unmarked, unofficial singletrack that splits off the Pomona Mine Trail around 0.2 miles up from Brown Canyon Trail and goes to the edge of Fort Huachuca Military Reservation.]*

4.1 Near the bottom of the Brown Canyon Trail descent, the trail splits. Take a deep breath and take the climb to the right. The left split continues until it hits the Fort Huachuca Military Reservation, as well as some other unnamed, unmarked singletrack options outside the base. *[Side-trip. The singletrack to the left eventually enters Fort Huachuca and becomes the "Perimeter Trail." There's a very inviting sign just inside the base that says the Perimeter Trail is a cooperative effort between the U.S. Army, Coronado National Forest, and the city of Sierra Vista. This is a big fat lie. Expect to be hassled, and possibly arrested, by the military police if you enter the base—it's the Army's most sensitive intelligence analysis base, and they're supremely paranoid. On the other hand, if you're curious about receiving a body cavity search administered by uniformed men with guns, ride on! It eventually exits about 1.5 miles northwest of where you entered.]*

5.3 Arrive back at the Brown Canyon trailhead parking lot.

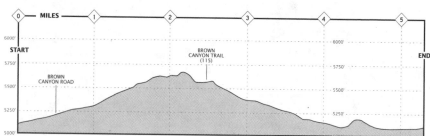

gravel road off Ramsey Canyon Road (one of the main paved accesses into the mountain range). It's only a mile and a half, but you'll gain several hundred feet in elevation. After a short road descent, the route reaches a water crossing (there's only water in this crossing during the spring) and a stock tank (there's always water in the tank, but it's unsafe to drink). The two-plus mile descent down Brown Canyon Trail proper is the real treat. Except for the very steep, very challenging climb to return to the lot, the work-to-fun ratio is such that this ride deserves multiple laps.

Brown Canyon was named after a miner named John Brown who moved to the canyon in 1880 (prospectors had worked the area at least a decade prior). One of the most distinctive landmarks of the canyon is the tailings pile from the Pomona Mine, which is near the top of the ridge and can be seen for miles.

This mine, once known as the James Group, was worked during World War I. The mine produced tungsten and galena, though gold was also present. In 1946 the Pomona Mining Company acquired the property and built a road from the canyon bottom to the mine site. They also put in an aerial tram, but operations were abandoned about a year later. Today, the old road can still be ridden up to the mine; it's

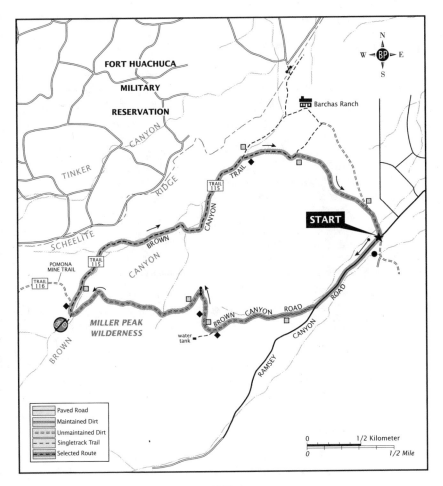

237

now called the Pomona Mine Trail 116, and is an exceedingly steep 1.4-mile grind up the side of the mountain.

Most of the Huachuca Mountains are wilderness, preserve, or military reservation. In fact, the Brown Canyon ride is nestled into one of the only corners of the mountain range that is not wilderness. The Huachuca Mountains are famous among bird-watchers—more than 170 species have been spotted in the range. Also seen are javelina, black bear, mountain lion, and coatimundi.

To the north of the Brown Canyon Trail, the Fort Huachuca Army Reservation takes up whatever portions of the mountain are not wilderness or preserve. Fort Huachuca was built in 1877 as an advanced military base the U.S. Army used during its campaign against Apache raiders led by Geronimo. The army closed all the other forts in the area but left Fort Huachuca in place in order to deal with bandits and renegade Indians near the Mexico border. Today, Fort Huachuca is one of the U.S. Army's primary intelligence schools, and houses the U.S. Army's Military Intelligence Museum.

Local Attractions

- **Fort Huachuca Museum & Military Intelligence Museum:** *(520) 533–5736 – Learn about Fort Huachuca's history through period rooms and dioramas highlighting memorabilia dating from the base's Apache-fighting days to the present. The Military Intelligence Museum has exhibits on intelligence history and the equipment used to crack the other side's secrets. The museums are about 2.5 miles in from the base's main gate in Sierra Vista.*

- **Coronado National Memorial:** *(520) 366–5515 – On AZ 92, continue south of the turnoff to Brown Canyon about 12 miles to Coronado Road. The Coronado National Memorial marks where Francisco Vásquez de Coronado marched through the area in 1540 in search for the Seven Cities of Cibola. The Coronado National Memorial is also the southern starting point of the Arizona Trail (see the Arizona Trail Project sidebar on page 103). Today, the Coronado National Memorial features nature walks, hiking, and a scenic drive in the Huachuca Mountains.*

- **Town of Bisbee** *– Head south, and then east, on AZ 92 to reach this charming little mining town. Historic buildings hug the steep hillsides of Old Bisbee; the Bisbee Mining and Historical Museum are quite interesting as well. Lots of good, tourist-friendly restaurants. What Sierra Vista may lack in personality, Bisbee more than makes up for.*

- **Tombstone** *– From central Sierra Vista, head northeast on Charleston Road to make a direct shot to the town of Tombstone about 40 minutes away. This is the home to many Old West stories, including the infamous shootout at the OK Corral. The Tombstone Cemetery holds the remains of many gunslingers and other legendary historical figures. Downtown Tombstone features re-creations of famous gunfights on the streets every week.*

Ride Information

❶ Trail Contacts:

Coronado National Forest: Sierra Vista Ranger District, Hereford, AZ (520) 378–0311 or *www.fs.fed.us/r3/corona-do/svrd*

❷ Schedule:

Open year round – *Only rarely receives snow, but in the summer, temperatures can reach the mid-90s on the hottest days, though it is still generally cooler than nearby Tucson.*

❸ Fees/Permits:

No fees or permits required

❹ Local Information:

Sierra Vista Chamber of Commerce, Sierra Vista, AZ (520) 458–6940 or *www.sierravistachamber.org* • **Bisbee Chamber of Commerce:** (520) 432–5421 or *www.bisbeearizona.com – Bisbee is a charming little mining town-tourist trap community 30 minutes east of Sierra Vista, hidden behind the Mule Mountains* • **Fort Huachuca Homepage:** *http://huachuca-www.army.mil – Read all about this army base's storied past.*

❺ Accommodations:

Rail Oaks Ranch Bed & Breakfast, Hereford, AZ (520) 378–0461 or *www.railoaksranch.com – a charming little B&B just 10 miles south of Sierra Vista in the Huachuca Mountains.*

❻ Group Rides:

Dawn to Dust Mountain Bike Club, Sierra Vista, AZ or *www.primenet. com/~tomheld/dd.html – Started in 1993, this club has about 30 members and up to 15 rides each week. Very friendly crowd.*

❼ Local Bike Shops:

Sun 'n Spokes, Sierra Vista, AZ (520) 458–0685

❽ Maps:

USGS maps: Miller Peak, AZ

Mount Graham

Ride Specs

Start: From the Grant Hill Loop/Cunningham Loop trailhead, about 26 miles up Mount Graham outside of Safford. The trailhead is about 1.5 miles past the Hospital Flat Campground. However, Hospital Flat is a nicer place to park, and features bathrooms and water. The ride up the dirt road to the trailhead is a very mellow climb.

Length: The two loops combined come out to about 10 miles. However, checking out some of the sub-loops and bailouts within the Grant Hill Loop can bring the total up to 17 miles or more.

Approximate Riding Time: 3 hours to do just the two loops, 5+ hours to ride everything

Difficulty Rating: Aerobically challenging due to the altitude of the rides (9,000–9,500 feet) and a couple steep mile-long climbs within each ride. Technically moderate, with the exception of some very tight switchback segments on both loops that are quite difficult.

Trail Surface: The trail is a mix of old logging roads that are being converted to singletrack, and some fresh new singletrack that's been recently cut by the Forest Service specifically for mountain bikers.

Lay of the Land: These trails wind through old-growth Douglas firs, white fir, Engelmann spruce, and tall stands of quaking aspen.

Elevation Gain: Cunningham Loop–2,114; Grant Hill–804

Land Status: National forest

Nearest Towns: Safford and Willcox

Other Trail Users: Hikers theoretically, although the trails are so underused that you'll rarely see anyone else up there.

Canine Compatibility: Dogs permitted, but be sure to bring lots of food and water—it's a high altitude trail, and your riding buddy will feel it as much as you.

Wheels: Hardtails are probably ideal for dealing with the big climbs involved.

Getting There

From Tucson: Head toward Willcox on I-10 eastbound. Pass through Willcox. Once past Willcox, take U.S. 191 north (Exit 352) toward Safford. Just south of Safford, turn left on AZ 366. (There's a sign that says "Mount Graham.") Drive up this twisty road to the top of the mountain range. About 22 miles up from the AZ 366 junction, this pavement ends. Continue ahead. About a mile later, there's a sign for "Hospital Flat Campground." Park here if you prefer a well-organized campground (water, bathrooms, picnic/camping areas), or continue to the actual trailhead parking lot for the Grant Hill Loop about 1.5 miles ahead.

From Phoenix: Head east toward Globe on U.S. 60. In Globe, take U.S. 70 southeast to Safford. In Safford, turn south on U.S. 191 and drive 7 miles to AZ 366. From the AZ 366 junction, follow the directions above. *DeLorme: Arizona Atlas & Gazetteer:* Page 68 B3

At 10,700 feet, Mount Graham is the tallest of the "sky islands" of Coronado National Forest. Due to the conspicuous lack of wilderness designation on the mountain, it is also perhaps the most overlooked riding area in all of Arizona.

For most Arizonans who have ever heard of it, "Mount Graham" is shorthand for the Pinaleno Mountains (the range within which the mountain resides) just as "Mount Lemmon" is shorthand for the Santa Catalinas north of Tucson. There are hundreds of cabins scattered across its slopes, and tens of thousands of visitors escape the heat every year out here. Still, the Pinalenos are three hours away from both Tucson and Phoenix, so the mountains aren't as populated as the Catalinas north of Tucson.

There are two distinct loops in the Pinalenos, recently built by the Forest Service specifically for mountain bikers. The loop to the north, the Cunningham Loop, follows old logging roads around a steep slope, providing incredible views into the desert 5,000 feet below. The trail fades back and forth between singletrack and doubletrack; after a few more years it will all be singletrack. The thorny bushes that grow on the other track and in the median between the ruts are huge incentives to stay on the singletrack—bring tube sealant! There's also one substantial climb, ending with a wild set of switchbacks back down.

As you make the turn eastward on Cunningham Loop and begin the ascent to the top of the trail, Mount Graham International Observatory is visible to the north. During most days, it looks like a massive concrete box perched atop a ridge about a thousand feet higher than the trail. The "box" opens up at night high above the interfering heat and light of the valleys below. There are two telescopes in operation today, with a third under construction. This third telescope has been a source of tremendous controversy—Mount Graham is considered a holy site to the San Carlos Apache tribe, and the construction site endangers a habitat of the Mount Graham red squirrel, thought to be extinct until they reappeared in the 1970s. Today, between 100-300 of the endangered red squirrels live atop Mount Graham.

The second loop, which meanders around and up Grant Hill to the south, features more original singletrack and mellower climbs. More importantly, it features a vista point a couple miles in from the start that puts you on the top of a cliff—at least 4,000 feet straight down to the lowest slopes of the Pinalenos. The vast red desert spread out before this viewpoint is the Willcox Playa, a major bird-watching mecca and geological oddity. Once a shallow lake, the playa's surface today epitomizes flatness—never deviating more than a foot in elevation.

Grant Hill Loop also features three bail-out trails that cut across the outer loop, each providing a distinct ride experience and opportunities to extend the ride into an all-day event. Most of Grant Hill is covered in deep, thick old-growth forest, so bring along your orange/yellow lenses.

The weather can change dramatically and very quickly atop the sky islands, and Mount Graham is no exception. Bring a windbreaker or rain jacket, especially during the monsoon season (May–August).

Both rides begin at the Grant Hill Loop trailhead, just beyond the Hospital Flat campground. Hospital Flat is the site of a hospital facility that served Fort Grant at the end of the nineteeth century. Fort Grant was established at the base of Mount Graham at the direction of General Crook in 1872 as part of his military campaign to suppress the local Apache tribes (*see Ride 36: Highline to Christopher Creek* for more history about General George Crook). Fort Grant was the base of operations for General Crook's campaign against Geronimo, which ended in Geronimo's surrender in 1886. Fort Grant ceased operations in 1905, and eventually became a state prison.

Ride Information

🌑 Trail Contacts:
Coronado National Forest, Safford Ranger District, Safford, AZ (520) 428–4150 or *www.fs.fed.us/r3/coronado/srd/ index.htm*

☀ Schedule:
Open April 15–November 15

💲 Fees/Permits:
No fees or permits are required to ride the trails or enter the forest. However, if you want to camp at Hospital Flat or any other campsite in the Pinaleno Mountains, there is a $10/car/night fee, payable at self-pay stations all over the mountain.

❓ Local Information:
Eastern Arizona Collége Thatcher & Safford information pages: *www.eac.cc. az.us/thatcher.html* • **City of Safford:** *www.ci.safford.az.us/* • **Graham County Chamber of Commerce,** Safford, AZ (520) 428–2511 or 1–888–837–1841 or *www.graham-chamber.com* • **Willcox Chamber of Commerce,** Wilcox, AZ (520) 384–2272 or 1–800–200–2272 or *www.willcoxchamber.com/*

🔎 Local Events/Attractions:
Mount Graham International Observatory, Safford, AZ (520) 428–6260 Ext. 17 or *www.discovery park.com* – Check out the world-famous observatory atop Emerald Peak in the heart of the Pinaleno Mountains or take an all-day tour through Discovery Park.

🍴 Restaurants:
Mechy's Mexican Restaurant, Safford, AZ (520) 348–9711 – Tiny, tiny little blue building on the main drag, heading west out of town, serves up cheap and yummy authentic Mexican fare. A secret favorite among locals—check out the line for the drive-through on any day of the week.

🚲 Local Bike Shops:
Cycle Path, Safford, AZ (520) 428–4666

Other Resources:
🅱 **Mount Graham International Observatory:** *http://medusa.as.arizona. edu/graham/graham.html*

Maps:
Ⓝ **USGS maps:** Webb Peak, AZ; Mount Graham, AZ

MilesDirections

Cunningham Loop

0.0 START from the Grant Hill/Cunningham trailhead, 1.5 miles past the Hospital Flat Campground. Cunningham Loop begins across AZ 366, to the north of the trailhead. Head up the gravel road and, in a couple hundred yards, go around a gate.

0.3 Pedal around the "road closed" gate. There's a sign indicating the Cunningham Loop Trail continues ahead.

2.3 The trail splits just past a crossing over Grant Creek. The signs at this split indicate that the trail goes either up the hill to the right

or continues ahead to the left. Turn left! *[FYI. The right is the loop's return, and will prove extremely difficult to climb if you went this way.]*

4.0 A short connector trail splits off to the left and goes down to the Cunningham Campground. Continue to the right, around the corner. *[Bailout. The connector puts you back onto AZ 366 in about 0.3 miles. Turn left and head back to the trailhead if you need to quit.]*

4.7 A trail sign points to the right and up a switchback. This is the beginning of the mile-long climb to the top of the loop. Take a deep

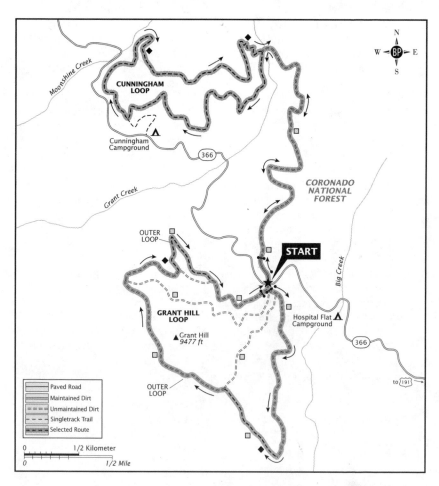

breath and start climbing.

5.9 Begin the technical switchback descent back to the doubletrack below.

6.1 Reach the bottom of the switchbacks. Turn left onto the doubletrack and head back to the trailhead.

8.3 Return to the trailhead.

Grant Hill Loop

0.0 START from the Grant Hill/Cunningham trailhead. Grant Hill Loop begins on the south side of AZ 366, directly behind the wooden map sign. The trail can be ridden in either direction, although the climb in the clockwise direction is more mellow. This description assumes a clockwise ride. Pick up the trail beyond the gate to the left of the sign and head up the doubletrack. There's a split-off to the right just a few yards beyond the gate; this is one of the bailout inner loops, so don't take this. Continue ahead.

1.2 A trail sign points to the right. *[Side-trip. There's a singletrack to the left that goes out to an incredible vista in about 100 yards. Check it out— it's a worthy side-trip.]*

1.7 The trail intersects with a doubletrack that goes left and right. Turn left and continue up the Outer Loop. *[Bailout. The right is the first bailout, and puts you back toward the trailhead in about 1.4 miles.]*

2.4 A doubletrack splits off to the right. *[Bailout. This is a quick, two-mile bailout back to the trailhead. Continue ahead and around the corner.]*

2.7 A very easy-to-miss singletrack splits off to the left and heads quickly down the hill. Turn left here on the singletrack. *[FYI. Believe it or not, this is the Outer Loop of the Grant Hill Loop Trail! It's not well marked and is very easy to miss as you come barreling down the doubletrack. Look for a rock pile and a sign about a hundred yards down from the topmost portion of the doubletrack you're about to descend.] [Bailout. Another bail-out option is to continue ahead, down the doubletrack. You'll save about 0.5 miles over taking the singletrack on the Outer Loop.]*

3.4 Reconnect with the doubletrack heading back to the trailhead. Turn left and continue toward the trailhead.

4.5 Reach the trailhead.

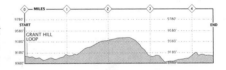

Honorable Mentions

Sky Islands

Compiled here is an index of great rides in Sky Islands that didn't make the A-list this time around but deserve recognition. Check them out and let us know what you think. You may decide that one or more of these rides deserves higher status in future editions or, perhaps, you may have a ride of your own that merits some attention.

Ⓠ Elephant Head

This is a designated mountain bike trail built by the U.S. Forest Service in the Santa Rita Mountains (the range south of Tucson; *see Ride 30: Gold Country*) just for us. It's a long, hard ride that may take up most of a day to accomplish.

Start riding up Proctor Ranch, which is a dirt road, and keep your eyes open for the nice mountain bike signs indicating the Elephant Head Trail, which will be singletrack as soon as you get off Proctor Ranch (about 1.2 miles). The trail changes from singletrack to doubletrack about five miles later, and the trail begins to climb the west face of the Santa Ritas. There's a gate at about seven miles; go through, make the steep climb, and again start looking for bike route signs. The signs will point you to singletrack that will take you up to a saddle. Once at the saddle, either turn around (it's about eight miles back to the car at this point) or continue ahead to FS 183. You can take either FS 183 up to the radio towers to your left (east) or turn right (west), heading down the dirt road toward Mt. Hopkins Road, which goes up to the Smithsonian Observatory atop Mt. Hopkins (it's a very, very long ride—about 20 more miles if you choose to go that way). Recommended route is to be happy with the radio towers and head back the way you came. Total ride is about 23 miles.

Getting there: From Tucson, head south on I-19 for 25 miles to the Continental exit. Go down Madera Canyon Road for 11 miles. The parking lot is just before Proctor Ranch Road. *Delorme: Arizona Atlas & Gazetteer:* Page 73 B5

Ⓡ Patagonia

Patagonia has served as the secret training ground for Cannondale's mountain biking team, as well as Cannondale-sponsored Dirt Camp mountain biking clinics. There are several interesting rides around the mountains near Patagonia worth exploring if you find yourself in the area.

Temporal Gulch is a fairly rugged out-and-back that simply follows Temporal Canyon Road (FS 72) up into the Santa Rita Mountains until it narrows into singletrack and hits wilderness area. Temporal Gulch is a *long* ride, about 30 miles round trip if you ride to the bitter end. To get to it, take Temporal Canyon Road north out of town and just keep riding. There are some other roads up in the mountains that split off the forest road and are worthy of exploration: FS 72A is a nasty, steep climb about halfway up the road, and FS 4100, which splits off just north of town, will take you to Squaw Gulch and other old mining roads.

Red Mountain is a hidden gem of the Patagonia trails, featuring some sweet singletrack that's virtually unknown to any but local riders. Take Harshaw Road (FS 58) east out of town to the turnoff to Red Rock Canyon Road (FS 138). Follow this road until you reach the singletrack trail right before Red Rock Ranch. Explore and enjoy the twisty trail.

Getting there: Patagonia is most easily reached by taking AZ 82 south off I-10, heading east out of Tucson. It's a very small town, but there's some great food and even some hotels. *Delorme: Arizona Atlas & Gazetteer:* Page 73 C5

(S) Sierra Vista

There are many biking opportunities around Sierra Vista and near Fort Huachuca. Most of the rides are down AZ 92, south of Sierra Vista in the Huachuca Mountains. Much of the mountain range, one of the Coronado National Forest "sky islands," is taken up by the Miller Peak Wilderness and is therefore off-limits to bikes. However, bikers both on and off the army base have sussed out dozens of trails all over the range that are perfectly legal to ride.

Bicycling magazine named Sierra Vista one of "America's 10 Best Bike Towns," both for mountain bikers and road riders, in its August 1999 issue. Besides the excellent Brown Canyon loop (*see Ride 31: Brown Canyon*), another riding opportunity in the Huachuca Mountains is Carr Canyon, a rugged doubletrack that quickly switchbacks up the mountain until it hits the wilderness boundary in about six miles. You can also take a right turn at the first switchback going up the mountain and take the Clark Springs Trail, a fairly steep and technical singletrack, back down to the bottom. To get to Carr Canyon, go one mile south of Ramsey Canyon Road (*see Ride 31: Brown Canyon*), and look for the Mesquite Tree Restaurant. The dirt road up the mountain begins on the west side of the road, just past the restaurant.

The best contact for more information about Sierra Vista mountain biking is the Dawn to Dust Mountain Bike Club. Check them out at *www.primenet.com/ ~tomheld/dd.html*. They have maps and additional information. Sierra Vista also has an excellent bike shop, Sun 'n' Spokes, at 164 East Fry Boulevard, (520) 458–0685. The other shop in town is M&M Cycling, at 1301 East Fry Boulevard, (520) 458–1316. *DeLorme: Arizona Atlas & Gazetteer:* Page 74 D1

(T) San Pedro River

There's a nice 14-mile stretch of flat bike trail along the San Pedro River, one of Arizona's only running rivers and one of North America's few north-flowing rivers. The San Pedro Riparian National Conservation Area is popular with hikers, bird-watchers, and mountain bikers.

There are many historic and archaeological sites along the San Pedro River Trail. For example, there's an undisturbed 40,000-year-old stratigraphic record at a site

called Murray Springs. Spear points from the Clovis people, present 11,000 years ago, have been found at this site as well. Murray Springs is off Monson Road, 1.2 miles north of the turnoff onto Monson from AZ 90 (the highway from Sierra Vista to Bisbee).

Another historic site along the San Pedro River Trail is the Spanish Presidio Santa Cruz de Terrenate. This is the most intact example of an extensive network of presidios that once stretched throughout southern Arizona, marking the northern extension of New Spain into the New World. All that remains today is a stone foundation and some adobe wall remnants. This site is accessible from the Terrenate trailhead: From the historic ruins of Fairbank where AZ 82 crosses the San Pedro River, drive about two miles west on AZ 82, and then turn right (north) on Kellar Ranch Road. The trailhead is about three miles north of the intersection. The Terrenate ruins are about two miles in from the trailhead.

Getting there: There are numerous trailheads on the San Pedro River Trail. The most popular is the San Pedro House trailhead, located nine miles east of Sierra Vista on AZ 90 where the highway crosses the river. From this trailhead, you can ride either north or south. *Delorme: Arizona Atlas & Gazetteer:* Page 74 C2 & D2.

(U) Chiracahua Mountains

This mountain range occupies the southeastern corner of the state. Rising to 8,400 feet from the desert floor, the Chiracahuas are largely taken up by wilderness but still have some great biking opportunities—especially if you want to go camping for a few days and explore the forest roads atop the mountain.

The Onion Saddle Campground, atop the Chiracahuas via Pinery Canyon Road, is ground zero for mountain biking. There are numerous forest roads that crisscross the mountain. There are also some singletrack trails, Trail 336 and Trail 251, that are accessible from Onion Saddle Campground and do not enter wilderness. The "Onion Saddle Loop" ride is to take Trail 251 out of the campground to its intersection with Trail 336, turn left/west on Trail 336 to Pinery Canyon Road (FS 42), and take the forest road back to the campground—about nine miles total. Trail 251 also continues north past its intersection with Trail 336, eventually hitting FS 356. It's a long, long climb via FS 42 back to the campground this way, though—maybe six solid miles of climbing up Pinery Canyon.

If you're looking for a longer, less technically challenging tour of the mountain, the Pinery Canyon Loop is another option. Take FS 42 up the mountain to Onion Saddle, and then turn onto FS 42D heading south out of Turkey Park. Turn right (west) at the intersection with FS 357 and enter Pine Canyon. Just past Downing Pass, you rejoin with FS 42 and bomb back down Pinery Canyon Road to the beginning. Depending on where you start, this can be a 15-20 mile loop, all on forest roads.

The top of the Chiracahuas, like all the Sky Islands, is shrouded in deep pine forests. One of the most distinctive aspects of the Chiracahuas is the standing rock formations that crop up here and there; the biggest collection of them is unimaginatively called the Standing-Up Rocks Formation, and can be found in the national monument portion of the forest.

Getting there: From Tucson, head east on I-10 to Willcox. From Willcox, take AZ 186 southeast (it'll be signed) toward Chiracahuas National Monument. AZ 181 heads directly up the mountain to the national monument, a lookout tower and ranger station, and the Standing-Up Rocks formation. You can either start riding up Pinery Canyon Road to the Onion Saddle Campground, or drive up to the campground and poke around the forest roads at the top. Setting up a shuttle ride so you can take Pinery Canyon Road (FS 42) all the way down out of the mountain—about 20 miles of straight downhill—is a cheap, very scenic, thrill. **Delorme: Arizona Atlas & Gazetteer:** Page 68 D3

Ⓥ Santa Catalina Mountains

There are many other mountain biking opportunities in the Santa Catalinas in addition to the Butterfly and Crystal Springs trails (see Ride 26: Mt. Lemmon Top to Bottom). Generally, all the rides in the Catalinas are technically and aerobically very demanding. If you're a glutton for punishment, try some of the following trails as well:

Green Mountain: This is an extremely challenging technical trail, and is perhaps one of the most difficult trails in this entire book. Drive up Catalina Highway to the General Hitchcock Campground; it's the second campground on Catalina Highway, and is 16.7 miles from the beginning of the highway. Park and ride up the Catalina Highway about 5.8 miles to San Pedro Vista Point. Look for the Brush Corral Trail sign to the right, and start descending the Brush Corral Trail. Stay on the Brush Corral Trail at the first junction with the Green Mountain Trail and continue down the switchbacks, which are terrific fun if you can hold on. Take the Brush Corral Trail 21 shortcut up and connect with the Green Mountain Trail at the top. Descend on the Green Mountain Trail to the General Hitchcock Campground and your vehicle. Total distance is 11.7 miles. *Bring body armor if you own it, otherwise plan on walking long stretches of this trail.*

Molino Basin: The Molino Basin Campground is the first campsite on the Catalina Highway as you drive up toward Summerhaven. It's about 12 miles from the start of the highway, in a small basin (surprise!) to the side of the highway. A couple trails start from here—Molino Basin Trail heading west, and the Bellota Trail, across the highway heading east. Molino Basin Trail is a very nice eight-mile climb/descend out-and-back ride that starts right from the campground and heads due west. The trail is very well marked and is virtually impossible to get lost on. Molino Basin Trail is aerobically challenging to climb, and technically moderate-to-challenging to descend. You reach the end of the ride when you reach Prison Camp Road. You can either continue on the road until you hit the wilderness boundary, or turn around whenever you feel like it.

Shuttle Ride: If you want to set up a shuttle ride, there's an opportunity to reach the La Milagrosa Ridge Trail from the Molino Basin Campground. Head east up a very steep climb on the Bellota Trail (it's signed), back down Bellota Ridge, and to a gate. From there, the biggest challenge is finding La Milagrosa: Past the gate, you'll walk about 200 yards down a wash, looking for La Milagrosa Ridge Trail, then head right (south). Once you're on the trail, La Milagrosa takes you down a very narrow, dangerous sliver of rock to the end of Snyder Road, off Soldier Trail Road. Snyder is where you'll park your shuttle car—get a Tucson road map to figure out the road portion. Again, wear body armor on this ride if you own it.

This is by no means a comprehensive guide to the bikeable trails of the Santa Catalinas. An excellent resource is *The Map: Trails of the Tucson Area* by the Arizona Mapping Kompany.

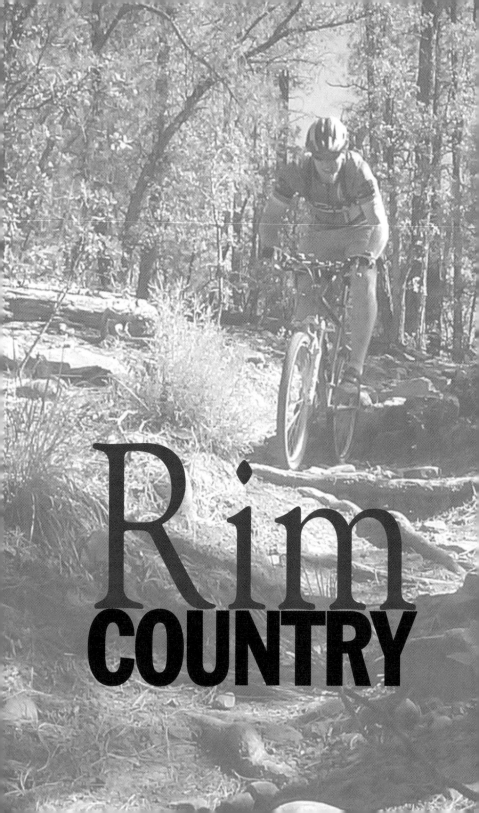

Rim
COUNTRY

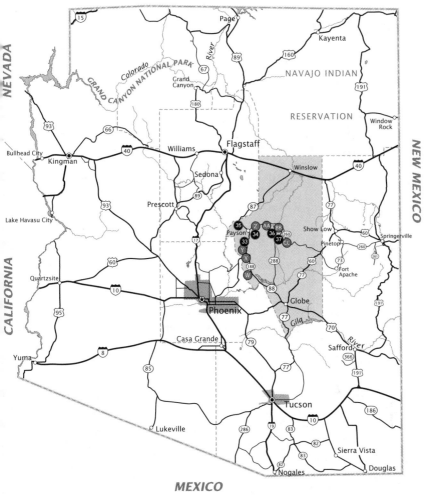

Rim Country

The Rides	Honorable Mentions
Cypress Thicket **33.**	**W.** Four Peaks Road
Houston Mesa Horse Camp Trails **34.**	**X.** Sunflower
Strawberry Mountain **35.**	**Y.** Mazatzal Mountain Loop
Highline to Christopher Creek **36.**	**Z.** Stewart Pocket/"The Boulders"
Willow Springs Lake **37.**	**AA.** Road 235 Trail
	BB. Carr Lakes Trails
	CC. Valentine Ridge

Rim Country

The Mogollon Rim juts out of the landscape just north of Payson and continues across the state into New Mexico. It's the southern edge of the Colorado Plateau, and is so massive and stark that it catches weather patterns passing over it. The land below the rim is wet and green; above the rim, the land is pine-covered and quite a bit dryer.

Settlers, explorers, soldiers, and criminals have lived along the Rim for centuries now. Various Apache tribes once populated the green, fertile land as well, until they were rounded up and chased out by the U.S. Army, who was charged with "protecting the settlers" who came to "civilize" the place. The U.S. Army only partially succeeded in civilizing the area along the Mogollon Rim—although there are some very nice communities here, most of the area is still quite wild and green.

The towns of Pine and Strawberry sit at the westernmost edge of the Mogollon Rim. They're small, iconoclastic communities with some minor tourist trade and long histories—both were among the first settlements in this part of the state, and haven't grown much in the past hundred-plus years. Strawberry features several very nice, very large homes up the road, away from AZ 260. The locals keep to themselves, but they don't act surprised to see Lycra-clad bikers wandering into the little diners and general stores.

Just down the road is Payson, the center of life on the Rim. Surprisingly, there's not a particularly active local biking community in Payson—the town seems to have many more motor-sports devotees. There's one bike shop in town, Manzanita Cyclery, and second shops have consistently failed to take hold. Given how fast Payson is growing, this may soon change. Houses are sprouting up west of town at a quick pace, and Payson—the closest pine-covered town to metro Phoenix—is becoming an extension of the Valley of the Sun.

The riding in a 30-minute radius around Payson is a mix of very, very nice singletrack and some long-ish but interesting forest road loops. There are hundreds of miles of forest road to explore, both above and below the Rim and south of Payson in the rolling high Sonoran desert. Just a few of the most attractive forest road rides are included in this book, but pick up any *DeLorme: Arizona Atlas & Gazetteer* and you'll find plenty of exploration opportunities. As far as singletrack goes, pretty much everything that's legal can be found in this book.

Head up the Rim a pace, and AZ 260 winds its way to the top of the Colorado Plateau as it approaches Show Low. Campsites and small fishing lakes abound atop the Rim; if you get a chance to camp right on the Mogollon Rim take it and enjoy some of the most dramatic views in the state.

As AZ 260 approaches Show Low, the land becomes sandy and dry. The trails give way to ATV areas the further east you go along the Rim. By the time you reach the towns of Heber and Overgaard—mostly small truck stops and stores for the nearby summer cabin communities—the trees have thinned out and you're in high plateau.

Section Overview

Cypress Thicket

The Cypress Thicket loop/lollipop enthralls visitors with a view of the sprawling Mazatzal Mountains few people get to experience. The ride starts and ends with significant climbs—bring your spare lungs—and some long, thrilling descents. It also skirts the Mazatzal Wilderness, one of the largest wilderness areas in Arizona. (*See page 258.*)

Houston Mesa Horse Camp Trails

The Houston Mesa Horse Camp Trails are favorites of local riders. Fast, bermed singletrack winding through juniper and hellishly dangerous descents await riders of all skill levels. The Shoofly Ruins atop Houston Mesa harbor some great views of the rim and surrounding mountain ranges. (*See page 264.*)

Strawberry Mountain

Strawberry Mountain is an extremely mixed trail. The beginning is a dirt road, then there's doubletrack, then there's pavement, and then there's hellacious singletrack. If you avoid the singletrack and take AZ 87 back to your vehicle, this is a moderately difficult ride (due to long climbs at the beginning and at the end). The singletrack all by itself is very difficult and dangerous. (*See page 268.*)

Highline to Christopher Creek

The Highline Trail is a destination trail for riders throughout the Southwest. The Highline itself, and all of its attendant loops and spurs, is a technically challenging journey along the base of the Mogollon Rim. The views of the valleys and ranges below the Mogollon Rim are spectacular all along the Highline. Cyclists can also choose to ride atop the rim via the General Crook Trail, which skirts the cliff's edge for miles and miles. Any mountain biker anywhere in Arizona with strong skills and lots of courage owes it to him or herself to try these trails out. (*See page 274.*)

Willow Springs Lake

Atop the Colorado Plateau above the Mogollon Rim, Willow Springs Lake was the first official mountain bike trail established in Arizona. The loop follows some old doubletrack as well as some very new singletrack, edging Willow Springs Lake and crossing atop a high rock dam that separates it from Horse Trap Gulch. For cyclists looking for cooler climes (temperatures 25 degrees lower than metro Phoenix or Tucson), this is the place. (*See page 280.*)

Cypress Thicket

Ride Specs

Start: From the beginning of FS 406, at the west end of Main Street
Length: 18-mile loop
Approximate Riding Time: 3 hours
Difficulty Rating: Technically easy, but physically strenuous due to long climbs, including one sketchy ascent.
Trail Surface: Gravel roads and jeep roads
Lay of the Land: High desert, cypress thicket
Elevation Gain: 2,387 feet
Land Status: National forest
Nearest Town: Payson
Other Trail Users: Off-road vehicles
Canine Compatibility: Dogs permitted, but the ride is too long to be dog friendly
Wheels: Hardtail, rigid, or hybrid is fine. A trailer might be nice for an extended exploration of the thicket, but don't forget that final climb out!

Getting There

From Payson: From the corner of AZ 87 (Beeline Highway) and Main Street, head west on West Main Street. In one mile, you will pass through Green Valley Park, a municipal park. At 1.7 miles, West Main Street becomes Doll Baby Ranch Road as you pass the Payson Golf Course on your right. At 1.9 miles, the road surface changes to dirt and becomes FS 406. At 2.3 miles, drive past a bridge that splits off to your right toward a waste treatment plant. Continue ahead on FS 406. At 2.6 miles, enter Tonto National Forest. Park on the other side of the cattleguard.
DeLorme: Arizona Atlas & Gazetteer: Page 50 B2/3

The city of Payson is near the geographic center of Arizona, even though it is thought of as being in the eastern part of the state. Nestled at the base of the Mogollon Rim, Payson is at the intersection of a variety of terrain and climate. The Mogollon Rim—which is actually the southern edge of the Colorado Plateau—bisects the state, but nowhere else is the line as obvious as in Payson, and along the AZ 260 as it slowly ascends the cliff face. Adding further complexity, the Payson area sits near the junction of three national forests: Tonto, Coconino, and Apache-Sitgreaves.

Payson's rides can be divided into several distinct regions. There are the below-the-rim rides (specifically all the variations on the mighty Highline Trail; *see Ride 36: Highline to Christopher Creek*), the above-the-rim rides (*Horse Trap Lake*), the Strawberry-Pine forest rides (*Strawberry-Pine Trail*) to the northwest, and finally the mine country rides. Cypress Thicket is exemplary of Payson's mine country: Rolling hills of high chaparral foliage, not quite desert and not quite forest. There isn't much coverage in mine country, and temperatures can get really high in the summer. This trail cuts through the desert, so cyclists should prepare themselves for arid and hot conditions.

The Cypress Thicket is, literally, a thicket of Arizona Cypress trees stretching several miles along the base of the Mazatzal Mountains. The thicket is visible from the descent atop Snowstorm Mountain, which separates Payson from the beautiful moun-

tain ranges to the west. The foliage starts out pretty sparse at the top, which is typical of Payson's mining country. About halfway into the long descent the forest becomes noticeably thicker. The Cypress Thicket is at its densest as the road skirts the Mazatzal Wilderness, following Rye Creek. Cyclists may note several opportunities to duck into the wilderness area, such as the trailhead to Mineral Springs (FS 414A). But as always, designated wilderness is no-bikes-allowed. The Mazatzal Wilderness includes portions of both Tonto National Forest and Coconino National Forest.

The Mazatzal (locally mispronounced "mad as hell") Mountains are this ride's western barrier. They're not really visible from Payson, so it may come as some surprise when you turn a corner and see them for the first time. There are three opinions on the origin of the word "Mazatzal;" one is that it is an Apache word meaning "bleak" or "barren," another is that it's Paiute for "Land in Between," and yet another is that it is a Nahuatl (Aztec) phrase meaning "Land of the Deer." While the cliff faces are certainly barren, the visible eastern face of the Mazatzals is lush with Arizona Cypress and other chaparral growth. The entire range lies within designated wilderness.

The Cypress Thicket ride begins with a fairly steep grind up Snowstorm Mountain. The good news is, you'll get to bomb down this dirt road at the end. Once atop a saddle in Snowstorm, it's a very long descent into Cypress Thicket. The bad news is, you'll have to grind your way back out. If you just don't feel like storming the

MilesDirections

0.0 START in the parking area just past the Forest Service sign. Begin by heading west and uphill along FS 406.

1.2 A doubletrack splits off to the left. Continue ahead on the main dirt road. *[Note. There will be several split-offs along this road, so as a rule always stick to the main road.]*

2.3 Cross over a cattleguard. This is the first of three cattleguards you will pass over before you make a turn onto FS 193 (a different forest road) to return.

2.5 FS 406 comes to a fork. A sign at the intersection indicates that heading right along FS 406 takes you to East Verde River. Turning left on FS 414 goes to Cypress Thicket. Turn left at this fork and continue along FS 414 toward Cypress Thicket.

3.2 FS 414 comes to a fork with FS 193. Turn right and continue on FS 414 toward Cypress Thicket.

4.4 Cross over the second cattleguard.

7.6 There's a Forest Service sign on the right for Mineral Creek Trailhead (FS 414A). Pass this and continue heading down the hill on FS 414. *[FYI. There are several other Forest Service signs in this area, each explaining what road you're on and how far it is to various things. For this ride, stay on FS 414 until after you cross the third cattleguard and turn north onto FS 193.]*

9.3 Cross over the third cattleguard. This third cattleguard is your cue to begin looking for the left turn that will reconnect with FS 414 and eventually return you to the parking area.

10.1 FS 193 intersects from the left. It's off the road a little, so if you're cooking down the hill you could easily miss it. *[FYI. If you miss this turn-off, you'll wind up about 10 miles south along FS 414 in the town of Rye.]* Turn left on FS 193 and grind your way up the steep, difficult hill. The road becomes unimproved doubletrack at this point.

10.5 Nearing the top of the climb, the trail splits. Bear left continuing along FS 193. *[FYI. As you continue to climb, look to your right and you'll see Table Mountain—it'll be self-evident if you look.]*

11.6 Cross over a cattleguard.

12.0 Arrive at a barbed-wire gate. Disengage the gate, ride through, reattach the gate, and continue down the hill.

13.3 As you're riding along the tops of softly rolling hills, FS 193 turns to the left. It's joined by another road from the right. Just stay left and continue climbing.

13.6 Pass a private mining community (Excursion Mine) on your left (mostly consisting of water tanks and trailers). Stay out of this area and continue along FS 193.

14.0 Pass a corral on your left. Stay on the main road, which continues ahead.

14.7 Reach the intersection with FS 414. Turn right on FS 414.

15.4 Reach the intersection where FS 406 splits off to the East Verde River. Turn right onto FS 406 and begin the long grind up the hill. The climb is about two miles long.

18.0 Reach your vehicle.

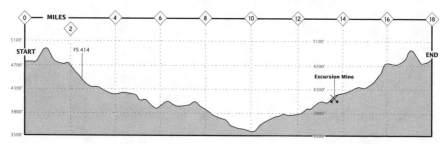

ramparts, you can drive any vehicle up and down FS 406 (Doll Baby Ranch Road). The Doll Baby Ranch drive is actually a local attraction visitors may consider driving or biking to. The ranch, started in 1882 by Napoleon "Poley" Bonaparte Chilson, is still in operation much as it was at its founding—it has never had phone or electric service. George Smith named Baby Doll Ranch in 1906, but the name has been turned around over the years.

Turning up FS 193, the road becomes narrower, unimproved doubletrack. This is really the only technically "difficult" portion of the trail, due to loose rocks and a few ledges you'll have to navigate. The doubletrack eventually widens as it approaches

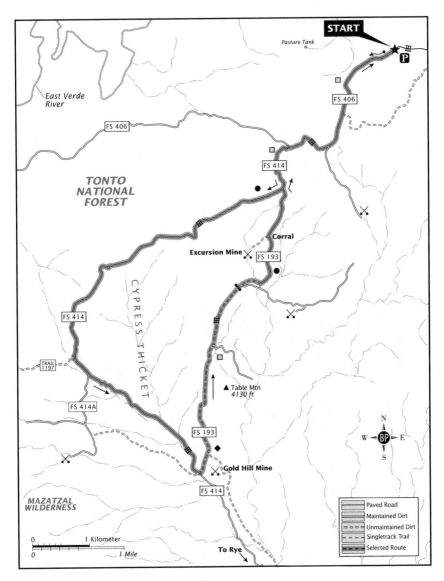

Storm seasons

Monsoons *are the annual shift of wind direction, bringing summer rains that flood the desert and high forests of the southwest. Monsoon season is officially July 1 through September 15; meteorologists also define the start of the monsoon season as the third day in a row that the dew point averages 55 degrees or higher. Payson and the rest of the Mogollon Rim gets hit very hard by monsoons—expect a rainstorm every day at 3 P.M., and plan accordingly. The White Mountain town of Greer is Arizona's wettest, averaging 11.48" of rain.*

Winters also bring regular rains, as well as snow in mountainous areas such as Flagstaff, Prescott, the "sky islands" of Coronado National Forest (Santa Catalinas, Mt. Graham, Santa Ritas), and the White Mountains. Arizona's winter seasons are extremely unpredictable; Flagstaff's ski season has run as late as April. The bulk of the rain/snow season usually hits January through early March, although snow can persist in the highest parts of the mountains as late as May.

Table Mountain, which rises to the right of the trail. Keep the mountain to your right and you'll find your way out of the thicket without much trouble.

Views of the Mazatzals from any point on this ride are breathtaking. The only man-made structure on the entire ride is the Excursion Mine on FS 193. It's private property, a scattering of water tanks and trailer homes. Off the road a bit, red steel posts dot the landscape. Each post is an official federal mine claim. Don't mess with these posts or even mention the phrase "claim jumper" very loudly; Arizona's miners are notoriously protective of their stakes.

Payson's mine country has had a long and troubled past. Most of the area's mines did not pay off very well, and the land is so rugged that it was difficult to move people and equipment into and out of the countless gulches and hills. The best part of Payson's mining history is that visitors can now explore the remains of various mines: Oxbow, Zulu, Midget, Thompson, etc.

Ride Information

☻ Trail Contacts:

Tonto National Forest, Payson District, Payson, AZ (928) 474–7900 or www.fs.fed.us/r3/tonto

☻ Schedule:

Open year round

⑤ Fees/Permits:

No fees or permits required

❓ Local Information:

Rim Country Regional Chamber of Commerce, Payson, AZ (928) 474–4515 or www.rimcountrychamber.com • **Town of Payson,** Payson, AZ (928) 474–5242

♀ Local Events/Attractions:

Mazatzal Casino 1–800–777–PLAY or www.777play.com – south of Payson on the Beeline Highway (AZ 87) on the Tonto Apache Reservation • **Rim Country Museum** (928) 474–3483 – open Wednesday through Sunday, 12:00 A.M.–4:00 P.M.

● Accommodations:

Trails End Motel, Payson, AZ (928) 474–2283

⑪ Restaurants:

El Rancho, Payson, AZ (928) 474–3111 • **The Small Café** (928) 474–4209 – a little hard to find, but unbeatable home-made-style breakfasts

⑫ Other Resources:

National Wilderness Preservation System: www.wilderness.net/nwps/wilderness.cfm/Mazatzal – some interesting information about the Mazatzal Wilderness

⑬ Group Rides:

Manzanita Cyclery runs a group ride out of its shop every Saturday morning. Call for more information.

⑭ Organizations:

Mogollon Mountain Bicycle Association – contact Dan Basinski: (928) 474–5354

⑮ Local Bike Shops:

Manzanita Cyclery, Payson, AZ (928) 474–0744

Ⓝ Maps:

USGS maps: North Peak, AZ; Payson South, AZ

Houston Mesa Horse Camp Trails

Ride Specs

Start: From Houston Mesa Trailhead
Length: 6.8-mile loop
Approximate Riding Time: 1.5 hours
Difficulty Rating: Moderately difficult, with an extremely difficult ascent up to, and descent down from, Houston Mesa. Aerobically moderate, with steep climbs on the main loop as well as on some of the optional connectors
Trail Surface: Bermed, fast singletrack, and rocky and difficult doubletrack
Lay of the Land: Juniper forest
Elevation Gain: 664 feet
Land Status: National park
Nearest Town: Payson
Other Trail Users: Equestrians, ORVs (specifically quads and motorcycles), and hikers
Canine Compatibility: Dogs permitted
Wheels: Full suspension strongly advised

Getting There

From Payson: Traveling north on AZ 87 past the junction with AZ 260, look for a brown sign that says Houston Mesa Campground at 1.8 miles. Turn right (east) onto Houston Mesa Road. At 2.7 miles, you'll see a sign for the Houston Mesa Trailhead. Turn right and park.
DeLorme: Arizona Atlas & Gazetteer: Page 50 B3

Within five minutes of downtown Payson, the Houston Mesa Horse Camp Trails comprise a network of bermed, smooth singletrack, ultra-rocky jeep roads, and walking paths. The network is fairly new, having been developed since new homes were built south of Tyler and north of Houston Mesa. In fact, the trail is a narrow wedge of national forest squeezed between housing developments.

The Shoofly Loop is the more difficult of the loop options. The start of the Houston Mesa is somewhat rocky and twisty. It eventually evens out and gets fast and smooth while winding through juniper and pine trees—welcome shade during the warmer months. The area is fundamentally dryer and rockier than along the Mogollon Rim (*see Ride 36: Highline to Christopher Creek Trail*), demanding different skills than the narrower, smoother rides of the lower rim itself.

Climbing to the top of Houston Mesa is a handful, indeed probably impossible for all but the most accomplished riders. The trail is loose, rocky, and fairly steep all the way up; coming down the same ascent is a popular challenge for local downhill nuts. But once on the top, the views prove to be worth every step. Luckily the climb is just a couple hundred feet long.

The jeep roads atop Houston Mesa are very rocky and rough; full suspension will take the bite out of the rubble, so bring it if you've got it. There are no clean "lines" to pick between the babyheads that lie half-buried beneath the road's surface.

Take the time to visit the Shoofly Ruins at least once if you're in the area and on this trail. Although the descent to the Ruins' parking lot is rocky, it's a great place to rest after doing battle with the jeep roads up on the mesa. Shoofly Village was built and occupied more than 1,000 years ago by a tribe with close ties to the vanished Hohokam people, and consists of 87 rooms and several courtyards. The ruins are surrounded by a walled compound that encloses about four acres. The Shoofly Village

Ride Information

🍷 Trail Contacts:
[See Ride 36: Highline to Christopher Creek Trail]

🕐 Schedule:
Open year round

$ Fees/Permits:
No fees or permits required

❓ Local Information:
[See Ride 36: Highline to Christopher Creek Trail]

🅽 Maps:
USGS maps: Payson North, AZ

petered out through about 1250 AD, along with most of the Payson-area tribes; nobody is sure what caused this exodus.

A fair amount of caution should be used while descending Houston Mesa. The jeep "road" on this trail is a field of loose boulders and rocks; the trail never looks the same twice from week to week. Add to this fact the steepness—as well as being several hours away from medical help—and you'll see this task is not to be taken lightly. Maybe you'll get lucky and arrive when the trail is clearer than normal.

Most of the "good" (that is, fast and smooth) trails are within Lockwood Gulch below Houston Mesa proper. The forest becomes much thicker and greener in the Gulch; Houston Mesa itself barely has any trees on it at all. The various connectors below the Mesa, and Houston Loop itself, are much smoother and faster. Indeed you can get a heck of a lot of speed going if you take the connector down to Tyler Parkway. Be careful of hikers and other trail users, as this is a primary access from the housing development to the south.

Although designated for equestrian use, the trails don't host horses often. The area south of the Mesa is a favorite of homeowners from the new developments along Tyler Parkway; expect to see walkers with dogs on almost any day of the week. As you go further north, the trails are a playground for quads and dirt bikes.

MilesDirections

0.0 START from the Houston Mesa Equestrian Trail Center off Houston Mesa Road. The trail goes southeast out of the parking lot. Just after you get on the trail, it splits left and right. Turning right takes you up to the Horse Camp; turning left takes you to the Shoofly Trail. Turn left.

0.5 Arrive at a barbed-wire gate and an angled walk-through. Lift the bike over, walk through, and continue.

1.1 Arrive at another barbed-wire gate. Just beyond the gate, the trail splits. The left is marked with an equestrian sign; the right is not. Turn left here. Just beyond this turn, there's another split. The right is marked "Shoofly"; turn right here and continue.

1.4 Arrive at another split. To the left is Shoofly Trail; to the right is Houston Loop. Turn left onto the Shoofly Trail.

1.9 As you climb—or more likely hike—a very rocky ascent, a trail splits off to the left. This left-hand trail is not so rocky, and connects back to Houston Mesa Drive. Continue on the right fork, up the bouldery climb. *[Bailout: If you need to get out fast, turn left on the trail that splits off here, which will get you back to Houston Mesa Drive in about 500 yards.]*

2.1 Top out on Houston Mesa. From up here you can see the entirety of the Mogollon Rim to the north, Christopher Mountain to the south, and the Mazatzals to the southwest. A sign indicates the trail turns toward the right. Follow the sign.

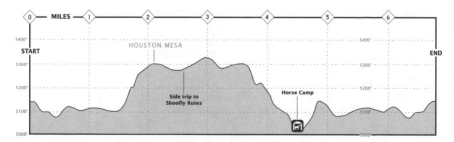

2.6 The trail crosses a very rocky, dirt road and continues on the other side. If you go ahead, you'll get to the Shoofly Ruins. If you turn right, you'll continue on the Houston Mesa Loop. If you turn left, it'll take you to a corral and eventually back to Houston Mesa Drive. Turn right (east), following the "Horse Camp" sign.

3.5 After a descent off the top of the mesa, the rocky dirt road reaches a split. The left heads south to the Houston Loop (see map); the right is marked with a "Horse Camp" sign. Turn right and continue down the hill

3.9 Reach a barbed-wire gate. Go through the gate and continue.

4.5 At the bottom of the hellish decent, look for a Forest Service sign with a bright yellow arrow pointing to a singletrack off to the right. If you look a little deeper into the brush, you'll see the "Horse Camp" signs again. Turn right here, continuing to follow the horse camp signs. [*Side-trip/option: Continue down the doubletrack here to visit the Houston Loop, a moderately difficult singletrack loop just a bit south. Add +2.5 miles to your route.*]

4.6 Pass through another gate.

5.4 Return to the split you saw at mile 1.4. The trail to the right goes back up the Shoofly Trail (should you want to make another lap), the left continues to the Horse Camp. Turn left.

5.7 Return to the crossroad at 1.1. Turn left and go down the singletrack. Just around the corner, there's another gate. Go through the gate and continue. Just past the gate, there's a right-hand turn that says "Horse Camp." If you go straight, you'll get to the Tyler Parkway. To continue along this route, turn right.

6.6 Return to the split that takes you either back to the Houston Mesa Trailhead or up to the Horse Camp. Turn right to return to the trailhead.

6.8 Return to the Houston Mesa Trailhead.

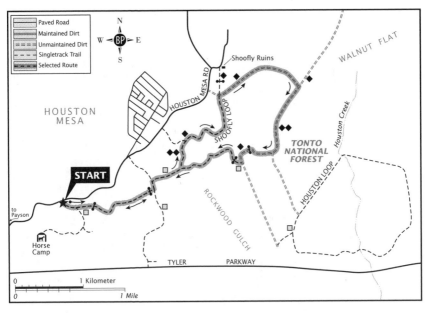

Strawberry Mountain

Ride Specs

Start: From the parking area on FS 428/Strawberry Mountain Road—just past the entrance to Tonto National Forest

Length: 15-mile loop

Approximate Riding Time: 2–2.5 hours

Difficulty Rating: Aerobically and technically moderate, with a difficult climb in the beginning and a technically difficult portion at the end.

Trail Surface: Dirt road, pavement, and singletrack, creating a loop

Lay of the Land: Ponderosa pine and piñon pine forest

Elevation Gain: 2,411 feet

Land Status: National forest, cities of Strawberry and Pine

Nearest Town: Pine

Other Trail Users: Hikers, cars (except on the Strawberry/Pine Trail)

Canine Compatibility: Dogs permitted

Wheels: Hardtail is fine; hybrid is also fine if the Strawberry-Pine trail back to your car is avoided

Getting There

From Payson: Head north on AZ 87 out of Payson toward Pine. At 14.5 miles past the intersection of AZ 87 and AZ 260, turn left on Hardscrabble Road. If you enter Pine proper, you've gone too far. On Hardscrabble Road, drive about one mile until the pavement ends and the road becomes dirt. At this point, the road is considered FS 428. Park on any turnoff you can find; there are several pull-offs to the right and left of the dirt road. There's a good spot just past the "Limited Use Road" sign. *DeLorme: Arizona Atlas & Gazetteer:* Page 50 A2

T his little-used loop around Strawberry Mountain is a favorite among local riders. The initial climb is a lung-burner, but the payoff is the long, fast descent into the vacation town of Strawberry. The Strawberry-Pine Trail that leads back to your vehicle is a hidden treasure—five miles of technical singletrack tucked away beneath a canopy of pine trees.

Strawberry Mountain, near the westernmost end of the distinct Mogollon Rim cliff's edge, is fairly typical for pine-covered mountains in the Rim area. Strawberry Mountain and Hardscrabble Mesa have been home to miners and ranchers for a century. This means the Pine-Strawberry area is a rather recent addition to the European domination of the area. Apache lived on the mountain and in the valleys below the Mogollon for several hundred years (perhaps even thousands of years), and fought hard to keep their land once the Army arrived. One of the first European settlements in the area was Mazatzal City near Doll Baby Ranch (*see Ride 33: Cypress Thicket*), but once the Army left, the Apache harassed the settlers out of the area. The settlers ended up in the Pine-Strawberry area with not much more than cattle and hogs.

Today, Strawberry Mountain features some palatial homes nestled among the trees, as well as a few working cattle and horse ranches in the valley between the mountains. And yes, there are wild strawberries for those willing to look hard enough.

The ride begins on an unfortunately steep climb up Strawberry Mountain Road (FS 428). It's a well-used dirt road; indeed it's the only access to the ranches atop Hardscrabble Mesa—so be aware of traffic. The road tops out near the split in the road that leads to the ranches. Feel free to ride to the gate, but you'll have to turn around when you reach it. When FS 428 splits, the ride gets more fun—a very slight downhill grade and virtually no traffic means riders can hammer out the miles in the

MilesDirections

0.0 START from the dirt parking area just past the Limited Use Road sign. Start biking up the dirt road toward Strawberry Mountain.

0.6 To your right, there's a brown Forest Service sign indicating a trail crossing. You'll be coming out here later. For now, continue ahead on FS 428.

1.5 The trail splits, becoming FS 428 and FS 428A. At the split in the trail, take the left split and continue on FS 428. To the right, the trail passes through a gate and becomes 428A. This road leads to several ranches and eventually dead-ends at a locked gate.

2.5 FS 427 splits off to the left. It's undeveloped doubletrack that heads west and south. Continue on FS 428 as it bends to the right.

4.9 A barbed-wire gate crosses the trail. Disengage the gate, cross over, and hook the gate up again. Just past the gate, you can see a watering hole and a wooden sign for FS 428. As you approach the sign, you'll see your current trail intersects with a road going left and right. The right heads back to the locked gate. You want to turn left, westward, and con-

tinue working your way around Strawberry Mountain.

5.6 After passing a corral on your left, you'll arrive at a gate. Pass through the gate, close it, and continue ahead.

5.9 The trail splits. To the left is a road that goes toward Twin Buttes. You will continue ahead on FS 428 and cross over the cattleguard.

6.5 Pass some very nice homes on your left. Continue on FS 428, going up a short hill toward a stop sign. At the stop sign, FS 428 terminates at FS 708 (also called Fossil Creek Road), which goes left and right. Turn right, heading toward Strawberry.

7.0 The road changes to asphalt. Continue ahead.

9.4 Fossil Creek Road ends at AZ 87. Turn right and ride the shoulder through Pine.

10.0 Just beyond the turnoff to the Black Bear Restaurant, AZ 87 widens briefly with a slow truck pullout. Look for a paved turnoff to the right, which ends at a parking lot and some

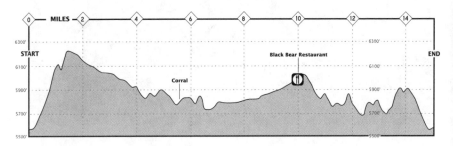

trail signs. In the parking lot, look for a wooden sign indicating the beginning of the Strawberry-Pine Trail. It'll be to the left of the parking lot signs.

10.7 Look for a white arrow painted on a tree, pointing to the right toward the trail. Follow this and all other painted arrows you see along the trail.

12.4 The trail splits. To the left, there's a deep gully with a dead tree crossing it and a very large, very old tree stump. A trail appears to descend quickly toward the left. However, there are several painted white arrows directing you toward the right. Take the right following the arrows and continue ahead.

13.0 There's a major manmade blockage across the trail, constructed of rocks and logs. Carry the bike over this block and continue ahead. Just beyond this portage, the trail splits left and right. For this ride, take the right, heading upward along Strawberry Mountain. The left descends into Pine; you'll have to bike up the pavement to where you parked if you take this.

14.3 Arrive at FS 428. *[Note. There's a tricky descent down to the dirt road, so be careful!]* Once you're on the dirt road, turn left and bomb back down to your vehicle. Listen for approaching cars!

15.0 Return to your vehicle.

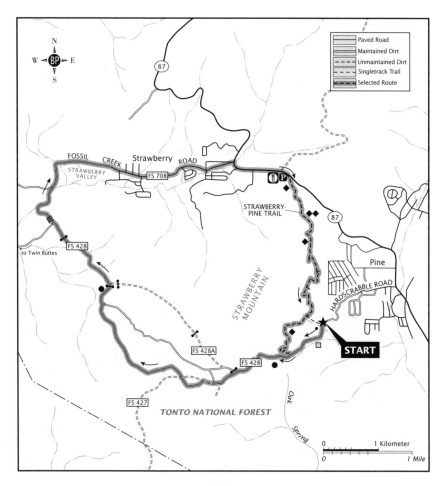

big ring all the way around Strawberry Mountain until the brief climb to the town of Strawberry. After that, cyclists are back on paved road, pedaling through the quiet hamlets of Strawberry and Pine en route to the Pine-Strawberry Trailhead off AZ 87.

You can easily stick to the main road, turning onto Hardscrabble Mesa Road and returning to your vehicle. However, the Pine-Strawberry Trail is a little-known but wild ride that's well worth the trip. Hidden off AZ 87 behind a tiny four-car parking lot, the Pine-Strawberry Trail cuts along Strawberry Mountain under a heavy canopy of pine trees. Because the trail is little used, it can be quite rocky and root-strewn, with a few death-defying descents featuring big rocky drops. This trail will demand a complete skill set; don't try it if you think you're tired from the loop around the mountain. The Pine-Strawberry Trail would make a good, if short, shuttle ride as well.

> *Strawberry School is the oldest school-house still standing in Arizona. It's a classic one-room schoolhouse, complete with chairs, a desk, and chalk boards that cover one wall. For those wanting to stop in and visit the little schoolhouse, it can be found less than two miles west on Fossil Creek Road in Strawberry. It's open May through September.*

The trail split at mile 13 is critical. Going left offers a great singletrack descent back down to Pine…but then cyclists will have to grind back up Hardscrabble Mesa Road to get back to the vehicle. The right fork ascends a series of rocky, little-used switchbacks up Strawberry Mountain. It's so rocky in fact, riders should expect to walk much of this trail. The views of the Mogollon Rim, once the trail tops out, are unmatched.

Ride Information

🌑 Trail Contacts:
[See Ride 33: Cypress Thicket]

🕐 Schedule:
Open year round – *may be snowy in the winter, rainy during the summer monsoon season*

💲 Fees/Permits:
No fees or permits required

❓ Local Information:
Pine-Strawberry Chamber of Commerce, Pine, AZ (928) 476–3547 or *www.pine-strawberry-az.com*

🌐 Local Events/Attractions:
Tonto Natural Bridge State Park, Payson, AZ (928) 476–4202 – *Tonto Natural Bridge is the world's largest travertine bridge, a limestone arch that is 183 feet high over a 400-foot long tunnel. Travertine is a kind of dissolved limestone. The turnoff to the park is 13 miles north of Payson •* **Strawberry Festival,** Pine, AZ (928) 476–3547 – *Each June brings the Strawberry Festival, featuring local arts and crafts, music, food, games, and other fun (if touristy) activities. A great excuse to escape the heat elsewhere in the state.*

🛏 Accommodations:
Windmill Corner Inn: (928) 476–3064 – *18 miles north of Payson on AZ 87 •* **Strawberry Lodge,** Payson, AZ (928) 476–3333

🎫 Other Resources:
The Pine-Strawberry Archaeological and Historic Society: *www.geocities.com/ pinestrawhs*

🅝 Maps:
USGS maps: Strawberry, AZ; Pine, AZ; Buckhead Mesa, AZ; Cane Springs Mountain, AZ

36

Highline to Christopher Creek

Ride Specs

Start: From the AZ 260 trailhead—off AZ 260, four miles east of Christopher Creek
Length: 13-mile loop
Approximate Riding Time: 2–2.5 hours
Difficulty Rating: Technically difficult, requiring moderate physical exertion. A few short, steep climbs
Trail Surface: Singletrack that quickly changes from smooth to rocky. A portion of the trail is on AZ 260. There are numerous loop opportunities.
Lay of the Land: Below-the-rim pine forest
Elevation Gain: Highline to Christopher Creek Loop–2,114 feet; George Crook Loop–804 feet
Land Status: National forest
Nearest Town: Christopher Creek
Other Trail Users: Hikers/runners, equestrians
Canine Compatibility: Dogs permitted
Wheels: Hardtail with a good fork; full suspension strongly recommended

Getting There

From Payson: Starting from the intersection of AZ 87 (Beeline Highway) and AZ 260, go east on AZ 260 and follow the Mogollon Rim. Drive 26.5 miles east. The trailhead is on the north side of AZ 260, four miles after passing through the town of Christopher Creek and about one mile after AZ 260 splits into a multi-lane highway. *DeLorme: Arizona Atlas & Gazetteer:* Page 51 B4

Cutting Arizona in half like a massive tectonic scar is the Mogollon Rim. The rim is in fact the southern edge of the Colorado Plateau, upon which much of northern Arizona rests. While the Mogollon Rim stretches from New Mexico through Arizona, nowhere is it more obviously a "rim" than in the Payson area. Volcanic action has hidden the cliff's edge in the White Mountains and points east, and the rim is merely a trace by the time it reaches Prescott to the west. But for nearly one hundred miles, the Mogollon Rim is an obvious and visible cliff.

The Highline Trail was established in the late 1800s to connect early homesteads and ranches along the Mogollon Rim. It became a national recreation trail in 1979. The total trail length is 51 miles, running from the Pine Trailhead at the west end to the AZ 260 Trailhead at the east end.

Today, the Highline Trail is an extremely popular national recreation trail. It's technically difficult in spots, but not impossible to bike. If you stay in your seat and push yourself, this trail *will* make you a better rider. The rewards follow each hard section— smooth and fast singletrack. The Highline's hypnotic path weaves toward the rim and down into a drainage gulch, then away from the rim and up to a rocky viewpoint. In and down, out and up, over and over until reaching the Christopher Creek split.

The descent to Christopher Creek is steep, rooted, and occasionally dangerous for those not paying attention. You can work on your switchback skills, your getting-your-butt-behind-the-seat skills, and your sudden-transition-to-vertical-climb skills all at once on this trail. For an especially exciting downhill adventure worthy of the most expensive long-travel downhill racing bike, check out the continuous downhill from atop the rim via the Drew Trail, and then down Christopher Creek.

The General George Crook Trail is another major trail in the area, and a necessary component for many of the most popular loop options. General Crook was the Army officer in charge of moving provisions to forts throughout the region; his "trail" began as a military road between Fort Apache (now in the middle of the San Carlos Apache reservation) to the territorial capital of Prescott, for a total length of 140 miles. The trail was abandoned until the mid-1970s when a Boy Scout troop resurrected it. The General Crook Trail is now a mix of dirt road and singletrack that runs along the very edge of the Mogollon Rim; the eastern end of the General Crook Trail connects to the White Mountain Trail system.

The views from atop the rim via the General Crook Trail are quite camera-worthy. Parts of the General Crook Trail are actually FS 300 (Rim Road), while there are many narrow—often forgotten and overgrown—remnants of singletrack shooting off

the road here and there. Bring thorn-resistant tubes and plenty of bug repellant if you want to explore the little-used singletrack bits. Keep your eyes open for cairns that hikers and bikers have piled to mark the trail as it fades into the brush.

The forest below the rim is thick ponderosa pine. Needles and pinecones cover much of the trail throughout the year, sometimes hiding roots and vital rock drop-offs. While there are no Bengal tiger trap-type holes completely hidden on the trail, stay alert.

In the spring, hordes of horned toads come out of hiding to sun themselves on the trail's red rocks. They're slow and stupid early in spring, and they won't get out of your way like sleek geckos will. Again, stay alert and don't squash the toads.

While approaching Christopher Creek (the creek itself, not the village), the forest gives way to lush ferns and grasses. A rainforest-like canopy covers the bottom of the trail, though much of its lush flora and fauna was jeopardized by the Dude Fire of 1990. A lightning strike below the rim ignited an inferno that engulfed more than 24,000 acres across three national forests (Coconino, Tonto, Apache-Sitgreaves). Sixty-three homes were destroyed, including author Zane Grey's historic home, and six firefighters died fighting the flames. Although such fires are natural—indeed are necessary—to the forest ecosystem, the Dude Fire is considered the worst fire in Arizona history. The fire location was several miles east of this loop, although it did cross a portion of the 51-mile-long Highline Trail.

MilesDirections

There are numerous loop options that use combinations of the Highline, Christopher Creek, General Crook, and Drew Canyon trails with AZ 260 acting as a connector. The first route described in this chapter takes you from the AZ 260 trailhead north along Highline Trail to Christopher Creek Trail; down Christopher Creek Trail to AZ 260; and then east along AZ 260 back to the trailhead. The second route described takes you to the top and along the Mogollon Rim on Rim Road, down a crazy descent on Drew Canyon Trail, and then back along Highline Trail to you car.

Highline/Christopher Creek Loop:

0.0 START from the AZ 260 trailhead. The Highline Trail heads due west out of the parking lot, just beyond the bathrooms and corral (the trailhead is behind the map kiosk); For this ride, head straight down Highline Trail, descending a shallow hill along singletrack. Every couple of miles, there's a white diamond nailed into a tree. *[FYI. The Military Sinkhole Trail/FS 317 splits off to the right* and ascends quickly and painfully to the top of the Mogollon Rim.]*

4.2 The Highline Trail reaches an old, rotten gate. There are several trail options here. To your right, before you pass through the gate, is the Drew Canyon Trail, coming down off Mogollon Rim and FS 9350. Dead ahead, through the gate, is the continuation of the Highline Trail (all 51 miles of it). *[Note. This trail has a wooden sign that says "Christopher Creek," but it is not the trail you want!]* To your left, after you've passed through the gate, is the Christopher Creek Trail. Head south down this trail, south...very quickly down, down, down.

6.3 Reach an intersection. To the right is a trail marked with a sign reading, "See Canyon Trail." To the left is the Highline National Recreation Trail. Turn left, heading toward Christopher Creek.

6.4 Cross Christopher Creek. It's a steep and slippery hike-a-bike section, especially dangerous when wearing SPD-type shoes with hard soles. Keep following the white diamond

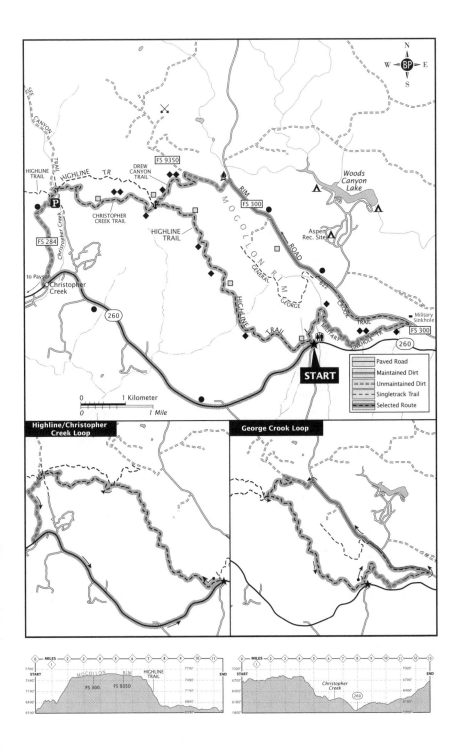

Highline/Christopher Creek Loop

George Crook Loop

N
W — E
S
BP

*Woods
Canyon
Lake*

HIGHLINE
TRAIL

HIGHLINE TR

FS 9350

DREW
CANYON
TRAIL

CHRISTOPHER
CREEK TRAIL

HIGHLINE
TRAIL

FS 300

Aspen
Rec. Site

FS 284

to Payson

Christopher
Creek

260

HIGHLINE

TRAIL

GENERAL

GEORGE

CROOK

TRAIL

MILITARY

SINKHOLE TR

Military
Sinkhole

FS 300

260

START

	Paved Road
	Maintained Dirt
	Unmaintained Dirt
	Singletrack Trail
	Selected Route

0   1 Kilometer

0   1 Mile

HIGHLINE
TRAIL

MOGOLLON   RIM

FS 300   FS 9350

MILES

7790'
START
7490'
7190'
6890'
6590'

7790'
7490'
7190'
6890'
6590'
END

MILES

7000'
START
6700'
6400'
6100'
5800'

*Christopher
Creek*
260

7000'
6700'
6400'
6100'
5800'
END

blazes nailed into the trees and take the trail that heads due south, directly across the creek.

6.5 Reach the "See Canyon Trail" trailhead kiosk. Ride into the parking lot and make a left turn onto the gravel road (FS 284). You will bomb very quickly down to AZ 260 and civilization.

8.0 Exit onto AZ 260 and turn left. Cross over the highway—careful of speeding RVs!—and grab a bite to eat at the Tall Pines Market. Head east on AZ 260, pedaling up the long ascent.

13.0 Turn onto the AZ 260 trailhead and return to your car.

George Crook Loop:

0.0 START from the AZ 260 trailhead. Military Sinkhole Trail starts at the same place the Highline Trail begins, except you'll need to turn right (east) at the bathrooms and corral instead of left. (There's a sign.) *[FYI. About 200 yards up the trail, you'll reach a clearing atop a granite shelf. You might see a little*

game trail heading straight up the rim. Do not take this trail. Instead, look to the right of this clearing for a trail that continues due east. Because of unpredictable deadfall during the rains and snows every winter, Military Sinkhole may involve quite a bit of portage over fallen trees.]

1.4 Military Sinkhole Trail joins the remains of an old wagon road that heads straight up to Mogollon Rim. This wagon road is very rocky and loose, and the ascent is relentless.

2.3 Reach the end of the climb! Military Sinkhole Trail connects with the General George Crook Trail atop Mogollon Rim. Look for the little wooden sign that says "Military Sinkhole Trail." Turn left past the sign, riding along the rim's edge.

3.3 General George Crook Trail parallels Rim Road (FS 300) and becomes Rim Lakes Vista Trail (Trail 622), which is paved for wheelchair access. Get ready for some mind-blowing views from the edge of the Mogollon Rim!

3.6 When the pavement runs out, hop onto the dirt road (FS 300/Rim Road) and head for the sign that says "9350 Camping Area." *[Side-*

Popular Loop Options for the Highline Trail

• *Highline Trail west starting from the 260 Trailhead, down Christopher Creek Trail to AZ 260, back up the highway to the trailhead. Very fun, very fast. The descent down Christopher Creek Trail is technically difficult in spots but is one of the best singletrack trails in the state. Approximate ride time: 2.5 hours.*

• *Starting from the 260 Trailhead, head up Military Sinkhole to George Crook Trail, down Drew Canyon, back to 260 Trailhead via Highline Trail. Physically difficult, due to the God-awful climb up the Military Sinkhole Trail to the rim. Technically difficult descent down the Drew Canyon Trail. Approximate ride time: 3.5 hours.*

• *From the town of Christopher Creek, go up FS 284, up Christopher Creek Trail, turn right (east) on the Highline Trail to the 260 Trailhead, up Military Sinkhole, down Drew Canyon Trail, Christopher Creek Trail, and FS 284 back to the town of Christopher Creek. The best of everything, and a true epic. Don't go into this one without lots of endurance and guts. Approximate ride time: 5+ hours.*

Ride Information

● Trail Contacts:
Tonto National Forest, Payson Ranger District, Payson, AZ (928) 474–7900 or *www.fs.fed.us/r3/tonto* – *The Payson Ranger District handles everything below the Rim, including the Highline and Christopher Creek Trails* • **Apache-Sitgreaves National Forest,** Chevelon-Heber Ranger District, Overgaard, AZ (928) 535–4481 or *www.fs.fed.us/r3/asnf/* – *The Heber Ranger District handles the "Rim Lakes Recreation Area," which includes trails above the Rim such as the General George Crook Trail.*

● Schedule:
Open year round – *Winters can be wet,* cold, and potentially snowy, particularly atop the Rim.

● Fees/Permits:
No fees or permits required

● Local Information:
[See Ride 33: Cypress Thicket]

● Accommodations:
The Village at Christopher Creek, Payson, AZ 1–800–950–6910 or *www.thevillageatcc.com* – *very nice cabins right on the Rim*

● Maps:
USGS maps: Promontory Butte; AZ Woods Canyon, AZ

---

trip. *You can continue on the singletrack out of the parking lot where Trail 622 ends. This is the continuation of the General George Crook Trail, which can be taken all the way to Prescott with time and persistence (it's several hundred miles long). General George Crook Trail becomes overgrown and very hard to follow shortly after the end of Trail 622, and it gets progressively farther away from Rim Road. Feel free to explore this trail, as it will give you views off the rim few ever see. It's just very hard to get back on track to reach the Drew Trail, which takes you down the cliff side.]*

5.4 Turn left onto FS 9350 [**FYI.** *This is a very well marked area for camping].* Take the dirt road heading toward Mogollon Rim; the road splits at the bathrooms but quickly rejoins.

6.2 Turn left at the large sign that says "Drew Canyon Trail." Look for a pair of poles off the road a bit, indicating the start of the trail.

[Note. Drew Canyon is extremely steep and dangerous; be prepared to walk some parts if you're not a certified Rad Downhiller.]

7.3 Arrive at the gate where the Christopher Creek Trail descends. Turn left at the gate (but don't go through it; it's to your right after you've descended the Drew Canyon Trail) and head down Highline Trail back to the AZ 260 trailhead (4.2 miles of sweet singletrack). *[**Side-trip.** Continue straight and head down to the town of Christopher Creek (3.8 miles of primo singletrack and fast forest road to the highway). Follow the directions from Highline/Christopher Creek Loop back to the trailhead.]*

Willow Springs Lake

Ride Specs

Start: From the first parking area to the left of FS 237
Length: 15.8-mile loop
Approximate Riding Time: 2 hours
Difficulty Rating: Moderate technical difficulty, with a long, shallow climb at the end. Aerobically moderate.
Trail Surface: Singletrack and doubletrack
Lay of the Land: Pine forest
Elevation Gain: 593 feet
Land Status: National forest
Nearest Town: Heber
Other Trail Users: Hikers
Canine Compatibility: Dogs permitted
Wheels: Hardtail is okay; a bit too rough for hybrids

Getting There

From Payson: From the intersection of AZ 87 and AZ 260 in Payson, drive 34.4 miles east on AZ 260. Drive past AZ 288 (the turn to Young) and start looking for FS 237 on your left, about three miles up the road. Pass the Willow Springs Lake turnoff—this just gets you to the lake's marina. If you reach the Canyon Point Campground turnoff, you've gone too far. In a few yards, FS 237 has a sign that reads "Sitgreaves National Forest Rim Lakes Recreation Area." Turn left here; don't turn on the split to the right immediately past the Forest Service sign. You're looking for a parking area and bathrooms about 0.4 miles in on your left. If you pass a gated road on your left, you've gone too far. Park next to the bathrooms. *DeLorme: Arizona Atlas & Gazetteer:* Page 51 B5

W illow Springs Lake was Arizona's first trail designated for mountain biking. Although a bit hard to find the way sometimes, it's worth a visit both for the scenery and the weather. Temperatures run at least 10 degrees cooler than Payson atop the Mogollon Rim.

Atop the rim, the winds are incessant. Any time of year, regardless of the prevalent weather, there's a good chance some strong winds will be blowing. The first part of the trail cuts across open meadows and exposes you to the wind, but dense stands of pine block most of it while you're riding.

The meadow portion of the ride continues as the trail follows the power lines. Just as the trail reaches AZ 260 again, the trail makes a hard right and enters the trees. Depending on the time of year, there's an excellent chance of seeing elk within the forest, even this close to the highway. Typically springtime is the best time to see the elk—they're usually heading up to the top of the rim, where its temperatures are cooler during the summer months.

Heading into the ride, there's a bike symbol along the trail every mile for the first four miles. For the rest of the ride, there are little blue diamonds tacked onto the trees. Good thing, because the Forest Service doesn't often perform trail maintenance here. Shortly after making the turn away from the highway and into the forest, there's one good set of signs...and then you're on your own. Many of the signs are facing the other direction—our way is the better way to ride the loop, honest—so you're look-

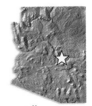

ing not for bike signs, but the *backs* of bike signs. This skill will come in especially handy around mile four or so: Multiple downed trees and manmade rock blockages cut across the trail, but it's still definitely the trail (the rangers say the blockages are remnants from when they were shutting down old forest roads to vehicles, and not meant to be taken as bike-proofing).

Willow Springs Lake is a small, attractive fishing lake that's popular with boaters in the summer. It's too small, really, to cruise around on but it's perfect for fishing and sunning. Indeed, the entire top of the rim is dotted with many lakes, perfect for rowboats and lazy days. Willow Springs Lake is actually much larger and more scenic than the more-popular Woods Canyon Lake to the west, just a couple miles off AZ 260 but a half-hour closer to Payson.

When the trail reaches the dam at the far eastern edge of the lake, there's an unmarked turn to the right that goes up a loose climb to continue on the loop. However, there are a couple of exploration options here: Bikes can ride across the top of the dam and over to the other side of the lake (there's a boat launch and more trees), or enter the Horse Trap Wildlife Enclosure. The enclosure, which includes the extremely deep Horse Trap Gulch, is completely closed to motorized vehicles but is open to mountain bikes. It's worth poking around in, but don't go too deep into the gulch—it's a steep climb out!

The trail makes its way northeast and returns to an old forest road. The road is off-limits to trucks now and is a fairly flat ride in both directions. It's about four miles to

the end, but worth the trip to see Chevelon Canyon. The trees at the end are usually too dense to see through, so leave the bike and explore on foot for a while. It's a beautiful and little-seen part of the state.

The improved dirt road returns more-or-less straight back to the parking area. The dirt road by itself is a pretty good "date ride," if riding with somebody who's not an experienced rider but wants to be on a bike in the dirt. It's a 10-mile out-and-back, and the dead end, among the pines, is a great place for a picnic. Keep in mind the area is more than 6,500 feet up, and may leave inexperienced riders a bit breathless from altitude alone.

MilesDirections

0.0 START from the parking area. Ride back out onto FS 237, turn left, ride about 50 feet, and turn immediately left onto the gated dirt road. The gate has a mountain biking sign posted, as well as other indications that the trail begins here. Lift the bike over the gate and begin riding along the power lines that enter the forest.

0.2 The trail forks. Although there's a bike sign on the right fork, stay to the left, which will take you clockwise around the loop. You'll eventually come back out on the right fork.

1.5 A doubletrack splits off to the right, marked with a gray diamond and numbered 9505E. Continue ahead, following the power lines.

2.5 The power line trail takes you almost back to AZ 260. You can see the highway just beyond a barbed-wire fence. Look to your right and you'll see bike symbols along a single-track. Turn right here, and follow the trail.

2.7 The trail intersects with singletrack. If you turn left, you'll get back to AZ 260. There's an

excellent wooden sign with a bright white arrow pointing you right. Turn right and continue down the singletrack. Just beyond this turn, there's a little singletrack to your left that can take you down to the lake. For this ride, continue ahead on the main singletrack.

3.0 After a short, loose climb, the trail appears to continue ahead. However, look to the right and you'll see numerous blue diamonds and bike signs pointing you to an unobvious fork. To make matters worse, there are two manmade rock blockages across the trail. Regardless, this is the trail! Take the right fork and continue. [*FYI. If you go left, the trail eventually peters out at a gorge.*]

3.2 The trail seems to split left and right. There are rock dams across either trail. Although there are no blue diamonds visible, you want to take the left split. Yes, there's a massive downed tree across the trail (it's been there for years). Go over it. In about 30 yards, you'll be rewarded with the *back* of a bike sign and several blue diamonds pointing back in the direction from which you came.

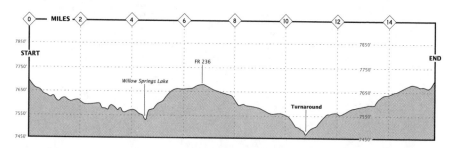

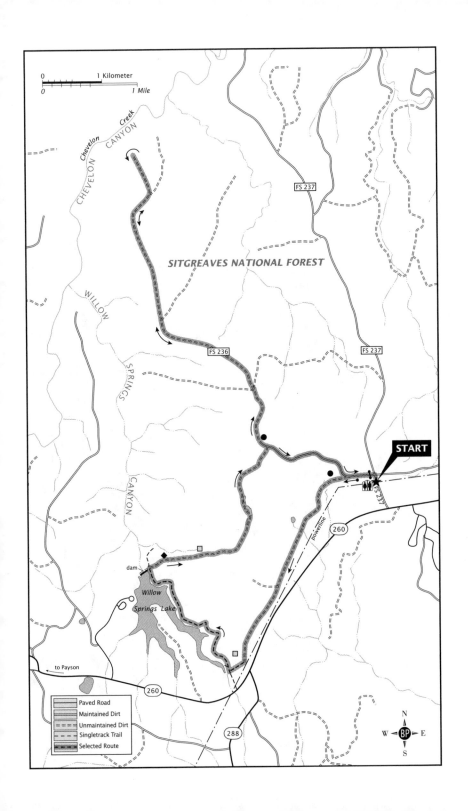

0 ——— 1 Kilometer
0 ——— 1 Mile

Chevelon Creek

CHEVELON CANYON

FS 237

SITGREAVES NATIONAL FOREST

WILLOW

FS 236

FS 237

SPRINGS

START

FS 237

CANYON

260

powerline

dam

Willow Springs Lake

to Payson

260

288

	Paved Road
	Maintained Dirt
	Unmaintained Dirt
	Singletrack Trail
	Selected Route

N
W — BP — E
S

Many of the signs you see are set up for riding the trail counterclockwise.

4.0 Dead tree across the trail. Somebody has built a little rock bridge so you can ride over the tree. Just beyond the downed tree, there's another big log—this one you'll have to carry the bike. As always, keep your eyes open for bike signs and blue diamonds pointing in both directions.

4.5 As you come down a hill, you'll arrive nearly on the shoreline of Willow Springs Lake. Turn right and follow the lake's edge until you reach a massive dam at the end of the lake. For the Willow Springs Lake trail, look for a dirt road that comes down a hill directly across from the edge of the rock dam, to your right. Ride up this road. *[FYI. You can ride along the dam if you want to get a better view of the lake. There's also a fence beyond the dam*

and it appears you can proceed forward—which you can, but it takes you into the Horse Trap Wildlife Enclosure and a difficult climb back out.]

6.0 Reach a series of little stagnant ponds. The trail passes between these ponds. There's a split to the right marked with a hand-painted signpost that says "Spur #3." Instead, turn left and ride between the ponds.

6.9 Reach the improved FS 236. Turn left and follow the road until it dead-ends at the edge of Chevelon Canyon. If you turn right, you'll get back to your car in a couple miles.

10.8 Reach the end of the road. There's a wooden signpost but no sign. Park the bike for a while and hike along the edge of Chevelon Canyon. *[FYI. Depending on the time*

of year, there are some spectacular views of the canyon from up here. During the spring and summer, though, it's so heavily treed that you can just barely see the canyon at all.] When you're done, turn around the way you came.

14.6 Return to the turnoff to the Willow Springs Lake bike trail, now on your right. Continue ahead to get back to your car.

15.5 A doubletrack splits off to your right. This is the road you rode in on earlier, and now you can see you're on the road you saw split off before at mile 0.2. Continue left and head toward the gate.

15.8 Return to the gate. Lift the bike over and return to your vehicle.

Ride Information

🌙 Trail Contacts:
Apache-Sitgreaves National Forest, Chevelon-Heber Ranger Districts, Overgaard, AZ (928) 535–4481

⏰ Schedule:
Open year round – *possible snow in winter*

💲 Fees/Permits:
No fees or permits required

❓ Local Information:
Heber/Overgaard Chamber of Commerce, Heber, AZ (928) 535–5777

🍴 Restaurants:
Hermanas Mexican Food, Heber, AZ (928) 535–4863

🗺 Maps:
USGS maps: Woods Canyon, AZ; OW Point, AZ; Porcupine Ridge, AZ

Honorable Mentions

Rim Country

Compiled here is an index of great rides in Rim Country that didn't make the A-list this time around but deserve recognition. Check them out and let us know what you think. You may decide that one or more of these rides deserves higher status in future editions or, perhaps, you may have a ride of your own that merits some attention.

(W) Four Peaks Road

The road up to the top of the Four Peaks Wilderness Area is an infamous grind that's popular with racers in the metro Phoenix area. It's awfully long and steep, if that's what turns you on. It's also the only way to ride a bike into the wilderness area. The views back down into the Valley are terrific, so bring a camera. Total ride is about 20 miles, and is very aerobically challenging. Give yourself about five hours.

Getting there: Heading north on U.S.87 toward Payson, turn right on FS 143; the first right turn about four miles past the Bush Highway turnoff. Either park here, or drive in two miles to a split in the road. Take the left (north) road, Cline Cabin Road, and head up. The road becomes more rugged the higher you go. Stop when you reach the wilderness area signs at the top.

(X) Sunflower

There are a couple hidden gems around the small town of Sunflower, on U.S. 87 headed toward Payson. Both require substantial climbing, as they take you up the southern Mazatzal Mountains into ponderosa pine country.

Starting in Sunflower, head east on FS 22 (a very popular route for off-road vehicles and trucks). Look for the turnoff onto singletrack Trail 73 at a corral. Follow this singletrack up, up, up until it hits FS 422. You can either follow the road around Boulder Mountain and head all the way to the Four Peaks Wilderness Area (see Four Peaks Road, above), or turn around and head back down the singletrack. The total route from Sunflower to the wilderness area is 17.5 miles one way.

Another ride out of Sunflower is up to the lookout tower on Mount Ord. Go north of Sunflower about five miles on U.S. 87. The highway climbs quite a bit, with a safety pullout for trucks at the top. Then the highway drops again. At the very bottom, look to the right for FS 626. Park in the lot and begin climbing. It's a 7.5-mile, 4,000-foot climb to the top of Mt. Ord. There's a lookout tower at the top, and the ranger may let you up into the tower when you get there.

Getting there: Sunflower is about 30 miles north of metro Phoenix on U.S. 87. *Delorme Arizona Atlas & Gazetteer:* Page 50 D2 and C2.

(Y) Mazatzal Mountain Loop

Although the Mazatzal Mountains lie almost entirely within a wilderness area, there is a nice 14-mile forest road loop that heads up into the mountain range. There's lots of climbing, but they payoff with the views and green piñon/juniper forest, making the trip well worth it.

Getting there: From Phoenix, head north on U.S. 87 toward Payson. North of Sunflower, look for a turnoff about eight miles later to your left, which is FS 201. Look for milepost 218. The loop is to take FS 201 due north toward the Mazatzal Mountains and take FS 201A back. Make sure you take FS 201 north, and not FS 25 west (although there are some good exploration opportunities down this road as well). All these roads are marked with backroads signs. There are several smaller trails into the wilderness area; stay off those trails while on your bike. *Delorme Arizona Atlas & Gazetteer:* Page 50 C2.

(Z) Stewart Pocket/"The Boulders"

Southeast of Payson, there's a sweet little segment of singletrack well hidden behind a ridge of boulders and new housing development. Stewart Pocket is the valley that follows a minor creek; the singletrack crosses back and forth over the creek, eventually climbing up into the boulders.

Starting from the corner of Granite Dells Road and Sutton Road, bomb down Sutton Road, known to the locals as "roller coaster road" for the four sizeable whoop-de-dos you can launch from on the way down. Sutton Road takes a hard right at the bottom of the drop; look for a trail behind a gate right at the turn, and head up this trail. Follow it until you hit the creek, and then look for where the trail picks up on the other side. It's well hidden, but keep looking and you'll find it.

Follow the trail until it climbs into the boulders—you may need to hike-a-bike up—and enjoy the views from atop the granite. Continue heading southeast, down out of the boulders, until you have to cross the streambed one last time. The stream is extremely washed out at the far end. Look for the hike-a-bike up and out of the streambed and back up to Granite Dells Road. Turn left (northwest) and head back up the road.

Stewart Pocket is about 7.5 miles round trip back to the intersection of Granite Dells and Sutton. The trail is easy, with some moderately technical spots and a long, shallow climb at the end of the ride.

Getting there: This very cool ride is practically inside Payson's city boundaries. You can either ride to it from Manzanita Cyclery's shopping center at the corner of AZ 260 and AZ 87, or drive down Granite Dells Road (first road east of the intersection, heading southeast) to the intersection with Sutton Road. *Delorme Arizona Atlas & Gazetteer:* Page 50 B3.

AA Road 235 Trail

This is an extremely easy out-and-back ride to the edge of Chevelon Canyon. It would be perfect for fit non-bikers or for a bike-assisted picnic. FS 235 is a designated mountain bike trail, following an old forest road that shoots due north 5.2 miles from Rim Road onto a finger of land between Chevelon Canyon and Willow Springs Canyon. It's pretty flat the whole way, and well marked. Give yourself a couple hours of riding time.

Getting there: From Payson, head east on U.S. 260. Turn onto Rim Road, marked with Forest Service signs as a recreation area. Park in the lot just after you turn onto Rim Road. The trail heads due north out of the parking lot. *Delorme Arizona Atlas & Gazetteer:* Page 51 B4 and A4.

BB Carr Lakes Trails

The U.S. Forest Service has built three brand-new loops atop the Mogollon Rim, near Carr Lake. These trails are so new that they're marked only with colored flags; expect rough conditions on the trails themselves until they're worn in.

The three loops are unimaginatively named Loop A, B, and C. Loop A is 5.8 miles long; loops B and C are simply extensions of this same loop, adding 0.2 and 3.2 miles respectively. You can ride these loops in various combinations and drag the ride out to 12 miles or more. The trails are currently moderate-to-difficult, due both to trail finding problems and the newness of the trail surface.

Getting there: Drive up FS 300, also known as the Rim Road, heading west atop the Mogollon Rim, to the turnoff to FS 9350. This is the same turnoff you take to get to the Drew Canyon Trail (*see Ride 36: Highline to Christopher Creek*). The loop begins at the intersection of FS 300 and FS 9350, and heads northwest. All three loops are within the triangle defined by FS 300, the Mogollon Rim, and the back edge of Loop C, so you can't get too lost. Contact the Chevelon-Heber Ranger District at (928) 535-4481 for more information. *Delorme Arizona Atlas & Gazetteer:* Page 51 A4

CC Valentine Ridge

The Mountain Biking Association of Arizona (MBAA) has adopted a trail system on Valentine Ridge, a camping area east of Payson just north of the small town of Young. The trails consist of old logging roads that wind their way through ponderosa pine and fir forests. Everything is well marked with signposts, and the Pleasant Valley Ranger District (520–462–4300) says it's very hard to get lost.

There are two trails on Valentine Ridge. The first is Valentine Trail 551, a two-mile long stretch of road between FS 188 and FS 109. The entrance off FS 188 is about two miles west of the Valentine Ridge campground, and is marked with a map kiosk. The second trail, Dan's Trail 550, does not have a developed trailhead but is very easy to find. It is a 4.8-mile-long trail that starts very close to where Trail 551 ends on FS 109, goes due south, and winds back and forth until it again ends on FS 109.

There are many, many opportunities to explore the network of old logging roads below the Mogollon Rim. These trails are an excellent starting point. One good loop would be to start in the Valentine Ridge campground and head west on FS 188. Turn left (south) on the Valentine Trail and take it to FS 109. At FS 109, turn right (west) until you reach Dan's Trail, and head south on it until it takes you back to FS 109. Take FS 109 back to the Valentine Trail, and follow it back to the campground. The ride is about 16 miles long.

Getting there: From Payson, take AZ 260 east toward Heber. Turn right (south) on the road to Young and follow it for six miles. Turn left on FS 188. Continue to the Valentine Campground. *Delorme Arizona Atlas & Gazetteer:* Page 51 B5.

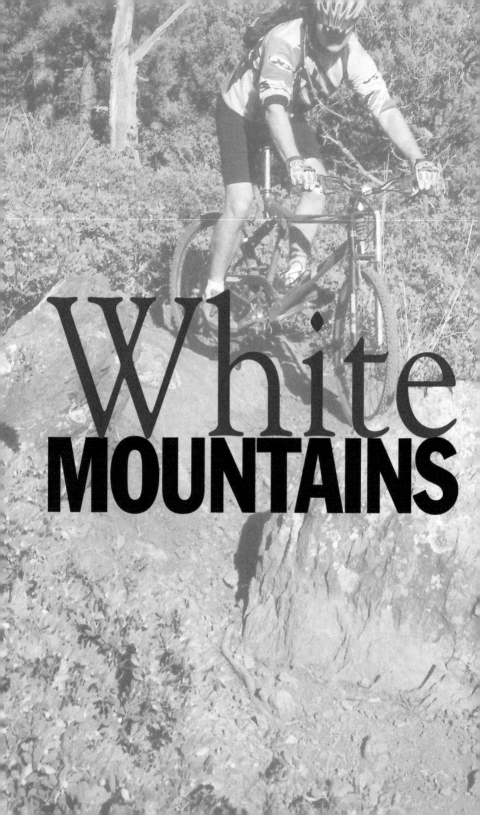

White
MOUNTAINS

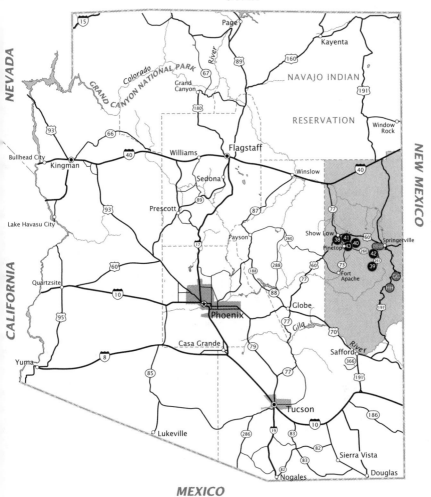

UTAH

NEVADA

CALIFORNIA

Page

Kayenta

NAVAJO INDIAN

RESERVATION

Window Rock

NEW MEXICO

Grand Canyon

GRAND CANYON NATIONAL PARK

Colorado River

Flagstaff

Winslow

Williams

Bullhead City

Kingman

Sedona

Prescott

Lake Havasu City

Payson

Show Low

Springerville

Pinetop

Fort Apache

Quartzsite

Phoenix

Globe

Gila

Casa Grande

Safford

River

Yuma

Tucson

Lukeville

Sierra Vista

Douglas

Nogales

MEXICO

The Rides

Buena Vista Trail 637 **38.**
Indian Spring/West Fork **39.**
Los Burros **40.**
Porter Mountain Trails **41.**
South Fork Shuttle **42.**
South Pinetop **43.**

Honorable Mentions

DD. Pole Knoll Recreation Area
EE. Sunrise Ski Resort
FF. Murray Basin
GG. Alpine
HH. Hannagan Meadow

White Mountains

White Mountains

There was never a more tragic tale of overlooked, underused single-track than that of the White Mountain Trail System. Miles and miles of singletrack languish unused among the pine forests and rolling hills of the White Mountains. Some easy, lots hard, and all really, really high up—at least 7,000 feet, some going up to nearly 10,000 feet in altitude.

Unfortunately, this mother lode of trails is four hours away from the main population centers of Phoenix, Tucson, and Flagstaff. You'll have to commit to an overnight stay if you're traveling to the White Mountains for biking, and unfortunately there's not enough work in the area (unless you're into logging or construction) to live here.

Called the "redneck Alps" by one anonymous city worker, the White Mountains aren't particularly mountainous. There are no snow-capped peaks, no dramatic altitude changes. Instead, the area is mostly rolling hills and lots of pine trees. Sort of a letdown when you first arrive. But don't let first impressions fool you: The riding here is really top-notch. The TRACKS trail maintenance organization (all volunteers) deserves huge credit for developing such nice trails on the west side of the mountains near Pinetop-Lakeside and Show Low.

Large super-luxury cabins are starting to show up in the Pinetop-Lakeside area, steadily changing the tone of the place from rustic-rural to Scottsdale-tourist. Show Low, up the road a bit (the two towns are separated by about a quarter-mile of undeveloped forest), still retains its rural cowboy-rancher feel. To the south, the San Carlos Apache Indian Reservation is fairly bleak except for the Hon-Dah Casino on the edge of town (and there's no biking allowed). Tensions between the Native Americans from the reservation, the Show Low locals, and the wealthy cabin owners sometimes run high.

On the biking scene, there are very few local mountain bikers in Pinetop-Lakeside/Show Low. There's a good shop in town—Cycle Mania—that runs group rides every week and attracts about a half-dozen regulars. And that's about the extent of the local organized mountain bike community. There are also a few die-hard individualists on the outskirts of town who are terrific riders but, much like most of the area residents, are fiercely independent.

On the eastern side of the White Mountains down in the foothills you'll find Springerville and Eagar. No snow-capped peaks on this side either, although one of Arizona's largest ski resorts—Sunrise—is on the reservation just west of town. Springerville and Eagar are even more rural (and Mormon) than Show Low and Pinetop-Lakeside on the other side of the mountain. Again, the one shop in town—Sweat Shop—is sufficient for the small, but dedicated, core of local riders. The local U.S. Forest Service office is very biker-friendly, and at least one of the rangers is himself a mountain biker, and is overseeing construction of more single-track in the area every year. The premier ride on this side of the White Mountains—Indian Spring—was built with mountain bikers in mind. Eagar also hosts a very nice family-oriented mountain biking festival each year in late August called the Valle Redondo Fat Tire Fiesta.

Section Overview

Buena Vista Trail 637

Buena Vista Trail 637 is a climb-heavy workout loop around the Buena Vista region of the Sitgreaves National Forest. Once the loop is completed, consider exploring the many other trails within this triangular region, defined by U.S. 60, FS 73, and the northern border of the San Carlos Apache Reservation. *(See page 296.)*

Indian Spring/West Fork

This relatively new addition to the White Mountains trail inventory starts out buffed, groomed, and very fast, leading through forest and across meadows. For those looking for a truly punishing trail, the West Fork spur becomes a lovely death march and should not be missed while visiting this part of the state. *(See page 302.)*

Los Burros

The local all-time favorite route, the Los Burros trail is an aerobically and technically demanding adventure up some of the highest points in the White Mountains area. Difficult climbs are always rewarded by thrilling downhill drops. This is probably one of the top five singletrack rides in the entire state. *(See page 308.)*

Porter Mountain Trails (Panorama and Timber Mesa trails)

The trails that begin along Porter Mountain Road offer something for every rider. There are some amazingly tricky lines hidden among the Timber Mesa Trail's treacherous rock gardens.

There are switchbacks and downhills that will challenge even seasoned riders. There are broad, fast doubletrack climbs that ascend several hundred painless feet up from the trailhead. Best of all, there's miles and miles of twisty singletrack hidden atop Timber Mesa darting between trees, over logs, down little rocky drops, and across the rooted pine-needle-covered forest floor. A bit further east, the Panorama Trail is an excellent introduction to what the White Mountains have to offer. It's fairly easy, taking cyclists through a variety of terrain and one long climb that will introduce novice lungs to climbing at altitude. Bring the camera to capture some spectacular mountaintop views. *(See page 314.)*

South Fork Shuttle

The South Fork Shuttle is a decadent treat for anyone who likes to go down through twisty singletrack, dodging through trees as you drop the hammer in the big ring. It's fast, it's fairly effortless (after some initial very rocky climbs at 9,000 feet—don't get dizzy from oxygen deprivation!), and it's a shuttle—so bring a buddy and factor in about 40 minutes for the trip to position vehicles at both ends of the trail. *(See page 320.)*

South Pinetop (Springs, Blue Ridge, and Country Club trails)

There are three excellent, short loops at the southern end of Pinetop-Lakeside that can be ridden individually or together in any configuration you wish. Short, sweet, tricky, and fast in some spots, the Springs Trail makes for a nice introduction to what the White Mountains has to offer bikers of all skill levels. Some of the trail weaves through rock gardens—an excellent place to hone your technical skills. Country Club Trail is easier and faster, although at four miles, is also a short trail. Finally, the Blue Ridge Trail, accessible via the Springs Trail, FS 187, or the super-abusive Ice Cave Trail to the northwest, is an overall more difficult trail. Because the trails are so close to town, they enjoy regular maintenance and use. *(See page 326.)*

Buena Vista Trail 637

Ride Specs

Start: From the Buena Vista trailhead, a couple hundred yards east of U.S. 60/FS 77
Length: 10.4–mile loop
Approximate Riding Time: 2 hours
Difficulty Rating: Physically moderate, with some difficult passages due to altitude, sand, and seven significant steep climbs. Technically moderate, with some tricky spots where quads have washed out the trail.
Trail Surface: Mixed doubletrack and singletrack
Lay of the Land: Pine and juniper forest
Elevation Gain: 1,360 feet
Land Status: National forest
Nearest Town: Show Low
Other Trail Users: Equestrians, ATVs, hikers, and hunters
Canine Compatibility: Dogs permitted
Wheels: Hardtail, with or without suspension, would be good for all the climbing

Getting There

From Show Low (the intersection of AZ 260 and U.S. Route 60): Take U.S. Route 60/AZ 77 (the road to Globe), approximately 4 miles south to FS 300. Look for the brown Apache-Sitgreaves National Forest sign. Turn left at the sign onto FS 300 and park at the Buena Vista trailhead. *DeLorme: Arizona Atlas & Gazetteer:* Page 52 B2

"Buena Vista" means "nice view" in Spanish, and this ride is packed with plenty of buena vistas. The Buena Vista Trail, a central piece of the White Mountain Trail System, loops within a triangular segment of a national forest. But to get to those nice views, riders have to go up. And up.

Buena Vista's defining aspect is its climbs. There are seven significant climbs on this trail, the first being by far the steepest and most strenuous. Cyclists shouldn't be surprised if they count more than seven climbs while riding the Buena Vista: What mere mortal riders consider a lung-busting climb, the high-altitude bike studs who frequent the trail simply view as a short rise. And remember, what goes up always comes down. There are few users on the trail (typically hikers and ATV enthusiasts), so enjoy ripping downhills after each climb (with caution).

The primary draw of Buena Vista isn't the official loop, which has been badly worn by unmonitored ATV use, but the secret singletrack network that crisscrosses the area. To get the inside scoop on these hidden trails, check out the color map at Cycle Mania in Show Low. That shop also organizes weekly rides along these awesome trails. Ask specifically about the Grindstone and Differential trails. A guided tour is the best—and maybe the only—way to find these singletrack treasures. This network of secret trails was created almost entirely by Cycle Mania's owner Tom Barrett, who is also the TRACKS volunteer responsible for this segment of the

White Mountain Trail System. All of the trails are watched over by TRACKS volunteers, who sort of take "ownership" of the trails and perform regular maintenance as well as create expansions of the network. Don't be surprised to find improved game trails and rediscovered old logging roads being used by bikers and hikers throughout the Apache-Sitgreaves National Forest.

Secret singletrack aside, the main Buena Vista Trail itself can be hard to follow. It crisscrosses over several old roads, so expect to get lost. If you do, simply backtrack until you find the blue diamonds indicating the official trail. Even if you do get lost,

MilesDirections

0.0 START from the Buena Vista trailhead, a few yards off U.S. Route 60/AZ 77. Head due east on the doubletrack.

0.5 Reach a T-intersection with the Buena Vista Trail 637. Wooden signs point back to the trailhead and indicate the trail goes left and right. Follow the sandy doubletrack to the left, heading north on the Buena Vista Trail 637. Follow the blue diamonds all the way around the loop—you can't get lost unless you start exploring some of the trails that crisscross through the forest. In this case, always remember that the Buena Vista Trail loops around the entire area and you *will* cross it eventually if you keep heading out along the same trail.

0.8 The trail reaches an intersection. A blue diamond with an arrow points to the right, toward narrower singletrack up a short hill. Follow the blue diamond—they're present for the entire trail—up the short hill.

1.0 The trail splits. The right split, marked with a yellow-dotted blue diamond, indicates a shortcut across the loop. To stay on our described route, take the trail to the left, where the blue arrows point up a hill.

1.3 Crest the first and most difficult uphill.

1.8 Cross a doubletrack. To the right is a shortcut across the forest to the other side; you pick up the Buena Vista Trail again in about two miles if you take this. Continue straight across and pick up the trail again (marked with blue diamonds).

1.9 Intersect with a rocky doubletrack. Blue

arrows point you right, up a hill.

2.6 Reach another intersection. Turn right, up the hill.

3.9 The trail splits. Turn right, following the blue diamonds.

4.4 A complicated intersection of marked and unmarked trails. Shoot straight through the gully at the bottom of the hill and pick up the doubletrack, marked with blue diamonds, on the other side. Continue going right on the other side of the gully. A few yards ahead of the gully, the trail splits left and right. Take the jaunt to the right and visit the Lost Tank, a small water hole that's full only some parts of the year. Once you've reached the Lost Tank, bear left and pick up the trail again. Shortly after returning to the Buena Vista Trail from the Lost Tank side trip, veer to the left at a split. Blue diamonds, logs, and a stone cairn mark the correct trail.

5.4 Reach a trail intersection. Turn right. Reach another intersection at the bottom of the hill. Behind you is a singletrack marked with yellow dots. This connects with the shortcut at mile 1.0.

5.8 Turn down and to the left at the intersection. Don't go straight. Keep following those blue diamonds!

6.6 Reach a three-way intersection. Follow the rock cairn and blue diamond to the right. Just past that intersection, reach another intersection. Continue straight ahead. Just ahead of this intersection, follow the doubletrack that veers to the left. Follow the blue diamonds.

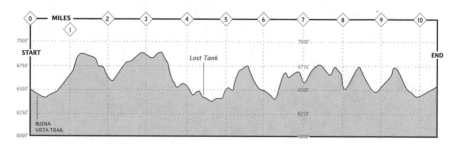

you're never that far from civilization. Feel free to explore the roads and make up your own route.

Around the turn of the century, the Buena Vista area was logged almost clean. Loggers found numerous Native American ruins in the area, and marked remaining nearby trees with white rings so they could come back and steal artifacts. Many of these ruins are still unexplored. Just remember, it's illegal to remove ruins from

---

7.1 Reach the crest of a long climb and an intersection. Follow the blue diamonds to the right.

7.2 Another veer to the left. Stick to the blue diamonds, to the right. The trail will take several trips off the established doubletrack through there for the next mile and a half; just

keep following the blue diamonds and you can't get lost.

9.9 Rejoin the junction back to the Buena Vista trailhead, to the left where the sign indicates.

10.4 Return to the trailhead.

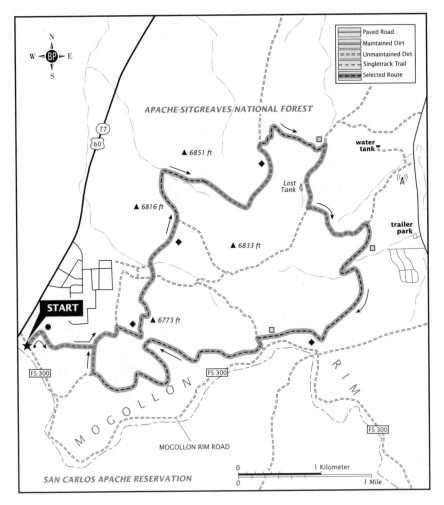

public lands. Looking is legal, though, but good luck finding these "marked" ruins; long-time local explorers still haven't found all the sites.

There is some private land around the trail where cyclists need to be careful. The entire southern border of the Buena Vista area is along the San Carlos Apache Reservation and is fenced off with barbed wire. Visitors must buy a recreation pass from the tribe or hire a tribal tour guide to enter this land. Also, the eastern edge of the area abuts trailer parks and cabins, all private land. It's difficult to get really lost in the Buena Vista area, but respect the privacy of land owners should you need to finish the ride quickly. There are several access points that take you out of the national forest and onto private drives and roads in the trailer parks. Homeowners don't want to see bikers using these roads as regular access, but generally don't care if they see you leaving their property.

Ride Information

◐ Trail Contacts:

Lakeside Ranger Station, Lakeside, AZ (928) 368–5111 • **Apache-Sitgreaves National Forests Supervisor's Office,** Springerville, AZ (928) 333–4301 or *www.wmonline.com/attract/asforest.htm*

◐ Schedule:

Open year round – *However, winters are extremely cold and snowy.*

◐ Fees/Permits:

No fees or permits required

◐ Local Information:

Show Low Chamber of Commerce, Show Low, Arizona 1–888–SHOW LOW (746–9569) or *www.showlow.com* • **White Mountains Online:** *www.wm online.com*

◒ Accommodations:

Apache Pines, Show Low, AZ (928) 532–1688

◐ Restaurants:

Branding Iron Steakhouse, Show Low, AZ (928) 537–5151

◐ Group Rides:

Contact Cycle Mania about group rides into the Buena Vista area (928) 537–8812

◐ Local Bike Shops:

Cycle Mania, Show Low, AZ (928) 537–8812

◐ Maps:

USGS maps: Show Low South, AZ

39

Indian Spring/ West Fork

Ride Specs

Start: From Indian Spring trailhead—southeast of Big Lake on the south side of FS 249E
Length: 13.6-mile loop
Approximate Riding Time: 3 hours
Difficulty Rating: Physically moderate, with the West Fork spur being a very difficult climb due to altitude (9,000 feet or more). Technically not demanding, unless you take the West Fork spur, which has some challenging rocky passages.
Trail Surface: Singletrack and Rails-To-Trails conversion
Lay of the Land: Pine forest
Elevation Gain: 1,511 feet
Land Status: National park
Nearest Town: Eagar
Other Trail Users: Hikers
Canine Compatibility: Dogs permitted
Wheels: Hardtails, hybrids, even rigid bikes are okay for this trail

Getting There

From Eagar: Take AZ 260 west to the Big Lake turnoff (AZ 261). Head south for about 25 miles. Go past Big Lake, visible to the right. Just past the lake, turn right on FS 249E and drive about half a mile to the trailhead. Look for the Indian Spring trailhead on the right. Park here. *DeLorme: Arizona Atlas & Gazetteer:* Page 53 D5

The Indian Spring Trail 627 was built by the Forest Service in the mid-1990s with mountain bikes in mind. The trail is immaculately groomed, with shallow berms on the turns and fun little hops here and there. However, hikers still use it (but not equestrians), so keep speeds in check.

Indian Spring begins with a shallow climb alongside Big Lake Knoll, a hill that overlooks nearby Big Lake. There's a short side trip about a half-mile from the start of the ride that you can hike to reach the Big Lake lookout tower. The trail up isn't really bikeable; either leave your bike at the gate to the side trail, or plan on carrying it up. You can go up the lookout tower for some incredible views of Big Lake and the surrounding mountains, but ask the tower's attendant first.

After a screamingly fast stint through meadows and trees, Indian Spring joins with the Old Apache Railroad rail bed, a product of a Rails-To-Trails Conservancy project. Rails-To-Trails is an effort to convert old, usually historic, rail systems into hiking and biking trails. Its effort is controversial among some conservative land-owning groups around the country, because tax dollars are spent to convert the railbeds into public trails without input from nearby property owners. These property owners then complain about the "land grab," called such because some railbeds were placed on easements privately negotiated with land owners who didn't sell the land but only

lent it to the railroad, and about the new easy access the public has to areas so close to their private property. This controversy did not play a part in the creation of the Indian Spring Trail, which resides entirely on national forest land.

The transformation from railbed to trail sometimes meets with mixed success, particularly if the cinders that make up the rail bed are too deep for bike tires. The first effort to transform the Old Apache railbed had this problem, and the cinders were

MilesDirections

0.0 START from the Indian Spring trailhead. The trail heads to the left of the trailhead kiosk.

0.6 A trail splitting off to the left leads to an optional walk (or ride, if you enjoy steep climbs up to nearly 10,000 feet) up to the Big Lake Lookout Tower. The climb is about half a mile each way (one mile total to make the side trip). *[WARNING. Don't climb the tower during a lightning storm!]*

2.2 Cross over FS 24, a wide, well maintained dirt road. The trail continues on the other side and is marked.

3.5 To your left is Indian Spring, a small pond.

3.8 Intercept with the Old Apache Railroad Rails-to-Trails project. Turn right.

5.3 Reach the junction with the West Fork Trail to your left. Turn here if you want to add the West Fork out-and-back to your excursion. This route includes the West Fork out-and-back and consequently the rest of the mileage is based on taking this trail. *[Bailout: If you're not up for a technical descent or the lung-busting ascent, skip the West Fork Trail and continue ahead on Trail 627. Subtract 5.3 miles from the total ride distance.]*

5.7 The West Fork Trail intersects with Conklin Spring Road (FS 68). Either cross over this road and pick up the singletrack, or take the driveway up to the West Fork trailhead.

7.9 Cross a wooden bridge that carries you over an old avalanche site. The trail is extremely rocky and treacherous, but still rideable with the right practice.

8.2 Reach the bottom of the descent to the West Fork Black River. Turn around here and head back toward Conklin Spring.

10.6 Reach the West Fork trailhead. Head across Conklin Spring Road and pick up the singletrack on the other side (the trail is marked).

11.1 Return to the Rails-to-Trails portion of the Indian Spring Trail. Turn left and continue up the hill.

12.1 Reach the end of the rail bed. The trail continues right as singletrack.

12.8 Cross FS 249E. Pick up the singletrack on the other side. Look for the trail sign.

13.4 Trail comes to a fork. Take the right fork. *[Side-trip: The left takes you to the Big Lake campground in about 0.3 miles.]*

13.6 Reach the trailhead.

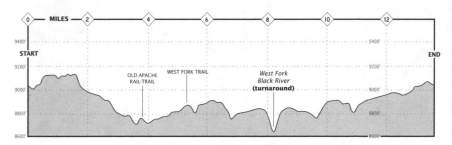

too deep for bikers initially. The railbed was then resurfaced and now the conversion is an unqualified success. The climb up the railbed is gentle and eminently rideable by bikers of all skills and fitness levels. The Old Apache Railroad used to run between a logging camp at the town of Maverick, and the Apache Logging Company's base in McNary, on the western side of the White Mountains. (*See Ride 40: Los Burros for more information about the Apache Logging Company.*)

The West Fork out-and-back portion of this ride descends into a canyon where overheated cyclists can soak their feet in the west fork of the Black River (not to be confused with West Fork Trail 94, also known as West Baldy Trail, which starts in Greer and follows the west fork of the Little Colorado River). The descent to the West Fork starts as rolling, easy singletrack and then becomes a series of rugged switchbacks as the trail drops into the canyon. While crossing a bridge over the rubble of an old avalanche, bike tires

> *Eagar features the only domed high school football field in the country—the Round Valley High School Ensphere. The facility is open for tours most of the year.*

sound like they're rolling over broken dishes. Be warned: The climb out of West Fork is steep, long, and technically difficult near the bottom of the canyon.

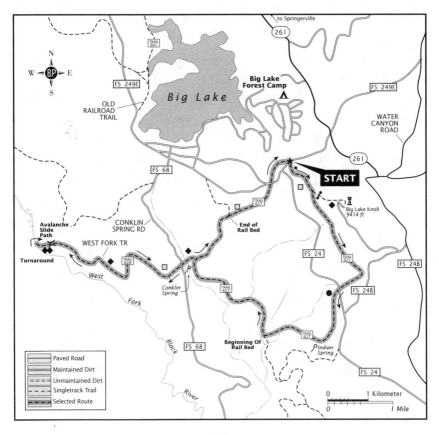

305

The Black River and White River join to become the Salt River, which cuts across the state and passes through metro Phoenix.

Indian Spring is just south of the Big Lake Recreation Area, a major summertime attraction for fishermen and outdoor enthusiasts from across the state. This area is approximately equidistant from Phoenix, Tucson, and Flagstaff.

Ride Information

📞 Trail Contacts:
Springerville Ranger District, Springerville, AZ (928) 333–4372 or www.fs.fed.us/r3/asnf/

🕐 Schedule:
Open year round

❓ Local Information:
Round Valley Chamber of Commerce, Springerville, AZ (928) 333–2123 or www.az-tourist.com – has information on Springerville, Eager, Greer, Alpine, and Nutrioso • **Town of Springerville,** Springerville, AZ (928) 333–2656 or www.springerville.com • **Town of Eagar,** Eagar, AZ (928) 333–4128 or www.eagar.com

🎉 Local Events/Attractions:
Valle Redondo Fat Tire Fiesta: (928) 333–1640 or www.z-com.com.fiesta – Three days of singletrack, racing, dining and other mountain biking fun. Late August, which is a perfect time to escape the heat of Phoenix and Tucson—it's usually in the mid-80s in the Springerville area that time of year.

Sponsored by Eagar Parks and Recreation and Sweat Shop Bike & Ski • **Casa Malpais Indian Ruins:** www.wmonline.com/attract/casam.htm – Get a peek at the lives of one of the "vanished" tribes of Arizona. Two miles north of Springerville on U.S. 180/191. $3 entry to the Casa Malpais Museum (in Springerville on Main Street) for adults, $2 for children.

🛏 Accommodations:
Best Western Inn, Eagar, AZ (928) 333–2540 or 1–800–528–1234 • **Corral Motel,** Springerville, AZ (928) 333–2264

🍴 Restaurants:
Los Dos Molinos, Springerville, AZ (928) 883–8152 – excellent Mexican fare, very hot!

🚲 Local Bike Shops:
Sweat Shop Bike and Ski, Eagar, AZ (928) 333–2950 – bike rentals, service, gear, apparel

🅽 Maps:
USGS maps: Big Lake South, AZ

Los Burros

Ride Specs

Start: From the trailhead kiosk at the end of Los Burros Campground
Length: 13.8-mile loop
Approximate Riding Time: 3-4 hours
Difficulty Rating: Technically moderate, with some technically challenging rock gardens and descents. Physically moderate to difficult, with three difficult climbs at high altitude.
Trail Surface: Mixed singletrack and double-track
Lay of the Land: Mixed conifer and ponderosa pine forest
Elevation Gain: 1,441 feet
Land Status: National park
Nearest Town: McNary
Other Trail Users: Hikers, off-road vehicles, equestrians, and hunters
Canine Compatibility: Dogs permitted
Wheels: Full suspension is recommended, because of some long, rocky downhills

Getting There

From McNary: Heading east toward Springerville on AZ 260 through the town of McNary from the town of Pinetop-Lakeside, look for the grocery store on the right of AZ 260, and just beyond that a sign for the local fire department. To the left of these signs, look for a small green sign that says "Vernon." The road marked "Vernon" is FS 224. Turn onto this road. Drive 7.5 miles down an extremely rutted dirt road to the Los Burros campground and trailhead on the right. Park at the end of the campground, park, and leave from the trailhead kiosk. **DeLorme: Arizona Atlas & Gazetteer:** Page 52/54 C3/C4

The Los Burros trail begins at the Los Burros Campground, 7,900 feet up, and climbs to 8,300 feet. Cool to cold year-round, this is the White Mountain area's must-ride adventure. The ride starts out with some easy climbs, long, lazy singletrack through meadows, rock gardens, and three moderately hard climbs. Once past the first steep climb, there's an insanely fast (remember IMBA rules) downhill. The singletrack roller coaster that wraps around Wishbone Mountain (the mountain the trail goes around) about three-quarters of the way into the ride makes the whole trip worth it ... but don't expect to have lots of energy left over. Los Burros is a physically demanding ride, especially if you're used to lower altitudes.

In 1997, Los Burros was the Subaru Arizona Race Points Series trail. It's also a major component of the annual Tour of the White Mountains 67-mile mountain bike race (*see Sidebar*). True gluttons for punishment can take a 6.5-mile long connector to the Country Club Trail (*see Ride 43: South Pinetop*) and add that loop for a total of about 24 miles.

This trail offers many wildlife viewing opportunities. At various points in the year (especially in late fall, when the wildlife migrate to the warmer climes of the Mogollon Rim), visitors can see elk, wild turkey, mule deer, and black bears. Since

MilesDirections

0.0 START from the Los Burros trailhead.

0.2 Pass through a gate and close it behind you. Just beyond the gate, turn right on the doubletrack next to the power line. Always remember to follow the blue diamonds that mark the trail the whole way.

0.5 A doubletrack splits off the Los Burros Trail. Go left and follow the blue diamonds. Turning right takes you up a hill—don't take that.

1.0 The trail intersects with FS 9, a dirt road. Go straight through; Los Burros Trail continues on the other side of road. *[FYI. The area you're now riding into is known as Indian Flat or Reservation Flat, comprised of smooth, flat singletrack across meadows and through groves of aspen.]*

3.0 Reach a fork. The doubletrack goes to the left, the singletrack goes immediately right. Turn right onto the singletrack, continuing along Los Burros Trail.

4.4 There's an intersection of old forest roads. As always, follow the blue diamonds to stay on Los Burros Trail as you pass through the intersection.

4.5 Reach Bear Wallow Tank, a small, muddy pond (a good rest area). Bear left at the pond, looking for the blue diamonds.

7.1 Pass through a gate and close it behind you. Shortly after the gate, you'll reach an intersection. Turn left, following the blue diamonds.

7.4 Small singletrack off to the left: Ignore this singletrack! Continue on the doubletrack about

50 feet, then pick up a singletrack off-shoot on your right. It climbs a short, steep hill.

8.1 Pass through a gate and close it behind you.

9.0 Cross the wide dirt road (FS 224) and continue on the other side. *[**Bailout:** Turn left onto FS 224 and you'll be able to ride on a dirt road all the way back to Los Burros Campground, about 2.5 miles west].*

9.8 Cross a doubletrack and continue along the singletrack on the other side.

10.0 Take a small singletrack turn to the left.

10.2 Near the cattleguard, cross over a dirt road and continue on the doubletrack.

11.1 Cross doubletrack, and pick up the singletrack across the road.

11.8 Arrive at a cluster of small wooden signs indicating various nearby trails. Follow the Los Burros trail, which points you straight ahead. Just past the cluster of signs, cross over FS 224 again; singletrack continues on the other side and is marked with a blue diamond.

12.1 Big hairy descent down a rocky power line road. Extremely dangerous! *[**FYI.** At the bottom of the hill, look for a gate to your right. This is the first gate you passed through at the beginning of the ride. Pass through and close the gate behind you.]*

13.8 Return to Los Burros trailhead.

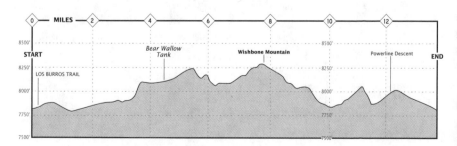

bears can run upward of 25 mph, don't try to run from them. Bear sightings are very rare, but if you're really worried about them, consider bringing along pepper spray. If you run into a bear, stay calm and quiet. Don't look into its eyes, which it will take as a sign of aggression. Don't turn your back on the bear, but instead quietly back away to indicate that you're trying to get out of its territory. You'll know you're in bear country by the bears' claw marks in the trunks of aspen trees.

Nearby McNary is an old lumber town with an interesting history. Back in 1916, a Flagstaff businessman named Tom Pollock chose the area as a base of operations for the Apache Lumber Company, so named because he leased the land from the Apaches. He ran a railroad into the new town, called Cooley (named for one of the two ranchers of the famous Show Low card game); this is the same rail line on which a portion of the Indian Spring Trail's rails-to-trails segment is built (*see Ride 39: Indian Spring*). Meanwhile, a thousand miles east in McNary, Louisiana, another lumber company was quickly running out of timbered land. The easterners came in and bought out the Apache Lumber Company, and renamed the town McNary. The town became known for its harmonious mix of blacks, whites, Latinos, and Indians. McNary's sawmill burned down in 1979 and was rebuilt near Eagar, on the eastern

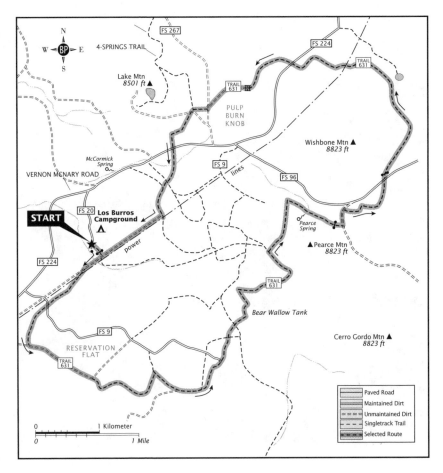

NRMC Tour of the White Mountains

If you're bored with the regular race circuit, and if eight grueling hours of high-altitude climbing sounds like lots of fun, this race/festival is for you. This massive 63-mile endurance race through many routes of the White Mountain Trail System is one of the toughest of its kind. On the same day, you can also take a 50-mile variation, as well as shorter loops of 46 and 25 miles. Held during the second weekend of October, the temperatures start out crisp but warm up nicely as the day gets on. Proceeds from the race go to the Navapache Regional Medical Center. Contact (928) 537–6319, Cynthia Clements, or register for the race at www.nrmc.org/twmreg.htm.

- *7-8 mile breeze ride*
- *25, 35, 45-mile singletrack challenges*
- *25- 50-mile tours on Forest Service roads*
- *63-mile singletrack endurance race*

This family event also has a kid's rally. The atmosphere is pretty accommodating with showers, bunks, and "barn and breakfast" arrangements available. Camping onsite, evening barbeque, and a Sunday breakfast. There are also various fun rides on Sunday.

side of the White Mountains.

The Los Burros trail is named after the Los Burros Campground, which also serves as the trailhead. The campground was once the site of the Los Burros Ranger Station, built in 1909; the ranger's original house and barn are all that still exist. It's a very popular campground with the trucks-and-guns crowd who come to party on Reservation Flat, a large meadow up the trail a bit. The campground is not otherwise notable, but is in a very pretty part of the national forest and provides great access to the trail. With McNary and Pinetop-Lakeside so close by car, the Los Burros trail makes a great bike-camping trip.

Ride Information

🕿 Trail Contacts:
Lakeside Ranger Station, Lakeside, AZ (928) 368–5111 • **Apache-Sitgreaves National Forests Supervisor's Office,** Springerville, AZ (928) 333–4301 or www.wmonline.com/attract/asforest.htm

⏱ Schedule:
Open year round – *Call first to check for snow.*

❷ Local Information:
Pinetop/Lakeside Chamber of Commerce, Lakeside, AZ (928) 367–4290 or 1–800–573–4031 or www.pinetoplakesidechamber.com

❶ Local Events/Attractions:
The Tour of the White Mountains: (928) 368–6700 – *A 48-mile long tour of all the singletrack trails that comprise the White Mountain Trail System. Contact the Pinetop-Lakeside Parks and Recreation Department for more information. Held in early October* • **Hon-Dah Resort Casino,** Hon-Dah, AZ (928) 369–0299 or www.hon-dah.com – *At the intersection of Highways 260 and 73—just past the Pinetop city limits, and just within the border of the Fort Apache Indian Reservation, you can find one of Arizona's shiny new casinos. Not as lavish as the Las Vegas Strip, but Hon-Dah makes for a ritzy home base while you're exploring the area by bike.*

❿ Other Resources:
On-line Mountain Guide, McNary, AZ: www.mtn-guide.com/sumovu.cfm/az103.htm

❸ Maps:
USGS maps: McNary, AZ, Sponseller Mountain, AZ, Boundary Butte, AZ, Horseshoe Cienega, AZ

Porter Mountain Trails
(Panorama and Timber Mesa trails)

Ride Specs

Start: There are two trails off Porter Mountain Road. The 636 Trailhead, for the Timber Mesa Trail, is 2.5 miles east of the turnoff from White Mountain Boulevard. The Panorama Trail is around the mountain, another 3.5 miles beyond Timber Mesa (for a total of six miles).

Length: Timber Mesa is a 6-mile loop; Panorama is an 8.3-mile loop. There are also options to combine the trails into one large ride.

Approximate Riding Time: 1.5 hours

Difficulty Rating: Timber Mesa is technically moderate, with difficult rocky sections and switchbacks, and physically moderate-to-difficult due to the altitude. The Panorama Trail is easy-to-moderate, due to a couple moderately difficult rocky sections and one long climb at altitude.

Trail Surface: Timber Mesa starts as singletrack and turns into gravel road at the end. Panorama Trail is a mix of singletrack and doubletrack. The connector trails between these two rides are rugged doubletrack.

Lay of the Land: The entire Porter Mountain area is in pine-juniper forest.

Elevation Gain: Panorama–574 feet; Timber Mesa–555 feet

Land Status: National park

Nearest Town: Pinetop-Lakeside

Other Trail Users: Hikers, hunters, and off-road vehicles

Canine Compatibility: Dogs permitted, but exercise caution during the hunting season

Wheels: Front suspension recommended for Timber Mesa; a rigid (but not a hybrid) is fine on the Panorama Trail

Getting There

From Show Low: From the intersection of U.S. 60 and AZ 260 (White Mountain Boulevard) in Show Low, head south on White Mountain Boulevard 8.3 miles to Porter Mountain Road. Look for the Navopache Power Company yard to the left. Turn left on Porter Mountain Road and drive 2.5 miles to the 636 Timber Mesa Trailhead on the left (the sign is on the right). Enter the Sitgreaves National Forest. Drive on the dirt road about a quarter mile before it dead-ends at the trailhead parking lot. *DeLorme: Arizona Atlas & Gazetteer:* Page 52 B3

Completed in August 1999, Timber Mesa 636 trail is an extremely recent addition to the White Mountain trail system. Constructed from a combination of existing singletrack, doubletrack segments, and old hunting and game trails, this trail is a favorite of the local hard-core riding crowd. Not that there's much of a crowd here—there are maybe a half-dozen really committed riders native to the White Mountains, and a dozen more semi-regulars scattered throughout the region.

Elk are plentiful in this portion of the Sitgreaves National Forest, especially during the summer. They'll usually dart away, but some will run alongside the bike trail for a bit before darting off in another direction.

Like all of the White Mountain area, riding is nearly year round. This trail gets some snow in the winter, but as often as not it warms up to 45 degrees a day later, melting the snow away. During the summer monsoon season, expect a downpour

almost daily. Timber Mesa is the easiest to ride during this season, because the trail's base is mostly comprised of cinder.

Blue diamonds—imprinted with the White Mountain Trail System logo—are trail markers, while blue diamonds with green dots indicate connector routes. The local trail maintenance folks ran short of blue diamonds in some cases and cut them in half. Look also for blue triangles, sometimes turned on their side like arrows, when trying to pick out the singletrack.

If you ride the broad doubletrack out of the trailhead, you'll come across the ruins of Jacques Ranch, now just a pair of freestanding chimneys. The ranch was built as a summer home for the Jacques family in the late 1800s, but burned down shortly after construction.

Visitors planning on spending more than a day riding in the White Mountains can make the Panorama Trail either the first or last visit. It's a great introduction to the area, and serves as a nice wind-down after riding some of the more exciting roller coasters in the area.

Panorama Trail is a loop north of Porter Mountain, the large mountain east of

Pinetop/Lakeside dotted with radio towers. The loop connects the dots between two tanks and a pair of hills called Twin Knolls. The trail comes by its name honestly—once at the top of the Twin Knolls, the view extends to the San Francisco Peaks to the west, Winslow to the north, and well into New Mexico to the east. Get ready for some spectacular photo-ops.

The area east of Porter Mountain is divided between squirrel-infested pine forest and grazing fields with cattle. Most times of the year, cows wander the trail—usually near the tanks that define the outer boundaries of this trail.

A portion of the trail passes through the Woolhouse Wildlife Habitat Area, which is closed to motorized vehicles (but not mountain bikes) for habitat protection. Not that it matters much; you'll see many signs of illegal 4x4 and motorcycle use in the area.

A local organization called TRACKS (it doesn't seem to be an acronym for anything), a coalition of hikers, equestrians, and bikers, is responsible for designating and maintaining the 200-plus miles of the White Mountain Trail System. The organization is always looking for maintenance volunteers, so if you're from the area or even just passing through, contact the group and ask how you can help.

White Mtn Trail System Signage

Trails in the White Mountain Trail System are marked with blue diamonds on trees. A blank blue diamond indicates a primary trail. A diamond marked with a green dot means a connector trail. A yellow dot indicates a shortcut back to the trailhead. A red dot indicates a side route to a vista or other areas of interest.

Ride Information

🌐 Trail Contacts:
Lakeside Ranger Station, Lakeside, AZ (928) 368-5111 • **Apache-Sitgreaves National Forests Supervisor's Office**, Springerville, AZ (928) 333-4301 or *www.wmonline.com/attract/asforest.htm*

🕐 Schedule:
Open year round – winters can be very cold

❓ Local Information:
Pinetop/Lakeside Chamber of Commerce, Lakeside, AZ (928) 367-4290 or *www.pinetoplakesidechamber.com*

👥 Organizations:
TRACKS: (928) 368-6700 (Pinetop-Lakeside Parks and Recreation Department) – *This volunteer organization, comprised of bikers, hikers, and equestrians, works in partnership with the Forest Service. The volunteers built the majority of the White Mountain Trail System (to which many of the White Mountain area rides belong), and they handle all the trail maintenance. Contact the Lakeside Ranger District or the Pinetop-Lakeside Parks and Recreation Department.*

🍴 Restaurants:
Matta's Too Mexican Restaurant, Pinetop-Lakeside, AZ (928) 368-6969

🇳 Maps:
USGS maps: Lakeside, AZ

MilesDirections

Timber Mesa

0.0 START from Timber Mesa Trail 636 trailhead. There's a large wooden national forest sign and what appears to be a wide doubletrack to the left of that sign. Do not take the doubletrack—this is the return route if you follow the Timber Mesa Trail loop as it's mapped. Instead, look for a narrow, hidden singletrack route to the right of the sign, bearing almost due east.

0.6 Pass a lookout point to the left with a view of the Pinetop-Lakeside area from this rocky crag.

0.7 Cross the Flume Trail, a doubletrack connector to the Panorama Trail. Ride through this intersection and stick to the singletrack; do not veer left or right. *[Side-trip. Turn right onto the Flume Trail to head over to the Panorama Trail in 2.5 miles.][Bailout: Turn left if you want to quickly hook up with the doubletrack that takes you back to the trailhead.]*

2.1 Reach a closed gate. Just beyond the gate is a doubletrack that loops westward and eventually takes you back to the trailhead. The trail turns to the left and hooks into a wide gravel road. Follow this road back to the trailhead.

2.3 Cross the Sawmill Trail, a doubletrack connector to the Panorama Trail. Continue ahead. *[Side-trip. Turn right to take the Sawmill Trail over to the Panorama Trail in 4.0 miles.]*

4.0 To your right, you can see Frost Tank.

5.8 Look for the twin chimneys (the last remnants of the Jacques Ranch ruins) to the right of the trail.

6.0 Return to the parking lot.

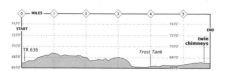

Panorama Trail

0.0 START from the Panorama Trail trailhead. The Panorama Trail heads due north, to the right of the trailhead kiosk; follow the sign that says "Porter Tank 2.5 miles." A few yards north of the trailhead, you'll come across wooden signs pointing left toward the Timber Mesa Trail via the Flume connector (note the green dots on the blue diamonds—remember, green dots are connectors!). Follow all the blue diamonds without green dots to find the Panorama Trail. Keep going straight toward Porter Tank. *[Side-trip. Turn left on the Flume Trail connector to reach the Timber Mesa Trail in 2.5 miles.]*

0.4 Reach a split in the trail. Go straight to take the Panorama Trail clockwise. You'll end up here at the end of the ride.

0.7 Reach an intersection with lots of doubletrack. Blue diamonds point you to the farthest right of all the choices.

1.2 The road splits just a few yards past fenced-in private property. Follow the blue diamond, which leads you along the trail to the left.

1.4 The road splits after a descent down a lava-covered hill. To the right is a wilderness area—no bikes allowed! Continue left at the split along the barbed-wire fence.

2.4 Reach Porter Tank. The tank itself is hidden behind a slight rise, camouflaging it from bike-height view. Look for the wooden sign that points you to the right and northward of the tank. Sign indicates South Tank is 1.5 miles east (right). *[Side-trip. Continue following the doubletrack westward and up the rocky incline to take the Sawmill connector to the Timber Mesa Trail. The connector is 4 miles long.]*

4.1 Arrive at South Tank. Look for the hidden wooden sign (it isn't facing you as you arrive) that points south (right) immediately at the sign. Look carefully for the blue diamonds that mark the trail southward. Turn right, following the blue diamonds.

5.8 After passing through the most technically challenging portion of the trail (lava-rock gardens and water bars), the trail turns left and up the hill.

6.3 Arrive at the top of the saddle between the Twin Knolls. There's a poorly marked right-hand turn that takes you up a singletrack around the westernmost Knoll. Take this turn and continue up and around the hill.

6.8 Reach the highest point of the ride, overlooking the entire western White Mountains region. Porter Mountain is due west, notable for its radio towers and the cinder pit that scars its side.

7.2 Watch out for a tight, unmarked dogleg at the bottom of the hill. Carefully work your way around it and continue.

7.8 Rejoin the doubletrack you were already on at the beginning of this trail. Go left to return to the parking lot.

8.3 Return to the Panorama Trail trailhead kiosk.

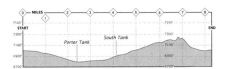

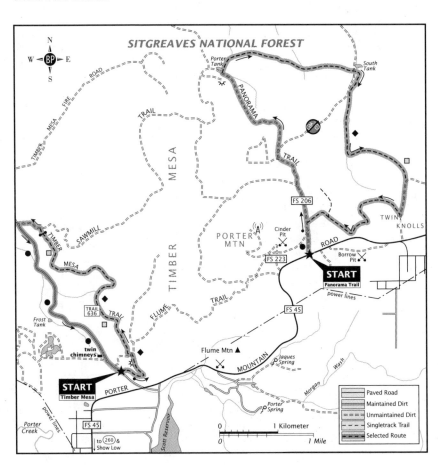

319

South Fork Shuttle

Ride Specs

Start: From Mexican Hay Lake
Length: 7-mile shuttle or 14-mile out-and-back
Approximate Riding Time: 1 hour as a shuttle, 2–3 hours as an out-and-back
Difficulty Rating: Moderately difficult descents, with one extremely dangerous hike-a-bike
Trail Surface: Singletrack
Lay of the Land: Aspen and conifer forest
Elevation Gain: 459 feet
Land Status: National forest
Nearest Town: Eagar
Other Trail Users: Hikers
Canine Compatibility: Dogs permitted
Wheels: Full suspension recommended

Getting There

From Springerville: Travel west on AZ 260 for about eight miles. Turn south on South Fork Road (FS 560), which leads to the South Fork Campground. Leave one vehicle at the South Fork Campground. The campground-use fee is $2. Pay the campground host, which is just down the road a short distance from the trailhead. Although this ride can be done as an out-and-back—and many riders do it this way—the climb from the South Fork Campground up to Mexican Hay Lake is very steep, difficult, and at high altitude. Figuring out the out-and-back is a snap based on these instructions and the map.

Shuttle: Take the shuttle vehicle from the South Fork Campground back to AZ 260. Turn right on AZ 260 heading east for about five miles toward Springerville/Eagar. Turn right on AZ 261 at the Big Lake exit—look for brown Forest Service signs. Head south for about seven miles on AZ 261 toward Mexican Hay Lake. At the top of a big climb, you'll see a "No Passing" sign and a turn-off for a rugged dirt road up a hill and to your right. This road is best driven with a high-clearance truck (if you're driving a sedan, park it on the road and ride your bike up this road). Turn right onto this road and drive up to the gate where you'll park off the road a bit. You'll know that you've missed this turn-off if, at around seven miles along AZ 261, you pass Mexican Hay Lake on your right. At the top of the hill, there's a cattleguard. The trail begins at about 9,000 feet. Go through the gate and head west. ***DeLorme: Arizona Atlas & Gazetteer:*** Page 53 C5

Valle Redondo Fat Tire Fiesta

The town of Eagar, a suburb of Springerville on the eastern end of the White Mountains, throws this event during the last week of August every year—a perfect time to get away from the heat in Phoenix and Tucson, and a nice change of pace from Flagstaff. Events include guided tours of the area's terrific, hidden rides, a hill climbing race up Flat Top Mountain, lots of swag giveaways, and a generous pasta dinner on Saturday night. Visit www.z-com.com/fiesta for more information.

While Show Low and Pinetop-Lakeside rule the western face of the White Mountains, the eastern face is Eagar's domain. Eagar, a small town south of Springerville, is becoming a hotbed of mountain biking (read about the Valle Redondo Fat Tire Fiesta in the sidebar).

The South Fork Shuttle, about 13 miles south of Eager in the Apache National Forest, is a favorite trail for bikers and hikers in the eastern half of the White Mountains. At the top of the trail, the beginning of the ride skirts Mexican Hay Lake, one of many shallow fishing holes atop the White Mountains. The tall reeds that give the lake its name make it a magnet for waterfowl. The lake is surrounded by meadow on one side and an aspen/conifer forest on the other. Ducks and Canada geese can be seen throughout most of the year and bald eagles winter here. Elk, deer, beaver, and turkey are all common sights along the trail.

The singletrack runs down to the South Fork Campground from Mexican Hay Lake. As a shuttle, it's generally a drop straight down to the campground except for a short climb from the gate outside the lake. No matter what your condition, 9,000 feet means really thin air. Even long-time local riders gasp like asthmatics as they climb the rocky ascents at the beginning of the ride. Cyclists should pace themselves and take solace knowing there will be more air at the lower elevations.

Views from the upper portion of the trail are spectacular, particularly the vista point just before a very steep—probably hike-a-bike—descent. From the southwest to the northwest, Mount Baldy, Green's Peak, and all the mountains between are visible, while the vast grassland to the north stretches to the horizon. To the southeast, Escudilla Mountain rises near the New Mexico state line.

MilesDirections

0.0 START from the cattleguard atop the hill overlooking Mexican Hay Lake. Immediately past the gate, the doubletrack splits off left and right. Go to the left, as the doubletrack heads down toward Mexican Hay Lake.

0.9 A hiking sign to your right points up a rocky hill, indicating the South Fork Campground is six miles away. Head up this hill, following the singletrack.

4.1 A dangerous rocky passage drops about a hundred yards. Do not attempt to ride this without lots of backup and body armor. Despite the challenge, you're rewarded with excellent views over the canyon that holds the Black River. Be careful descending this passage.

4.4 The singletrack intersects with a doubletrack that continues up the mountain. Cross the doubletrack and continue on the single-track, marked with trail signs. Just beyond this, pass through a gate (close it behind you).

4.8 Portage across the South Fork Creek. On the other side of the creek, there's a trail sign pointing right. Go right following the sign.

4.9 Reach a crossroads with FS 70A. The singletrack continues straight through. Follow the signs.

6.7 As you travel along the South Fork Creek, the trail suddenly splits left and right. Go left! If you go to the right, you'll probably end up dropping 20 feet into the rocky creek bed.

7.0 Reach the northern trailhead and your shuttle vehicle at South Fork Campground.

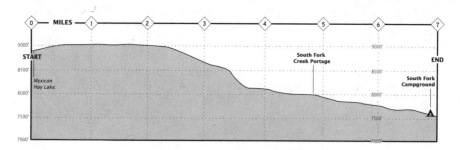

Once past this dangerous descent, the trail follows the South Fork of the Little Colorado River for several miles. This is a fast-moving river fed by runoff and springs throughout the area. There are many pools along the way, popular with anglers for their plentiful trout. Beavers also live along the Little Colorado; look for gnawed aspen stumps and their intricately built dams.

The trail itself along the river is very fast, very smooth, and a lot of fun. Hikers are fairly common, so watch your speed. There are also a couple false turns that look like

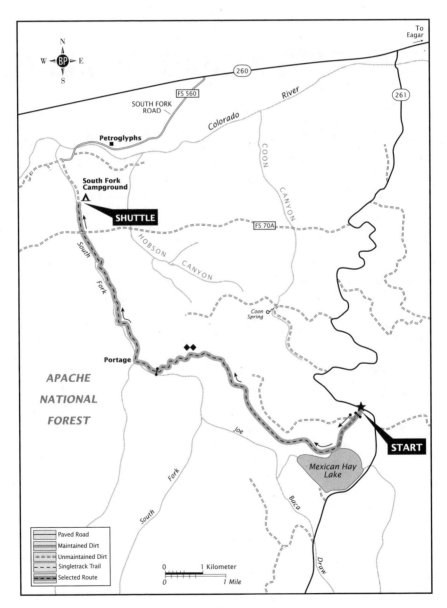

323

shortcuts along the river, but will in fact take you off the trail entirely and drop you 10 feet into the water below.

The lower part of the trail passes through stands of cottonwood, sycamore, pine, aspen, and oak. Several grassy meadows open up the scenery and make ideal picnic spots, offering a change from the steep-sided canyon that dominates most of the lower trail.

South Fork Trail can be ridden as an out-and-back as well, starting from the South Fork Campground. Allow two hours to climb up to Mexican Hay Lake from the campground.

Ride Information

● Trail Contacts:
Springerville Ranger District, Springerville, AZ (928) 333–4372 or www.fs.fed.us/r3/asnf/

● Schedule:
Open year round – *winters are extremely snowy.*

● Fees/Permits:
$2 to enter the campground. $6 to camp overnight at South Fork Campground.

● Local Information:
Round Valley Chamber of Commerce, Springerville, AZ (928) 333–2123 or www.az-tourist.com – has information on Springerville, Eager, Greer, Alpine, and Nutrioso • **Town of Springerville,** AZ (928) 333–2656 or www.springerville. com • **Town of Eagar,** AZ (928) 333–4128 or www.eagar.com

● Local Events/Attractions:
Sunrise Park Resort, McNary, AZ (928) 735–7669 or *1–800–772–7669 or*

www.sunriseskipark.com – One of Arizona's great skiing destinations, the Apache-owned Sunrise Park Resort is also ground zero for Arizona's downhill mountain biking scene. During most of the summer, Sunrise runs its lifts to the top of the ski area, so bikers can bomb down the ski runs without having to huff up to the top of the run (at about 10,000 feet) • **Little House Museum** (928) 333–2286 – On the way into the South Fork Campground off AZ 260, there's a little museum, a guest ranch, and cabins in the meadows and forests along the Little Colorado River. The Little House Museum features exhibits in a series of buildings at X Diamond Ranch, including a cabin and a granary dating from the 1890s. 90-minute tours are available May 25 through Labor Day. Admission is $4 for adults, $1.50 for kids.

● Maps:
USGS maps: Greer, AZ, and Eagar, AZ

About Social Trails

First, a definition: "Social trails" are trails that aren't strictly illegal but also aren't part of a maintained, established trail network. They're called "social trails" because their locations get passed along socially—among friends and clubs.

Once widely publicized, these so-called "social trails" often become more trouble than they're worth: The trails don't have any formal maintenance, and because of the sudden increase in use (often by those who don't have a vested interest in the trail's survival) these trails quickly get ruined. We've seen social trails dredged up, logged over, plowed, fenced off, and patrolled by rangers—not because they're illegal, but because they're too much trouble to deal with once the masses start showing up.

And that's why you won't find social trails in this book.

During the course of research, I've been introduced to literally hundreds of miles of social trails. In almost every case, they've been shown only with the promise that I wouldn't include them in the book. I'm honoring that promise.

That said, I'm not morally or ideologically opposed to the idea of legal social trails. Instead, they should be the prize, the common goal that brings dedicated bikers together—and not just an opportunity to sell more books.

Want to learn where these social trails are? Be social! Meet other riders, chat with local shops, make friends, and join clubs. And if you know of some social trails of your own, be discriminating about who you share them with—today's social trail may become tomorrow's trail access fight.

South Pinetop
(Springs, Blue Ridge, and Country Club trails)

Ride Specs

Start: Off numerous trailheads on Bucksprings Road
Length: Varies with route taken
Approximate Riding Time: 45 minutes–3 hours (depending on which trail and combination of trails you select)
Difficulty Rating: The Springs Trail is moderately difficult, due to technically challenging rocky sections. The trail is not physically taxing, because it's so short. A great trail for honing technical skills. Country Club Trail is an overall easy trail, while Blue Ridge is an overall more difficult trail (both physically and technically).
Trail Surface: Singletrack
Lay of the Land: Pine forest
Elevation Gain: Springs–162 feet; Blue Ridge–860 feet; Country Club–227 feet
Land Status: National forest
Nearest Town: Pinetop-Lakeside
Other Trail Users: Equestrians, hunters, and runners
Canine Compatibility: Dogs permitted
Wheels: Hardtail okay

Getting There

From Pinetop: Heading south on White Mountain Boulevard (AZ 260) on the way out of Pinetop-Lakeside, turn left on Bucksprings Road. About one mile in, turn left on Sky High Road (also called FS 182). The pavement ends in about half a mile along FS 182. Cross a cat-

tleguard and enter Sitgreaves National Forest. One mile in, find Trail 633 trailhead to the left (west). This trailhead provides access to both the Springs and Country Club trails, and to Blue Ridge Trail via the Springs Trail. Park in the parking lot. The Springs Trail is the trail that goes to the left of the trailhead kiosk. The connector to the Country Club Trail is across Sky High Road.

To get to the Blue Ridge Trail 107 trailhead 2 (the easiest to access), keep going north past the Springs Trail trailhead on Sky High Road/FS 182, following the Apache railroad bed. Turn west (left, again) when the road stops, intersecting with FS 187. The total distance from the turn onto Sky High Road to the trailhead is about three miles. Look to the right (north) for Trailhead 2, which is about a quarter mile west on FS 187.

Although Country Club Trail 632 can be reached via connector from the Springs Trail trailhead, it has its own trailhead as well. At the intersection with FS 187, turn right instead of left (which goes to Blue Ridge Trail) and cross over the Apache railroad bed. The trailhead is about a quarter mile east, at the junction of FS 185 and FS 187. The total distance from the turn onto Sky High Road to the trailhead is about three miles. **DeLorme: Arizona Atlas & Gazetteer:** Page 52 B3

The three loops in south Pinetop-Lakeside are an excellent example of why people—not just retirees—are starting new lives in the White Mountains. Just a mile away from condo and housing developments resides Sitgreaves National Forest. The first really cool mountain biking route as you enter Sitgreaves from Bucksprings Road is Trail 633, the Springs Trail. This trail is an even mix of super-fast flat singletrack weaving through pine and juniper forest, and tricky, technical passages through rock

gardens. Racers blasting through full-throttle can finish the entire trail in about 45 minutes. However, few riders will be able to ride this route without dabbing. One switchback in particular is sure to kick off even the most experienced riders.

The Springs Trail crosses Billy Creek and Thompson Creek riparian areas, for a total of three water crossings. Each water crossing is a rocky wheel trap. Rookies splashing through them for the first time should consider walking.

From Springs Trail, you can connect to the Blue Ridge and Country Club trails. The Blue Ridge Trail 107, which ascends Blue Ridge Mountain, was the first trail built in the White Mountain trail system. Portions of the trail follow old logging

roads, but most of it is technical singletrack. The loop is about nine miles long and quite remote once you get away from the forest roads. The trail was recently rerouted, adding a few hundred yards and bumping up the total mileage. Blue Ridge Trail is an important, and difficult, portion of the mighty Tour of the White Mountains, a 67-mile long off-road endurance race that uses several of the trails around Pinetop-Lakeside. Maintenance on the Blue Ridge Trail is the exception to the norm. It truly is an ongoing challenge—some would say a losing battle—and portions of the Blue Ridge are becoming close to unrideable.

East of Blue Ridge and Springs trails is the Country Club Trail 632. At 3.5 miles long, Country Club is probably the easiest trail, both physically and technically, of all the trails in the White Mountain Trail System. There's a nice side-trip about a third of the way into the loop that takes you up to the top of Pat Mullen Mountain, a 300-foot climb in about a quarter-mile—quite a grunt at 7500 feet. There's also a connector trail between Country Club and the wonderful Los Burros Trail (see page 308).

One popular variation on the Springs Trail ride is to connect it to the Country Club Trail 632. This trail has its own trailhead, about a half-mile up the road, but you can get to it from the Springs Trail trailhead—look for a doubletrack connector directly across the road from the Springs Trail trailhead. This connector crosses over the old Apache railroad bed.

All the trails in this portion of the White Mountain trail system are accessible from numerous trailheads, both off Bucksprings Road and the various forest roads that crisscross the forest. South Pinetop-Lakeside is becoming quite developed, with very large homes coming ever closer to the edge of the forest. Expect users—usually hikers—to be on all these trails throughout the year.

Ride Information

◑ Trail Contacts:

Lakeside Ranger Station, Lakeside, AZ (928) 368-5111 • **Apache-Sitgreaves National Forests Supervisor's Office**, Springerville, AZ (928) 333-4301 or www.wmonline.com/attract/asforest.htm

◔ Schedule:

Open year round – may be prohibitively cold in the winter

❷ Local Information:

Pinetop/Lakeside Chamber of Commerce, Lakeside, AZ (928) 367-4290 or 1-800-573-4031 or www.pinetoplakesidechamber.com

◒ Events/Attractions:

Tour of the White Mountains, Show Low, AZ (928) 537-4375 – contact Cynthia Clements or www.nrmc.org/twm.htm – A series of races and fun rides are held in early October and sponsored by Navapache Regional Medical Center Foundation. The longest race is 67 miles, and uses several of the singletrack loops in the White Mountain trail system. There is also a 50-mile race and shorter loops.

◉ Maps:

USGS maps: Indian Pine, AZ

MilesDirections

Springs Trail

0.0 START from the Springs Trail trailhead. Take the left trail.

0.4 Cross a doubletrack but stay on the singletrack.

1.1 Cross two wooden bridges. Continue bearing right. The singletrack and doubletrack that intersect Springs Trail will take you back to an equestrian center, just off the trail to the right about a hundred yards.

1.8 Cross Billy Creek.

2.6 To the left is a rocky, steep connector to the Blue Ridge Trail. Keep right. *[Option. Turn left and head up—probably a hike-a-bike—to join the Blue Ridge Trail in 0.2 miles.]*

3.7 Return to the trailhead.

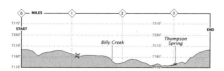

Blue Ridge Trail

0.0 START from the Blue Ridge Trail trailhead 2 (see Getting There in this chapter). Cross FS 187 and pick up the singletrack on the other side, heading south.

0.7 Connector with the Springs Trail joins from the left. Continue ahead. *[Option. Turn left to join up with the Springs Trail in 1.2 miles.]*

1.0 Pass a singletrack connector that joins from the left. Continue ahead on the marked Blue Ridge Trail. *[Side-trip: There's some super-cool singletrack buried in the little sliver of forest between the Blue Ridge Trail and the edge of Pinetop-Lakeside. It's the Billy Creek Trailpark, which doubles as a goshawk refuge. Too many little trails to map, but it's worth checking out.]*

4.0 After a rough but gradual climb, cross FS 187 and arrive at trailhead 1. Pick up trail on the other side. The Blue Ridge Trail will cross over several other jeep roads as you go around the north side of the mountain. Keep a lookout for the blue diamond trail markers used by TRACKS to designate the trails.

4.9 The Ice Cave Trail joins from the left. Continue ahead. *[Option. Turn left to explore the Ice Cave Trail 608. It's a difficult, rocky, somewhat dangerous descent down to Scott Reservoir, visible from both the top of Blue Ridge Mountain and from the Timber Mesa Trail (see Porter Mountain Trails). The Ice Cave itself is about halfway down the 3.5-mile long trail to the right, but it's been fenced off and dynamited shut.]*

5.5 The trail joins an old jeep road for a few hundred yards, and splits off to the right. Watch for trail markers.

6.5 Reach the top of Blue Ridge Mountain. Follow the jeep road south for a bit less than a mile, and then jump back onto singletrack to the right.

9.0 Return to the trailhead.

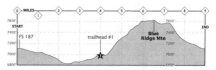

Country Club Trail

0.0 START at the Country Club Trail trailhead (see Getting There in this chapter). Head north, across FS 185, and pick up the single-track on the other side of the dirt road.

1.0 The trail up to Pat Mullen Mountain splits off to the left. Continue ahead. [*Side-trip. Turn left to get to the top of Pat Mullen Mountain in about 0.3 miles.*]

1.8 Get onto FS 185 for a short bit. In about 0.2 miles, the Country Club Trail will split off to the right (west) and continue on single-track. [*Option. Continue ahead on FS 185 to*

join with the Los Burros Trail in 7.0 miles.]

2.5 A doubletrack connector to the Springs Trail joins from the left. Continue ahead. [*Option. Turn left to reach the Springs Trail trailhead in about 1.5 miles.*]

3.5 Return to the trailhead.

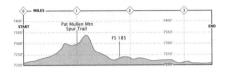

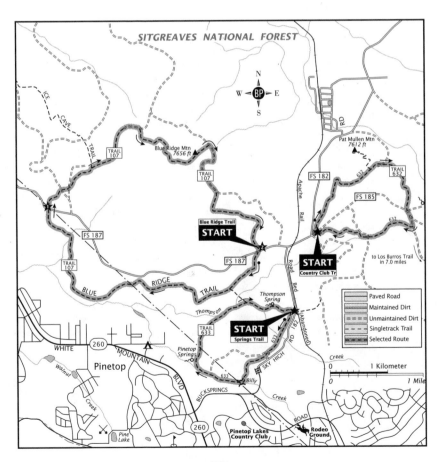

Honorable Mentions

White Mountains

Compiled here is an index of great rides in White Mountains that didn't make the A-list this time around but deserve recognition. Check them out and let us know what you think. You may decide that one or more of these rides deserves higher status in future editions or, perhaps, you may have a ride of your own that merits some attention.

DD) Pole Knoll Recreation Area

This recreation area is designed for cross-country skiing, but expect to see all sorts of users there throughout the year. The trails are very tame old doubletrack, making them an easy alternative to some of the more difficult stuff in that part of the White Mountains (*see Ride 39: Indian Spring* and *Ride 42: South Fork* for examples). Most of the trails are on old logging roads, and it's hard to get lost in the recreation area. Follow the cross-country ski markers. There are sometimes maps available at the sign-in kiosk.

Getting there: From Springerville, head west on AZ 260 to FS 112; it's the turnoff between AZ 373 (to Greer) and AZ 273 (to Sunrise Ski Resort), about 14 miles west of Springerville. *DeLorme: Arizona Atlas & Gazetteer:* Page 53 C4

EE) Sunrise Ski Resort

The White Mountain Apache Tribe manages Sunrise Ski Resort, and has hosted MBAA's downhill race series in the past. If you like taking a ski lift to the top of a mountain just to hurtle yourself down 30 degree grades at 40 miles per hour, Sunrise is the place for you. Theoretically the resort is open all summer long, but sometimes this means just weekends and sometimes it means whenever the tribe feels like opening up shop. When the resort *does* open, they may or may not be operating the lift for bikers. Call the resort before you tie up a whole weekend hauling yourself out there: (928) 735–7669.

In addition to the downhill runs, there are also 13 miles' worth of high-altitude cross-country trails in and around the resort. Everything at the resort is at the 8,000–10,000 foot level, so bring both lungs and lay off the cigarettes.

Admission to the resort is free. An all-day lift ticket is $15.

Getting there: Find your way to the AZ 260 en route to Springerville. Turn right (south) on AZ 273. Sunrise Park Lodge is four miles south on AZ 273. *DeLorme: Arizona Atlas & Gazetteer:* Page 53 C4

(FF) Murray Basin

The U.S. Forest Service has been building a new network of trails southeast of Eagar, behind and around Flat Top Mountain.

For now, the trails can be reached from the Homestead Trailhead (see *Getting there*, below). The trailhead is behind the gate at the far eastern end of the parking lot. The Homestead Trail features bathrooms and ramadas. At the trailhead, the road also continues south to a designated OHV trailhead.

There are two trail choices at the Homestead Trailhead. If you go right, you'll start out on the Homestead Trail, an easy-to-moderate 4.5-mile loop that visits two historic trailheads. Go left from the trailhead, and you'll take the moderate-to-difficult Flat Top Trail, a climbing-intensive cross-country trail with terrific views onto wildflower fields and historic ranch properties.

On Flat Top Trail, there are a couple choices to make. The first split you reach (at about two miles), turn left to continue on Flat Top Trail. Turning right takes you to Picnic Hill Trail and the Picnic Hill Trailhead near the intersection of U.S. 180 and AZ 260. At the second split, about a mile past Picnic Hill, take the right to continue on Flat Top Trail. The left hooks back with the Homestead Trail.

The Flat Top Trail eventually summits at a saddle on Flat Top Mountain, where the trail joins with Flat Top Road and bombs you back down into town. The total loop, starting and ending at the stoplight, is about 12 miles.

According to Ranger Vincente Ordoñez, the project coordinator on the Flat Top Trails, the Forest Service will be adding one more singletrack to this new network: Just before the summit on the Flat Top Trail, the new Robinson Hollow trail will split off west, careen down the side of Flat Top Mountain (he says the trail will be "very technical"), and exit near the gate at the bottom of Flat Top Road. The distance will be around two miles.

Getting there: Starting from the Eagar stoplight (there's only one in town), take Main Street south. Main Street turns 90 degrees west and turns into School Bus Road; continue on School Bus Road until you reach the first left, Water Canyon Road. Head left (south) on Water Canyon Road about two miles; once you leave the residence, the road turns to dirt and is then called FS 285. Turn left (east) on FS 76. Go about 1.5 miles to the dead-end, where you'll find the Homestead Trailhead. *DeLorme: Arizona Atlas & Gazetteer:* Page 53 C5/C6.

ⓖⓖ Alpine

The tiny village of Alpine serves as a center of snow recreation during the cold, white winters of the White Mountains. During the summer, nearby cross-country ski areas become popular, easy mountain biking trails.

Luna Lake Loop is the largest of several trails in the Alpine area. There is a Lower and Upper Loop; ridden in combination, you can squeeze out 10.5 miles. The ride features some mellow climbs and descents as the trail follows old jeep roads. All the trails are well marked, and exit the Luna Lake Campground. To get to the campground, drive five miles east from Alpine on U.S. 180. Turn left (north) on the Luna Lake entrance road just east of the lake. Drive one mile in, to the trailhead.

Georges Lake Trail is a 7.5-mile out-and-back that's also quite close to Alpine. The quickest way to start the ride is to head out of Alpine itself: Starting north on U.S. 666, take the first forest road to your right past the intersection with U.S. 180. Take the forest road around the back of Georges Lake and the hill behind Alpine. Georges Lake Trail connects with the Luna Lake trails via a forest road between the Luna Lake campground and FS 275; get a map from the local ranger station for details.

Williams Valley is another trail system close to Alpine. There are five miles of marked trails looping through big meadows and between old-growth forest. Drive 1.5 miles north of Alpine on U.S. 666 and turn left (west) 4.5 miles on FS 249 to Williams Valley. There are two parking lots here: One at the crest of the hill, the other at the west end of the valley on the south side of the road. The trail system is well marked and has established trailheads.

Terry Flat Loop, an easy six-mile ride at 9,600 feet, is to the north of Alpine about 5.5 miles. Go north out of Alpine on U.S. 666 to FS 56. Turn right (east) on FS 56 and follow it 4.5 miles to Terry Flat. Take the left fork past Tool Box Draw 0.5 miles to a parking lot at the Escudilla National Recreation Trail trailhead. The trail follows unused forest roads that loop around the meadows of Mt. Escudilla. The Forest Service recommends you ride the loop clockwise. While you're in the area, check out the hike up Escudilla National Recreation Trail—it goes to the top of Arizona's third-highest mountain, but it's not open to bikes.

Getting there: Alpine is seated at the intersection of U.S. 191 and U.S. 180, just a few miles west of the state border. The various trails describe their specific trailheads. **DeLorme: *Arizona Atlas & Gazetteer*:** Page 53 D6.

(HH) Hannagan Meadow

South of Alpine on the infamously twisty U.S. 666 (now called U.S. 191; they're marked both ways in some places), Hannagan Meadow is another very popular winter recreation area with summertime biking opportunities. There are two trails in the Hannagan Meadow area: the Hannagan Meadow Loop and the Ackre Lake Trail.

Hannagan Meadow Loop is a 5.5-mile ride defined by the U.S. Forest Service as "easy", and that's quite accurate. Even at 9,000 feet, this forest road loop's strongest selling point isn't a workout but some beautiful scenery: The fields of wildflowers that bloom in the summer can be breathtaking. The described loop follows primitive doubletrack, and is marked with blue diamonds. If you have lots of juice, there are many exploration opportunities up old logging roads that crisscross the area.

Ackre Lake Trail is a seven-mile out-and-back that leaves directly south from the Hannagan Meadow Campground and drops down to Ackre Lake. It's super-easy and a nice date ride for non-biking spouses and companions. About 1.8 miles south of the trailhead, the trail splits. Take the right to go to Ackre Lake. The left enters the Blue Range Primitive Area, the last designated "Primitive Area" in the United States, and is closed to bikes.

Getting there: Hannagan Meadow Lodge and Campground is 17 miles south of Alpine on U.S. 666/U.S. 191. The Hannagan Meadow Loop begins one-quarter mile north of the lodge. **DeLorme: *Arizona Atlas & Gazetteer*:** Page 61 A5.

The Art of MOUNTAIN BIKING

The Art of Mountain Biking

Welcome to the new generation of bicycling! Indeed, the sport has evolved dramatically from the thin-tired, featherweight-frame days of old. The sleek geometry and lightweight frames of racing bicycles, still the heart and soul of bicycling worldwide, have lost much ground in recent years, unpaving the way for the mountain bike, which now accounts for the majority of all bicycle sales in the U.S. And with this change comes a new breed of cyclist, less concerned with smooth roads and long rides, who thrives in places once inaccessible to the mortal road bike.

The mountain bike, with its knobby tread and reinforced frame, takes cyclists to places once unheard of—down rugged mountain trails, through streams of rushing water, across the frozen Alaskan tundra, and even to work in the city. There seem to be few limits on what this fat-tired beast can do and where it can take us. Few obstacles stand in its way, few boundaries slow its progress. Except for one—its own success. If trail closure means little to you now, read on and discover how a trail can be here today and gone tomorrow.

With so many new off-road cyclists taking to the trails each year, it's no wonder trail access hinges precariously between universal acceptance and complete termination. But a little work on your part can go a long way to preserving trail access for future use. Nothing is more crucial to the survival of mountain biking itself than to read the examples set forth in the following pages and practice their message. Then turn to the maps, pick out your favorite ride, and hit the dirt!

MOUNTAIN BIKE BEGINNINGS

It seems the mountain bike, originally designed for lunatic adventurists bored with straight lines, clean clothes, and smooth tires, has become globally popular in as short a time as it would take to race down a mountain trail.

Like many things of a revolutionary nature, the mountain bike was born on the west coast. But unlike Rollerblades, purple hair, and the peace sign, the concept of the off-road bike cannot be credited solely to the imaginative Californians—they were just the first to make waves.

The design of the first off-road specific bike was based on the geometry of the old

Schwinn Excelsior, a one-speed, camel-back cruiser with balloon tires. Joe Breeze was the creator behind it, and in 1977 he built 10 of these "Breezers" for himself and his Marin County, California, friends at $750 apiece—a bargain.

Breeze was a serious competitor in bicycle racing, placing 13th in the 1977 U.S. Road Racing National Championships. After races, he and friends would scour local bike shops hoping to find old bikes they could then restore.

It was the 1941 Schwinn Excelsior, for which Breeze paid just five dollars, that began to shape and change bicycling history forever. After taking the bike home, removing the fenders, oiling the chain, and pumping up the tires, Breeze hit the dirt. He loved it.

His inspiration, while forerunning, was not altogether unique. On the opposite end of the country, nearly 2,500 miles from Marin County, east coast bike bums were also growing restless. More and more old, beat-up clunkers were being restored and modified. These behemoths often weighed as much as 80 pounds and were so reinforced they seemed virtually indestructible. But rides that take just 40 minutes on today's 25-pound featherweights took the steel-toed-boot- and-blue-jean-clad bikers of the late 1970s and early 1980s nearly four hours to complete.

Not until 1981 was it possible to purchase a production mountain bike, but local retailers found these ungainly bicycles difficult to sell and rarely kept them in stock. By 1983, however, mountain bikes were no longer such a fringe item, and large bike manufacturers quickly jumped into the action, producing their own versions of the off-road bike. By the 1990s, the mountain bike had firmly established its place with bicyclists of nearly all ages and abilities, and now command nearly 90 percent of the U.S. bike market.

There are many reasons for the mountain bike's success in becoming the hottest two-wheeled vehicle in the nation. They are much friendlier to the cyclist than traditional road bikes because of their comfortable upright position and shock-absorbing fat tires. And because of the health-conscious, environmentalist movement of the late 1980s and 1990s, people are more activity minded and seek nature on a closer

front than paved roads can allow. The mountain bike gives you these things and takes you far away from the daily grind—even if you're only minutes from the city.

MOUNTAIN BIKING INTO SHAPE

If your objective is to get in shape and lose weight, then you're on the right track, because mountain biking is one of the best ways to get started.

One way many of us have lost weight in this sport is the crash-and-burn-it-off method. Picture this: you're speeding uncontrollably down a vertical drop that you realize you shouldn't be on—only after it is too late. Your front wheel lodges into a rut and launches you through endless weeds, trees, and pointy rocks before coming to an abrupt halt in a puddle of thick mud. Surveying the damage, you discover, with the layers of skin, body parts, and lost confidence littering the trail above, that those unwanted pounds have been shed—*permanently*. Instant weight loss.

There is, of course, a more conventional (and quite a bit less painful) approach to losing weight and gaining fitness on a mountain bike. It's called the workout, and bicycles provide an ideal way to get physical. Take a look at some of the benefits associated with cycling.

Cycling helps you shed pounds without gimmicky diet fads or weight-loss programs. You can explore the countryside and burn nearly 10 to 16 calories per minute or close to 600 to 1,000 calories per hour. Moreover, it's a great way to spend an afternoon.

No less significant than the external and cosmetic changes of your body from riding are the internal changes taking place. Over time, cycling regularly will strengthen your heart as your body grows vast networks of new capillaries to carry blood to all those working muscles. This will, in turn, give your skin a healthier glow. The capacity of your lungs may increase up to 20 percent, and your resting heart rate will drop significantly. The Stanford University School of Medicine reports to the American Heart Association that people can reduce their risk of heart attack by nearly 64 percent if they can burn up to 2,000 calories per week. This is only two to three hours of bike riding!

Recommended for insomnia, hypertension, indigestion, anxiety, and even for recuperation from major heart attacks, bicycling can be an excellent cure-all as well as a great preventive. Cycling just a few hours per week can improve your figure and sleeping habits, give you greater resistance to illness, increase your energy levels, and provide feelings of accomplishment and heightened self-esteem.

BE SAFE—KNOW THE LAW

Occasionally, even the hard-core off-road cyclists will find they have no choice but to ride the pavement. When you are forced to hit the road, it's important for you to know and understand the rules.

Outlined below are a few of the common laws found in Arizona's Vehicle Code book.

- **Bicycles are legally classified as vehicles in Arizona.** This means that as a bicyclist, you are responsible for obeying the same rules of the road as a driver of a motor vehicle.
- **Bicyclists must ride with the traffic—NOT AGAINST IT!** Because bicycles are considered vehicles, you must ride your bicycle just as you would drive a car—with traffic. Only pedestrians should travel against the flow of traffic.
- **You must obey all traffic signs.** This includes stop signs and stoplights.
- **Always signal your turns.** Most drivers aren't expecting bicyclists to be on the roads, and many drivers would prefer that cyclists stay off the roads altogether. It's important, therefore, to clearly signal your intentions to motorists both in front and behind you.
- **Bicyclists are entitled to the same roads as cars (except controlled-access highways).** Unfortunately, cyclists are rarely given this consideration.
- **Be a responsible cyclist.** Do not abuse your rights to ride on open roads. Follow the rules and set a good example for all of us as you roll along.

THE MOUNTAIN BIKE CONTROVERSY

Are Off-Road Bicyclists Environmental Outlaws? Do We have the Right to Use Public Trails?

Mountain bikers have long endured the animosity of folks in the backcountry who complain about the consequences of off-road bicycling. Many people believe that the fat tires and knobby tread do unacceptable environmental damage and that our uncontrollable riding habits are a danger to animals and to other trail users. To the contrary, mountain bikes have no more environmental impact than hiking boots or horseshoes. This does not mean, however, that mountain bikes leave no imprint at all. Wherever man treads, there is an impact. By riding responsibly, though, it is possible to leave only a minimum impact—something we all must take care to achieve.

Unfortunately, it is often people of great influence who view the mountain bike as the environment's worst enemy. Consequently, we as mountain bike riders and environmentally concerned citizens must be educators, impressing upon others that we also deserve the right to use these trails. Our responsibilities as bicyclists are no more and no less than any other trail user. We must all take the soft-cycling approach and show that mountain bicyclists are not environmental outlaws.

ETIQUETTE OF MOUNTAIN BIKING

When discussing mountain biking etiquette, we are in essence discussing the soft-cycling approach. This term, as mentioned previously, describes the art of minimum-impact bicycling and should apply to both the physical and social dimensions of the sport. But make no mistake—it is possible to ride fast and furiously while maintaining the balance of soft-cycling. Here first are a few ways to minimize the physical impact of mountain bike riding.

- *Stay on the trail.* Don't ride around fallen trees or mud holes that block your path. Stop and cross over them. When you come to a vista overlooking a deep valley, don't ride off the trail for a better vantage point. Instead, leave the bike and walk to see the view. Riding off the trail may seem inconsequential when done only once, but soon someone else will follow, then others, and the cumulative results can be catastrophic. Each time you wander from the trail you begin creating a new path, adding one more scar to the earth's surface.
- *Do not disturb the soil.* Follow a line within the trail that will not disturb or damage the soil.
- *Do not ride over soft or wet trails.* After a rain shower or during the thawing season, trails will often resemble muddy, oozing swampland. The best thing to do is stay off the trails altogether. Realistically, however, we're all going to come across some muddy trails we cannot anticipate. Instead of blasting through each section of mud, which may seem both easier and more fun, lift the bike and walk past. Each time a cyclist rides through a soft or muddy section of trail, that part of the trail is permanently damaged. Regardless of the trail's conditions, though, remember always to go over the obstacles across the path, not around them. Stay on the trail.
- *Avoid trails that, for all but God, are considered impassable and impossible.* Don't take a leap of faith down a kamikaze descent on which you will be forced to lock your brakes and skid to the bottom, ripping the ground apart as you go.

Soft-cycling should apply to the social dimensions of the sport as well, since mountain bikers are not the only folks who use the trails. Hikers, equestrians, cross-country skiers, and other outdoors people use many of the same trails and can be easily spooked by a marauding mountain biker tearing through the trees. Be friendly in the forest and give ample warning of your approach.

- **Take out what you bring in.** Don't leave broken bike pieces and banana peels scattered along the trail.
- **Be aware of your surroundings.** Don't use popular hiking trails for race training.
- **Slow down!** Rocketing around blind corners is a sure way to ruin an unsuspecting hiker's day. Consider this—If you fly down a quick singletrack descent at 20 mph, then hit the brakes and slow down to only six mph to pass someone, you're still moving twice as fast as they are!

Like the trails we ride on, the social dimension of mountain biking is very fragile and must be cared for responsibly. We should not want to destroy another person's enjoyment of the outdoors. By riding in the backcountry with caution, control, and responsibility, our presence should be felt positively by other trail users. By adhering to these rules, trail riding—a privilege that can quickly be taken away—will continue to be ours to share.

TRAIL MAINTENANCE

Unfortunately, despite all of the preventive measures taken to avoid trail damage, we're still going to run into many trails requiring attention. Simply put, a lot of hikers, equestrians, and cyclists alike use the same trails—some wear and tear is unavoidable. But like your bike, if you want to use these trails for a long time to come, you must also maintain them.

Trail maintenance and restoration can be accomplished in a variety of ways. One way is for mountain bike clubs to combine efforts with other trail users (i.e. hikers and equestrians) and work closely with land managers to cut new trails or repair existing ones. This not only reinforces to others the commitment cyclists have in caring for and maintaining the land, but also breaks the ice that often separates cyclists from their fellow trailmates. Another good way to help out is to show up on a Saturday morning with a few riding buddies at your favorite off-road domain ready to work. With a good attitude, thick gloves, and the local land manager's supervision, trail repair is fun and very rewarding. It's important, of course, that you arrange a trail-repair outing with the local land manager before you start pounding shovels into the dirt. They can lead you to the most needy sections of trail and instruct you on what repairs should be done and how best to accomplish the task. Perhaps the most effective means of trail maintenance, though, can be done by yourself and while you're riding. Read on.

ON–THE–SPOT QUICK FIX

Most of us, when we're riding, have at one time or another come upon muddy trails or fallen trees blocking our path. We notice that over time the mud gets deeper and the trail gets wider as people go through or around the obstacles. We worry that the problem will become so severe and repairs too difficult that the trail's access may be threatened. We also know that our ambition to do anything about it is greatest at that moment, not after a hot shower and a plate of spaghetti. Here are a few on-the-spot quick fixes you can do that will hopefully correct a problem before it gets out of hand and get you back on your bike within minutes.

Muddy Trails. What do you do when trails develop huge mud holes destined for the EPA's Superfund status? The technique is called corduroying, and it works much like building a pontoon over the mud to support bikes, horses, or hikers as they cross. Corduroy (not the pants) is the term for roads made of logs laid down cross-wise. Use small-and medium-sized sticks and lay them side by side across the trail until they cover the length of the muddy section (break the sticks to fit the width of the trail). Press them into the mud with your feet, then lay more on top if needed. Keep adding sticks until the trail is firm. Not only will you stay clean as you cross, but the sticks may soak up some of the water and help the puddle dry. This quick fix may last as long as one month before needing to be redone. And as time goes on, with new layers added to the trail, the soil will grow stronger, thicker, and more resistant to erosion. This whole process may take fewer than five minutes, and you can be on your way, knowing the trail behind you is in good repair.

Leaving the Trail. What do you do to keep cyclists from cutting corners and leaving the designated trail? The solution is much simpler than you may think. (No, don't hire an off-road police force.) Notice where people are leaving the trail and throw a pile of thick branches or brush along the path, or place logs across the opening to block the way through. There are probably dozens of subtle tricks like these that will manipulate people into staying on the designated trail. If executed well, no one will even notice that the thick branches scattered along the ground in the woods weren't always there. And most folks would probably rather take a moment to hop a log in the trail than get tangled in a web of branches.

Obstacle in the Way. If there are large obstacles blocking the trail, try and remove them or push them aside. If you cannot do this by yourself, call the trail maintenance hotline to speak with the land manager of that particular trail and see what can be done.

We must be willing to sweat for our trails in order to sweat on them. Police yourself

and point out to others the significance of trail maintenance. "Sweat Equity," the rewards of continued land use won with a fair share of sweat, pays off when the trail is "up for review" by the land manager and he or she remembers the efforts made by trail-conscious mountain bikers.

RULES OF THE TRAIL

The International Mountain Bicycling Association (IMBA) has developed these guidelines to trail riding. These "Rules of the Trail" are accepted worldwide and will go a long way in keeping trails open. Please respect and follow these rules for everyone's sake.

1. Ride only on open trails. Respect trail and road closures (if you're not sure, ask a park or state official first), do not trespass on private property, and obtain permits or authorization if required. Federal and state wilderness areas are off-limits to cycling. Parks and state forests may also have certain trails closed to cycling.

2. **Zero impact.** Be sensitive to the dirt beneath you. Even on open trails, you should not ride under conditions by which you will leave evidence of your passing, such as on certain soils or shortly after a rainfall. Be sure to observe the different types of soils and trails you're riding on, practicing minimum-impact cycling. Never ride off the trail, don't skid your tires, and be sure to bring out at least as much as you bring in.

3. **Control your bicycle!** Inattention for even one second can cause disaster for yourself or for others. Excessive speed frightens and can injure people, gives mountain biking a bad name, and can result in trail closures.

4. **Always yield.** Let others know you're coming well in advance (a friendly greeting is always good and often appreciated). Show your respect when passing others by slowing to walking speed or stopping altogether, especially in the presence of horses. Horses can be unpredictable, so be very careful. Anticipate that other trail users may be around corners or in blind spots.

5. **Never spook animals.** All animals are spooked by sudden movements, unannounced approaches, or loud noises. Give the animals extra room and time so they can adjust to you. Move slowly or dismount around animals. Running cattle and disturbing wild animals are serious offenses. Leave gates as you find them, or as marked.

6. **Plan ahead.** Know your equipment, your ability, and the area in which you are riding, and plan your trip accordingly. Be self-sufficient at all times, keep your bike in good repair, and carry necessary supplies for changes in weather or other conditions. You can help keep trails open by setting an example of responsible, courteous, and controlled mountain bike riding.

7. **Always wear a helmet when you ride.** For your own safety and protection, a helmet should be worn whenever you are riding your bike. You never know when a tree root or small rock will throw you the wrong way and send you tumbling.

Thousands of miles of dirt trails have been closed to mountain bicycling because of the irresponsible riding habits of just a few riders. Don't follow the example of these offending riders. Don't take away trail privileges from thousands of others who work hard each year to keep the backcountry avenues open to us all.

THE NECESSITIES OF CYCLING

When discussing the most important items to have on a bike ride, cyclists generally agree on the following five items.

Helmet. The reasons to wear a helmet should be obvious. Helmets are discussed in more detail in the Be Safe—Wear Your Armor section.

Water. Without it, cyclists may face dehydration, which may result in dizziness and fatigue. On a warm day, cyclists should drink at least 30 ounces during every hour of riding. Because of this, a hydration backpack (such as those made by Camelbak™, Hydrapak™, Platypus™, or Blackburn™) is strongly recommended for desert riding—the bladders can hold at least 70 ounces, and some packs are designed to hold 100oz. bladders or larger. Remember, it's always good to drink before you feel thirsty—otherwise, it may be too late.

Cycling Shorts. These are necessary if you plan to ride your bike more than 20 to 30 minutes. Padded cycling shorts may be the only thing preventing your derriere from serious saddle soreness by ride's end. There are two types of cycling shorts you can buy. Touring shorts, also known as "baggies," are good for people who don't want to look like they're wearing anatomically correct cellophane. These look like regular athletic shorts with pockets, but have built-in padding in the crotch area for protection from chafing and saddle sores. Baggies also put another layer between you and the ground, providing extra protection during crashes – between the sharp rocks and thorny plant life that is present on many Arizona rides, this extra protection matters. The more popular, traditional cycling shorts are made of skin-tight material, also with a padded crotch. Whichever style you find most comfortable, cycling shorts are a necessity for long rides.

Gloves. Just as cycling shorts are necessary for avoiding soreness at the end of a ride, gloves are necessary for protecting your hands during crashes. Full-finger gloves are a little warm in the summer, but they provide the best protection from rocks, gravel, and cactus. There are too many ways to crash to not wear gloves.

Food. This essential item will keep you rolling. Cycling burns up a lot of calories and is among the few sports in which no one is safe from the "Bonk." Bonking feels like it sounds. Without food in your system, your blood sugar level collapses, and there is no longer any energy in your body. This instantly results in total fatigue and light-headedness. So when you're filling your water bottle, remember to bring along some food. Fruit, energy bars, or some other forms of high-energy food are highly recommended. Candy bars are not, however, because they will deliver a sudden burst of high energy, then let you down soon after, causing you to feel worse than before. Energy bars are available at most bike stores and are similar to candy bars, but provide complex carbohydrate energy and high nutrition rather than fast-burning simple sugars.

BE PREPARED OR DIE

On the following page is a list of essential equipment that will keep you from dying alone in the woods. To carry these items, you will need a backpack. If you're carrying lots of equipment, you may want to consider a set of panniers. These are much larger and mount on either side of each wheel on a rack. Many cyclists, though, prefer not to use a pack at all. They just slip all they need into their jersey pockets, and off they go. Of course, these are the guys who are always asking to borrow my tools for trailside repairs.

BE SAFE—WEAR YOUR ARMOR

While on the subject of jerseys, it's crucial to discuss the clothing you must wear to be safe, practical, and—if you prefer—stylish. The following is a list of items that will save you from disaster, outfit you comfortably, and most important, keep you looking cool.

Be Prepared Or Die

- Spare Tube
- Tire Irons: See the Appendix for instructions on fixing flat tires.
- Patch Kit
- Pump
- Money: Spare change for emergency calls.
- Spoke Wrench
- Spare Spokes: To fit your wheel. Tape these to the chain stay.
- Chain Tool
- Allen Keys: Bring appropriate sizes to fit your bike.
- Compass
- First-Aid Kit
- Rain Gear: For quick changes in weather.
- Matches
- Guidebook: In case all else fails and you must start a fire to survive, this guidebook will serve as excellent fire starter!

Helmet. A helmet is an absolute necessity because it protects your head from complete annihilation. It is the only thing that will not disintegrate into a million pieces after a wicked crash on a descent you shouldn't have been on in the first place. A helmet with a solid exterior shell will also protect your head from sharp or protruding objects. Of course, with a hard-shelled helmet, you can paste several stickers of your favorite bicycle manufacturers all over the outer shell, giving companies even more free advertising for your dollar.

Shorts. Let's just say Lycra™ cycling shorts are considered a major safety item if you plan to ride for more than 20 or 30 minutes at a time. As mentioned in The Necessities of Cycling section, cycling shorts are well regarded as the leading cureall for chafing and saddle sores. The most preventive cycling shorts have padded "chamois" (most chamois is synthetic nowadays) in the crotch area. Of course, if you choose to wear these traditional cycling shorts, it's imperative that they look as if someone spray painted them onto your body.

Gloves. You may find well-padded cycling gloves invaluable when traveling over rocky trails and gravelly roads for hours on end. Long-fingered gloves may also be useful, as branches, trees, assorted hard objects, and, occasionally, small animals will reach out and whack your knuckles.

Glasses. Not only do sunglasses give you an imposing presence and make you look cool (both are extremely important), they also protect your eyes from harmful ultraviolet rays, invisible branches, creepy bugs, dirt, and may prevent you from being caught sneaking glances at riders of the opposite sex also wearing skintight, revealing Lycra™.

Shoes. Mountain bike shoes should have stiff soles to help make pedaling easier and provide better traction when walking your bike up a trail becomes necessary. Virtually any kind of good outdoor hiking footwear will work, but specific mountain bike shoes (especially those with inset cleats) are best. It is vital that these shoes look as ugly as humanly possible. Those closest in style to bowling shoes are, of course, the most popular.

Jersey or Shirt. Bicycling jerseys are popular because of their snug fit and back pockets. When purchasing a jersey, look for ones that are loaded with bright, blinding, neon logos and manufacturers' names. These loudly decorated billboards are also good for drawing unnecessary attention to yourself just before taking a mean spill while trying to hop a curb. A cotton T-shirt is a good alternative in warm weather, but when the weather turns cold, cotton becomes a chilling substitute for the jersey. Cotton retains moisture and sweat against your body, which may cause you to get the chills and ills on those cold-weather rides.

First Aid

- Band-Aids
- mole skin
- various sterile gauze and dressings
- white surgical tape
- an ace bandage
- an antihistamine
- aspirin
- Betadine® solution
- a First aid book
- Tums®

- tweezers
- scissors
- anti-bacterial wipes
- triple-antibiotic ointment
- plastic gloves
- sterile cotton tip applicators
- syrup of ipecac (to induce vomiting)
- a thermometer
- a wire splint

EXTREME HEAT

If you're stuck in the desert, or really anywhere in Arizona, there's a good chance you're going to need to deal with the prospect of riding in extreme heat. Given a choice, stay out of the sun if it's going to be more than 90 degrees Fahrenheit – your heart rate jumps about 10 beats per minute at this temperature, which can be dangerous if you're already stressing your body. Until you're really acclimated to the heat, stay away from rides that demand a lot of energy output, such as a stressful climb or a really long ride.

Sunscreen. You will get a sunburn you will never forget if you ride in the sun without sunscreen. The real danger periods are from about 9 a.m. to 5 p.m.; before and after this, the sun is low enough on the horizon that most UV rays are blocked by the atmosphere. However, at high altitudes (anything over 5000'), the UV index is often much higher because the air is much thinner.

Fluids. You need to drink like a fish to stay well. See the sidebar on the following page for more details.

Clothing. Sleeveless jerseys are a good choice when the going gets hot, but the fashion police might frown if you don't have the guns to look good in them. Baggy shorts are also a little warm in the extreme heat. In short, wear as little as possible.

AND AT THE OTHER END OF THE THERMOMETER

There are many opportunities to ride in extreme cold around Arizona, especially in the mountains in the winter.

Layers. Depending on how cold a ride you're contemplating, you should wear two or three layers of fabric over your torso. The innermost layer should be a

Hydration

Simple fact of mountain biking in Arizona: You have to drink a whole lot of water. Dehydration is a real risk, even on a short ride. When you're dehydrated, your energy levels get low, aches become more acute, and overall health and endurance quickly goes south.

Get this—by the time you feel thirsty, you may already be too dehydrated to adequately recover on this ride! One good way to measure how well hydrated you are is urination frequency and color. You should need to pee about once an hour, and the color should be pale or colorless.

A good rule of thumb to follow is to bring at a minimum 20 oz. water per hour of riding. That may be too little for some (hydration requirements increase with fitness), but it's a good place to start. This means a typical 24 oz. water bottle will get you through a little more than one hour of riding, a standard Camelbak™-style 70 oz. hydration bag is good for about 3.5 hours, and a big 100 oz. bladder should get you through a five-hour epic.

Increase this amount by 25 to 30 percent during very hot weather, and at higher (7,000 feet+) altitudes.

Pre-hydrating is always a good idea, especially if you know you're going on a long (3+ hours) or remote ride. Try to drink two to three quarts of water throughout the day before the ride, and a Gatorade™-type drink immediately before the ride.

Water is not the last word when it comes to fighting dehydration. According to Nutrition for Health, Sport, and Fitness (Williams, 1999), the body needs carbohydrates after just one hour of exertion. One eight ounce "serving" of a diluted carb and electrolyte drink (such as Gatorade™) per hour should be sufficient. Without this extra boost, electrolyte imbalances in your body may lead to cramping and disorientation even if you do drink enough water. Either take the carb drink straight or mix it into your water supply.

There are some situations where it's impractical—if not impossible—to carry enough water for a ride. Check first to see if you can make a water drop somewhere along the trail before riding it. Word to the wise: In any situation where you're out of water and more than an hour away from help, mooch water off anyone you come across on the trail. Doesn't matter if it's a hiker, biker, 4x4 rider, equestrian, whomever. Many clubs, in particular the 4x4 clubs, have bylaws that state the members must render assistance to other trail users. Other outdoor enthusiasts are generally thrilled to help a fellow adventurer.

Polypropylene™ or Capilene™ long-sleeved shirt, which will wick away the sweat as you ride. The outermost layer should be a Goretex™ or similar shell, to keep the wind from providing you with extra evaporative cooling. Between these layers, something wooly and breathable is good. Try to avoid wearing cotton or baggy clothing when the temperature falls. Cotton, as mentioned before, holds

moisture like a sponge, and baggy clothing catches cold air and swirls it around your body. Good cold-weather clothing should fit snugly against your body, but not be restrictive.

Socks. A pair of wool, or better still Smartwool™, socks feels wonderful in the cold. Don't wear more than one pair under your shoes, though. You may stand the chance of restricting circulation, and your feet will get real cold, real fast.

Thinsulate or Gortex™ gloves. We may all agree that there is nothing worse than frozen feet—unless your hands are frozen. A good pair of Thinsulate™ or Gortex™ gloves should keep your hands toasty and warm.

Skull cap. Ventilated helmets are designed to keep heads cool in the summer heat, but they do little to help keep heads warm during rides in sub-zero temperatures. Cyclists should consider wearing a hat on extremely cold days. Capilene Skullcaps are great head and ear warmers that snugly fit over your head beneath the helmet. Head protection is not lost. Another option is a helmet cover that covers those ventilating gaps and helps keep the body heat in. These do not, however, keep your ears warm.

All of this clothing can be found at your local bike store, where the staff should be happy to help fit you into the seasons of the year.

TO HAVE OR NOT TO HAVE... *(Other Very Useful Items)*

Though mountain biking is relatively new to the cycling scene, there is no shortage of items for you and your bike to make riding better, safer, and easier. We have rummaged through the unending lists and separated the gadgets from the good stuff, coming up with what we believe are items certain to make mountain bike riding easier and more enjoyable.

Tires. Buying yourself a good pair of knobby tires is the quickest way to enhance the off-road handling capabilities of your bike. There are many types of mountain bike tires on the market. Some are made exclusively for very rugged off-road terrain. These big-knobbed, soft rubber tires virtually stick to the ground with unforgiving traction, but tend to deteriorate quickly on pavement. There are other tires made exclusively for the road. These are called "slicks" and have no tread at all. Use the right tire for the job: Knobby tires are required for most of the rough terrain in Arizona, while slicks provide superb traction on slickrock like that found in Sedona.

Tube sealant. The abundance of thorny plant life and razor-sharp rocks makes sealed tubes, such as those made by Slime™ and Wrench Force™, necessary for desert riding. They'll make your wheels heavier and roll slower, but frankly it's more fun than stopping every half hour to fix punctures. An even heavier alternative is to go with thorn-resistant tubes, which are built from thicker material.

Toe Clips or Clipless Pedals. With these, you will ride with more power. Toe clips attach to your pedals and strap your feet firmly in place, allowing you to exert pressure on the pedals on both the downstroke and the upstroke. They will increase your pedaling efficiency by 30 percent to 50 percent. Clipless pedals, which liberate your feet from the traditional straps and clips, have made toe clips virtually obsolete. Like ski bindings, they attach your shoe directly to the pedal. They are, however, much more expensive than toe clips.

Bar Ends. These great clamp-on additions to your original straight bar will provide more leverage, an excellent grip for climbing, and a more natural position for your hands. Be aware, however, of the bar end's propensity for hooking trees on fast descents, sending you, the cyclist, airborne.

Back Pack. These bags are ideal for carrying keys, extra food, guidebooks, tools, spare tubes, and a cellular phone, in case you need to call for help.

Suspension Forks. These days, it's actually quite hard to find a trail-ready mountain bike that does not come equipped with a suspension fork. Few trails in this book are appropriate for fully rigid bikes, although hardcore bike rats riding rigid single-speed bikes have been known to ride just about everything in the book. For general-purpose trail riding, you don't need more than about 3" to 4" of travel in your fork. For more technical rides and brutal descents, 4" or more is strongly recommended. If you're considering a downhill-specific fork, you need to do more research than this book can provide you. Check with your local bike shop for more details.

Bike Computers. These are fun gadgets to own and are much less expensive than in years past. They have such features as trip distance, speedometer, odometer, time of day, altitude, alarm, average speed, maximum speed, heart rate, global satellite positioning, etc. Bike computers will come in handy when following these maps or to know just how far you've ridden in the wrong direction.

Water Pack. This is an essential item for cyclists pedaling for more than a few hours, especially in hot, dry conditions. The most popular brand is Camelbak™, and these water packs can carry in their bladder bags as much as 100 ounces of water. These packs strap onto your back with a handy hose running over your shoulder so you can be drinking water while still holding onto the bars on a rocky descent with both hands. These packs are a great way to carry a lot of extra liquid on hot rides in the middle of nowhere (like most everything in this book).

Disc Brakes. Not strictly necessary, because most trails in Arizona are dry throughout the year, disc brakes do provide generally superior braking power. This is a very good thing when it comes to the more technical rides in the state. They also allow you to ride the bike even when the rims are tweaked way out of true. Upgrading a bike to use disc brakes is usually too expensive to justify, but strongly consider this upgrade when buying a new bike.

TYPES OF OFF-ROAD TERRAIN

Before roughing it off road, we may first have to ride the pavement to get to our destination. Please, don't be dismayed. Some of the country's best rides are on the road. Once we get past these smooth-surfaced pathways, though, adventures in dirt await us.

Rails-to-Trails. Abandoned rail lines are converted into usable public resources for exercising, commuting, or just enjoying nature. Old rails and ties are torn up and a trail, paved or unpaved, is laid along the existing corridor. This completes the cycle from ancient Indian trading routes to railroad corridors and back again to hiking and cycling trails.

Unpaved Roads are typically found in rural areas and are most often public roads. Be careful when exploring, though, not to ride on someone's unpaved private drive.

Forest Roads. These dirt and gravel roads are used primarily as access to forest land and are generally kept in good condition. They are almost always open to public use.

Singletrack can be the most fun on a mountain bike. These trails, with only one track to follow, are often narrow, challenging pathways through the woods. Remember to make sure these trails are open before zipping into the woods. (At the time of this printing, all trails and roads in this guidebook were open to mountain bikes.)

Open Land. Unless there is a marked trail through a field or open space, you should not plan to ride here. Once one person cuts his or her wheels through a field or meadow, many more are sure to follow, causing irreparable damage to the landscape.

TECHNIQUES TO SHARPEN YOUR SKILLS

Many of us see ourselves as pure athletes—blessed with power, strength, and endless endurance. However, it may be those with finesse, balance, agility, and grace that get around most quickly on a mountain bike. Although power, strength, and endurance do have their places in mountain biking, these elements don't necessarily form the complete framework for a champion mountain biker.

The bike should become an extension of your body. Slight shifts in your hips or knees can have remarkable results. Experienced bike handlers seem to flash down technical descents, dashing over obstacles in a smooth and graceful effort as if pirouetting in Swan Lake. Here are some tips and techniques to help you connect with your bike and float gracefully over the dirt.

Braking

Using your brakes requires using your head, especially when descending. This doesn't mean using your head as a stopping block, but rather to think intelligently. Use your best judgment in terms of how much or how little to squeeze those brake levers.

The more weight a tire is carrying, the more braking power it has. When you're going downhill, your front wheel carries more weight than the rear. Braking gently with the front brake will help keep you in control without going into a skid. Be careful, though, not to overdo it with the front brakes and accidentally toss yourself over the handlebars. And don't neglect your rear brake! When descending, shift your weight back over the rear wheel, thus increasing your rear braking power as well. This will balance the power of both brakes and give you maximum control.

Good riders learn just how much of their weight to shift over each wheel and how to apply just enough braking power to each brake, so not to "endo" over the handlebars or skid down a trail.

If you're one of those beginners who is convinced that a pair of ultra-powerful, fine-tuned brakes will transform you instantly into a World Cup champion downhiller, you're barking up the wrong tree. Other factors—like experience, good vision, and confidence—are far more important. Riders who possess these qualities don't have to think much about their brakes.

GOING UPHILL—Climbing Those Treacherous Hills
Shift into a low gear. Before shifting, be sure to ease up on your pedaling so there is not too much pressure on the chain. With that in mind, it's important to shift before you find yourself on a steep slope, where it may be too late. Find the gear best for you that matches the terrain and steepness of each climb.

Stay seated. Standing out of the saddle is often helpful when climbing steep hills on a bike, but you may find that on dirt, standing may cause your rear tire to lose its grip and spin out. Climbing is not possible without traction. As you improve, you will likely learn the subtle tricks that make out-of-saddle climbing possible. Until then, have a seat.

Lean forward. On very steep hills, the front end may feel unweighted and suddenly pop up. Slide forward on the saddle and lean over the handlebars. Think about putting your chin down near your stem. This will add more weight to the front wheel and should keep you grounded. It's all about using the weight of your head to your advantage. Most people don't realize how heavy their noggin is.

Relax. As with downhilling, relaxation is a big key to your success when climbing steep, rocky climbs. Smooth pedaling translates into good traction. Tense bodies don't balance well at low speeds. Instead of fixating grimly on the front wheel, look up at the terrain above, and pick a good line.

Keep pedaling. On rocky climbs, be sure to keep the pressure on, and don't let up on those pedals! You'll be surprised at what your bike will just roll over as long as you keep the engine revved up.

GOING DOWNHILL—The Real Reason We Get Up in the Morning
Relax. Stay loose on the bike, and don't lock your elbows or clench your grip. Your elbows need to bend with the bumps and absorb the shock, while your hands should have a firm but controlled grip on the bars to keep things steady. Breathing slowly, deeply, and deliberately will help you relax while flying down bumpy singletrack. Maintaining a death-grip on the brakes will be unhelpful. Fear and tension will make you wreck every time.

Use Your Eyes. Keep your head up, and scan the trail as far forward as possible. Choose a line well in advance. You decide what line to take—don't let the trail decide for you. Keep the surprises to a minimum. If you have to react quickly to an obstacle, then you've already made a mistake.

Rise above the saddle. When racing down bumpy, technical descents, you should not be sitting on the saddle, but hovering just over it, allowing your bent legs and arms to absorb the rocky trail instead of your rear. Think jockey.

Remember your pedals. Be mindful of where your pedals are in relation to upcoming obstacles. Clipping a rock will lead directly to unpleasantness. Most of the time, you'll want to keep your pedals parallel to the ground.

Stay focused. Many descents require your utmost concentration and focus just to reach the bottom. You must notice every groove, every root, every rock, every hole, every bump. You, the bike, and the trail should all become one as you seek single-track nirvana on your way down the mountain. But if your thoughts wander, however, then so may your bike, and you may instead become one with the trees!

LAST-MINUTE CHECKOVER

Before a ride, it's a good idea to give your bike a once-over to make sure everything is in working order. Begin by checking the air pressure in your tires before each ride to make sure they are properly inflated. Mountain bikes require about 45 to 55 pounds per square inch of air pressure. If your tires are underinflated, there is greater likelihood that the tubes may get pinched on a bump or rock, causing the tire to flat.

Looking over your bike to make sure everything is secure and in its place is the next step. Go through the following checklist before each ride.

- **Pinch the tires to feel for proper inflation.** They should give just a little on the sides, but feel very hard on the treads. If you have a pressure gauge, use that.
- **Check your brakes.** Squeeze the rear brake and roll your bike forward. The rear tire should skid. Next, squeeze the front brake and roll your bike forward. The rear wheel should lift into the air. If this doesn't happen, then your brakes are too loose. Make sure the brake levers don't touch the handlebars when squeezed with full force.

- **Check all quick releases on your bike.** Make sure they are all securely tightened.
- **Lube up.** If your chain squeaks, apply some lubricant.
- **Check your nuts and bolts.** Check the handlebars, saddle, cranks, and pedals to make sure that each is tight and securely fastened to your bike.
- **Check your wheels.** Spin each wheel to see that they spin through the frame and between brake pads freely.
- **Have you got everything?** Make sure you have your spare tube, tire irons patch kit, frame pump, tools, food, water, foul-weather gear, and guidebook.

Festivals and Races

Valle Redondo Fat Tire Fiesta: The Town of Eagar, a suburb of Springerville on the eastern end of the White Mountains, throws this event during the last week of August every year—a perfect time to get away from the heat in Phoenix and Tucson, and a nice change of pace from Flagstaff. Events include guided tours of the area's terrific, hidden rides, a hill climbing race up Flat Top Mountain, lots of swag giveaways, and a generous pasta dinner on Saturday night. Contact Rye Sluiter at (520) 333-1640 for more information.

NRMC Tour of the White Mountains: If you're bored with the regular race circuit and if eight grueling hours of high-altitude climbing sounds like lots of fun, this race/festival is for you. This massive 63-mile endurance race through many routes of the White Mountain trail system is one of the toughest of its kind. On the same day, you can also take a 50-mile variation, as well as shorter loops of 46 and 25 miles. Held during the second weekend of October, the temperatures start out crisp but warm up nicely as the day gets on. The atmosphere is pretty accommodating—showers, bunks, "barn and breakfast" arrangements. Camping onsite, evening BBQ, Sunday breakfast and various fun rides throughout the day. Proceeds from the race go to the Navapache Regional Medical Center. Contact (520) 537-6319, Cynthia Clements, or register for the race at www.nrmc.org/twmreg.htm.

7-8 mile breeze ride
25, 35, 45 singletrack challenges
25, 50 mile tours on Forest Service road
63-mile singletrack endurance race

Great Pumpkin Fat Tire Festival: Oro Valley's mountain biking festival, held during the third week of October each year, features races in all categories, kids' events, and clinics. The races take place in Catalina State Park, north of Tucson. Call (520) 297-2191 for more information.

Cosmic Soulstice: Two days of racing and touring in Flagstaff in mid-September—just in time to escape the last of the desert heat. The epic stage race is 43 miles long; there is also a hill climb race up Mt. Elden and a long tour of the jeep roads around the San Francisco Peaks. Call Cosmic Cycles at (520) 779-1092 for more information.

24 Hours in the Old Pueblo: Arizona's first 24-hour endurance race takes place in the foothills of the Tortolita Mountains, north of Tucson. The race is held the second week of February. Check out www.epicrides.com for more details, or call (520) 579-7829.

MBAA Series: This is Arizona's statewide eight-race series for NORBA points. MBAA holds races in Flagstaff, Phoenix, Tucson, and smaller towns like Prescott and Williams. The series begins each year in late January and ends in late June. Mountain Bike Association of Arizona has the scoop: (602) 351-7430 or www.mbaa.net.

Dirt Devil Series: Sponsored by Maricopa County Parks & Recreation and Landis Cyclery, the Dirt Devil Series is a nice three-race series that also serves as a warm-up to the longer MBAA series. Call any Landis Cyclery for information: (480) 839-9383 and (480) 730-1081 in the East Valley, (602) 264-5681 in central Phoenix, or (480) 948-9280 in Paradise Valley.

Repair and
Mainte

Repair and Maintenance

FIXING A FLAT

TOOLS YOU WILL NEED

- Two tire irons
- Pump (either a floor pump or a frame pump)
- No screwdrivers!!! (This can puncture the tube)

REMOVING THE WHEEL

The front wheel is easy. Simply open the quick release mechanism or undo the bolts with the proper sized wrench, then remove the wheel from the bike.

The rear wheel is a little more tricky. Before you loosen the wheel from the frame, shift the chain into the smallest gear on the freewheel (the cluster of gears in the back). Once you've done this, removing and installing the wheel, like the front, is much easier.

REMOVING THE TIRE

Step one: Insert a tire iron under the bead of the tire and pry the tire over the lip of the rim. Be careful not to pinch the tube when you do this.

Step two: Hold the first tire iron in place. With the second tire iron, repeat step one, three or four inches down the rim. Alternate tire irons, pulling the bead of the tire over the rim, section by section, until one side of the tire bead is completely off the rim.

Step three: Remove the rest of the tire and tube from the rim. This can be done by hand. It's easiest to remove the valve stem last. Once the tire is off the rim, pull the tube out of the tire.

CLEAN AND SAFETY CHECK

Step four: Using a rag, wipe the inside of the tire to clean out any dirt, sand, glass, thorns, etc. These may cause the tube to puncture. The inside of a tire should feel smooth. Any pricks or bumps could mean that you have found the culprit responsible for your flat tire.

Step five: Wipe the rim clean, then check the rim strip, making sure it covers the spoke nipples properly on the inside of the rim. If a spoke is poking through the rim strip, it could cause a puncture.

Step six: At this point, you can do one of two things: replace the punctured tube with a new one, or patch the hole. It's easiest to just replace the tube with a new tube when you're out on the trails. Roll up the old tube and take it home to repair later that night in front of the TV. Directions on patching a tube are usually included with the patch kit itself.

INSTALLING THE TIRE AND TUBE
(This can be done entirely by hand)

Step seven: Inflate the new or repaired tube with enough air to give it shape, then tuck it back into the tire.

Step eight: To put the tire and tube back on the rim, begin by putting the valve in the valve hole. The valve must be straight. Then use your hands to push the beaded edge of the tire onto the rim all the way around so that one side of your tire is on the rim.

Step nine: Let most of the air out of the tube to allow room for the rest of the tire.

Step ten: Beginning opposite the valve, use your thumbs to push the other side of the tire onto the rim. Be careful not to pinch the tube in between the tire and the rim. The last few inches may be difficult, and you may need the tire iron to pry the tire onto the rim. If so, just be careful not to puncture the tube.

BEFORE INFLATING COMPLETELY

Step eleven: Check to make sure the tire is seated properly and that the tube is not caught between the tire and the rim. Do this by adding about 5 to 10 pounds of air, and watch closely that the tube does not bulge out of the tire.

Step twelve: Once you're sure the tire and tube are properly seated, put the wheel back on the bike, then fill the tire with air. It's easier squeezing the wheel through the brake shoes if the tire is still flat.

Step thirteen: Now fill the tire with the proper amount of air, and check constantly to make sure the tube doesn't bulge from the rim. If the tube does appear to bulge out, release all the air as quickly as possible, or you could be in for a big bang.

When installing the rear wheel, place the chain back onto the smallest cog (furthest gear on the right), and pull the derailleur out of the way. Your wheel should slide right on.

LUBRICATION PREVENTS DETERIORATION

Lubrication is crucial to maintaining your bike. Dry spots will be eliminated. Creaks, squeaks, grinding, and binding will be gone. The chain will run quietly, and the gears will shift smoothly. The brakes will grip quicker, and your bike may last longer with fewer repairs. Need I say more? Well, yes. Without knowing where to put the lubrication, what good is it?

THINGS YOU WILL NEED
- One can of bicycle lubricant, found at any bike store.
- A clean rag (to wipe excess lubricant away).

WHAT GETS LUBRICATED
- Front derailleur
- Rear derailleur
- Shift levers
- Front brake
- Rear brake

- Both brake levers
- Chain

WHERE TO LUBRICATE

To make it easy, simply spray a little lubricant on all the pivot points of your bike. If you're using a squeeze bottle, use just a drop or two. Put a few drops on each point wherever metal moves against metal, for instance, at the center of the brake calipers. Then let the lube sink in.

Once you have applied the lubricant to the derailleurs, shift the gears a few times, working the derailleurs back and forth. This allows the lubricant to work itself into the tiny cracks and spaces it must occupy to do its job. Work the brakes a few times as well.

LUBING THE CHAIN

Lubricating the chain should be done after the chain has been wiped clean of most road grime. Do this by spinning the pedals counterclockwise while gripping the chain with a clean rag. As you add the lubricant, be sure to get some in between each link. With an aerosol spray, just spray the chain while pedalling backwards (counterclockwise) until the chain is fully lubricated. Let the lubricant soak in for a few seconds before wiping the excess away. Chains will collect dirt much faster if they're loaded with too much lubrication.

Index

Euphoria...
in many different states.

COLORADO · OHIO · WASHINGTON BALTIMORE · PHILADELPHIA

WASHINGTON · VIRGINIA · BOSTON · OREGON · INDIANA

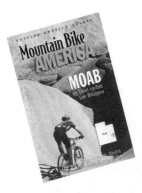

The most beautiful, challenging and exhilarating rides are just a day-trip away.

Visit **www.outside-america.com** to order the latest guides for areas near you – or not so near. Also, get information and updates on future publications and other guidebooks from Outside America™.

For more information or to place an order, Call **1-800-243-0495.**

OUTSIDE AMERICA GUID

Mountain Bike

AMERICA

Meet the Author

Arizona native Paul Beakley is a full-time writer and graphic designer living in Tempe, Arizona, and a partner in a marketing and public relations firm. Being self-employed provides both the free time to ride and the constant ambient stress to chase him out of the office.

Paul has been writing magazine features for more than a decade. His work has appeared in *Urban Land Magazine*, *Harnett's Sports Arizona*, *Vim & Vigor*, *The Business Edge*, *eHealth*, *Future*, and *Arizona Business*, among others.

When he's not writing, Paul is also a freelance mountain bike tour guide for several tour companies around the state. In the course of working on this book, Paul rode an average of 4,000 miles each year for two years. Consequently, he consumed three complete drive trains (chainrings, cogs, derailleurs), more than 100 tubes, three sets of clipless pedals, nine front tires, 20 rear tires, six chains, four rims, 30-some spokes, three bottom brackets, three sets of grips, several gallons of chain lube, a headset, three derailleur hangers, two multi-tools, six complete sets of cables and housing, 18 brake pads, two brake systems, two saddles, three seat posts, three stems, one set of shifter pods, two seatpost collars, two rear shocks, seven hydration bladders, two hydration backpacks, three bike computers, and more than 200 energy bars (Clif Bar™ Carrot Cake being da bomb, followed closely by the one that tastes like Oreo cookies).

Please buy this book so he can get out from under his bike debt.